THE URBAN ORDER

JANET ADAMSON CRAIG SHORT (1895–1966)

I dedicate this book to the memory of my grandmother. She started her working life as a servant in a big house, but she was the grandest lady of them all. She, along with my Aunt Nana, looked after me after my mother died and instilled a sense of social obligation as well as a love of learning. She had a great belief in the emancipatory qualities of education. She taught me that educational achievement was not simply a personal matter, it had to have a social purpose; learning was not a private activity but a social obligation, and scholarship, to have any real meaning, should be transmitted to as wide an audience as possible.

She used to tell me about words and poetry. She was gentle and tough as befits a woman who had eleven children, many grand-children, lived through wars and economic depressions and survived personal tragedies. Sometimes, in my dreams, I hear her calling my name. I loved her dearly. And I think of her often.

THE URBAN ORDER

An Introduction to Cities, Culture, and Power

JOHN RENNIE SHORT

BLACKWELL *Publishers*

First published 1996
2 4 6 8 10 9 7 5 3 1

Blackwell Publishers Inc.
238 Main Street
Cambridge, Massachusetts 02142, USA

Blackwell Publishers Ltd
108 Cowley Road
Oxford OX4 1JF
UK

Library of Congress Cataloging-in-Publication Data

Short, John R.
The urban order / John Rennie Short.
    p.   cm.
Includes bibliographical references and index.
ISBN 1–55786–360–1. – ISBN 1–55786–361–X (pbk.)
1. Cities and towns.   I. Title.
HT151.S477   1996
307.76–dc20   95–307
                                                   CIP

Typeset in 10 on 14pt Linotype Galliard

Printed in Great Britain by T. J. Press Limited, Padstow, Cornwall

This book is printed on acid-free paper.

CONTENTS

PART III
THE PRODUCTION OF THE CITY

INTRODUCTION

THE CITY, TOO, BOMBARDS HIM. HE SEES DECADES AND CENTURIES, POVERTY AND WEALTH, GRACE AND VULGARITY. HE SEES A KALEIDOSCOPE OF TIME AND MOOD: BUILDINGS THAT APE GOTHIC CATHEDRALS, THAT REMEMBER GREEK TEMPLES, THAT PARADE SYMBOLS AND IMAGES. HE SEES COLUMNS, PEDIMENTS AND PORTICOS. HE SEES VICTORIAN STUCCO, TWENTIETH-CENTURY CONCRETE, A SNATCH OF GEORGIAN BRICK. HE NOTES THE RESILIENCE AND TENACITY OF THE CITY, AND ITS INDIFFERENCE.

HE SEES, TOO, THAT THE CITY SPEAKS IN TONGUES . . . A CACOPHONY OF SOUND THAT RUNS THE WHOLE GAMUT FROM YIDDISH TO URDU, A GLOBAL TESTIMONY REACHING FROM MOSCOW TO SYDNEY BY WAY OF GREECE AND TURKEY AND REMOTE BIRTHPLACES IN IRELAND AND INDIA OR THE CARIBBEAN. THE RESONANCES OF THE PLACE ARE UNIVERSAL. IF THE CITY WERE TO RECOUNT ITS EXPERIENCE, THE ENSUING BABBLE WOULD BE THE TALK OF EVERYTIME AND EVERYWHERE, OF PERSECUTION AND DISASTER, OF SUCCESS AND MISFORTUNE.

PENELOPE LIVELY, CITY OF THE MIND (1991, 3–4)

In 1986 I was in Sydney, Australia, doing research on commercial office development. I was walking around the central business district trying to take photographs of construction sites. The film must have got jammed because the final four photographs, as I discovered later, were superimposed one on another. Illustration 1.1 is the result. It is hard at first glance to make sense of the image. It looks confused, chaotic. But stay with it and you can make out buildings and people. The accidental collage presents fragments of a city, each of them recognizable.

Our experience of the city is like this photograph. Go to a big city. You can make out the buildings, see the crowds, identify the places, and know one street leads to all the others. But the big picture tends to elude us. The bigger the city the less it hangs together in our mind's eye. I do not want to take the analogy beyond a sustainable level, but this book is also much like this photograph.

This books aims to look at various fragments of the urban experience. They include the relationships between:

Illustration 1.1
The urban order?
(photograph: author)

■ the city and the economy. Here, I want to consider the economic functioning of the city. Particular topics include the economy of the city (as a point in the production landscape as well as a site of investment), the changing international division of labor and the consequent effects on specific urban economies;

■ the city and society. Here the focus is on the city as an arena of social interaction, the distribution of social groups, residential segregation, the construction of gender and ethnic identities

and patterns of class formation. I want to consider urban neighborhoods and the reproduction of ways of life;
- the representation of the city and power. I want to look at the relationships between urban structure and social power. I will develop the theme that the city is a system of communication, a recorder of the distribution of power and an arena for the social struggles over the meaning and substance of the urban experience.

The book is predicated on the assumption that we can impose some kind of order on the kaleidoscope of images, the myriad messages and competing interests that constitute the urban in contemporary society. The term "order" is interesting and its appearance in the title is deliberate. It is a simple word with complex meanings. According to the *Oxford English Dictionary* it has twenty separate meanings, from the nine grades of angelic beings (for the interested, they are seraphim, cherubim, thrones, dominations, principalities, powers, virtues, archangels and, top of the heap, angels) to the various definitions with more pertinence for our project. These include the use of the word as a verb to mean: to sequence, to arrange, to classify and to command. Order is used in architecture to refer to style, in mathematics to denote a degree of complexity, and in social studies to inform ideas about social class and rank. *Order*: a small word but large enough in meaning to capture a rich diversity of nuance, analysis, exposition, and method. It seems suitable enough for something as complex as the urban and gives us enough latitude to construct a diversity of narratives. And yet there is something paradoxical about the word and the intent. The term would seem to run counter to the notions of fragments and diversity outlined earlier. The definite article in the title suggests a singular reading. And is not the whole contemporary enterprise of scholarship critical of the attempt to impose order and generality? To have a word like order would seem to be a return to the discredited search for universal generalizations.

A more accurate, but more pompous, title would have been *My Urban Order*.

I have tried to show the personal nature of this order by including a series of case studies drawn from my researches over the past twenty-odd years. These case studies fill a number of requirements. They are historically specific and empirically grounded yet echo the broader themes in the other chapters. They anchor the more general chapters in specific places and particular times. The case studies allow the reader to see the focus, methods, and results of my research. These have changed over the years. Chapter 13, for example, based on work completed almost twenty years ago, is very different from chapters 14 and 15. The style, methods, and approach are different and these differences are both personal, reflecting my own development, and inclusive of the broader methodological and deeper philosophical changes in the discipline. The case study chapters indicate the nature of my changing position, the different cities I have been studying, the variety of topics that have interested me, the varied styles of research and exposition, the recurring themes, and the new obsessions. These snapshots allow the reader to see the building blocks of this particular order. The case studies are meant to be interesting in their own right, but they are also an act of positioning; they indicate the places I have written about – and from. Order is not revealed, it is imposed and this imposition always takes a particular direction. The case studies of this book and the general narrative come from my experience and my research. Some of the case studies are based on joint work with other people. By putting them in this volume I seek not to appropriate them for myself, rather the reverse: to show that academic work is a collective endeavor, embedded in communities of readers, writers, and fellow researchers. These chapters are only the more obvious manifestations of the collective nature of academic work. An even more accurate title for the book would be: *My (with the help of friends and colleagues) Urban Order*. I know it is now fashionable to have parentheses in academic works: Se(man)tic, (His)tory, and so on, but this more accurate title is something else. Despite its drawbacks, or maybe even because of them, I will stick with *The Urban Order*.

There is an order to the Order. In each of the three sections of the book I will examine the evolution of the order, its contemporary tensions and ambiguities, and possible trajectories of change. Across time the exposition looks backward as well as forward; over space, I will show the variety of the urban experience by examining material from around the world. Parochialism can be avoided in books, as in all things, only by lifting our eyes and minds beyond the present, the near, and the familiar.

The book is not a discussion of an implied universal city. My experience is biased toward the cities of the rich world, and this is reflected in both the case studies and the more general chapters. There is more in this book about the urban experience in the capitalist world than the urban condition of the Third World. This latter condition is not central to the book but neither is it ignored.

To undertake a general text on the urban order is an ambitious task which can sometimes fall uncomfortably between the heroic and the stupid. The topic is now so vast, the literature so voluminous, the approaches so varied, the discourses so different, and the critiques so many that a general text like this can only be a partial compromise, limited by the position and experience of a single author. The book, however, is not meant as a full stop, a definitive summing up. It should be read as a partial, selective, provisional text; a report of a discussion that is active, ongoing, endlessly fascinating and even sometimes illuminating.

There is an angle of vision and a mood that underpins the book. I want to highlight the role and importance of the city, and, above all, I want to celebrate the city. For many people the city has become a metaphor for the decline of civilization. Cities have had a bad press. It is assumed by many people that the terms "urban" and "problem" are synonymous, like "urban" and "decay". There are many things wrong in cities. But the easy juxtaposition of urban with problems and the automatic connection between cities and social ills have become so pervasive that they have clouded our judgment, polluted our language and infected our analysis. This book does not ignore the drawbacks of city living, but at the heart of it is a profound belief in the collective ability of people to make a civilized life. The built form, collective idea, and daily practice of this endeavor constitute our cities. They are a mirror of our societies, a part of our economy, an element of our environments. But above all else they are a measure of our ability to live with each other. When we examine our cities, we examine ourselves.

I have always had a fascination with cities. I came from a small village of no more than 5,000 souls, a significant number of whom were direct relatives. My paternal grandmother had 11 children, most of whom stayed in the village and had large families. I had over 40 cousins in the village. The exact number was always fluctuating as a steady birth rate continually added new family members and death exacted a tragic toll.

I remember a trip with my grandmother. I must have been no more than seven or eight. We went to Glasgow, at that time a city of almost a million people. I remember arriving at the train station in the center of the city. The immense railway steam engines, up against the buffers at the end of their journeys, were like primeval monsters momentarily at rest. Passing these huge, hissing, frightening metal giants and stepping out of the station and into the thronging crowds was an intense experience that has stayed in my memory. The smell of the crowds, the constant noise, the lights, the continual movement, the hustle, the bustle of a city both excited and terrified me. It still does.

After that trip my village never seemed the same. It was no longer the center of the universe. I now knew it was at the edge of something. Later, much later, I would know it was at the edge of an extended urban region whose center was over 30 miles away.

The village of my youth was a great place to grow up, and the extended family was a basis for mutual support and love. But as I grew older the bonds of support became so tight they seemed to block my growth. In my teenage years the road out of the village seemed to me its most pleasing and exciting prospect. Journeys up to Glasgow or Edinburgh were great adventures. Although only 30 miles away they could have been trips to another planet. The new people, the fancy shops, the cinemas where the actors spoke in foreign languages and you had to read the translations in little scripts at the bottom of the screen: it was a whole new world. Later, I went away to university in one city and then, for graduate work, to another, bigger city. My first academic post was in a town on the outermost edge of London. Now my urban trips were to one of the great cities of the world, where to see someone in brightly colored, flowing robes or an exotic turban was nothing out of the ordinary. London was a world city; voices, smells, fashions, and people from all over the planet. The city was more than a microcosm of society, it was a metaphor for the world. And then there were the foreign cities: Barcelona, Paris, Seville, Amsterdam, New York, Los Angeles, Prague, and Vienna. I was becoming more traveled, older, maybe wiser, but somehow cities still evoked that same response, that mixture of fear and excitement, repulsion and attraction, fascination and disgust that has stayed with me through my personal experiences and occupied much of my professional life.

People write books for many reasons: money, fame, promotion and, as they get older, to leave a record for when they have long gone. And these form part of the many reasons for my writing. But there is something else in this book. There is a genuine attempt to give meaning and order to the feelings of a little boy grabbing tightly onto his grandmother's hand as he walked along the railway platform, down the steps of the station, and into that noisy, weird, banal, bizarre, grubby, fantastic, vile, beautiful, and ultimately most human of places we call the city.

GUIDE TO FURTHER READING

At the end of every chapter I will provide a guide to further reading. At the end of this introductory chapter I provide a list of "urban" writers whom I have found particularly useful and interesting.

I am biased towards this author. He gave me my first academic job. I was in awe of him then and probably still am. He is one of the most enthusiastic people about cities and urban planning. His writing has all the enthusiasm of a young man yet all the virtues of a mature scholar. Among his many books my favorites are *Great Planning Disasters* (London: Weidenfeld & Nicolson, 1980), *The World Cities* (London: Weidenfeld & Nicolson, 1984) and my special favorite *Cities of Tomorrow* (Oxford: Blackwell, 1988), a book only he could have written. The style, the subject matter and the comprehensive coverage come from over thirty years of engagement with urban planning issues.

David Harvey

I first read David Harvey's *Social Justice and the City* (London: Edward Arnold, 1973) when I was beginning my graduate studies. It had a profound effect on me and provided a starting point for my subsequent work. I liked his writing style, applauded his commitment and respected his serious engagement with ideas. I have read most of his subsequent papers and books and always find them interesting and provocative. His *The Urban Experience* (Oxford: Blackwell, 1989) and *The Condition of Postmodernity* (Oxford: Blackwell, 1989) are important books. A fuller assessment of David Harvey's work appears in chapter 5.

Jan Morris

Jan Morris is one of the most gifted travel writers. Incisive comments are softened with smooth prose and a gentle compassion. She is one of the most astute commentators of cities, able to see the broad social processes and yet capture the local feel of a city. She has written full-scale biographies of *Venice* (1960; 2nd rev. edn, Harmondsworth, Middx: Penguin, 1983) and *Oxford* (London: Oxford University Press, 1965, rev. 1988). My favorite are her short essays (*Among the Cities*, New York: Viking Press, 1985; *Locations*, London: Oxford University Press, 1992). These descriptions of cities from around the world are a model of nonfiction writing. Be sure to read them a couple of times, many wise comments are made. Amongst many academics there is a belief that those who write clearly lack ideas, almost as if profundity is measured by the convolutions of the prose. This belief is wrong. Convoluted prose usually reflects an intellectual laziness, an inability to structure an argument, and nothing more.

Lewis Mumford wrote about culture, technology and cities. His *The Culture of Cities* (London: Secker & Warburg, 1938) sets out the benefits of careful urban planning and the construction of garden cities. *The Urban Prospect* (New York: Harcourt, Brace, 1968) is a collection of incisive essays, but it is his *The City in History* (New York: Harcourt, Brace, 1961) for which he is best known. And rightly. This book is a magisterial summary of the origins, transformations and prospects for the city. It is well written, argumentative and always rewarding. I have been reading it on and off for over twenty years and have yet to be bored.

William McIlvanney

We learn much about cities from the work of novelists; Honoré de Balzac, Charles Dickens and Sinclair Lewis all gave imaginative reconstruction to the urban experience. Amongst contemporary writers, Naguib Mahfouz gives us a feel for Cairo, while Tom Wolfe's *Bonfire of the Vanities* (New York: Random House, 1987) is a good read about New York. Compare it with Jay McInerney's two New York novels, *Bright Lights, Big City* (New York: Random House, 1984) and *Brightness Falls* (New York: Random House, 1992). But if I had to choose one novelist I would take the Scottish writer William McIlvanney. He writes in the language of my family and in a style so finely wrought as to demand rereading. Detective stories give us an opportunity to take a social transect through the city. In *Laidlaw* (London: Hodder & Stoughton, 1977), *The Papers of Tony Veitch* (London: Hodder & Stoughton, 1983) and *Strange Loyalties* (London: Hodder & Stoughton, 1991) the detective story reaches a classical standing. One of the greatest pleasures is that of anticipation and I look forward to new books by this writer.

Jonathan Raban

I first read *Soft City* (London: Hamish Hamilton, 1974) when I was a graduate student. Here was a celebration of the city, a reveling in the diversity and anonymity of the big city. The writing was punchy, accessible and always informative. Raban published other books, about boating trips and travels to the Middle East. He is one of the best travel writers. But it is his *Hunting Mister Heartbreak* (London: Collins Harvill, 1990) that I like the best. It is the mature work of an accomplished writer and an acute observer. His writing on US cities is always provocative yet fair. Take some time with this book. Compare the two books and witness the maturing of an important talent.

PART I
THE CITY AND ECONOMY

IN THIS PART OF THE BOOK I WILL CONSIDER THE RELATIONSHIPS BETWEEN THE CITY AND THE ECONOMY. CHAPTER 2 PROVIDES A LONG-TERM HISTORICAL PERSPECTIVE, WHILE CHAPTER 3 EMPHASIZES THE SPATIAL DIMENSION. CHAPTER 4 LOOKS AT THE CONNECTIONS BETWEEN THE CITIES AND THE EVOLVING GLOBAL ECONOMY. CHAPTER 5 CONSIDERS THE INSIGHTS PROVIDED BY A POLITICAL ECONOMY APPROACH. CHAPTERS 6 AND 7, A CASE STUDY FROM SYDNEY, AUSTRALIA, NOTE THE LINKAGES BETWEEN GLOBAL INVESTMENT PATTERNS AND THE CHANGING RELATIONSHIP BETWEEN CAPITAL AND LABOR. CHAPTER 8, A CASE STUDY OF LONDON DOCKLANDS, DISCUSSES THE RECENT SOCIAL AND SPATIAL RESTRUCTURING IN A WORLD CITY. ALL THREE CASE STUDY CHAPTERS MAKE THE LINK BETWEEN THE GLOBAL ECONOMY, NATIONAL SYSTEMS OF REGULATION, AND THE SOCIO-SPATIAL CONSEQUENCES FOR PARTICULAR CITIES.

Chapter 2
CITIES AND ECONOMIC DEVELOPMENT

Towns are like electric transformers. They increase tension, accelerate the rhythm of exchange and constantly recharge human life.

FERNAND BRAUDEL, *CIVILIZATION AND CAPITALISM* (1981, 479)

In his magisterial work *Civilization and Capitalism* the French historian Fernand Braudel describes the development of the first towns and cities as crucial turning points, important watersheds of human history.

Cities have an especially pivotal role in the history of economic development. It is a role, however, that has been given little serious treatment. The urban contribution has not been fully recognized because economists and economic historians have, in the main, been concerned with the abstract notion of the economy, and when they have looked at the real world they have concentrated on such objects as the firm or specific industries or the national economy. There are a few exceptions, but, by and large, cities as crucibles of economic change have not received the amount of attention they deserve. And yet there is a symbiotic relationship between urban development and economic development; economic growth and decline are intimately associated with urban expansion and contraction. The growth of cities is inextricably linked to economic development. The form of urban growth influenced and continues to influence the nature of economic change and development. The social organization of the economy was and is embodied in the spatial organization of society. There is a fascinating relationship between society and space that is most acute in the city. In this chapter I will look at the historical development of this relationship; in effect, I will plot the economic trajectory of the city in time.

THE FIRST CITIES

Cities appeared late in the human occupancy of the planet. During the Paleolithic and Mesolithic periods humans existed in small bands and lived off the land by hunting animals and collecting wild fruit and vegetables. The first cities developed in this context but emerged more fully with the agricultural revolution of the Neolithic period (10,000–5,500 Before Present (BP)). This revolution involved greater human control of the external environment, including the domestication of animals, the invention of cereal production, and the creation and management of irrigation systems. The very first cities developed in Mesopotamia sometime between 5,000 and 6,000 years ago. They were based on the agricultural surplus made available by the enhanced productivity of irrigated farming and the management of this surplus by a social elite.

At one time, city development was explained only with reference to the existence of agricultural surplus. City population, so the argument went, could not survive without the food of the agricultural producers. The urban revolution was thus based on the agricultural revolution. This argument has more than just archaeological interest; it sustains a much broader and very popular view that sees cities as exploiting the wealth, labor, and industry of honest rural workers. Even to this day there is a strong body of opinion that sees farming as natural and cities, especially big cities, as unnatural, parasitic, and ultimately places of economic and social degeneration.

This theory of agricultural primacy is simple and rather elegant. The only troubling thing about it is that it is wrong. Two points. First, why should farmers produce a surplus? To the modern reader this may seem a silly question. But remember, listening to market signals is a comparatively recent human attribute and one that implies the development of a market system as well as a market mentality. In his book *Stone Age Economics* (1972) the American anthropologist Marshall Sahlins suggests that hunting-gathering communities had a great deal of leisure; the bounty of the earth was enough to sustain the small communities with limited needs. In one sense, because their resources were greater than their needs, they lived a relatively secure and, one hesitates to say, perhaps happier life. He refers to them in one section of his book as the original affluent society. From this reading the Neolithic revolution becomes less a leap of progress and more a fall from grace. The production of agricultural surplus becomes less a mark of progress and more an indication of coercion. Agricultural surpluses are created through social relationships and in particular through the emergence of an elite that controls and allocates the food surplus. The first cities were the control centers of a hierarchical social system. The first cities were not so much a product of agricultural surplus as a cause.

Second, the argument can be reversed. Jane Jacobs, in her book *The Economy of Cities* (1969), provides a revisionist version of history. She suggests that cities created agricultural productivity. In a persuasive argument she indicates that commentators have confused the results of urban economic development with the preconditions of this development. In essence, she argues that it was the engine of urban trade that stimulated agriculture. *The agricultural revolution was not the cause of urban growth but a consequence.* In this revisionist urban view the sequence is reversed: towns develop on the basis of trade, and the agricultural production done by the town dwellers is then transplanted to the rural areas.

One of the earliest cities is Çatal Hüyük in Anatolia, Turkey, whose origins go back to the ninth millennium BP. Excavations have revealed a thriving agricultural and trade center, with obsidian flaking and polishing as a major industry. The evidence suggests a complex economy including agriculture, manufacturing, and trade with other places. There is also evidence of a continuation of the cultural symbols of the hunting period in the discovery of animal paintings, carvings, and displays of bull horns and skulls. The earliest city, then, suggests a continuation of the Paleolithic into the Neolithic and some possible validation of Jacobs' urban primacy argument.

Urban empires

Historian Paul Wheatley has identified seven centers of primary urban growth in the ancient world (see table 2.1). According to Wheatley, these were areas which developed independently from each other. They range across the globe and through time from the earliest settlements in Mesopotamia to the younger cities of Mesoamerica. Despite this enormous variation in time and space they have a number of common characteristics. The cities were the control centers and the ceremonial complexes of very hierarchical societies. They housed the social elite, the granaries, the temples and palaces. From here order was maintained and agricultural surplus was collected and distributed while the religious rituals sanctified the social order by connecting the population to the elite and the elite to the deities. Cities were crucial in the development of these early empires. They concentrated control, they sanctified the social order, and were both cause and effect of agricultural developments such as irrigation, domestication of plants and animals, and improvements in farming techniques. Along with these changes came improvements in technical knowledge, astronomy, forms of writing, history, geography,

TABLE 2.1	EARLY URBAN EMPIRES	
Area	*Beginnings*	*Cities*
Mesopotamia	6000–5500BP	Lagash, Ur, Uruk
Indus	5000–4500BP	Mohenjo-Daro
Egypt	5000BP	Memphis, Thebes
China	4000BP	Cheng-Chon
Central Andes	2500BP	Cuzco
Mesoamerica	1000BP	Tenochtitlan
Southwest Nigeria	1000BP	Sagamu

Source: After Wheatley (1971)

Illustration 2.1
*Babylon c.538 BC.
The central city
was the control
center of the
society in the
earliest cities (©
Mary Evans
Picture Library,
London)*

and mathematics. The urban empires became knowledge-based societies where information and the conscious, regular and systematic collection of data became an integral part of maintaining control. These early cities also gave us the first recorded literature. The *Gilgamesh Epic* is a poem which tells us of the hero Gilgamesh, probably based on a king of Uruk, a city in Mesopotamia, around 4600BP. At one point it reads:

In Uruk he built walls, a great rampart, and the temple of blessed Eanna for the god of the firmament Anu, and for Ishtar the goddess of love.

The poem is a story of human vanity. Gilgamesh, the great king and warrior, seeks eternal life. But even great kings cannot escape the mortality of human existence. The story is over 4,000 years old, but it is a universal story, a recurring motif that explores both the joy of life and the inexorable fact of death.

For many contemporary critics cities are irreligious places of material expression. It is a paradox, therefore, that the first big cities developed as centers of religious worship. Gilgamesh, for example, built walls, ramparts, and temples. Appeal was made to sacred laws to sanction the social order. The cities were the point of contact between the sacred and the profane. At the center of the early cities were the temples reaching up to the sky, connecting the worldly and the celestial, a pact in stone between the worshiped and the worshipers, an architectural point of communication between the here and the now, the past and the future. In these early cities began the development of religious beliefs that replaced the earlier animist traditions, which saw spirits and gods all around in all living things, with sky-centered religions that located the deities up in the heavens. The cities helped to break the bond between the people and their immediate environment. But the environment struck back. The empires waxed and waned sometimes in response to external threat, defeat, and conquest; but in many cases epidemics, flooding, and silting of irrigation channels caused their downfall. The plains of Sumer that saw the first cities are now windswept .ruins, the land exhausted by overexploitation and no longer able to support human life. The early urban civilizations could not escape the brute facts of the physical environment. It is a lesson not just for the first cities.

These first cities were based primarily on threat and religious appeal. Control extended only as far as the threat capability of the central authorities. Within the city, control was clearly visible: the walls were as much to keep people in as to keep others out. Further away from the city, the religious appeal was less significant. People on the periphery were not part of the regular rituals that reaffirmed the social order with reference to cosmic appeal. Toward the periphery power was more difficult to sustain. The first urban empires were based on the threat system, and the threat capability declined with distance from the center. This may explain why the first urban empires were relatively limited in size and were of regional significance, never to reach global significance. The costs of maintaining power over space acted as a limiting factor to the extent of these empires but the limitation was broken when the exchange system of the merchant cities supplanted the threat system. When exchange replaced threat regional systems could become global trading networks.

THE MERCHANT CITY

Merchant cities concentrated more on commercial exchange than on threat. Their development was an important element in the creation of a world economy, an economy created by the trading impulses emanating from what is now Western Europe. From the middle of the twelfth century trade began to flourish within Europe and between Europe and the East. The extension of a trading system implied the creation of a money economy, the emergence of a merchant class, and the growth of urban trading centers. Until about 1400 there were two interconnected trading centers in Europe. In northern Europe the Hanseatic League towns of Hamburg, Lübeck and Bremen were part of an extensive trading system throughout the North and Baltic seas. The term "Hanseatic" comes from the word *Hansa*, meaning group of merchants. The largest city in the north was Bruges. In 1340 it had a population of 35,000, which grew to 100,000 in 1500. In the south, Genoa, Pisa, and Venice were important centers for trade in the Mediterranean. The subsequent history is of competition between cities for prime position and the rise and fall of cities as they achieved and then lost that position (see table 2.2).

TABLE 2.2	DOMINANT MERCHANT CITIES OF EUROPE	
City	*Period of Dominance*	*Largest Population / (year)*
Bruges	1350–1500	100,000 (1500)
Venice	1400–1600	150,000 (1600)
Antwerp	1530s–1580	100,000 (1568)
Genoa	1570s–1630s	95,000 (1620)
Amsterdam	1630s–1750s	200,000 (1700)

Venice

By 1400 Venice had emerged as the leading city in the Mediter-ranean. Trade was conducted in cloth, cotton, wool, silk, and spices. The Venetian empire was part exchange, part threat. Forts were established around the inland seas and a powerful navy maintained Venetian preeminence. In fifteenth- and sixteenth-century Venice we see the creation of a commercial society, a society where trade, exchange, credit, and banking were established and encouraged. Between 1297 and 1797 a merchant class ruled the city. Venice may be one of the first and was definitely one of the longest-surviving mer-chant cities. It was a place of wealth and stability. There was a successful textile industry, and in the trading world the Venetians pocketed the difference between the cost of goods and the retail price. Money flowed into the city. It was also a city of culture that provided the artistic context from which arose such important figures as Palladio (1508–80), the man who influenced Western architecture, and such key figures in the Western artistic tradition as Bellini (1431–1516), Titian (1488–1576), Tintoretto (1518–76), and Canaletto (1697–1768). City economies not only produced money, they provided the context, the market and the finance for artistic endeavors. Wealth does not guarantee great art, but it helps.

The cities of Italy created a commercial society, but commerce also created a civic society. The merchant city was a constellation of shared interests and there was a collective purpose to the pursuit of private gain. Affairs had to be regulated and controlled, proper pricing agreed upon, rules established, deals struck, and contracts made. Commerce implied cooperation. The individual merchants created a civic culture, and the pursuit of civic virtue and the construction of public space became part of the Renaissance enterprise. Indeed, a large part of the Renaissance involved the development of civic art, public spaces, and collective rituals. The cities of the Italian Renais-sance were the setting as well as the reason for the pursuit of a public order – municipal governments, permanent city officials, the gener-ation and spending of public finances, the regulation of commercial affairs; in effect, the creation of a civic world.

The civic purpose of Venice, as of other Italian cities, was under-mined by systems of patronage and allegiances based on class, family, and gender. But the tempering of private loyalties with civic obligations and civic rights gave impetus to the Renaissance. Merchant cities were places of commerce and industry, the seedbed of a capitalist order; they also helped to create the Western concep-tion of the civic world and the public realm.

Illustration 2.2

Map of Venice in the sixteenth century. Notice the merchant ships in the harbor and the ruling class shown in the cartouche (© Mansell Collection, London)

Amsterdam

Between Venice and Amsterdam in the history of merchant cities came the sudden rise and quick fall of Antwerp and Genoa. It was a time of fluctuating trade: wealth from the Americas came and then went, new trading routes were being established, and economies waxed and waned. By the early seventeenth century, however, Amsterdam emerged as the center of a world economy. In 1550 the city had a population of only 20,000, but by 1700 the figure was close to 200,000. It was above all a trading city. Goods were brought from the Baltic, the Mediterranean, the Americas, and the Indies. Some were the basis for industry – tobacco curing, sugar refining, diamond cutting – and much was stored in giant warehouses around the city and reexported. Amsterdam was the hub of an expanding commercial system that was extending its circumference around the globe. Trading companies were established to organize trade, banks lent money, and credit fueled the system. A mercantile culture was created in the construction of a merchant city. Tolerance was not only a religious virtue but good commercial sense. Amsterdam became a center of religious and social tolerance; a characteristic it has maintained, as any visitor to today's city can attest. The art of this period owes less to pomp and majesty and more to restrained bourgeois sensibilities. The domestic interiors of Vermeer (1632–75), the portraits of Frans Hals (1582/3–1666), or the group sittings of Rembrandt (1606–69) bespeak a merchant class rather than patrician splendor.

The biggest building built in Amsterdam during the so-called Golden Age, and one of the biggest buildings of seventeenth-century Europe, was not a private mansion or a nobleman's castle but the Town Hall. The construction of the Town Hall exemplified the civic virtues as well as the private wealth of Amsterdam. Simon Schama has examined some of the consequences of that fabulous wealth. In *The Embarrassment of Riches* (1987) he shows how a modest community had to cope with becoming a world empire, how the making and spending of great wealth was filtered through the moral membrane of Calvinism. In their art, their culture, and their civic arrangements the citizens of the world city tried to be both moral and rich; they regulated excess through rites of cleanliness and charity. Foundling hospitals, charitable works, and attempts to minimize urban poverty were the results of moral disquiet as well as of Christian charity.

In coping with the moral implications of materialism, Amsterdam was perhaps the last commercial empire to be troubled by the ambiguity. As capitalism, individualism and the cult of the free market began to dominate, private wealth was not something to fret over.

The city and economy

Amsterdam of the seventeenth century was a city on the axis of a changing social world; it condensed the tensions of a society moving from a sense of community to a neglect of community, a shift from the notion that wealth is a moral solvent to a belief that poverty is an individual failing. In the Amsterdam of Vermeer and Rembrandt can be seen the clash of a money order with a moral order. In later centuries and other cities the battle was all too one-sided.

THE CITY AND THE INDUSTRIAL REVOLUTION

From the rise and fall of Bruges, Venice, and then Amsterdam to the expansion of London the steady enlargement of the world economy can be seen. Over this time European influence extended around the world as an embryonic global economy was established: the shadow of European economic expansion was extending around the globe.

Illustration 2.3
Amsterdam: the New Chapel and the Exchange in the seventeenth century (© Mansell Collection, London)

Britain was the first country to undergo that transformation of economy and society that we call the industrial revolution. The role of its major city was crucial. London was and still is a primate city, it

dwarfed the other cities in the nation, and it was the seat of economic, political, and social power. London housed Parliament, it was the seat of royalty, the center of finance, and the most important port. Up until the twentieth century 80 percent of all the country's imports and exports passed through the city. London was the hub of a vast commercial empire.

London's growth was extraordinary. In 1600 it had a population of 200,000, which increased to 675,000 by 1750, and to nearly 1 million by 1801, almost double the size of its closest rival, Paris. In an interesting paper that looks at the period 1650–1750 the historical geographer E.A. Wrigley (1967) examines the role of London in the transformation of the society (figure 2.1). London was demographically important: almost 11 percent of the country's population lived in the city in 1750. The comparable figures for other European countries and their largest city were approximately half this figure. Through migration one adult in six had experience of the city. The migratory population tended to be younger, more dynamic than the average. The leading edge of all social groups thus had an experience of life in the capital.

London's increasing population provided a huge and growing market for food producers and manufacturers. Wrigley argues that the trading wealth of commercial expansion fueled the growth of

Figure 2.1
The links between London's growth and the industrial revolution in London.
Source: *Wrigley (1967)*

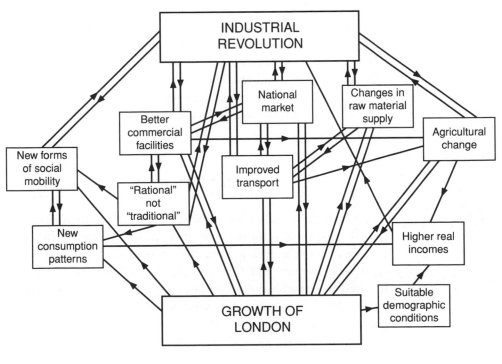

London, which in turn constituted a huge center of consumption, providing an effective demand for consumer goods. This demand was the basis for technological improvements. Agricultural improvements, for example, which predated the industrial changes, were prompted by the existence of this huge urban market, because the high and increasing demand was the inducement to greater investment, technological improvements and, ultimately, increased agricultural productivity. Between 1650 and 1750 there was a 75 percent increase in the demand for food. This gave stimulus to agricultural productivity and hence to the agricultural revolution, which was one of the bases of the industrial revolution. The need for fuel in the cold capital also generated coal production in the north of the country, and again we can see that the consumption power of the huge city created some of the preconditions for industrial take-off. To meet the demands of the urban population, better roads were built to link suppliers and the market; credit schemes were introduced that allowed the delay of immediate payment and thus made possible the creation of long links of commercial transactions stretching from the city to the smallest hamlet. By establishing a national market, fostering changes in agricultural methods, providing a wide range of commercial and credit facilities, and constructing an improved transport network that tied the supply and demand regions together, the city was an important element in the economic transformation of the country. In effect, Wrigley's findings underscore the Jane Jacobs (1969) thesis concerning the urban bias of economic change. Explanations of the industrial revolution often look to technological improvements or the Protestant ethic or some combination of economics and sociology. These all have a part, but it is important to remember that the enormous growth of London created a huge effective demand that was one of the most important stimulants to the industrial revolution.

THE CAPITALIST CITY

The coming of capitalist industrialization meant major changes to the urban order: urban growth, new cities, and new types of city. The great spurt of economic activity that took place at the end of the eighteenth century and flowered during the nineteenth century involved a tremendous concentration of people and fixed capital investment. The factory system was the most characteristic form. By concentrating production in factories the owners reduced production costs and increased profits. Housing for the workers clustered around the factories. In Europe urban growth took place as the old feudal systems of hierarchical community were collapsing. In the United States the ruling ideas were those of classic liberalism, which spoke more to property rights than to broader social goals. As capitalist urbanization was taking off the political consensus of the ruling elites stressed individual rights, not civic obligations, and a minimal state. The ruling ideology was stressing lack of government just when the urban condition was highlighting the need for government involvement. This tension is most apparent in the earliest industrial cities of the capitalist economy.

The first cities of the capitalist industrial order were found in Britain, Manchester being one of the most important. In 1760 this city had a population of 17,000. By 1830 it had increased to 180,000, and by the time of the census in 1851 it was a staggering 303,382. The structure of Manchester and other English cities at this time is recorded in an urban classic, Friedrich Engels' *The Condition of the Working Class in England in 1844.* First published in German in 1845, the book's first English edition had to wait until 1892. The subtitle, *From Personal Observation and Authentic Sources,* reflects Engels' visit to the city and his collection of empirical material culled from government reports and trade journals. The result is a committed piece of scholarship in which moral fervor and careful documentation are combined. The book is interesting in a number of respects. It is an invaluable record of the appalling housing conditions of the working class in the great cities. It is full of insights that link these conditions to the nature of the wider society. It is a snapshot of city living at the high point of an aggressive capitalism and an indictment of social inequality generated by the market system. The book is also interesting for what it represents. It is the work of a rich capitalist disgusted with the system from which he benefits. Engels was the son of a textile manufacturer, in England to run the family business and to manage a factory in Manchester. Later, in 1844 he met Karl Marx in Paris and began a lifelong friendship and collaboration that changed the world. Together they wrote the *Communist Manifesto,* which was published in 1848. Engels' money helped to subsidize Marx during his years of exile in London and his hours of study at the Reading Room of the British Museum. Thus the profits of capitalist industry helped to subsidize the greatest critic of the capitalist system. It can be argued that Engels' experience of cities like Manchester led, in small part, to the *Communist Manifesto* and Marx's monumental *Capital* which helped to transform the intellectual and political landscape of the twentieth century.

Industrialization and urbanization went hand in hand. Villages grew into towns and formerly quiet market towns exploded into cities; the predominantly rural landscape became dotted with the built form of the new order. The social as well as the physical land-scape was transformed. The industrial revolution involved the creation of an industrial proletariat. For Karl Marx and Friedrich Engels capitalist urbanization created a working class that, in their classic phrase, had nothing to lose but its chains. Denied power, marginalized by the ruling elite, and exploited by the market, this emerging class was, according to Marx and Engels, the gravedigger of the old order. Crowded around the factories in the industrial cities they achieved a sense of their collective power. Saved from what Marx and Engels described as "the idiocy of rural life," they were the future, the embodiment of social progress, the mechanism by which the forces of production and social relations of production would be brought into harmony and a new communist society be inaugurated. That was the dream. For the rich and powerful it was a nightmare. Alexis de Tocqueville noted in 1835 that

> *in cities men cannot be prevented from concerting together and awakening a mutual excitement that prompts sudden and passionate resolution. Cities may be looked upon as large assemblies of which all the inhabitants are members; their populace exercise a prodigious influence upon the magistrates and frequently execute their own wishes without the intervention of public officer.*
>
> (Tocqueville, 1835, I: 290)

If you listen carefully you can almost hear the fear in Tocqueville's words as he contemplates an urban mob breaking all the rules of "civilized" society. It was a fear shared by many in the nineteenth century, and it continued to resound in the twentieth.

In one of the most influential and powerful pieces of historical writing in the twentieth century, the English social historian E.P. Thompson surveyed the experience of the English working class in the crucial period of early capitalist urbanization. His book, first published in 1963, is entitled *The Making of the English Working Class*. The book is important in three respects. First, it was one of the most sustained pieces of research that looked at history "from below" and gave a voice and a story to those normally excluded by traditional emphasis on the powerful and influential; in this regard it was one of the leading lights in the new social history that tried to rescue the marginalized "from the enormous condescension of posterity." Thompson's book helped to establish a new angle of historical vision. Second, it looked at class and class relations as pivotal concepts in our understanding of historical change; not just class as defined by statistics but class as an historical moment, class as a process rather than a thing. Finally, and perhaps more relevant for our purposes here, it put an emphasis on the *making* of class. This part of the title is an indication that classes are not simply the result of grand historical processes; classes also make themselves. The English working class, the result of rapid industrialization and inhuman urbanization, also forged themselves in their culture of football clubs, self-help societies, burial clubs, codes of behavior, in religious affiliation to Nonconformist groups such as the Methodists, in trade union organizations, and in political representation; civic socialism and the British Labour Party grew from the urban radicalism of the organized working class. The English working class made themselves through and by and in their culture.

Classes make themselves as much as they are made by historical circumstances. And this fact has important implications. It suggests that the simple Marx and Engels model is mediated by the nexus of cultural factors by which economic categories are turned into social classes. This process of mediation allows us to explain the quite different experience of the United States and much of Western Europe. In Europe capitalist urbanization produced a working class that had

Illustration 2.4
Covent Garden market, London, c.1820. The capital's demand for food was a major stimulus to the agricultural revolution. The growth of London in general was intimately connected with the industrial revolution (© Mansell Collection, London)

both radical and conservative forces. The mix varied through time and over space, but in general we can say that in Europe the cities were the hearth of political radicalism and trade union organization. Things were different in the United States, where working-class organizations, despite some early successes, never achieved the prominence or importance they did in Europe. The reason lies in the very different experience. US cities of the late nineteenth and early twentieth centuries witnessed waves of immigration from Europe. The politics of race and ethnicity cut across class lines of identification. The ethnic diversity of US cities worked against the emergence of explicit class ideology.

The paradox of the capitalist city

In one chapter of his book, entitled "The Great Towns," Engels moralizes on city living in capitalist society:

> *The brutal indifference, the unfeeling isolation of each in his private interest becomes the more repellent and offensive, the more these individuals are crowded together, within a limited space. And, however much one may be aware that this isolation of the individual, this narrow self-seeking is the fundamental principle of our society everywhere, it is nowhere so shamelessly barefaced, so self-conscious as just here in the crowding of the great city. The dissolution of mankind into monads, of which each one has a separate principle and a separate purpose, the world of atoms, is carried out to its utmost extreme . . . What is true of London, is true of Manchester, Birmingham, Leeds, is true of all great towns. Everywhere barbarous indifference, hard egotism on one hand, and nameless misery on the other.*
> (Engels, 1973, 64–5)

Engles' words identify the important paradox at the heart of the capitalist city. There are antithetical elements implied by the two words: *capitalism* implies private property and the private appropriation of wealth; *city*, in contrast, is, in essence, a shared space where people come together for mutual benefit. The paradox was most clearly demonstrated in the nineteenth century, when an increasing urbanization was taking place against an ideology and a political practice that stressed minimum public involvement. The result was what Peter Hall (1988) refers to as "The City of Dreadful Night." The term comes from a poem of that title by the Victorian poet James Thomson in 1880. As urban growth continued apace, problems of overcrowding, disease and social unrest surfaced onto the political agenda. For

the more astute observers of the late nineteenth century the city was
like a volcano rumbling away on the brink of a catastrophic explosion.
The insanitary conditions, the declining health of the work force, the
fear of social revolution and the perception of the enormous social
and economic costs of unplanned, unregulated urbanization were the
background to government reports, social experiments and subsequent legislation. In Britain the searing indictment of Andrew
Mearns' *The Bitter Cry of Outcast London* (1883) led to the creation
in 1884 of the Royal Commission on the Housing of the Working
Class, which in turn led to legislation allowing city authorities to build
new housing for the "labouring classes." There was also pressure
from below. In 1886 and 1887 there were demonstrations by unemployed workers in London, bringing home to the ruling elite that the
problem had serious political implications. In 1890 there was another
Housing Act. The story was roughly the same in other cities. In Berlin
and Paris similar tensions were emerging, but in the United States
the slums of Chicago and New York did not provoke legislation
similar to that being passed in Britain. The strong belief in the market, the lack of organized working-class political representation and
the fear of an interventionist state all inhibited a greater role for the
state. Despite the important differences, these early responses and
nonresponses were the opening scenes in a drama of the city as an
arena for the generation and implementation of public policies that
is still unfolding.

The experiences of these nineteenth-century shock cities are of
great and enduring importance. In *Cities of Tomorrow* Peter Hall
argues that "twentieth-century city planning, as an intellectual and
professional movement, essentially represents a reaction to the evils
of the nineteenth-century city" (198, 7). I feel we can extend the
argument beyond planning. The experience of the nineteenth century created the context for government intervention. The reality of
the cities undermined the belief in the advantages of an unfettered
private market. From the slums, disease, and fear of the early capitalist city there arose a body of theory, ranging from the Communists
to the Fabians, and a legislative framework, ranging from greater
interventionism of Britain at one end to the more *laissez-faire*
response in the United States at the other, which transformed both
the economic workings of the market and the very notion of what
government should and could do. It is not too fanciful to argue for
the urban cause of the mixed economy, the welfare state, and the
acceptance of a legitimate role for public authorities. The acceptance
of this legitimacy is still not total and continues to fluctuate, but the
costs and benefits of the argument are most clearly shown in the big

cities of the capitalist world. The city condensed the searing ambiguities of capitalism and community and the emerging tensions between public and private, market and community, money and morality, economy and society. The city was the terrain in which the contradictions of a *capitalist society* were created, identified, and played out. The city in capitalist society was the arena of social tension and the crucible of economic change.

THE POSTMODERN CITY

In recent years the use of the term "postmodern" has become more common. It means different things to different people; however, the usage reflects a transformation, a sense of major change, a shift in both society and in the world of ideas about society. Here I will limit myself to brief comments on what we may term the postmodern city. The postmodern city has three important elements:

- the "new" look;
- the new enclosure movement;
- the "new" civic culture.

The "new" look

In the past 25 years the whole look of central cities has been changed. The straight-lined, flat-topped modernist towers now have to compete with buildings in a variety of shapes and colors, office blocks designed as Greek temples and government offices as Renaissance palaces. The modernist blocks look austere in comparison with this riot of color, shape, and ornamentation. Square buildings have been given new angles, flat roofs have been given pediments, glass walls now have holes in them or baroque-heavy detailing. We can understand this shift as one more round of architectural fashion. In the 1960s modernist architecture was all the rage; by the 1990s a post-

Illustration 2.6
Post-modern building: AT&T Building, New York; architect: Philip Johnson (© Peter Mauss Esto/1988, Arcaid)

31

modern look was the fashion. Mies van der Rohe, one of the gurus of modernist architecture, once said that less is more. Charles Jencks, who writes about postmodern architecture, turned the phrase around to read "less is a bore." It is the fate of all new fashions to be seen as revolutionary, then standard, and then merely boring. In architecture, as in much of life, nothing dates so quickly as the most recent.

But there is something more than a shift in style. There is a deeper message to be drawn than the fickleness of design. The shift from modern to postmodern, which we can date around the early 1970s, came at a time of increasing competition between cities. When a sharp cleavage occurs, as in the modern/postmodern shift, buildings and cities can look very dated very quickly. The building boom of the 1980s gave an added opportunity for the new look. The postmodern shift was part of an attempt at differentiation between cities at a time of growing global competition. There was a surge of both new building and refurbishment all in the new styles in an attempt to seem still connected to the global culture of capital. As cities chased after mobile capital they wanted to present a contemporary view, an image of being at the cutting edge. The postmodern look gave that image. Behind the shift in style was an attempt not to be caught in the past. The competition of the present helps explain the dive into the architectural past.

The new enclosure movement

The postmodern city is more than just a collection of new buildings. There is a new syntax as well as new words to this architectural shift. There is what I will refer to as the new enclosure movement. The first enclosures occurred in England, reaching their peak in the last half of the eighteenth and first part of the nineteenth centuries. Enclosures meant the privatizing of open common lands, the enclosing of open fields, and the private appropriation of public pastures. The modern enclosure occurs in urban areas and can be seen in many different ways. There has been the creation of what we may rightly call *bunker architecture*. More and more buildings seek to regulate access. More than this, they seek to hide access. An increasing number of hotels in downtown locations, for example, seek to hide their entrances, to block them or restrict them to the ordinary citizen. Walls come down to the street, entrances are taken away from direct street level, and access has to be negotiated. The result is the closing off from public space. The blank wall signifies as well as embodies the withdrawal from a civic culture.

There has also been the rise of "gated" communities. These have gates to keep out all but the residents and their friends. Private security guards, walls, gates, and electric fences all reflect a concern with safety and a palpable expression of fear of the urban other. The gates reinforce the fear we have of one another. The shared space of the city becomes the segmented segregation of tiny communities fearful of the rest of the city. There is a shattering of the notion of a collective good into the kaleidoscope of individual fears. Our cities now reflect our sense of fear more than our sense of hope. In his book on Los Angeles Mike Davis (1990) has a chapter on Fortress L.A. Some of the section headings tell us much about the contemporary enclosure movement: "The Destruction of Public Space," "The Forbidden City," "Sadistic Street Environments," "Frank Gehry as Dirty Harry," "The Panopticon Mall," "From Rentacop to Robocop," "The Fear of Crowds." In varying degrees these heading would also be appropriate for many other cities around the world.

The "new" civic culture

The new look of cities reflects and embodies a "new" civic culture which involves a decline in the benevolence of national and urban governments towards welfare, public goods, and many of those things that add to the quality of urban life. Public transport has been cut back, as has spending on cultural affairs and environmental quality, and the creation and maintenance of urban public spaces has been reduced. There are exceptions. French cities, and Paris in particular, have emerged as major exceptions to this trend. And the base point varies around the world. Swedish and Dutch cities, for example, still have an incomparably higher level of public expenditure than cities in the United States.

In the "new" civic culture more emphasis has been placed on revenue-generation than on revenue-disposal. The needs of business have been returned to a dominating primacy while footloose capital has been wooed with all manner of incentives, grants, and tax breaks. As recession deepens the bidding intensifies as cities compete one with another. City governments have also taken a more active role in land-development deals and the encouragement of revenue-generating activities. The redistributional city of late modernism is turning into the entrepreneurial city of early postmodernism.

There are countervailing tendencies. In the cities of the rich countries many people are just as concerned with the quality of employment as with the quantity of employment. As social and personal goals, economic growth and income maximization are competing with ecological responsibility and maximization of the quality of life. There is a concern with questions of environmental quality, social equity, and political empowerment. The "new" civic culture of the 1990s and beyond will be a curious mixture of a return to a domination by business interests and the evolution of a new enlightened public interest. The "welfare" state, at least in its most expansive phase, may be seen as a thing of the past, a curious time when rising real incomes and sustained economic growth allowed a social contract based on the need and the ability to create domestic harmony. But the demise of the old welfare state will not imply a return to the pre-welfare state. There are too many articulate and powerful people who rely on the range of public services. A new set of business ethics will also be forged, just as a new fiscal agenda for the public sector is being created. Perhaps the "new" civic culture will be a mixture of the imperatives of business, ecological responsibility, and quality of life. They will increasingly be seen as interrelated rather than separate considerations. A city with a healthy environment and a good quality of life will be more likely to attract and retain business. The more enlightened business will see the business sense of spending money on environmental cleanup and good education. There will be variations. The richer cities are likely to get richer; those left out of the benign cycle of growth and investment may languish. And the patterns of investment will, as usual, pay more heed to the rich and powerful than to the poor and needy. However, the "new" of the emerging civic culture does at least allow an opportunity for debate and criticism. When things are in flux, as they are now, alternative voices have a greater opportunity to be heard.

The modernist city was one dominated by single objectives and grand narratives. The postmodern city is likely to be of richer texture and more varied hues. Some good, some bad, and many in between. An examination of the evolution of this new urban form is one of the more interesting items likely to appear on the research agenda for many years.

GUIDE TO FURTHER READING

An excellent general introduction to the city is:
Mumford, L. (1961) *The City in History*, New York: Harcourt.

The role of the city in economic development is the subject of two well-written books:
Jacobs, J. (1969) *The Economy of Cities*, New York: Random.
Jacobs, J. (1984) *Cities and the Wealth of Nations*, New York: Random.

For an interesting look at the ancient city consider:

Sjoberg, G (1960) *The Pre-industrial City*, Chicago: Free Press.

Wheatley, P. (1971) *The Pivot of the Four Quarters*, Edinburgh: Edinburgh University Press.

The rise of the merchant city is covered by:

Braudel, F. (1981) *The Structures of Everyday Life*, London: Collins.

Braudel, F. (1984) *The Perspective of the World*, London: Collins.

Girouard, M. (1985) *Cities and People*, New Haven, Conn., and London: Yale University Press.

On the role of the city in the transformation of traditional society:

Wrigley, E.A. (1987) *People, Cities and Wealth*, Oxford and New York: Blackwell.

Still the best introduction to the capitalist city is:

Engels, F. (1973) *The Condition of the Working Class in England in 1844*, Moscow: Progress Publishers.

For a brief sample of writing on the postmodern city consider:

Davis, M. (1990) *City of Quartz*, London: Verso.

Ellin, N. (1995) *Postmodern Urbanism*, Oxford: Blackwell.

Harvey, D. (1989) *The Condition of Postmodernity*, Oxford: Blackwell.

Robins, K. (1991) Prisoners of the city: whatever could a postmodern city be?, *New Formations* 15, 1–22.

Watson, S. and Gibson, K. (eds) (1994) *Postmodern Cities and Spaces*, London: Routledge.

Zukin, S. (1988) The postmodern debate over urban form, *Theory, Culture and Society* 5, 431–46.

Other works cited in this chapter:

Hall, P. (1988) *Cities of Tomorrow*, Oxford: Blackwell.

Mearns, A. (1883) *The Bitter Cry of Outcast London*, London: James Clark.

Sahlins, M. (1972) *Stone Age Economics*, Chicago: Aldine-Atherton.

Schama, S. (1987) *The Embarrassment of Riches*, London: Collins.

Thompson, E.P. (1963) *The Making of the English Working Class*, Harmondsworth, Middx: Penguin.

Tocqueville, A. de (1835) *Democracy in America*, 2 vols, New York: J. & G.H. Langley.

Wrigley, E.A. (1967) A simple model of London's importance in changing English society and economy, 1650–1750, *Past and Present* 37, 44–70.

Chapter 3

THE URBANIZATION OF THE ECONOMY

SOCIETIES AND CIVILIZATIONS IN WHICH THE CITIES STAGNATE DON'T
DEVELOP OR FLOURISH FURTHER. THEY DETERIORATE.

JANE JACOBS, *CITIES AND THE WEALTH OF NATIONS* (1984, 232)

In chapter 2 I looked at the relationship between the city and economy over time. In this chapter I want to examine this relationship over space.

Economic transactions do not occur in a vacuum. They take place in space, over space, through space. Even the basic economic term "market," for example, is drawn from the spatial nexus of buying and selling. Cities, as points in space, reflect, condense, restrain, and enhance economic relationships and tensions. As the previous chapter concentrated on the economic trajectory of the city through time, so this chapter examines its economic position in space.

Let us begin with the concept of the urban hierarchy. Cities vary in size. The words we use to describe urban places contain some indication of the differences: "village;" "town;" "city;" "megalopolis." The words suggests an upward movement in size and influence. They imply that urban places are part of a hierarchical structure. This observation is not recent: over a thousand years ago in AD 985 the Arab geographer Al Muqaddasi, in a book entitled *The Classification of the Knowledge of Regions*, classified cities, towns, and villages in terms of a nested hierarchy. Three distinct levels of the urban hierarchy can be identified:

- international;
- national;
- regional.

Any one city can be seen in terms of its location within each of these hierarchies. The bigger the city the greater its role at all levels. A big city has a major part to play in a region and a country, and is an element in the international urban circuit.

Each level has been associated with a particular emphasis. At the international level the focus is on the emergence of a global economy and spatial modes of incorporation of peripheral economies into the world system. At the national level the dominant concern is the spatial manifestation of the economic history and economic geography of particular national economies. At the regional level the concern is more with local connections over space and the elaboration of concepts such as scale and threshold. Academic fashions come and go. In the early 1960s the focus of urban geography was on the regional level; more recently, the focus has shifted to understanding the position of individual cities within a global economic perspective. But to understand a city we need to be aware of its changing position at all of the levels.

THE GLOBAL HIERARCHY

Cities have been growing in size and number over the past 300 years. In 1800 only about three in every hundred people lived in towns with a population greater than 5,000. The population of the world was overwhelmingly rural, living on the land. Cities were small, like tiny pinprick islands in a vast rural sea. There were only a handful of cities with a population greater than half a million. By 1900 almost one in every ten people lived in towns, and the number of cities with more than half a million increased to twenty. By 1990, of the 5,300 million on the planet, four out of every ten lived in towns, and the number of cities with over half a million people had increased to almost 600.

A global hierarchy of cities can be identified. At the top are the command centers of the world economy. Three world cities can be identified: London, New York and Tokyo. These three constitute the main nodes of a global circuit of information, capital, and investment flows. They represent the centers of global power of the last 100 years. Below this the secondary financial centers compete for dominance and in some cases edge close to the world cities in influence and power. Such cities include San Francisco, Hong Kong, Zurich, and Paris. Mere size does not correspond with global influence. Some of the largest cities in the world do not have great world influence. Mexico City, for example, had a population of 5 million in 1950; in 1990 this had increased to 16 million, and estimates suggest that the figure will reach 25 million by the end of this century. However, this population growth reflects demographic shifts rather than changing global positions.

The global hierarchy reflects and embodies social, economic, and demographic changes. Let us consider just one example; cities and the emerging global economy.

The global economy did not just happen, it was constructed. Cities had an important role in this construction. Whenever the colonial powers grabbed territory they set about establishing towns and cities as control centers. New towns were established or old ones were transformed with the infrastructure of imperial and colonial control – barracks, prisons, courthouses, government offices, the residential quarters of the ruling elite. In Latin America, for example, the Spaniards created scores of urban centers with a characteristic pattern of gridiron streets, a central plaza containing the church, town council offices, viceregal palaces and, surrounding the center, the homes of the Spanish elite. Indians were kept to the periphery of the settlement. The cities were the control centers of the imperial system and the embodiment of the new political and cultural order.

Cities also had a key role in the economic system of empires. Urban hierarchies were reorganized to favor the coastal cities, whose primary commodities could be easily exported and manufactured goods could be cheaply imported. Colonial cities were the prime link between the economic core and periphery, the concrete manifestation of the emergent capitalism and what Anthony King (1990) has described as "global pivots of change." In the India of British control, for

Illustration 3.1
Colonial Calcutta: the social and radical differences of the colonial city are well illustrated in this nineteenth-century print (© Mary Evans Picture Library, London)

example, urban development was geared toward the supply of raw materials for British industry and the establishment of markets for the import of British manufactured goods. Bombay was planned and redeveloped so that by 1900 over three-quarters of India's raw cotton was shipped through the city. Calcutta exported jute to Dundee while Madras sent coffee, sugar, indigo dyes, and cotton to Britain.

Cities were and still are the point of contact between the periphery of the world economy and the core. They face both the traditional and the contemporary worlds. Around the world many cities have traditional areas, such as the marketplace, the inner city of traditional architecture. Superimposed on this vernacular tradition is the spatial manifestation of foreign economic control: the grid street pattern, the ornate public buildings and, more recently, the architecture of international modernism, the central business districts (CBDs) that look the same all over the world. The dual cities of the Third World embody the incorporation of the periphery into the core of the world economy. In the past this was done through formal imperialism and colonialism. Today it is achieved by the operation of multinational corporations, investment and disinvestment, capital flows, and the workings of the capitalist market.

The urbanization of the economy

Illustration 3.2
Commuters in London: arriving from the suburbs, the working day begins (photograph: Joanne O'Brien)

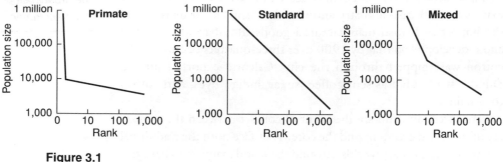

Figure 3.1
Rank size regularities

THE NATIONAL HIERARCHY

Cities and towns are the spatial manifestation of a national economy. The national urban hierarchy consists of all those villages, towns, and cities within one country. Ranked together they record the distribution of population throughout the different levels of the hierarchy. Empirical regularities in the distribution can be noted by plotting population size against rank on double logarithmic paper. The largest city is ranked 1, the second largest 2, and so on (figure 3.1). A country's economic history, as well as its economic geography, is made manifest in the changing form of its urban hierarchy. Although each country has its own distinctive patterns three general types can be identified:

- primate;
- standard;
- mixed.

The best way to discuss these different types is to provide some specific examples. Detailed case studies are often more illuminating than abstract remarks.

Britain and South America

Primate distributions are those in which the urban hierarchy is dominated by one large city. Let me elaborate with reference to one national system.

For the past 600 years, if not more, the urban history of the British Isles has been dominated by London. Throughout all the massive changes the one constant has been the overwhelming dominance of the London region in the urban hierarchy.

In 1800 Britain was still essentially an agricultural society. The bulk of the population worked on the land and lived in villages or small towns. Almost three-quarters of the population lived in places with less than 2,500 souls. Cities such as Norwich and Bristol were important regional centers, providing a market for local producers and trading points in the national economy. At the top of the hierarchy was London, the capital city of the country. London dominated not only because of its national prominence but also because it was the capital of a huge trading web that stretched around the world. London was a vast clearinghouse for the economic life of the British Empire, the hub of a giant wheel whose spokes stretched to Canada, Australia, South Africa, and numerous islands around the world. Even in 1800 London was a world city.

The dominance has continued. London is bigger than the combined populations of the next 15 biggest cities in the United Kingdom. One in every three people in the country lives either in London or in the south-east region of the country, which to all intents and purposes is within London's sphere of influence. The bias is apparent in the concentration of nationwide functions in the capital city. London is not only the largest city in the region, it is the seat of government of the United Kingdom, and the location of the headquarters of most major British, and indeed many foreign, companies and corporations. London is the center for the English legal system, the center for banking and insurance, the center for publishing, fashion and advertising. The list goes on and on, a litany of the concentration of money, power, and influence.

Population in the London of the officially designated administrative region has declined over the years. The population of Greater London was 8.6 million in 1939, but this figure had fallen to approximately 6 million by 1991. Growth in London has taken place outside the administrative region. The combined population of London and the south-east region of the country was almost 17 million in 1990. The total national population was 57.4 million. Because of transport connections many people now work in London but live outside the city. Long-distance commuting is a fact of life for those who work in the city. Housing is cheaper outside the city, and many people are willing to travel up to three hours a day to live in more spacious surroundings than they could afford in the capital. Home and work are connected by an intricate system of rail, road, and underground systems, which allow commuters to live throughout and beyond the south-east region. Many towns are little more than dormitory settlements from which thousands of people leave every morning by train, car or bus to work in the city. The commuting flows are like a great tide of humanity that brings in people in the morning, depositing them at their place of work, and then takes them back at the end of the working day.

The influence of the capital stretches even wider across the country. London is the home of the media. Because of the good transport connections and the relatively small size of the country, newspapers published in London can be bought every morning in most towns, cities, and even villages throughout the land. The chattering classes, the intellectual elite who give shape and substance to dominant ideas, are concentrated in the capital, with the result that the experience of London is magnified to national significance. The view from London, however, is not the same as that from Bristol or Leeds, let alone Nether Wallop or Tullibody. "National" debates have a significant metropolitan bias. Visitors to Britain are concentrated in London. One out of every three foreign tourists never even leave the city. But all visitors should remember that London is not Britain. It is not even England. It is a global metropolis, a world city. But behind this cosmopolitanism lies a metropolitan provincialism.

The variety of urban experience in Britain was evident in the varied response to different places – to be more precise, of the people and economy of these places – to the large-scale economic and social changes of the 1980s. Phil Cooke (1989) edited a collection of essays which looked at the local impacts of economic restructuring in seven localities. The studies highlighted the variety of change, from the decline in the old industrial areas in the north-east of England to the affluence and growth of such southern towns as Swindon. These locality studies pointed to the differences caused by the intersection of global and local economic and social factors.

The case of Britain illustrates a primate urban hierarchy in a rich country. It is much more common to find this pattern in the poorer countries of the world, where urban primacy is the rule rather than the exception. This is the case in South America, where urban growth has been dramatic. In 1940 two-thirds of the people in South America lived in the countryside. By 1990 two-thirds of a hugely expanded population lived in cities, especially the big cities. The biggest cities grew fastest because they were the scene of industrial activity and government functions. This provided job opportunities that in turn attracted migrants. The economic weight of particular countries became skewed toward the big city, a pattern maintained and reinforced by powerful vested interests. The big cities became the home of an emerging middle class, which drew more consumer-oriented industries. A powerful cycle of growth attracting more growth spiraled city populations. São Paulo in Brazil increased from 2.8 million in 1950 to 16 million in 1990, while Caracas, over the same period, increased from an insignificant 700,000 to 4 million. The big cities contained job opportunities and better provision of basic services, such as health care and education, all of which attracted migrants from the rural areas and other towns and cities. The end result is national hierarchies dominated by one giant city. In Uruguay one out of every two people live in Montevideo, while in Argentina one of every three people live in Buenos Aires. Colombia has population of 31 million, but over 4 million live in the capital and largest city, Bogotá. The concentration is even more marked in Peru: of a population of 21 million, 6.5 million live in Lima.

Urban primacy causes congestion in the one big city while siphoning off migrants, capital, and services from the rest of the country; it results in a very uneven distribution of economic growth, apoplexy at the urban center and anemia in the national periphery.

The US urban system

A standard distribution can occur when no one city dominates and there is a more even spread. Take the case of the United States, with a total population of almost 250 million; the largest city, New York, even with the most generous definition for the whole urban region, has a population of 18 million. Fewer than 7 percent live in the biggest city. Compare that figure with Mexico, where Mexico City has 18 percent of the country's population, or Britain, where over 20 percent live in the Greater London region.

The United States is an urbanized country. More than 70 percent of the nation live in cities of more than 50,000. It is a country of big cities; there are more than 20 cities of over 1 million. No one city dominates the economic, political, and social life of the country. New York is the biggest city, but is not the center of federal power. The size of the country, the greater power of the individual states and the changing regional distribution of economic activity have all militated against concentration in one center. The changing economic fortunes are recorded in the growth and decline of different urban regions.

At the time of independence the United States was essentially a rural society. In 1790, the first datum point for the new republic, the total population was only 3.9 million, at a density of 4.5 persons per square mile. Less than 7 percent of the population lived in cities and the cities were small. In 1790 the largest city, New York, had a population of only 33,181.

Settlers pushed westward from the ports and cities of the east in the search for land and wealth. The attraction of the interior was continually reinforced by the discovery of gold, the prospect of open land cleared by the US Army of its original populations, and the encouragement of the government. The Homestead Act of 1862, for example, made public land available to settlers in blocks of 160 acres. The westward movement, the stuff of western movies and cowboy myths, shifted the center of gravity of the US population away from its East Coast bias; a process helped by the growth of San Francisco and Los Angeles in the west, which acted as small counterweights to such East Coast cities as New York and Boston.

The nineteenth century also saw the beginnings of industrialization in the United States and the consequent growth of industrial cities. There was the emergence of steel towns, such as Pittsburgh, and the development of manufacturing centers, such as Chicago, Buffalo, Detroit, and Cleveland. These cities were concentrated in the north-east of the country, where the coalfields and the mass of the population were located. The industrial heartland of America was in the towns of such states as New York, Ohio, Pennsylvania, Michigan, New Jersey, and Massachusetts. The southern states of the Union were overwhelmingly rural and nonindustrial.

During the first half of the twentieth century there was a continued growth of the population and a shift toward a more urban population. From 1890 to 1940 it increased from 63 million to 131 million. Immigration fueled this demographic surge. In the nineteenth century most migrants had come from Britain, Ireland and Germany, but in this latter period the source of immigration was predominantly southern and central Europe. Most of the migrants arrived in the big cities of the East Coast; for many the New York skyline was their first sight of America. The cities grew by leaps and bounds. By 1920 more people lived in urban centers than in rural areas. The growth of manufacturing, the development of urban economies, and the mechanization of agriculture were all leading to the growth of cities and a leveling-off of migration to the land. The frontier was closed, and wide open lands no longer beckoned the foolish, the desperate, and the brave. The United States was becoming a society of big cities. The early cities of the Republic were small, but throughout the nineteenth and early twentieth centuries cities such as Philadelphia and Chicago continued to grow and attract migrants. New York emerged as the single biggest city; it grew from a population of 33,181 in 1790 to 3 million in 1890 and to 7 million in 1950.

At the midpoint of the twentieth century 56 percent of the entire US population lived in cities with a population of more than 50,000. The overwhelmingly agrarian society at the time of independence had become a predominantly urban society.

The US Census Bureau makes data available for urban regions, called metropolitan statistical areas (MSAs). MSAs are counties that either have a city population of at least 50,000 or contained an urbanized area of 50,000 with a total metropolitan population of at least 100,000. This definition therefore includes not only the legally defined cities but also the built-up surrounding areas. In 1950 there were 109 MSAs; their combined population constituted 56 percent of the entire US population and almost 6 percent of the land area. By 1990 the number of MSAs had risen to 283 and constituted 70 percent of the nation's population and 16 percent of the land area. In this 40–year period, then, the United States experienced a massive increase in the number of medium and big cities.

Consolidated metropolitan statistical areas (CMSAs) are MSAs that have a population of at least 1 million and a measure of local support for separate recognition. Twenty CMSAs have been identified. The largest is the New York–Northern New Jersey–Long Island CMSA with a combined population of over 18 million. The smallest is Hartford–New Britain–Middletown in Connecticut with just over 1 million. CMSAs are the metropolitan heartland of the United States: large urban regions whose sphere of influence spreads over a wide area and, in the case of New York, includes millions of people. Almost 90 million people live in these giant urban regions, one in every three persons in the United States.

The number and size of urban regions have been growing across the country. The statistics at the national level, however, conceal marked regional variations: the growth of urban regions has not been uniform. In the past 20 years urban growth has been concentrated in the south and west, whereas urban decline has been most marked in the north-east and midwest. The fastest-growing cities have been in the so-called Sunbelt states of California, Arizona, Texas, Georgia, and Florida. Retirement migration, the movement of firms from other parts of the country and the establishment of new industries such as the computer industries in Silicon Valley in California have all helped to shift the US population away from its traditional north-east focus. Cities like Los Angeles (California), Phoenix (Arizona), Dallas-Fort Worth (Texas), Atlanta (Georgia), and Miami (Florida) have all experienced tremendous growth in the last three decades. From 1945 to 1980 the population of Phoenix, for example, increased from a mere 65,000 to 790,000, and by 1990 it was well over 2 million. The lure of the sun, the availability of air-conditioning, the access to cheap, nonunionized labor in some Sunbelt states, and indirect federal subsidies in the form of energy utilization, water provision and defense procurements have all been key factors.

Throughout much of the Sunbelt economic growth was caused partly by federal expenditure on the space program and armaments technology. Houston became the control center for the National Aeronautics and Space Administration (NASA) program, while Cape Canaveral was the site of rocket launches. Elsewhere, but particularly in southern California, the heavy spending on high-technology armaments development was a powerful boost to economic expansion. Reductions in defense expenditure caused by the decline of the Cold War pose severe problems for the continued economic health of this region.

The rapidity of growth has caused problems. Sensitive ecological habitats have been destroyed or seriously affected by rapid, large-scale urban development. Many of these hot-dry (south and west) or hot-wet (south and east) environments are very sensitive. In some cases the pressure for growth has stretched the ecological limits. The Sunbelt of southern California and the south-west, for example, is an area of water scarcity, and yet modern American homes require ready supplies of cheap water. In some places development is being halted, or at least being made more expensive, because water availability is becoming more limited.

Urban decline, in contrast, has been apparent in the older settlements of the north-east and mid-west. The urban areas of such Frostbelt states as Michigan, Ohio, Pennsylvania, Massachusetts, and New York developed on the basis of traditional manufacturing. Since the 1970s there has been a deindustrialization of the American economy. Traditional manufacturing employment has been undercut by cheaper foreign competition. In 1970 over 90 percent of cars driven in the United States were made in the United States. Cities like Detroit turned out thousands of cars every day, and the city was buoyed up by a large number of people in high-paying jobs. In 1990 less than 60 percent of cars were made in the United States. German and particularly Japanese cars were considered better value for money. Foreign car companies have also established their own plants within the United States. However, they have built them not in the old industrial areas like Detroit but in the cheaper-labor areas of the Sunbelt. The net effect has been the loss of manufacturing employment in the Frostbelt. Some of the most-affected cities are called the Rustbelt as formerly growing industrial areas begin the process of decline. The loss of employment means fewer jobs, less income, and an erosion of the economic bases of these old cities. A cycle of decline can then be initiated as their tax base decreases, making it more difficult to provide good public services, which makes more people move, and so the downward spiral gathers momentum. The problem for the declining cities in the former industrial heartland of the United States is how to revive their flagging economies and attract investment. It is a difficult task.

The regional shift in the industrial center of gravity of the United States has also been caused by the movement of firms and companies from Frostbelt urban regions to Sunbelt cities. The search for a more pleasant climate is only part of the reason. Wages are lower, trade unions are less organized and state regulation limits the scope of union activity and organization. Taxes vary dramatically among states and even within states. The Frostbelt states often have higher taxes because they tend to spend more on social welfare and education. California is a Sunbelt exception, and even here there is some evidence that firms are moving from high-tax California to lower-tax Arizona. The net effect has been a movement of firms away from the traditionally higher-tax, higher-labor-cost states towards the more business-oriented climate of the Sunbelt. People have voted with their feet to these changing employment opportunities, and the result is urban growth in the Sunbelt and urban decline in the Frostbelt.

There is both stability and change in the US urban system. The stability is most pronounced atop the urban hierarchy. New York, for example, has been the largest city in the country for over 200 years. Change is apparent in the meteoric rise of certain cities. In 1900 Los Angeles, for example, was a small, rather insignificant sleepy settlement with a population of only 100,000. There has been incredible growth in the twentieth century as economic developments in industry and commerce provided a magnet for interregional and international migration. By 1990 the metropolitan region of Los Angeles, spread over 450 square miles, had a population of almost 12 million. It is an example of a city's move up the urban hierarchy over the course of the twentieth century. There are even more meteoric rises at the next level of the hierarchy. In 1945 the population of Phoenix, Arizona, was only 65,000. By 1980 it had increased to 790,000 and to over 2 million by 1990. The establishment of firms and industries attracted by the cheap labor, plentiful land and low taxes turned a flyblown, dead-end town into a thriving metropolis.

The curious case of Australia

For many countries the pattern of their urban hierarchy is neither standard nor primate. They may be dominated by two or even three cities. The urban hierarchy of Australia is unusual. It is dominated by *five* big cities (table 3.1; see also figure 3.2). The explanation of this pattern tells us much about the economic development of the country.

TABLE 3.1 CITIES IN AUSTRALIA		
City	*State*	*Population, 1990 (in millions)*
Sydney	New South Wales	2.8
Melbourne	Victoria	2.5
Brisbane	Queensland	0.9
Adelaide	South Australia	0.8
Perth	Western Australia	0.8

The top-heavy character of the hierarchy is a result of economic history. In the early years of white settlement what is now called Australia was a penal colony. Prisons are about enclosing people, limiting their space. The 1788 foothold on the coast was confined to a limited area around Sydney. Captain Arthur Phillip, his mariners and convict charges were hemmed in by the nature of their business, ignorance of the terrain, fear of the indigenous population and the need to maintain links with Britain. The colony relied on Britain for food.

Figure 3.2
Australia, showing major cities

Throughout the nineteenth century more and more of the interior came under white control. The aborigines used the land for both

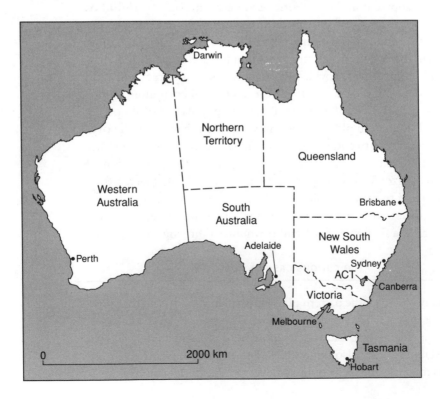

material and spiritual purposes. The whites used it only for material purposes – white control meant the "commodification" of the land. Sheep and cattle were grazed, wheat was grown and minerals were mined. These commodities were shipped overseas. Each state of Australia was a branch plant of an economic enterprise whose head office was in London.

The regional office was the major city in each state, the place of transshipment and the center for local finance and state government.

TABLE 3.2	URBAN PRIMACY IN AUSTRALIA	
State	*Largest City and population, 1990 (millions)*	*Second-largest city and population, 1990 (millions)*
New South Wales	Sydney 2.8	Newcastle 0.2
Victoria	Melbourne 2.5	Geelong 0.1
Queensland	Brisbane 0.9	Gold Coast 0.13
South Australia	Adelaide 0.8	Whyalla 0.002
Western Australia	Perth 0.8	Bunbury 0.002

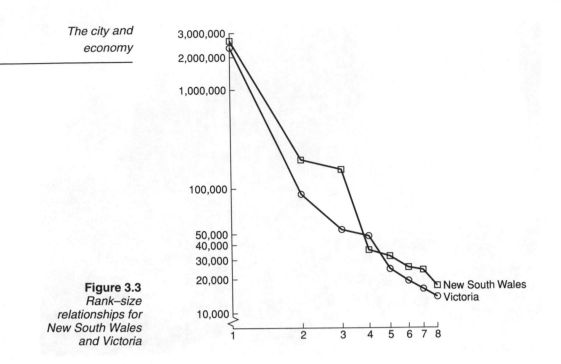

Figure 3.3
Rank–size
relationships for
New South Wales
and Victoria

Each state capital grew as a port for the import and export of goods. As more of the interior was commodified and trade increased, so did the cities. The cities grew bigger as the expansion of the trading system increased local earnings, which in turn created the demand for more goods and services: in each of the state capitals there was a process of cumulative causation of this kind. As table 3.2 shows, the size of towns declines markedly after the one big city in the state. Sydney, Melbourne, Brisbane, Adelaide, and Perth are primate cities within their states. Look how urban size falls away particularly in South Australia and Western Australia. Figure 3.3 highlights the primate rank-size distribution for New South Wales and Victoria.

In each state there was some development outside of the state capital. The discovery of gold in Victoria in 1851, for example, created a quick population increase in the goldfields. Tent sites became villages and villages grew into towns. There is, however, a critical population size for cities, sometimes termed the *urban ratchet*. Above this size, approximately a quarter of a million, cities can be self-sustaining. Below it, short-lived economic booms can just as quickly turn into slumps. In Victoria the landscape is littered with nineteenth-century goldfield towns whose fine buildings reflect a glorious past but now look onto a desultory present.

The Australian urban hierarchy is not yet dominated by just one

Illustration 3.4
*Penola, South
Australian outback
town: close to the
bottom of the
Australian urban
hierarchy*
*(© J. Carnemolla,
Australian Picture
Library)*

city. The reason for this pattern lies in the politics of the urban hierarchy. It was only in 1901 that the individual states federated to become one nation. Prior to this, the states were self-contained entities all looking more towards British and overseas markets than to each other. Their separateness was a function of distance (Perth is two time-zones away from Sydney), economic orientation and inclination. They had different railway gauges, different newspapers, and even different rugby codes. Rugby league was played in New South Wales, while Australian Rules, a sort of balletic game of organized violence, had its center in Victoria.

Each state was like a separate country, with very powerful state capitals responsible for trade, transport, education, and the vast bulk of public expenditure. State politicians used this power to maintain urban dominance. In New South Wales, for example, the state government, based in Sydney, fixed the railway charges so that it was always cheaper for wheat farmers to export their produce through Sydney rather than through any other port in New South Wales.

The different populations of the capitals are a function of the varying economic development, wealth, and population of their respective states. The richer states of Victoria and New South Wales can support the two largest cities, and the rivalry between them is intense. The two cities are often used to identify different character-istics of Australia. Melbourne is seen as more cultured and more civilized than brash, hedonistic, corrupt Sydney.

THE REGIONAL HIERARCHY

At the base level of the urban hierarchy are individual dwellings: the distance between them is a function of a variety of things, including the history of settlement and, in agricultural areas, the fertility of the soil. Where the soil is very fertile high population densities are found. In poorer areas, in contrast, only a thin scattering of population is possible. Compare the rich volcanic soils of Java in Indonesia, where average densities can reach 500 persons per square kilometer, with the more marginal farming areas of northern Canada, where densi-ties of one household per 500 square kilometers are commonly found.

At the next level of the settlement hierarchy we find groups of dwellings congregating together to form hamlets and small villages. This was the predominant level of settlement hierarchy before the industrial revolution; it still predominates throughout the rural areas of the world. The size and spacing of villages, like the individual dwellings, is a function of many factors, including history and such varied physical factors as soil fertility and agricultural productivity. Settlements are denser in richer agricultural regions than they are in areas where the soil is poor and unproductive.

The next level of the settlement hierarchy is the small town. Here are located urban services such as retail outlets and public services such as the town hall, post office, bars, and theaters. These facilities serve not only the town's population but also that of the surround-ing area. We are now in the urban section of the settlement hierarchy. In subsequent steps of the urban hierarchy the number of urban ser-vices increases, as does the population of the urban center. At one extreme there is the small town with a population of only a few thou-sand, a limited range of shops and only a few public services. At the other extreme is the giant city with a population in the millions, thou-sands of shops, and a whole range of urban services.

Central place theory

Early formulations The size and spacing of the regional urban hierar-chy has long been a source of fascination for observers. In 1915 a sociologist by the name of C.J. Galpin, in studying rural

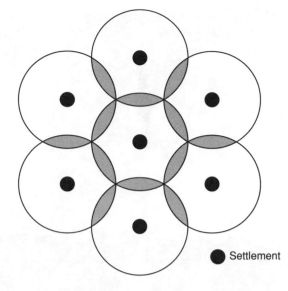

Settlement

Figure 3.4
*Galpin's model of
the spacing
settlements*

communities in Wisconsin, came to the conclusion that, under ideal
conditions, settlements with the same number of services would be
spaced at regular intervals across the landscape (Galpin, 1915). Each
settlement would have what he termed a complementary region (see
figure 3.4) In southern Germany the geographer Walter Christaller
(1966) wanted to discover what determines the number, size, and
distribution of towns. He answered the question with reference to
range and *threshold* of goods and services. The range of a good is the
distance people are prepared to travel to purchase it. People are willing to travel farther to buy a car than, say, a carton of milk. A car has
a greater range than milk. The threshold of a good is the minimum
population necessary to support the continued supply of the good.
Milk sales could survive in a small village but car sales need a bigger
population. Goods with large thresholds and extensive ranges are
called higher-order goods and services. Lower-order goods and services have smaller thresholds and more restricted ranges.

Christaller imagined a flat plain. The distribution of urban places,
which he called central places, would form a hierarchy. To service regular widespread demand, such as milk sales, a large number of widely
distributed small places would provide lower-order goods and services. Successive steps of the hierarchy would consist of larger central
places more widely spread, with both higher and lower goods and services. The complementary regions of central places would form a
hexagon. Why a hexagon? Because in the simple Galpin model (figure 3.4) there are areas of overlap. Christaller thought that most
people would only shop at one center, which would be the nearest

Illustration 3.5
*Stuttgart in the
1930s. This city
was one of the
higher-order urban
centers in
Christaller's study
of central place
theory (© Mansell
Collection, London)*

central place. The resulting spatial form is a hexagon (figure 3.5). Christaller proposed a number of hexagonal structures with different k values, where k refers to the number of lower-order centers served by one higher-order center (figure 3.6): in the market-optimizing structure, the emphasis is on minimizing consumer travel; in the traffic-optimizing structure the network is more efficient because routes link up higher-order centers with lower-order centers; and in the administrative-optimizing structure each lower-order place is within the boundary of a higher-order center.

Subsequent work   There have been subsequent theoretical and empirical contributions to central place theory. The German economist August Losch (1954) suggested a more flexible model in which k does not remain fixed for all levels of the hierarchy. For each good or service there is a different market area; the retail landscape is composed of the superimposition of various hexagonal market areas.

There have also been elaborations of the notion of the complementary region. Different terms have been used to describe the same

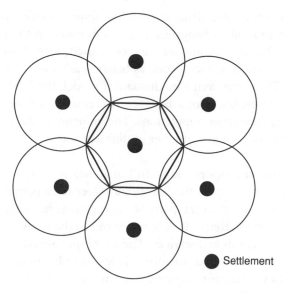

Figure 3.5
The derivation of hexagonal market areas

● Settlement

Figure 3.6
Different hexagonal structures
(a) Market optimizing k = 3
(b) Traffic optimizing k = 4
(c) Administration optimizing k = 7

● Higher order central place
○ Lower order central place
—— Complementary region
—— Highways

Derivation of *k* value

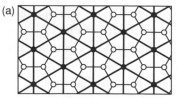

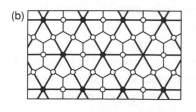

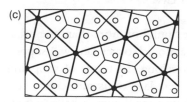

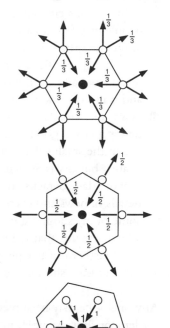

Shoppers in the smaller places divide into 3 equal groups when shopping in the 3 nearest larger places

Shoppers in the smaller places divide into 2 equal groups when shopping in the 2 nearest larger places

All shoppers in the smaller places shop in the nearest large place phenomenon: hinterland, ulmland, or sphere of influence. Attention shifted from identifying hexagons to discovering the extent of the region. Various techniques have been used, identifying the trading areas of various services, such as banking areas or school catchment areas. There was even a mathematical model, the Reilly model, that predicted the breakpoint between two cities based on their distance apart and respective populations. The influence in the sphere of influence can be seen in a number of different ways:

- allegiance to sports clubs. In Catalonia, the north-east region of Spain, support for the Barcelona soccer team permeates throughout the rural parts of the region as far as the Pyrenees;
- shopping patterns. People will travel to the nearest town or city to buy goods and services. The more specialized the service or the rarer the good the more likely it is to be found in a bigger urban settlement. Big cities thus attract shoppers from a wide sphere of influence;
- journey to work. Urban centers provide employment opportunities. People will travel into towns and cities for jobs. Journey-to-work patterns can be used to identify the sphere of influence of a city. At the outermost edges of the urban region people may find it easier to travel to work in another city. Sometimes the sphere of influence for journey-to-work patterns can stretch very far. In the case of London, for example, people travel from all over the south-east of England by car, tube, bus and train to work in the capital city;
- newspaper circulation. The circulation pattern of a city's newspaper is a good indicator of the city's sphere of influence. I live in the small village of Cazenovia in upstate New York. The nearest big city is Syracuse, twenty miles away, but I regularly buy the daily Syracuse newspaper because it provides me with details of news and events which affect my life. Since I also do some of my shopping in that city, I am interested in the advertisements that tell me about bargains and sales. Twenty miles farther out few people buy the newspaper because they do most of their shopping at another city.

Any one place may be subject to the "pull" of more than one urban settlement. For example, in rural Catalonia soccer fans will support the local village team as well as Barcelona. In terms of shopping, people will go to the local town for everyday goods and services, but if they want to hear a symphony or buy a car they may have to go to the nearest city. The same with newspaper buying. In any one week

I will buy three newspapers: the *New York Times* (New York is over 200 miles from where I live, but it gives me national and international news), the *Syracuse Herald-Journal* for local news, and the *Cazenovia Republican* to find out what my neighbors are up to. There are invisible lines across the landscape. Like magnetic fields the spheres of influence of towns and cities stretch throughout the land, encompassing smaller settlements and rural areas within their "pull of attraction."

While most of the work on hinterlands has been concerned with the social world, William Cronon (1991) has considered the physical environment. In particular, he examined the relationship between the city of Chicago and its hinterland in the period 1850 to 1890. He looked at the way the natural landscaping was turned into the human landscape in the harnessing of the hinterland to support economic growth. He focused on the growth of this major city relative to the natural systems that made its growth possible. The transformation of nature into commodity was studied with reference to grain, lumber, and meat and the respective role of merchants, rail and bank executives, and primary producers. The book is a well-documented study of the creation of a capitalist urban hinterland. Cronon's work is a rare example of an historical geography and of a geographical history.

Central place theory has also provided the basis for detailed empirical studies of particular regional hierarchies. Richard Preston (1971) identified the urban hierarchy in the Pacific north-west, Brian Berry (1967) looked at the evolution of the central place system in rural Iowa, and Bromley and Bromley (1979) uncovered the central place system in part of Ecuador by looking at bus services (figure 3.7). These studies are interesting because they provide an example of the elaboration of theory, detailed case studies of various and diverse urban regions and a creative use of techniques to uncover the different levels of the hierarchy and their spatial manifestation.

While central place theory has been important in the development of urban geography – and for many years it seemed to be the only theory in urban geography – there has been an eclipse of interest in recent years. There are two reasons. The first is that central place theory is most appropriate for preindustrial urban systems. The theory works best for central places in self-contained, agricultural regions. It has less relevance for urban systems affected by industrialization and rapid, large-scale "shocks" from the global economy. And yet it just these latter conditions that occur throughout much of the world as industrialization proceeds apace and the extension and strengthening of the global economy brings even the most remote

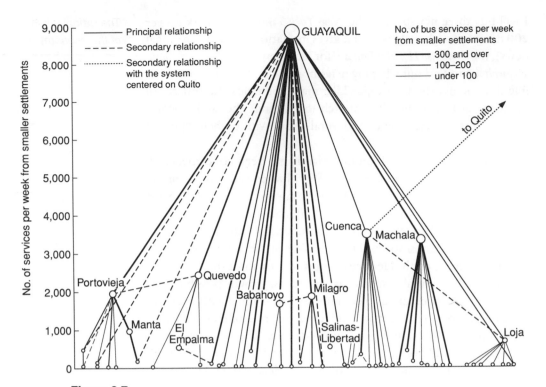

Figure 3.7
The functional structure of the system of centers focused on Guayaquil (1975)
Source*: Bromley and Bromley (1979)*

regions into the orbit of the world trading system. Central place theory is less appropriate in the modern urban world. And the second reason is that the spatial organization of society has been replaced by the social organization of space as a topic of interest; politics and culture rather than geometry and distance have become guiding lights in the new urban geography.

BEYOND CENTRAL PLACE THEORY: THE NEW GEOGRAPHY OF RETAILING

The early formulation and subsequent elaboration of central place theory was an important part of the earlier development of urban geography. While there is still a concern with retailing and shopping, the focus of more recent work has moved well beyond the confines of central place theory. Two areas can be identified. First, there is the *new geography of retailing* which is concerned as much with the social organization of retailing as with its spatial expression. A political economy approach can be identified in such writers as Wrigley and Lowe (1995) and Hallsworth (1992). In this approach emphasis is placed on such topics as the organization of retailing, the retail-supplier relations, retail employment, and examples of specific types of retailing. Let us look at each of these in turn.

In much of the advanced capitalist world an important trend has been the increasing size of retail companies. The small, family-run corner store has to compete with retail giants with thousands of employees, hundreds of outlets, and huge purchasing power. This trend is more marked in some countries. In Britain, for example, the level of market domination by just a few companies, such as Marks & Spencer, Tesco, and Sainsbury, is much greater than in the larger, more diverse and geographically more fragmented market of the USA. In his study of grocery retailing, Wrigley (1992) notes how this difference is partly a function of the antitrust legislation in the USA, which is hostile to the development of big capital in retailing, compared to the more benign regulatory environment experienced by the big UK grocery retailers. This increasingly oligopolistic market has a number of consequences. The locational strategies of these companies and the competition between them is one of the primary driving forces affecting the geography of retailing.

Another factor is the effect of retail-supplier relations. Retail-supplier relations are more complex than "a producer produces and a retailer sells." In many richer countries, the rise of large retail corporations has given them a huge bargaining advantage over producers, especially small-scale producers. And this increased power is reflected in the drive towards increasing costs and increasing quality of goods produced for the large retail chains. Markets are as influenced by retail power as by producer power. The increasing power of retailers reaches back through the production chain to affect the cost, timing, and quality of many goods sold in the retail sector.

Retailing employment has traditionally been one of the weakest sectors of organized labor. The wide dispersal of employees and the traditionally heavy reliance on occasional and part-time workers have not created the best conditions for the organization of labor. Employment in the retail sector, although access to it is easy, has traditionally been characterized by low wages, long hours and few promotion opportunities. As in other sectors of the economy, where there is intense competition and downward cost pressure companies want to lower their wage burden; this is a major factor behind the automation of the retail store. More open shelves and easier access to good allow consumers to look at the inventory without needing so much personal assistance. Computerized scanners allow companies to monitor their sales and inventory stock with fewer personnel.

The retail sector is very varied. The food sector is different from

(a) 1980

(b) 1985

Figure 3.8
*The location of
"coffee shops" in
Amsterdam
(a) 1980
(b) 1985*
Source*: Jansen
(1991)*

the fashion sector in terms of spatial location requirements, investment patterns and production chains. Some of these differences can
only be revealed by case studies of individual sectors. One interesting
example is the study by Jansen (1991) of cannabis retailing in
Amsterdam. The drug is legally sold in "coffee shops". Jansen's study
is an ethnographic account of the "coffee shops" as well as a spatial
analysis of the sector. The changing distribution of these shops is indicated in figure 3.8.

A second area of interest in the new geography of retailing is the
emphasis on *consumption* and *consumerism*. Shopping is not only a
necessity, it is a social activity, a cultural pursuit. Where we shop,
when we shop, and what we buy are important elements in social differentiation and individual identity. The importance of shopping is
evident in those slogans that percolated public discourse in the 1980s:
"When the going gets tough, the tough go shopping;" "Shop till you
drop;" "I could have shopped all night." Slogans like this were put
on the contemporary billboard, the T-shirt. Consumption is as much
an act of identity as production. What you buy identifies you as
much as what you do. Communities of consumption can be identified that result from the particular appropriations of consumer goods.
Certain goods and services have become an integral part of the changing definitions not of style and taste but of gender, age, sexual
orientation, and racial and ethnic identity. There are subtle connections between retail capital, consumer spending, and cultural
appropriation that link business, consumers, and communities
(Miller, 1995). An important element in this new research is the
analysis of the places and spaces of consumption (Shields, 1992). Jon
Goss (1993), for example, deconstructs the space and cultural meaning of the mall in the USA. Current work on shopping and retailing
has moved beyond the geometric focus of early central place theory
towards a more explicit consideration of the economic importance
and cultural significance of retail spaces.

MOVEMENT IN THE URBAN HIERARCHY

The urban hierarchy is never static. We can imagine it as a system in
continual motion. People, ideas, goods, and services are always
moving through the system. The net movement of population, for
example, gives us an indicator of wider economic changes. Movement
up the hierarchy, sometimes called rural-to-urban migration, is the
predominant form of population redistribution in urbanizing and
industrializing societies. Almost two-thirds of urban growth in big

cities in the Third World is due to people moving from rural areas to the bigger cities. In the opening scene of the 1992 movie *City of Joy* we are shown an Indian family leaving their village, boarding a bus and arriving in the huge, impersonal, sprawling city of Calcutta. The family gets ripped off, the man is unable to find work, and things look bleak. Through hard work – the man pulls a rickshaw through the smoggy traffic and flooded streets – and by the experience of living and coping in the big city, the family obtains accommodation and saves enough cash to afford a handsome dowry for their young daughter. Rural-to-urban migrants are driven by the hopes and expectations of making a better life for themselves and particularly for their children. While people move up the urban hierarchy money may move downwards as migrants remit some of their income back to the villages of their family. In Europe, for example, there are many houses constructed in rural Portugal, Greece, and Turkey funded by wages from work in the factories of Germany and France. Throughout the world rural migrants send some of their income back to the rural areas.

Figure 3.9 presents a general model of population movement in an urban region. In phase 1 people are attracted to the central city by the lure of jobs, better services and education. Most big Third World cities are in this phase at the present. In phase 2 jobs are no longer tied to the central core. With increasing affluence and transport improvements some people can move to the suburbs. This was the predominant movement in Western Europe and North America from 1950 to 1990. At this stage the predominant direction of movement is down the urban hierarchy and particularly from big cities to sub-urban towns and villages. Phase 3 shows a more complex pattern: suburbanization is still occurring, but there is also movement from the suburbs to the city center as younger households move back to selected city centers; while in the rural areas the process of counterurbanization may be occurring.

Counterurbanization refers to movement down the hierarchy to the more remote rural areas outside the sphere of influence of the big city. Counterurbanization is not just an extension of suburbanization but a reversal of the rural-to-urban shift that has been so dominant over the past 200 years. The evidence for counterurbanization is not conclusive. In an early paper Vining and Strauss (1977) suggested that a clean break was occurring in US population concentration since 1970. However, subsequent analyses of census did not reveal a sustained trend. For Europe, Hall and Hay (1980) found that rural-to-urban migration was still dominant. Counterurbanization may not be so widespread as first imagined, but in selected areas it is

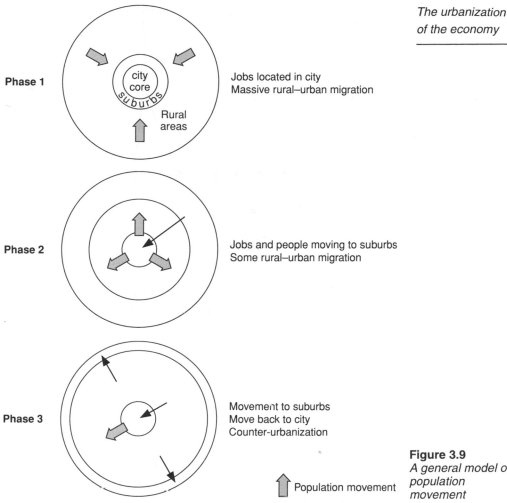

Phase 1

city core

suburbs

Rural areas

Jobs located in city
Massive rural–urban migration

Phase 2

Jobs and people moving to suburbs
Some rural–urban migration

Phase 3

Movement to suburbs
Move back to city
Counter-urbanization

Population movement

Figure 3.9
A general model of population movement

occurring (Coombs, 1989). The reasons include the telecommunications revolution, which allows people to be connected yet physically distant. The term *electronic cottage* captures this point. Telecommuting rather than travel commuting allows people to live far away from the central city. People's ability to live farther away from central places has been aided by domestic technology, which includes cars that enable them to travel far for shopping and fridges that lift the restriction of the need to shop on a daily basis. Counter-urbanization also occurs on a temporal basis in many countries, where the more affluent escape the urban summer and move to cottages and houses in the countryside. The population of many hamlets is boosted by such summer visitors.

The move back to the city is a selective process found particularly

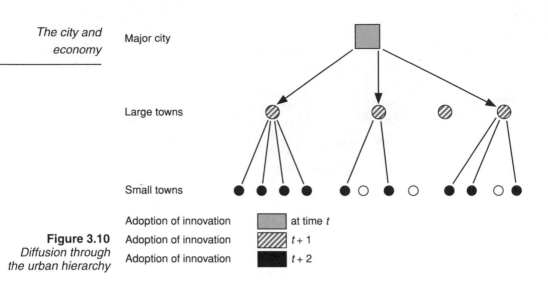

Major city

Large towns

Small towns

Adoption of innovation ▨ at time *t*

Figure 3.10
Diffusion through the urban hierarchy

Adoption of innovation ▨ *t* + 1

Adoption of innovation ■ *t* + 2

in bigger cities in North America, where there is still a substantial downtown service economy. Some developers have met this demand by creating apartment for singles. The resulting process of gentrification was one of the important topics of urban geography in the 1980s. It is considered more fully in chapter 9.

Ideas as well as people flow through the urban hierarchy. For example, big cities are often the incubators for ideas in fashion that percolate down through the smaller towns and villages (figure 3.10). Hierarchical diffusion through the urban system has also been identified for a number of phenomena, from measles (Cliff et al., 1993) to the adoption of technology (Robson, 1973). Peter Gould (1993), for example, shows how the HIV virus moves from city to city, creating urban regional epicenters and then spreading out into surrounding areas.

CHANGE IN THE URBAN HIERARCHY

Because the urban hierarchy is not static, a number of structural changes can be identified. *Thinning* of the hierarchy occurs when the provision of goods and services moves up the hierarchy. In his study of central places in Iowa, Berry (1967) showed how the settlement pattern reached its peak in 1904. Thereafter there was a thinning of the central place system as paved roads and automobile use allowed consumers to bypass smaller centers. As the small store is replaced by the out-of-town shopping center and as hypermarkets provide better bargains than the neighborhood grocery, then the provision of goods

moves up the hierarchy. Smaller centers lose some of their vitality.
Thinning has been a major process in the smaller towns and villages
of Western Europe and North America. The process creates real problems of accessibility for those with restricted access to automobiles in
societies where public transport is poor or expensive.

The *shrinking* of the urban network occurs when towns and cities
are brought closer together in space-time. In 1658 it took almost 14
days to travel or take a message between London and Edinburgh. The
journey was over rough roads by uncomfortable stagecoaches. By
1850 the same distance took 14 hours by train, and by 1990 it took
just one hour by plane. And a telephone call or electronic mail means
that conversations can be held between two people in the different
cities at exactly the same time. This technological wonder we now
take for granted. The urban network has been brought closer
together. In space-time terms the urban system has shrunk. And now
cyberspace has collapsed even further traditional notions of distance.
To measure urban centrality Walter Christaller, in the 1930s, used
the number of telephones in a town. It was a very prescient variable.
In the 1990s telecommunication has disrupted our traditional
notions of distance, centrality, and accessibility. When you can shop
over the phone, have things sent to you from a television catalogue,
then what constitutes a central place may be not at the junction of two
tarmacadam roads but at the intersection of two or more routes on
the information superhighway. Boyer (1995) argues that as cyberspace
pulls us together we tend to withdraw from the material world. It is
more an interesting hypothesis than a statement of fact. The full implications and consequences of this evolving information superhighway
on the urban hierarchy have yet to be fully developed and constitute
some of the more engaging research questions for the years ahead.

GUIDE TO FURTHER READING

Data on world urbanization, city populations and rates of growth for most
countries of the world are available in the annual United Nations
Demographic Yearbook. Other more convenient and more easily used
sources include:
Geographical Digest (published annually), Oxford: George Philip and
Heinemann.
World Development Report (published annually), Oxford and New York:
Oxford University Press.

On the global hierarchy, see:
Hall, P. (1984) *The World Cities*, London: Weidenfeld & Nicolson.
King, A.D. (1990) *Urbanism, Colonialism and the World Economy*, London:
Routledge.

Sassen, S. (1991) *The Global City*, Princeton, N.J.: Princeton University Press.
Sassen, S. (1994) *Cities in a World Economy*, Thousand Oaks, Cal.: Pine Forge Press.
Timberlake, M. (ed.) (1985) *Urbanization in the World Economy*, London: Academic Press.

The material on national and regional urban systems draws heavily upon my own writings on the subject:
Short, J.R. (1988) Urbanization in Australia, *Geography Review* 2, 7–11.
Short, J.R. (ed.) (1992) *Human Settlement*, New York: Oxford University Press.

Classic works on central place include:
Berry, B.J.L. (1967) *Geography of Market Centers and Retail Distribution*, Englewood Cliffs, N.J.: Prentice-Hall.
Bromley, R. and Bromley, R.D.F. (1979) Defining central place systems through the analysis of bus services: the case of Ecuador, *Geographical Journal* 145, 416–36.
Christaller, W. (1966) *Central places in Southern Germany*, Englewood Cliffs, N.J.: Prentice-Hall.
Galpin, C.J. (1915) *Social Anatomy of an Agricultural Community*, Research Bulletin 34, University of Wisconsin Agricultural Experiment Station.
Losch, A. (1954) *The Economics of Location*, trans. W.H. Woglom, New Haven, Conn.: Yale University Press.
Preston, R.E. (1971) The structure of central place system, *Economic Geography* 47, 135–56.

On counterurbanization:
Coombs, M. (1989) *Counterurbanization in Britain and Italy*, Oxford: Pergamon Press.
Hall, P. and Hay, D. (1980) *Growth Centres in the European Urban System*, London: Heinemann.
Vining, D.R. Jr and Strauss, A. (1977) A demonstration that the current deconcentration of population in the United States is a clean break with the past, *Environment and Planning* A9, 751–8.

On diffusions in urban systems, see:
Cliff, A., Haggett, P. and Smallman-Raynor, M. (1993) *Measles: A History*, Oxford: Blackwell.
Gould, P. (1993) *The Slow Plague: A Geography of the Aids Pandemic*, Oxford: Blackwell.
Robson, B. (1973) *Urban Growth: An Approach*, Cambridge: Cambridge University Press.

On the new geography of retailing, see:
Goss, J. (1993) The magic of the mall: an analysis of form, function and meaning in the contemporary retail economy, *Annals of Association of American Geographers* 83, 18–47.
Hallsworth, A. (1992) *The New Geography of Consumer Spending*, London: John Wiley.
Jansen, A.C.M. (1991) *Cannabis in Amsterdam*, Muiderberg: Dick Coutinho.
Miller, D. (ed.) (1995) *Acknowledging Consumption*, London: Routledge.
Shields, R. (ed.) (1992) *Lifestyle Shopping: The Subject on Consumption*, London: Routledge.

Wrigley, N. (1992) Antitrust regulation and the restructuring of grocery retailing in Britain and the USA, *Environment and Planning* A24, 727–49.

Wrigley, N. and Lowe, M. (eds) (1995) *Retailing, Consumption and Capital: Towards a New Retail Geography*, London: Longman.

On cybercities, consider:

Batty, M. (1990) Invisible cities, *Environment and Planning* B17, 127–30.

Boyer, M.C. (1995) *Cybercities*, New York: Princeton Architectural Press.

Graham, S. (1992) The role of cities in telecommunication development, *Telecommunication Policy* 16, 187–93.

Other works cited:

Cooke, P. (ed.) (1989) *Localities: The Changing Face of Urban Britain*, London: Unwin Hyman.

Cronon, W. (1991) *Nature's Metropolis: Chicago and the Great West*, New York: W.W. Norton.

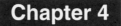

Chapter 4

THE CITY AND THE GLOBAL ECONOMY

CIVILIZATION AND PROFITS GO HAND IN HAND.
CALVIN COOLIDGE, *SPEECH* (1920)

One of the most obvious, and yet most important, facts of contemporary life is the internationalization of the economy. Economic trends, transactions, and processes now take place at a global level. International firms, multinational corporations, and transnational trading patterns link most of the globe in a tight web of economic interdependency. There has been such a globalization of production, consumption, and exchange that we can legitimately speak of a world economy. There are world markets, global production chains, and worldwide marketing strategies. The cities of the world are the nodes of this international circuit, the intersection points of various flows of information, capital, and commodities. In this chapter I want to focus on the connections between the city and the global economy.

THE WORLD CITIES

In 1915 the urban commentator Patrick Geddes coined the term "world cities" to refer to those places where the bulk of the world's most important business was conducted. It is still a useful working definition. We can make a distinction between megacities and world cities. Megacities have huge populations. Mexico City, for example, will by the year 2000 have a population approaching 30 million, making it the biggest single metropolitan area. Although it is a big city it is not a world city. Despite its huge population it does not have the same influence that London or New York has on the global economy or the international circulation of ideas and trends.

Three world cities can be identified: London, New York and Tokyo. They represent a snapshot of the dominant economic powers of the past 150 years. London grew as the capital not only of Britain but of an immense commercial empire that stretched from Hong Kong to the Caribbean, consisting of most of the Indian subcontinent and much of Africa. London was the center, a place where deals were done that connected tea drinkers with tea producers, the forests of Burma with the furniture makers of the world, the grain growers of America with the bread eaters of Europe. The city survived the collapse of the formal empire. Trading circuits, banking institutions, and marketplaces could operate without the infrastructure of colonialism. London maintained its hub position in the postcolonial world. There were competitors.

After the Second World War the United States emerged as the undisputed leader in the world economy. The strength of the US dollar, the competitive edge of US industry, and the exhaustion of European economies all secured a dominant position for the United States in the postwar trading system. New York was the major urban center for this new superpower with Wall Street becoming one of the world's financial centers. There were other US cities: Chicago had important commodities markets, while San Francisco and Los Angeles on the West Coast had increased trade with the emerging Pacific Rim. But New York maintained its dominance as the world city of the United States, the place where international corporations were most concentrated and where the control of money was most centralized.

In the 1960s and 1970s Japan emerged as an industrial power of world significance. Japanese manufactured goods established a reputation for quality, reliability, and price competitiveness that made

The city and the global economy

Illustration 4.1
Downtown Tokyo. Tokyo is now one of the most important world cities, home to the nine biggest banks in the world, a dynamic stock market with one of the highest costs of living (photograph: author)

Illustration 4.2
Shinjuku, Tokyo: two million people pass through this area every day (photograph: author)

them sell around the world. Japan became a major exporter of these goods, and the result was a huge balance of payments surplus that turned the country into a financial as well as an industrial power. Of the ten largest banks in the world, eight are Japanese and all of them are in Tokyo. By 1990 the Tokyo stock exchange had become the largest in the world.

These three cities now sit atop the global urban hierarchy. They are the command centers of the global economy and the main nodes of world business. In these cities deals are struck, contracts agreed upon, trends monitored and analyzed, money measured, made and exchanged. They are the centers of the international economy, world trade and transnational exchange. Saskia Sassen (1991) uses the terms "global cities" with reference to these cities. In her book she looks at the importance of financial services in their economies and notes how in each city, to varying degrees, there is a core of high-paying jobs concentrated in the financial services sector and an expanding periphery of poorly paid for jobs, especially in the nonfinancial service sector. She points to the growth of informal economies, the casualization of labor markets, and a marked dichotomy between the lives of the rich and the poor. The evidence she presents indicates a polarization between rich and poor; this is not unique to global cities, but there wealth and poverty reach their extremes in the same urban space. The global cities are also the most unequal cities.

THE PRODUCTION CITY

The city and long waves

Production in the city is a function of where the city is and when the city is. Capitalist economies change over time just as much as they vary over space. A distinct periodicity has been noted. Short-term fluctuations of between seven and ten years are called business cycles. The longer, 50 year cycles have been named Kondratieff cycles after the Soviet economist who wrote about them in the 1920s.

To understand these cycles and their implications for cities we can begin by making a distinction between an invention and an innovation. An invention involves the creation of a new technique, gadget, or process. Inventions occur on a random basis: they are the product of human ingenuity, genius, and sometimes plain pigheadedness. An innovation, in contrast, is the successful adaptation of an invention into a marketable commodity. Table 4.1, for example, shows the relationship between some electronic inventions and discoveries. Notice how one invention can spin off into a number of different innovations and also how there can be a long chain from the original invention to the most recent innovation. The basic argument is that while inventions occur randomly, innovations tend to cluster around a 50 year cycle. Why this should be we are not exactly sure. Indeed there are some who dispute this periodicity. But for those who accept the basic premise that such cycles exist, the agreed position is that four such waves can be identified (table 4.2). Notice how these waves involve not only technological changes but also changes in the social, spatial and political organization of economic activity. The term "wave" is interesting: the metaphor has a real significance. We can imagine these waves sweeping over the landscape, their shape and direction a function of the social and economic geography of the previous wave, forming a new sociospatial landscape that in turn is the context for the next wave. A study of industrial change in Britain concentrated on the older industrial areas (CDP, 1977). The resulting three-phase model shown in table 4.3 points to some of the connections between industry and community as one place moves from economic growth to economic redundancy. From this perspective it becomes easier to explain the booms and slumps of particular cities. Cities are located in time and space. While one wave may find them

TABLE 4.1   ELECTRONIC INVENTIONS AND INNOVATIONS

Original invention	Sample successor	Number of successor innovations	Dates of chain innovations
Phonograph	LP record Stereo record Compact disc	12	1877–1982
Telephone	PBX MODEM STD Digital systems	13	1876–1975
Wireless telegraphy	Broadcasting FM Packet switching	11	1896–1976
2–electrode valve	Klystron MASER	14	1909–74
Electronic TV	TV broadcasting	4	1919–36
Digital computer	IBM 701 Minicomputer Microcomputer Cray computer	21	1939–79

Source: After Dummer (1983)

	First 1787–1845	Second 1846–95	Third 1896–1947	Fourth 1948–2000 (?)
TABLE 4.2 THE FOUR KONDRATIEFF WAVES				
Key innovations	Power loom puddling	Bessemer steel Steamship	Alternating current Electric light Automobile	Transistor Computer CIT
Key industries	Cotton Iron	Steel Machine tools Ships	Cars Electrical engineering Chemicals	Electronics Computers Communications Aerospace producer services
Industrial organization	Small factories *Laissez-faire*	Large factories Capital concentration Joint stock company	Giant factories "Fordism" Cartels Finance Capital	Mixture of large "Fordist" and small factories (subcontract) Multinationals
Labor	Machine minders	Craft labor	Deskilling	Bipolar
Geography	Migration to towns (coalfields, ports)	Growth of towns on coalfields	Age of conurbations	Suburbanization Deurbanization New industrial regions
International	Britain, workshop of world	German, American competition Capital export	USA, German leadership Colonization	America hegemony Japanese challenge Rise of NICs New international division of labor
Historical	European wars Early railways	Opening of North America Global transport and communications	World wars Early mass consumption Great Depression	Cold war Space race "Global village" Mass consumption
Role of state	Minimal army/ police	Early imperialism	Advanced imperialism Science and education	Welfare state Warfare state Organized R&D

Source: After Hall and Preston (1988)

TABLE 4.3   A SIMPLE MODEL OF INDUSTRIAL CHANGE

Growth

Firms locate in the area on greenfield sites. (The capital to set this up comes from profits made elsewhere, therefore contributing to the decline of some older working-class area.) The industry expands and employment grows. All the available land is filled up.

A new population moves into the area. The new housing is partly financed by investors with a stake also in the new industry and so in ensuring that there is an adequate supply of labor available locally. Many of the new population have come from other areas of the country, where industry/agriculture is in decline.

Maturity

Local firms remain profitable. Few firms leave the area and new growth slows. (Meanwhile, a new generation of industrial investment is being laid down elsewhere on green fields, partly financed by the profits from local industry.)

Employment remains at a fairly stable level. The local population is well established and settled. There is little turnover of population, as local employment and housing opportunities are still relatively good.

Decline

Local industry begins to decline. There is little new investment in existing plant. Employment is cut.

The traditional manufacturing sector continues to decline, providing fewer and fewer jobs – especially skilled jobs. Several firms close altogether, leaving vacant sites.

Vacant sites remain derelict or are developed for warehousing, distribution or offices – for which the area is attractive because of its relatively central location. No new manufacturing enterprises comparable to the traditional industries are attracted to these sites as they are relatively expensive to buy, rent and develop, and also because there is now relatively little skilled labor available locally.

But the availability of cheap, old premises, together with a pool of low-income workers, does attract an inflow of small-scale, low-wage, low-productivity industry.

The housing stock is beginning to deteriorate and many of the better-paid and more-skilled workers move out to newer working-class areas. The reduction in job opportunities locally is an additional factor encouraging out-migration. More lower-paid and less-skilled workers move in from old working-class areas.

Rate of out-migration increases. Workers who lose their jobs in local industry cannot find equivalent jobs as local manufacturing employment continues to decline; they remain unemployed or find jobs outside the area. The housing stock is in a poor condition. The continued shift to a lower-income population means that the deterioration of the housing accelerates, as the residents are less able to afford improvements or the rent necessary to attract investment in improvement.

The emigration of younger, more skilled workers continues, leaving behind an increasingly unskilled, badly paid, insecurely employed or unemployed and badly housed population.

Source: After CDP (1977)

TABLE 4.4 PROPULSIVE INDUSTRIES AND NEW INDUSTRIAL SPACES

Propulsive sector	Typical Features	Cited examples
(a) labor-intensive craft industries (e.g., clothing, furniture)	Exploitation of "sweatshop" labor, often high level of immigrants; subcontracting and out-working	New York, USA Los Angeles, USA Paris, France
(b) design-intensive craft industries (e.g., jewellery)	High-quality products; extreme social division of labor (but class polarization subdued in some examples)	Jura, Switzerland Southern Germany Emilia-Romagna, Italy Central Portugal Jutland, Denmark
High-technology industries	Segmented local labor markets with (a) skilled managerial cadres, and (b) disorganized and malleable fractions of the labor force	Route 128, Boston, USA Orange County, CA, USA Silicon Valley, CA, USA M4 Corridor, UK Scientific City, France Austin, TX, USA Boulder, CO, USA Cambridge, UK Grenoble, France Montpellier, France Sophia Antipolis, France
Office and business services	Preferentially based on white-collar labor – including low-wage female labor; very diversified and prone to agglomeration	London, UK New York, USA Tokyo, Japan

Source: After Tickell and Peck (1992)

at the center of economic activity, the next wave may render them redundant. Detroit, the boomtown of the 1950s and 1960s, becomes the slump city of the 1980s and 1990s. The sleepy Silicon Valley of the 1950s becomes one of the buoyant centers of the computer industry in the 1970s and early 1980s.

Each Kondratieff cycle is associated with a number of key industries. In the first cycle from 1787 to 1845 it was cotton manufacturing and iron- and steel-making. Such industries had both a spatial component and social implications. There was increased urbanization and the growth of factory towns as well as the making of an organized working class, increased capital–labor cleavages, and the emergence of a state that underlined the rights of property at the expense of the rights of those without property. In the most recent cycle a number of key industries have been identified, referred to as *propulsive sectors* by Tickell and Peck (1992) (table 4.4). Three sectors have been identified:

- craft industries;
- office and business services;
- high-technology industries.

There are two main types of *craft industries*. The labor-intensive industries, including clothing and furniture, have a big-city location and very exploitative work practices. Wages are low and conditions are poor. In Los Angeles and New York, labor is often further weakened by being illegal. These workers, who do not have legal status, are poorly organized and cannot take their complaints to the authorities because they face deportation. Even when legal, the use of immigrant labor desperate to find a job in a new country weakens the bargaining power of the workers. In the more design-intensive craft industries, small, often family firms are tightly connected in regional agglomerations that respond quickly to changing customer needs. In both types of craft industry the emphasis is on agglomeration and flexibility; flexibility in a number of senses:

- flexible products: a range of specialized products are manufactured rather than a few products produced in bulk;
- flexible production: the number, range and type of products can be altered at short notice;
- flexible labor: there is no sharp demarcation of skills; workers do different types of jobs; work practices are also more flexible than in Fordist production.

In effect flexible production both reflects and embodies the power of capital over labor to speed and intensify the rhythm of work.

There was an increase in *office and business services* in the 1970s and 1980s. The informationization of the economy meant an increase in both the public and the private sector and involved an increasing demand for nonmanual labor. At the managerial levels this was mainly male, while much of the routine work was undertaken by women. It was urban-based, particularly in the world cities, the command centers of the world economy, although the same trend occurred in national and regional centers. Throughout the 1970s and 1980s the service sector saw large increases. However, it was affected by the world recession of the late 1980s and early 1990s. The manufacturing sector had already been extensively restructured in the early 1970s. This white-collar recession bit into the incomes, lifestyles and expectations of the white-collar, middle-income groups.

High-technology industries are the newest industrial form of the fourth Kondratieff cycle. A dual labor market can be identified: a small core of highly skilled workers involved in research and development and a larger pool of semi-skilled and unskilled workers involved in the routine manufacture of technological products. A separation in work is sometimes reflected in a separation of function, with routine manufacturing attracted to areas with a cheap and malleable workforce. Female workers in older industrial regions or in regions with no history of industrialization are a favored labor source. Much has been written about the industries associated with the research and development side of information technology. Table 4.4 shows some of the cited examples, which range in type but differ from the centers of innovation in previous waves. Castells (1989) refers to *milieux of innovation* to designate those centers which generate continual rounds of innovative products. He identifies a number of different types of milieux of innovation. Type 1 is based on a combination of university research, government markets and venture capital. Examples include Silicon Valley, California, Route 128 in Boston in the United States, and Cambridge, England. Type 1, including Orange County, California, focuses around large corporations and government-funded defense-related industries. Type 3 occurs within the confines of a large innovative corporation, such as IBM. Type 4, best exemplified by Austin, Texas, combines the technical branch plants of large corporations to create local spin-off, while Type 5 are those based on nonrecurring phenomena, such as the development of Minneapolis-St Paul, which derived from the presence of certain successful corporations and government markets. In all types there is an agglomeration effect as firms seek to stay close to their competitors and partners, and subcontract out legal accounting and financial services.

This typology is somewhat crude. However, it does allow us to move on from noting the importance of such factors as amenity-rich locations to attract high-quality labor, access to metropolitan services (especially banking), and the agglomeration tendency of such industries to explain their location in space. The typology also indicates the range of different factors that have been particularly important in the development of such centers. The role of government in funding research and development, especially in the defense industries, has been crucial. The presence of research universities or corporate research facilities is also important. The typology may change. The decline of defense spending, especially the lavish underwriting of research, and the fallout effects of corporate reorganization will all have their effects on restructuring the spatial location and relocation of high-technology industries.

The Silicon Valleys were the success stories of the later period of the fourth Kondratieff cycle. There was also the downside. For every Silicon Valley there was a Buffalo, New York, with economies dominated by big manufacturing firms, a declining manufacturing base and no tradition of entrepreneurship. Here things were bleaker. If the Silicon Valleys faced the problems of growth, the overheating of the local economy, rising house prices, and increasing congestion, then the Buffaloes faced the problems of decline: shrinking employment opportunities, a declining tax base, and a loss of economic vitality and confidence.

The city and production

Cities are an important site for the production of commodities. We can identify different types of production cities. In *cities of primitive accumulation* the whole nature of the city was orientated towards the creation and maintenance of profit. We can see such cities in the early phases of the industrial revolution, the Manchesters and Prestons that Engels was describing in his book *The Condition of the English Working Class* (see p. 25). In such cities working and living conditions were very poor. They were, in effect, centers of money-making for the rich with a poor quality of life for the majority of the workers. Such cities were not restricted to the early years of capitalist industrialization. Cities of primitive accumulation were also found in many of the centrally planned economies undergoing rapid urbanization and industrialization. In the early years of the Soviet Union Lenin and Trotsky spoke of the need for primitive social accumulation so that the fledgling socialist states could catch up with the capitalist West. Many of the burgeoning industrial cities of Eastern Europe had relatively poor living conditions. The emphasis was on rapid economic growth, with working and living conditions only a secondary consideration. Even into the 1970s and 1980s many socialist industrial cities had appalling living conditions because of the poor environmental standards. Cities of primitive accumulation can also be found in the contemporary capitalist world: in places where there is a concentration of industry and manufacturing, organized labor is weak, and governmental regulations are either weak or regularly flouted. Cities such as Tijuana in Mexico, which has attracted companies that wish to have easy access to the US market without having to pay US labor rates or to meet US environmental standards, are the new sites of primitive accumulation. Here organized labor is weak and governments are so eager to attract investment that few restrictions are put in place. The result is a labor market that is dominated more by the needs of capital than by labor, and urban living conditions that are placed secondary to the need for profit.

The *Keynesian city* is one in which the capital–labor relationship has been modified. Labor, because of greater organization and strength, technological developments, and new forms of regulation, has better working and living conditions. The state also has a more interventionist role in maintaining and improving living standards and forms of collective consumption like transport, health, and education. This type of city takes its name from the English economist John Maynard Keynes (1883–1946), who argued that the market left to itself would not necessarily ensure full employment. He maintained that the state could promote effective demand through direct spending; in effect, in some circumstances only the state could stimulate the economy. The implementation of his theories into government policy in the rich capitalist countries in the post-1945 world marked the acceptance that the state had an important and legitimate role in ensuring economic and social stability. Within the Keynesian city the booms and slumps of the capitalist economy were modified by government intervention. Welfare payments, for example, ensured relatively high standards of living, even for the unemployed. The power of the unemployed, a reserve army of labor, to depress the cost of labor was thus reduced. The Keynesian city was distinguished by relatively high incomes and the steady supply of high-quality public goods and services. It is permissible, I believe, to discuss the Keynesian city in the past tense. Its heyday was in the 1960s and early 1970s, especially in selected countries: Scandinavian, British, and US cities form a sort of hierarchy of Keynesian cities. Moving westward the welfare payments, social service provision, and quality of life for the very poor all declined.

The retreat from the Keynesian city was a function of the changing economic and political balance since the mid-1970s, which reduced the commitment to public spending, gave more power to capital over labor, and reduced the ability of government to support and maintain the public character of this type of city. Reaganomics in the United States and Thatcherism in Britain were in part a series of ideological and political attacks against the idea and practice of the Keynesian city.

The *post-Fordist city* is a comparatively recent phenomenon and reflects the general shift in capital–labor relations and government involvement since the mid-1970s. Urban labor markets are now much more likely to consist of a larger number of smaller firms, and the power of labor to disrupt production, compared to a market dominated by a small number of large production units, is lessened dramatically. Within these smaller production units, the large assembly-line techniques have been replaced by more flexible production systems, with a corresponding and consequent decline in the power of organized labor. There has been a shift toward lower wages and/or more intensive work practices. In the post-Fordist city the changing capital–labor relationship is also the backdrop for a reregulated state in which welfare provisions are reduced, public services are underfunded, and the dominant shift is toward various forms of privatization.

We can imagine an historical trajectory from the city of primitive accumulation through the Keynesian city to the post-Fordist city, a move resulting from the shifting power of capital and labor against a background of changing technology and shifts in the size and role of the state. The precise nature of the shift varies over space as well as time. Scandinavian cities, for example, have a greater Keynesian legacy than cities in the United States, and thus the post-Fordist city in Scandinavian countries differs from those in the United States. And even within individual countries there are variations. A city in New York State will have more spending per head on education, job training, and environmental protection than cities in Alabama or South Carolina. The post-Fordist city, with its reregulated state, exacerbates national, regional and local differences in capital–labor relations, local government involvement, and local community preferences and power structures. We should thus consider the post-Fordist city in broad outline, the precise details of its social and economic configuration as more a function of regional and local power structures and urban labor markets than the Keynesian city. The extent to which the post-Fordist city reflects the city of primitive accumulation rather than the Keynesian city is a function of capital–labor relations, the balance of social and political power, and the position of the city in the international economy.

Global shift

In the nineteenth century, when transport costs were high, industry was tied to sources of power or proximity to markets. Factory towns grew in Europe and North America close to waterpower, coalfields, or large urban centers. There was a definite division of the world into an industrial core, which manufactured goods, and the periphery, which exported raw materials and imported manufactured goods. In the twentieth century this pattern was overturned by industrialization in the periphery. World wars separated the core from the periphery and caused some protoindustrialization. More recently, the standardization of production techniques, the improvement in transport, and the relative ease of global capital investment have meant that the world, rather than a single nation, is the arena of decision-making for modern corporations.

One important factor in locational decision-making is the cost and militancy of labor. Labor in the older industrial centers of the core tends to be more expensive, better organized and more resistant to the introduction of techniques that increase the intensity of work and/or reduce the amount of labor. Because of the greater mobility of industrial production the net result has been a global shift of industry from the core to the periphery. The net effect has been industrialization of parts of the periphery and deindustrialization in the core. This has been a selective process: there have been the success stories of South Korea and the city-states of Hong Kong, Taiwan, and Singapore; the creation of import-substitution industries in such primate cities as Lima and Caracas; and, in a more localized example, the new industries of such cities as Tijuana, which sits on the Mexican border with the United States and where wage rates are only

Illustration 4.3
Singatronics, manufacturer of electronic medical products. The global shift of industry means that much industrial manufacturing is now undertaken in areas with cheap, docile labor (© Hutchinson Library/R. Ian Lloyd)

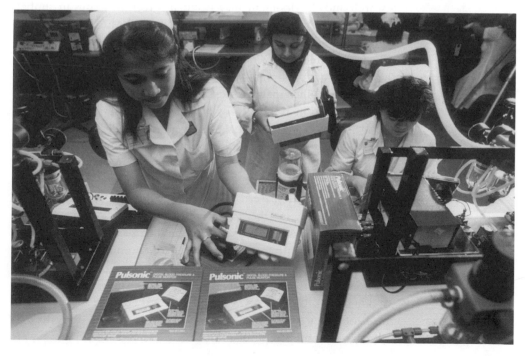

one-tenth of what they are just across the border, where environmental and job safety restrictions are more lax, and hence total costs are much less, and yet the location allows easy access to the North American market. The other side of the coin of global shift has been the loss of manufacturing employment in some of the older cities of the core. The decline of manufacturing employment in such places as the car cities of Detroit, United States, and Birmingham, United Kingdom, has been dramatic, with large negative multiplier effects on the local economies.

A new international division of labor has emerged in which more and more routine manufacturing production and employment is done in the cities of the Third World, while the older industrial cities have experienced employment loss and contraction of their economic base. Singapore and Syracuse, New York, Taiwan and Toledo, Ohio, are linked, their fortunes inseparably bound by a global economy which links all the towns and cities of the world in a fluctuating rhythm of growth and decline, expansion and contraction, investment and disinvestment.

The patterns and timing of global shift can be considered through an analysis of individual sectors or companies. The simple model shown in figure 4.1, for example, suggests different locations for different parts of a modern multinational enterprise. The administrative headquarters are often located in metropolitan areas of the rich world, research and development may occur in greenfield sites in sunbelt locations, while routine manufacturing follows the lure of cheap labor around the world. This is a simple model and the experience of individual companies may differ. Consider the example of Nike, one of the best-known names in the world for athletic shoes and sporting apparel (for a fuller analysis, see Katz, 1994). Nike grew enormously from its inception in the 1960s; by 1993 its annual turnover was just under $4 billion and its annual profit was $365 million. Nike grew as an importer of shoes. The founder Phil Knight imported shoes from Japan and sold them at athletics meetings throughout the Pacific north-west. The company grew to a multinational enterprise. Its headquarters are in Beaverton, just outside Portland, Oregon, a location determined by the founder. Over 6,000 people work in advertising and research and development in beautifully landscaped grounds crossed with jogging trails and containing such buildings as the Michael Jordan Building and the Bo Jackson Fitness Center. The location of the assembly plants that make Nike shoes are a case study in global shift. Only two US factories ever made shoes for Nike. In the 1960s they were made in Japan. As costs increased production shifted in the mid-1970s to South Korea. The factories in Pusan were

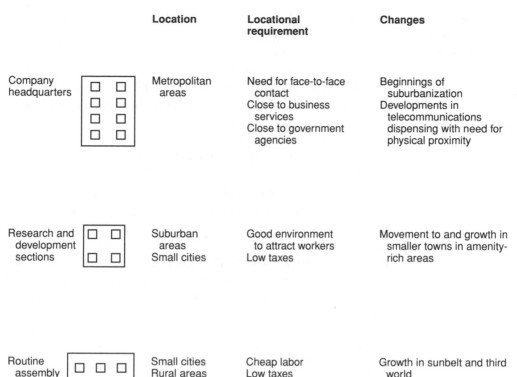

Location		Locational requirement	Changes
Company headquarters	Metropolitan areas	Need for face-to-face contact Close to business services Close to government agencies	Beginnings of suburbanization Developments in telecommunications dispensing with need for physical proximity
Research and development sections	Suburban areas Small cities	Good environment to attract workers Low taxes	Movement to and growth in smaller towns in amenity-rich areas
Routine assembly plants	Small cities Rural areas	Cheap labor Low taxes	Growth in sunbelt and third world

Figure 4.1
A simple model of the modern business enterprise

more modern, more efficient, and employed cheaper labor. In the competitive world of athletics shoes companies are continually looking to reduce production costs while still ensuring quality. Labor costs grew in South Korea, so in the 1980s production widened to Thailand and Indonesia. Factories in Bangkok and Jakarta were making shoes that were sold in New York and Paris. In the early 1990s factories opened in Dongguan, 40 miles outside of Guangzhou in South China. By 1993 there were 35,000 people employed in China making Nike shoes. By the 1990s Nike was also looking at areas in Europe such as the North of England where cheap labor could be found. Nike is a multinational enterprise whose changing and widening production sources are an exemplar of business practices in the contemporary global economy.

There have been tremendous changes in the social and spatial organization of employment in the last 20 years. We now have a reasonably accurate picture of the patterns of change. We also have vigorous theoretical debates; three in particular can be noted: long waves, regimes of accumulation, and modes of social regulation. There is a real need to find the theoretical connections between these three because together they can provide us with a more

comprehensive understanding of the relations between capital accumulation, technological developments, and social reorganization.
There are important connections to be made between Kondratieff
cycles, flexible production, and post-Fordism. As long as the debates
are Balkanized into separate academic republics the connections will
remain elusive and tantalizing rather than concrete and enlightening.

THE INFORMATION CITY

In his book *The Informational City* (1989) Manuel Castells suggests
that there is an informational mode of development. What he means
by this, I think, is that the generation, manipulation, and use of information has become much more central to economic development
than ever before. As well as internationalization, there has also been
the "informationization" of the economy. His view was widely shared
in the 1970s and 1980s when terms such as information technology,
the information age, and the information society became common
and were linked to the increasing use and sophistication of computers. However, information has always been central to economic
enterprises. To be sure, there is now more of it, but we should be
careful when assuming that our age is unlike any other age.

Information has become more important in all spheres of
economic and political life. In terms of production, the large, multi-
state corporations with international production chains now need a
mass of information to maintain and improve their production
processes. Indeed, we can see the improvements in information pro-
cessing, such as satellite connections, as being both a cause and an
effect of economic internationalization. There is a fascinating story
to be told of the connections and linkages between better communications and a more integrated global economy.

In the sphere of consumption, there is a need for market research,
surveys of consumer preferences, and an almost constant monitoring
of changing preferences and desires. Again, the causal connections
can flow both ways: constant monitoring, as in feeding into a central data bank details of purchases of goods as they happen, allows
both the measurement and the expression of changing consumer
preferences.

The rise of the state and its increasing size and growing involvement in all spheres of life are a function and consequence of the
growing ability to centralize and manipulate information. Most states
in the affluent world now have the names and addresses of their citizens in some form or other: electoral rolls, taxation registers, driving

license information, criminal records, ownership of property, school records. The list goes on and on.

We can picture the cities of the world, in one light at least, as points of information collection, transmission and manipulation. Two hierarchies can be identified. There is the political hierarchy: capital cities house not only the seat but also the brain of governments; not only the elected representatives, with their rumors and gossip and intrigue, but also the government agencies with their records, data banks, and information processors. From the small police station in a tiny village to the national police headquarters flow communication and information that maintain the power of the state. The different levels of this hierarchy function in different ways. The lowest levels send on information, while the upper levels not only receive information but use it to formulate policies, responses, and strategies. Capital cities are rich in political information, and this is part of their attraction and their strength. Washington, DC, makes few tangible commodities but is at the intersection of national and international information. And that is the source of its economic growth and vitality.

In the business world the flows are much more international. At the apex are the world cities, which contain the command functions, corporate headquarters, and banking institutions. The world cities that I discussed in chapter 3 are the nodes through which flow power, knowledge, and finance. New York, Tokyo and London provide a global coverage of financial information. Figure 4.2, for example, shows that together they provide a continuous time coverage of foreign exchange dealings. The three cities together give a continuous stream of information, a constant market for the buying and selling of money, and a total spatiotemporal coverage of the globe.

A complete coverage requires there to be at least three cities. No one city, or indeed pair of cities, can provide the necessary continuous coverage. This does not prevent competition for one of the three positions. London, for example, is under pressure from Paris and Frankfurt because it is hampered by the poor economic position of Britain, its declining infrastructure, and its more peripheral position within an increasingly integrated European Union. To date, London has maintained its position. The work of Nigel Thrift (1994) provides a picture of the information dynamics in a global city. He describes the City of London, the main financial and business center, as an upper-class craft community. It arose and continues to exist because for many corporations and financial institutions there is both the need for information in a rapidly changing world and the ability to act upon it quickly. The geographic center of a world city is a place-based community providing a meeting place for business interests on

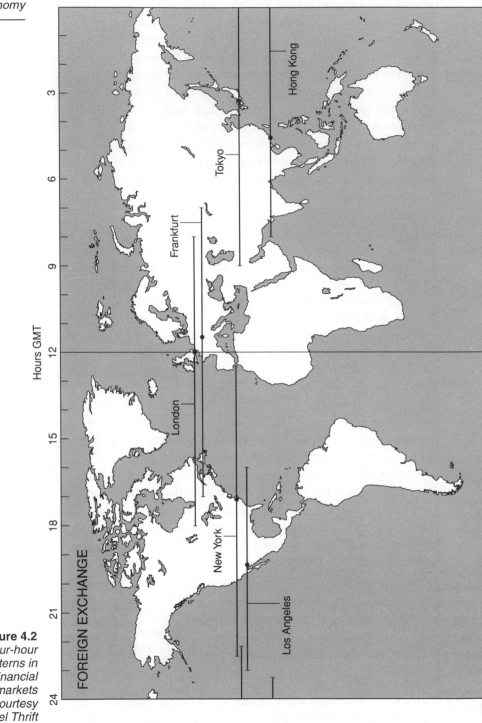

Figure 4.2
Twenty-four-hour
trading patterns in
global financial
markets
Source: courtesy
of Nigel Thrift

Illustration 4.4
*Interior of Lloyds
Building, London.
In the heart of the
City, Lloyds is a
major center for
commercial
insurance around
the world (© British
Architectural
Library, RIBA,
London;
photograph: A.C.
Cooper Ltd)*

a face-to-face basis that allows personal social interaction. Atop the
global hierarchy the business and financial centers of the three world
cities function as places for the gathering and sharing of information,
the tracking of innovations, the making of deals, and the representation and surveillance of the global economy. In summary, these
centers act as the meeting places, the hubs of discursive representation and product innovation in those knowledge-based industries
which service the world economy.

There is competition in space and time at the secondary level of the financial information urban hierarchy. Cities in the same approximate time zone, such as Sydney and Hong Kong, Frankfurt and Paris, San Francisco and Los Angeles, are competing for the same time slot of global coverage. There is also competition between cities of the same country for the dominant position as the national center connected to the world circuit. The competition takes place in primate urban distributions (see p. 40), but also in such countries as Australia and Canada with intense rivalry between Sydney and Melbourne and also between Vancouver, Toronto, and Montreal. Competition is severe and growing because of the increasing concentration of power in financial institutions. There are many cities but only so much power to be distributed. The internationalization and informationalization of the economy is leading to the concentration of command-and-control functions in only a small number of increasingly important cities.

The urban region as economic reality

The basic spatial economic unit is the urban region. It is the elementary building block of the world economy. This fact is often overlooked because of the weight and importance given to the nation-state. The nation-state was always more a political compromise and an emotional response than an economic arrangement. States are the unit of statistical analysis, economic policy, and political deliberation. They are political and military entities but not necessarily economic units. States are involved in economic policy, but where there is more than one city region in a country the effects can be counterproductive to some of the regions. For example, assume a country which has one urban region where the economy is dominated by service employment and another where manufacturing employment is most important. If the national state follows a policy of encouraging the manufacturing sector of the *national economy* then one region will probably benefit much more than the other. In any medium or large country there will be a number of different urban regions with varying rates of economic success and competitiveness in the world economy. To impose a *national* economic policy, say, in terms of trade restrictions, currency exchange or labor policy, will be to advantage some regions over others. Regional policies may be necessary to smooth out the imbalances. But whatever the policy adopted there is always the basic problem that urban regions are the functioning units of the global economy. The national level acts as an arena for political competition and lobbying; in effect, as a system of redistribution of the costs and benefits of growth and decline, and as the point of negotiation with the global market. When there is congruence between region and state then national economic policies can be beneficial. When they are not or when there is a variety of very different types of urban economies, some growing, others declining, then national economic policies may have deleterious effects. As nation-states move into larger and larger trade groupings the time may be ripe for the recognition of the city-state as the fundamental spatial economic entity.

THE NEW URBAN ORDER

We can summarize some of the relationships between socioeconomic change and spatial reorganization noted in this chapter with the notion of the *new urban order* (Short, 1989). The new order has its roots in the major economic changes that have occurred since the mid-1970s; these include new labor processes, labor markets, and systems of production marked by greater flexibility and reregulation. These economic processes have a marked effect on the spatial reorganization of society. At the international level there has been a global shift of industrial employment from the core countries to the semiperipheral and peripheral countries of the world economy. At the national level there has been a growth of service employment and a shift of industrial employment from traditional manufacturing regions to cheaper-labor, more business-oriented regions. New industrial regions have been identified in North America and Western Europe in which the new sociologies of production are concentrated (Scott, 1988; Sternlieb and Hughes, 1988). The economic consequences of this change are most marked in those cities in the old industrial regions of mature capitalist economies that have a heavy reliance on traditional manufacturing employment. Cities such as Detroit and Buffalo, for example, have experienced a real decline since the early 1970s; but even in larger cities, such as Los Angeles, New York, and Chicago, which have a broader economic base, the loss of manufacturing jobs has reduced the level of higher-income, manual, male employment. The jobs that have been lost have been skilled and unskilled, traditionally male employment with a history of strong unionization. The expanding job sectors have more female employment, more part-time workers, and a very distinct bifurcation between a core of highly paid, highly skilled, managerial-type workers and a semiperipheral and peripheral group of workers who have less-attractive conditions of employment.

At the urban level the changes vary by size and economic base of the city. At the apex of the urban hierarchy, the very largest cities are losing their status as manufacturing centers, and new employment growth is dominated by service employment. The effects of this on increased polarization and a deepening of the dual nature of the metropolitan labor market have been noted in a number of cities. The concept of the *dual city* has been invoked to describe the pattern (Mollenkopf and Castells, 1991). Large cities, such as New York, Chicago, and Los Angeles, have experienced growing polarization of the workforce as traditional manufacturing jobs disappear and employment moves to the suburbs while the central city fractures along the deepening divides of race and class. The work of Wilson (1987), for example, stresses the connection between a black underclass in inner-city United States and the loss of employment in these areas. The stark contrast is between the quality and number of jobs in the high-tech areas on the fringes of big cities and the restricted employment opportunities of poor inner-city residents trapped by low skills, restricted accessibility, and economic processes that drain the core of employment for all but a minority. While new-growth cities emerge, cities whose economy was based on traditional manufacturing lose their economic *raison d'être* and have to find new sources of investment and employment. Restructuring of the economy involves the spatial reorganization of society and the social reorganization of space.

Because of the globalization of production, consumption, and exchange in association with the decline of national regulation in wage-fixing and work practices, the "national" becomes a less significant unit of analysis (see Reich, 1991). The "global" becomes more significant as the unit for understanding general economic trends, while the "local" becomes the unit for appreciating the intersections between capital and labor, economy and society, polity and comity. The general effect is to make urban labor markets, just as much as the national economy, an important backdrop in negotiations between business and labor over wage rates and conditions of employment. The experience of similar groups of workers and hence particular types of households may vary from place to place. Where you live and work becomes an important determinant of standard of living and quality of life. As the local urban labor market becomes an important determinant of relative bargaining power, differences occur as much by city as by economic sector or socioeconomic position. The same locality has different communities, and similar communities may have varying fortunes in different localities. An understanding of these differences is vital to a fuller understanding of unemployment, poverty, economic growth, and decline.

On world cities:

Cybriwsky, R.A. (1991) *Tokyo: The Changing Profile of an Urban Giant*, Boston, Mass.: G.K. Hall.

Fainstein, S., Gordon, I. and Harloe, M. (eds) (1991) *Divided Cities: New York and London in the Contemporary World*, Oxford: Blackwell.

Hall, P. (1984) *The World Cities*, 3rd edn, London: Weidenfeld & Nicolson.

Markusen, A. and Gwiasda, V. (1994) Multipolarity and the layering of urban functions in world cities: New York City's struggle to stay on top, *International Journal of Urban and Regional Research* 18, 167–93.

Mollenkopf, J. (1993) *New York City in the 1980s*, New York: Simon & Shuster.

Sassen, S. (1991) *The Global City*, Princeton, N.J.: Princeton University Press.

Thrift, N. (1994) On the social and cultural determinants of international finance centers: the case of London. In S. Corbridge, R. Martin and N. Thrift (eds), *Money, Space and Power*, Oxford: Blackwell.

On the production city:

Dicken, P. (1986) *Global Shift*, London: Harper & Row.

Massey, D. and Allen, J. (eds) (1988) *Uneven Re-development: Cities and Regions in Transition*, London: Hodder & Stoughton.

Scott, A.J. (1988) *Metropolis: From Division of Labor to Urban Form*, Berkeley, Cal.: University of California Press.

Storper, M. and Walker, R. (1989) *The Capitalist Imperative: Territory, Technology and Industrial Growth*, Oxford and New York: Blackwell.

On the information city:

Castells, M. (1989) *The Informational City*, Oxford and Cambridge, Mass.: Blackwell.

On the connection between money and cities, look at some of the chapters in:

Corbridge, S., Martin, R. and Thrift, N. (eds) (1994) *Money, Space and Power*, Oxford: Blackwell.

A variety of perspectives on long waves include:

Berry, B.J.L. (1991) *Long Wave Rhythms in Economic Development and Political Behaviour*, Baltimore, Md: Johns Hopkins University Press.

Hall, P. and Preston, P. (1988) *The Carrier Wave: New Information Technology and the Geography of Innovation, 1846–2003*, London: Unwin Hyman.

Maddison, A. (1982) *Phases of Capitalist Development*, London: Oxford University Press.

Schumpter, J.A. (1928) *Business Cycles*, New York: McGraw-Hill.

On the urban geography of new industries:

Amin, A. (1994) *Post-Fordism*, Oxford: Blackwell.

Daniels, P. (1993) *Service Industries in the World Economy*, Oxford: Blackwell.

Scott, A.J. (1988) Flexible accumulation and regional development: the rise of new industrial spaces in North America and western Europe, *International Journal of Urban and Regional Research* 12, 171–86.

Soja, E. (1989) *Postmodern Geographies: The Reassertion of Space in Critical Social Theory*, London: Verso.

Sternlieb, G. and Hughes, J.W. (eds) (1988) *America's New Market Geography*, New Brunswick, N.J.: Center for Urban Policy Research, Rutgers University.

Tickell, A. and Peck, J.A. (1992) Accumulation, regulation and the geographies of post-Fordism: missing links in regulationist research, *Progress in Human Geography* 16, 190–218.

On the particular geographies of high-tech industries:

Castells, M. (ed.) (1985) *High Technology, Space and Society*, Beverley Hills, Cal., and London: Sage.

Castells, M. and Hall, P. (1994) *Technopoles of the World: The Making of 21st-Century Industrial Complexes*, London: Routledge.

Hall, P. and Markusen, A. (eds) (1985) *Silicon Landscapes*, Boston, Mass.: Allen & Unwin.

Hall, P., Breheny, M., McQuaid, R., and Hart, D. (1987) *Western Sunrise: The Genesis and Growth of Britain's Major High Tech Corridor*, London: Allen & Unwin.

Henderson, J. (1991) *The Globalization of High Technology Production: Society, Space and Semi-conductors in the Restructuring of the World Economy*, London: Routledge.

On the new urban order:

Mollenkopf, J. and Castells, M. (eds) (1991) *Dual City*, New York: Russell Sage.

Reich, R.B. (1991) *The Work of Nations*, New York: Alfred A. Knopf.

Short, J.R. (1989) Yuppies, yuffies and the new urban order, *Transactions of Institute of British Geographers* NS 13, 173–88.

Wilson, W.J. (1987) *The Truly Disadvantaged*, Chicago: University of Chicago Press.

Other works cited include:

CDP (1977) *The Costs of Industrial Change*, London: Home Office.

Dummer, G.W.A. (1983) *Electronic Inventions and Discoveries*, Oxford: Pergamon Press.

Katz, D. (1994) *Just Do It: The Nike Spirit in the Corporate World*, New York: Random House.

Chapter 5

THE POLITICAL ECONOMY OF
URBANIZATION

THE SUM TOTAL OF THESE RELATIONS OF PRODUCTION CONSTITUTES THE
ECONOMIC STRUCTURE OF SOCIETY – THE REAL FOUNDATIONS ON WHICH
ARISE LEGAL AND POLITICAL SUPERSTRUCTURES AND TO WHICH CORRESPOND
DEFINITE FORMS OF SOCIAL CONSCIOUSNESS. THE MODE OF PRODUCTION OF
MATERIAL LIFE DETERMINES THE GENERAL CHARACTER OF THE SOCIAL, POLITI-
CAL AND SPIRITUAL PROCESSES OF LIFE. IT IS NOT THE CONSCIOUSNESS OF
MEN THAT DETERMINES THEIR BEING, BUT, ON THE CONTRARY, THEIR SOCIAL
BEING DETERMINES THEIR CONSCIOUSNESS.

KARL MARX, A CONTRIBUTION TO THE CRITIQUE OF
POLITICAL ECONOMY (1859)

The city reflects and embodies the wider society. To understand the
city it is necessary to place it in a wider socioeconomic context. In
this chapter I will be concerned with the wider-angle look at the city
that is afforded by a political economy approach. It is an approach
that has yielded important, though not total, insights into the complexity of the city, and here I will give an outline of it and highlight
its contributions and its silences.

CITIES AND MODES OF PRODUCTION

Let us begin with the notion of the *mode of production*. This term was
first coined by Karl Marx (1818–83), who used it in a number of
different ways: to refer to the techniques involved in producing a
specific good; to the labor process in the capitalist system, and, in his
broadest definition, to the production, exchange, and consumption
relations along with the associated political and social arrangements
that reproduce an economic order. It is this broader definition that I
will use in this chapter. Marx suggested that history can be seen as
the rise and fall of different modes of production; in essence his work
was concerned with identifying the rise of the capitalist mode of

production from the feudal mode, and examining the contradictions inherent in the capitalist mode of production.

A mode of production contains both forces of production and relations of production. The forces of production refer to all those things that make up the productive capacity of the economy, including levels of technological development. The relations of production refer to the social relationships between the different economic actors and include property relations, work relations, and the ideological and political framework in which people buy and sell goods. Relations of production are ultimately class relations. Each mode of production, according to Marx, is characterized by a dominant class that owns the means of production. Property relations are structured to reinforce and maintain their ruling position but are subject to resistance and contestation from the dominated classes. For the capitalist mode of production a simple dichotomous model is initially proposed: the capitalists own the means of production while the workers own nothing but their labor power.

At the core of Marx's economic analysis of capitalism is the relationship between the capitalists and the workers. In simple terms, the capitalists purchase the labor power of the workers, which is harnessed in a system of production to create commodities. These commodities are sold for profit in a competitive marketplace. It is the competition and conflict between these two groups that provides the central dynamic of capitalist economies and is the essential key to our understanding of society. Capitalists want to keep wages as low as possible in order to make profits, whereas the workers seek to improve their wages and conditions of employment. The whole system is driven by the logic of profit. Capital is invested with an eye to reaping profit.

The system is unstable. The search for profit can be a disrupting influence on the established order. Capital needs a never-ending supply of investment opportunities. The competition between capitalists results in a constant struggle to improve productivity, which workers can try to resist. The endemic instability takes the form of periodic crises that threaten profit rates and the ability to sell commodities. The capitalist system is one of booms and slumps and of associated periods of social harmony and intense social conflict.

Marx's voluminous writings provide us with a rich and ambiguous source of both insight and fog. He starts with simple models that provide the basis for more sophisticated expositions. He was well aware, for example, that capitalist societies contain more than two classes. The two-class model was just that: a model that got to the very heart of the social and economic conflict in capitalist society. In his

Illustration 5.1
Karl Marx (© Mary Evans Picture Library, London)

historical writings on France, for example, he identified a whole variety of classes and class fractions. His method was dialectical. He was aware of the contradictions and changing realities of capitalist society. His concepts are used in different ways at different stages in his analysis and changed as his angle of vision altered. But there is also confusion. Marx wrote during most of his adult life. There are contradictions and confusion in his vast body of work. The labor theory of value has proved a problematic case, his writings on the role of the state are fragmentary, and there are places where technological determinism replaces the more sophisticated analyses found elsewhere. These criticisms are not meant to diminish his achievement. They are designed to see him as a scholar, not as a messiah. Too often there are only two simple readings of Marx: either his work has achieved the status of received text, to be carefully examined by a narrow band of academic acolytes to prove his continuing relevance and almost godlike stature, or he is summarily dismissed as a pompous, difficult writer and an irrelevant figure. Neither canonization nor easy dismissal is the appropriate response. The best way to see him is as an important commentator who cast a powerful gaze on capitalist society. His legacy is substantial. In the rest of this section I will consider this legacy in three ways: by looking briefly at the important themes in the Marxist and neo-Marxist literature on the city (these themes will be elaborated in later chapters); by examining the work of David Harvey, who is the most influential figure in this area; and by making comments on the rise and fall of the socialist city.

Important themes

There are a variety of topics that figure in the Marxist and neo-Marxist writings on the capitalist city. Here I will be concerned with just four:

- capital and capital flows;
- class and class conflict;
- regime of accumulation;
- urban conflict.

They are important because they have significance over and beyond the narrow range of explicitly Marxist-inspired work. Let us look at each of these in turn.

Capital and capital flows   A major objective of Marxist-inspired urban studies has been to unravel the relationship between the dynamics of capital accumulation and the production of the built environment.

This is part of a much broader aim to see the social production of space and the spatial reproduction of society as an interrelated process. The main thrust has been to establish the link between locational behavior, changing patterns of employment, and developments at the level of the process of capital accumulation. Capital is seen as a creative/destructive force that, in its search for profit, creates and recreates new landscapes, new divisions of labor, and new social relations. Linking social changes and economic restructuring in particular places to the rhythm and beat of capital is a major goal of this literature.

Capital responds to the uneven distribution of investment opportunities in the sociospatial landscape. Land beyond the city edge, for example, provides opportunity for speculative development. This investment involves new transport routes and new spatial divisions of labor. The transformed spatial structure in turn guides the flow of successive waves of capital investment. Patterns of fixed capital investment provide the decision-making context for successive waves of investment. Space not only is continually structured but also shapes the basis for subsequent capital restructuring.

The flows of capital have definite sociospatial outcomes. Capital is a social relationship. It is employed in specific technical, legal, and economic arrangements among different social groups and classes with varying attitudes, strategies, and resources. Gordon et al. (1983) refer to this terrain as the social structure of accumulation (SSA). There is a complex relationship between the SSA and cycles of capital investment/disinvestment. Over space, these cycles respond to the variable returns afforded by the uneven development of the SSA, which, in turn, is shaped by successive waves of capital flows. Through time, the size and direction of capital flows are both cause and effect of the SSA. A brief example: in the late nineteenth and early twentieth centuries factory towns were established in the industrial regions of Europe and North America. Cities such as Pittsburgh, Syracuse, Lille, Birmingham, and Essen grew as manufacturing centers. The factories needed labor around these points of production and an organized working class came into existence forged through struggle and adversity. By the last quarter of the twentieth century new technological developments allowed industry to be more footloose; it was no longer so tied to traditional sources of power or to pools of skilled labor. A crucial factor for capital was the cheapness of labor and its ease of control and management. Many of the older industrial cities had such a strongly organized labor movement that wages were kept high and limitations were set on the introduction of technologies that speeded up the rate of work. One effect was for capital to flow to cheaper labor regions and countries. Part of the decline of the Rustbelt and the rise of the Sunbelt in the United States was because of capital disinvestment from the cities of the north-east and investment in the cities of the south and west. In other words, the result of previous cycles of investment becomes the context for the most recent of investment decisions. Underlying these decisions are not inexorable iron laws but social relations and social consequences.

One benchmark study is the work of Baran and Sweezy (1966), who sought to show for the United States how investment in the built form of cities was an important outlet that delayed the long-term tendency toward stagnation. Baran and Sweezy suggest that state stimulation of suburbanization, through the construction of highways and associated infrastructural investment, encouragement of owner-occupation, and incentives to new housing construction played a vital role in buoying up the economy. Suburbanization undercuts the tendency of the economy to stagnate, reduces the problems of under-consumption, and promotes the complex of powerful industries involved in house-building, consumer durables, and automobile industries. Baran and Sweezy point to the stimulating effects of suburbanization on a capitalist economy. The main weakness of this line of argument is to see the production of particular types of built form as neatly dovetailed into the needs and interest of capital. Much Marxist work has seen the suburbs as ideally meeting the needs of capital accumulation while also providing the ideal form for social and political reproduction. The more sophisticated treatments are aware of the contingencies. Walker (1981, 34), for example, notes:

> *The construction of urban space is clearly a constitutive process . . . not a phenomenon to be relegated to an unmaterial, reflective superstructure . . . the social relations of the mode of production set limits and create pressures for a certain kind of spatial organization, but they do not determine spatial relations in any unique, non-contradictory or unidirectional way. Indeed, spatial relations are part of the internally structured whole of a mode of production.*

But the problem remains of analyzing the production of the city within a deterministic framework while also being sensitive to contingent factors. This is a problem central to Marxism as an explanatory theory of how history evolves and why particular spatial configurations emerge. We suggest that a move away from grand ahistorical generalizations toward more detailed analyses of specific agents operating in real time in specific places may be of more value.

Class and class conflict Class is a central, if a sometimes complex and often confusing, concept in the Marxist literature. At its simplest the notion of class is used to refer to the central rupture in capitalist society between those who own/do not own the means of production. Call it capital–labor or bosses–workers, but this cleavage is an important initial stage for analysis. Two strands can be identified.

The first is concerned with the city as a setting for capital–labor relations. Gordon (1984), for example, seeks to demonstrate, within a general model of urbanization and capitalist development in the United States, how industrial suburbanization was partly a response by capital to the increasing power of the working class within the city. Clark (1981) shows how spatial decentralization of production and the emergent division of labor are used as bargaining strategies by capital in their dealings with labor. Scott (1988) shows how an understanding of the capital–labor relationship allows us to explain the intraurban location of different types of industry and the decentralization of much industry toward the periphery.

There is a major difference between capital and labor. Capital is much more mobile than labor and is invested in specific sites in particular places. This fixed investment is just that: it "fixes" capital in particular locations. Capital, however, because of changes in technology and transport improvements, is becoming less fixed. Labor, on the other hand, is tied to particular locations. Movement is possible within countries but can be difficult between them. At the international level capital is much more mobile than labor.

The city is the site for the reproduction as well as the production of class and class relationships. The focus on class structure and residential segregation is the second strand of Marxist scholarship. In the broadest historical sense, urbanization is seen as a radical process. For Marx and Engels the city was pregnant with socialist consequences: urban life saved people from "the idiocy of rural life." In the long-term shift from rural living to urban life, Marx and Engels would seem to be correct. The process of urbanization does seem to involve a shift to social radicalism and constitutes a break with established ways. While there have always been examples of rural radicalism, from the Luddites of England in the last century to the Chiapas uprising in Mexico of the 1990s, cities have provided one of the most consistent points of resistance against the established order.

Within the city, the links between residential differentiation and class formation are more difficult to unravel. In smaller, more "closed" communities, such as coal-mining towns, local traditions of radicalism can emerge and be sustained and celebrated. In bigger cities, with a much broader social base, the easy identification of class and location, except at the extremes, is made more difficult. There is no clear-cut relationship between class formation and patterns of residential segregation. Part of the difficulty lies with similar spatial patterns, which can have very different social outcomes, and the more fundamental problem of the whole notion of class, class identity, and class consciousness. Sharply differentiated residential areas may produce intragroup cohesion, but the transformation of this cohesion into interclass conflict depends on a whole range of contingent factors that may lead either to acceptance, accommodation, or the practice of revolt. More rewarding have been the detailed case studies. Katznelson (1979), for example, looks at the experience of metropolitan United States and convincingly shows how the strength of residential segregation along ethnic cleavages is one reason behind the lack of class-conscious labor politics. The important point is that there is a complex relationship between society and space, class and locale. Untangling these connections can be a significant area of work and a fruitful avenue for further study.

Regime of accumulation   Mode of production is a very general concept. It is useful but not specific enough to capture changes in the precise form and organization of capitalist production. The term "regime of accumulation" refers to the dominant form of securing and accumulating profit. It is used often with reference to the distinction between Fordism and post-Fordism. The name Ford is associated with the mass-production of cars on controlled assembly lines, inflexibly geared toward the constant production of a standardized commodity. You could have the Model T Ford in any color as long as it was black. Post-Fordism involves greater flexibility of production for an increasing range of products with shorter runs. This implies more subcontracting, greater vertical integration between firms, and a more "flexible" use of labor. Flexible production is the response of capital to a tighter market, the declining power of organized labor, and rapid shifts in consumer preferences. It allows firms to adjust quickly to a more volatile market, permits high rates of productivity growth, and reduces employment costs. Flexible production involves a change in the relationship between labor and capital; in effect it gives capital greater control over the deployment of labor, the pacing of work, and the costs of labor. An increasing bifurcation has been noted between a core of highly paid, well-trained employees with good working conditions and generous benefits and a growing number of peripheral workers employed part-time, on a more irregular basis and with fewer benefits or advancement opportunities. Some of the most obvious changes are encapsulated in table 5.1.

Under conditions of flexible production more emphasis is placed on "just in time" delivery systems than on building up stock inventories. There is no point in building up reservoirs of stock in a volatile market because this may lead to unwanted goods. This implies greater circulation in space and is apparent in the greater volume of commercial traffic on the roads and the consequent urban congestion. Goods are traveling through space rather than accumulating over time. Flexible production also involves a new relationship between producer and retailer. The system of flexible production gives greater control to the large retailer in the producer–retailer nexus. In the Fordist system retailers simply sold what the producers created. In the new, more demand-driven system, greater emphasis is placed on speed and accuracy of delivery. Contracts tend to be for shorter runs of a large number of products, and the retailers, especially the larger retailers, have greater potential influence over both the design and the cost of the final product.

TABLE 5.1   CONTRAST BETWEEN FORDISM AND POST-FORDISM

Fordism	Post-Fordism
Mass production of homogeneous goods	Small-batch production
Uniformity and standardization	Flexible and small-batch production of a variety of product types
Large buffer stocks and inventory	No stocks
Resource driven	Demand driven
Single-task performance by worker	Multiple tasks
High degree of job specialization	Elimination of job demarcation
No job security	High employment security for core workers; no job security for temporary workers
Spatial division of labor	Spatial integration
Homogenization of regional labor markets	Labor market diversification
Discipline of labor force	Emphasis on cooperation and responsibility

Source: After Swyngedouw (1986) and Harvey (1989a and b)

Flexible production has also been linked to the evolution of new spatial agglomerations. A distinction can be made between two types of production space: standardized and vernacular. Standardized spaces of production include Detroit, Michigan, a landscape of giant factories set in a corporate culture. Vernacular production spaces have a large number of smaller firms, greater firm cooperation, and no single dominant company. Fordism involved the creation, spread, and deepening of standardized production spaces. The typical post-Fordist production space is vernacular: there are high-tech centers such as Silicon Valley in California and the artisanal skill centers of Italy.

The concept of flexible production, also sometimes referred to as flexible specialization, has taken hold in the urban and regional research literature. It has invigorated debates on production that for years suffered from crude locational models lacking much social sensitivity. But, like all sweeping intellectual trends, it has taken on the mantle of religious truth. In this context it is wise to consider some of the countervailing trends. Not every sector has been given over to flexible production. In the most successful capitalist economy, Japan, Fordist production techniques, although with such innovations as quality circles, still have a large part to play. Standardized spaces of

Illustration 5.2
Ford assembly line, 1929. "Fordism" is the name given to the mass-production on assembly lines (© Mary Evans Picture Library, London)

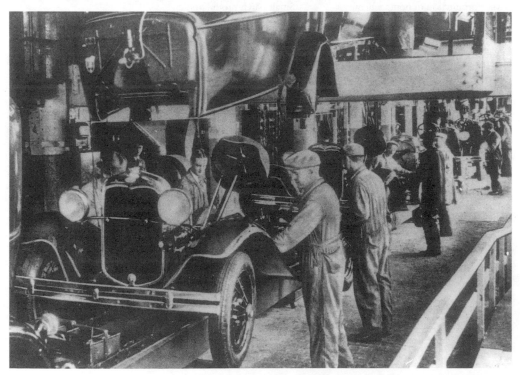

production continue to dominate the industrial landscape. Not all sectors show the same trends. If we consider retailing in the United Kingdom, for example, we see increasing concentration in a small number of very large firms: the opposite to the trend suggested by flexible production.

Urban conflict   The city had a special place in Marx's thought and writings. It was, after all, the built form of his object of study, industrial capitalism. In his work and in later Marxist-inspired and neo-Marxist literature a fundamental tenet was that the city was not something separate from the wider society. There is no separate "urban" discourse that can be abstracted from broader social considerations. The "urban" crisis or "urban" problems are crises of society, social problems that cannot be reduced to geographical explanation. The label "urban" is often used to spatialize rather than to socialize issues of great concern. The Marxist critique rejects the spatial definition or the independently "urban" explanation of social issues. We can see this at work in the earlier writings of Manuel Castells. In *The Urban Question* (first published in French in 1972 and translated into English in 1977) Castells sees the city as a scene of contradiction between competing classes and interests. Castells' starting point is to conceptualize the city as a scene of collective consumption. Items of collective consumption include transport, education, and other services that are consumed collectively, not privately; they are not produced by the market but are necessary to the reproduction of labor power and the smooth and efficient functioning of the city. Since the state provides these goods and services, issues of collective consumption become questions of political power encompassing the competing demands of various fractions of capital, consumers, residents, and organized labor. Castells distinguished between urban struggles and urban social movements. Urban struggles include such things as demonstrations against increases in urban transport fares or levels of educational provision. These struggles become urban social movements when, under the dominance of the working class, they seek to disrupt existing property arrangements and transform dominant political practice.

Castells' work has been the center of intense debate and his early work has been criticized for its mechanistic quality, in which contradictions call forth urban struggle, and for the hazy distinction between struggles and urban social movements. The context has changed from that in which his work was produced. He was writing when state provision was widely accepted as legitimate. However, with Reaganomics and Thatcherism in the 1980s and the rightward shift in ideology and practice, questions of collective consumption became issues of privatization as throughout North America and Europe the market rather than the state was argued to be the more efficient means of provision.

In his later work, *The City and the Grassroots* (1983), Castells becomes less structural and more concerned with human agency as a source of change. Castells dismisses his previous Marxist perspective, which he sees as too functional, too dominated by a view of the city as the outcome of the logic of capital. His focus is on urban social movements through time and across space. For each case study, from the Glasgow rent strike of 1917 to the gay movement in San Francisco, he seeks to show the connections with wider social forces, the stakes and strategies and the consequences for urban form, political practice, and social meaning. Questions of gender, sexual orientation, and ethnicity are now seen as sites of resistance and struggle as much as class.

To some extent Castells' work in these two books forms a coherent whole; a concern with the relationship between space and society. There is a change in emphasis: the first book is more concerned with social structure and social reproduction, whereas the second is focused more on social conflict and change. To a certain extent, however, his later work repudiates his Marxist commitment. His new approach is arrived at, he notes, "through the glorious ruins of the Marxist tradition." In this regard Castells exemplifies one trajectory: the explicit rejection of Marxism. The increased use of Marxist terminology and the concern with "Marxist" issues of the 1970s has been downplayed in the urban studies of the late 1980s and 1990s. Marxism has become less fashionable, criticisms of its silences and lacunae have led to an outmigration of interest. And because some of the basic notions of historical materialism have been incorporated into a taken-for-granted neo-orthodoxy, there is less need to spell out the Marxist terms. An alternative strand is represented in the work of David Harvey (1935–).

The work of David Harvey

David Harvey's first book, *Explanation in Geography* (1969), was published at a time of intense debate about the nature of method in quantitative social science. The book begins by drawing a distinction between philosophy and methodology. Harvey's main aim is to harness the then-growing quantitative, model-building approach, and he does this by formulating criteria for judging the soundness of arguments. The book is essentially concerned with understanding the process of scientific explanation. The best way to achieve this explanation is by taking the deductive approach with the use of models to suggest hypotheses that can then be verified. The testing of hypotheses allows the construction of theory, which provides the basis for subsequent model-building and hypothesis-testing.

Harvey's next book was *Social Justice and the City* (1973), which begins by taking up some of the same initial questions as the previous book on the separation between philosophy and methodology. This time, however, Harvey argues that the distinction should be avoided because the method of analysis conditions the objects of analysis; method and objective are not independent. *Social Justice* is really two books. The first part, "Liberal Formulations," is concerned with focusing geographical inquiry on socially relevant topics, such as social justice and income redistribution in the city. The second part, "Social Formulations," marks a distinct epistemological break. Now ideas are seen to be derived from a particular social context, and social justice cannot be discussed in the abstract; instead it must be placed within a consideration of the wider society. The concept of the city is radically altered. Rather than being a thing in itself, an independent object of inquiry, the city is seen as an important element mediating and expressing wider social processes. Through considerations of Marxist rent theory, the history of urbanism, and the notions of paradigm shift and consequent social science research, Harvey's main aim in the second part is to show the relationship between the city and society from the perspective of historical materialism.

Some commentators accept the notion of a rupture between the early and the later writings of Harvey. A more careful reading, however, reveals continuities. The Harvey of *Explanation* has the same concern with lofty theorizing, grand schemes, and general theories as the Marxist Harvey. The outlier is the Harvey of "Liberal Formulations" with its more directly social applications and empirical connections. Midlife crisis, the shock of metropolitan United States after provincial England, or whatever the reasons, it is the "Liberal Formulations" that stand out from a lifelong commitment to Grand Theory.

Two trends are apparent in Harvey's subsequent work. The first is one of maintaining orthodoxy, a repetition of Marx's ideas, phrases, and concerns. The second is a much more creative use of historical materialism, a concern to "update" Marx and in particular to explore the connections between space and society not discussed in orthodox Marxism. These connections are discussed in a series of papers. Let me consider some of them.

In one of the first papers after *Social Justice* Harvey (1974) critiques the concept of rent. In standard location studies and neo-classical economic views of the city, rent is seen as a harmonious device for sorting out different land uses. In criticizing this notion of rent Harvey resurrects Marx's three categories of differential, monopoly, and absolute rent. Although the terms and their application are problematic the most important point is to show that above all rent is a social relationship arising from the power afforded to landowners by the existence and maintenance of private property. Rent is a payment to private property, with the amount being fixed by the relative bargaining power between landowners, producers, and consumers. In a later paper Harvey (1976) sees the city as the arena of conflict between a landed fraction of capital, whose revenue comes from the power of landownership, a construction fraction of capital and labor, with the state acting as referee between the three although with the interests of capital predominating in its deliberations. This model prioritizes the capital–labor cleavage as the primary determining factor. It can be seen as complementary to Castells' more specific emphasis on consumption-based issues. Harvey also took up the matter of class in an attempt to integrate theories of residential differentiation with those of social stratification and class formation. In developing the ideas of Giddens (1973), Harvey (1975) sees residential differentiation as an important secondary force of social stratification: residential areas provide a common background of shared experiences, a locale for the maintenance and production of lifestyles, attitudes to work and education. Social inequalities and social images are produced and reproduced in the urban mosaic of the city. In effect, Harvey suggests a functional link between residential differentiation and the reproduction of a class-based society.

In a paper entitled "The Urban Process under Capitalism" Harvey (1978) identifies two circuits of capital. The first circuit involves investment in the production of commodities, and the second circuit involves investment in fixed capital items such as roads and buildings. Investment in the second circuit provides a temporary solution to the crisis of overaccumulation in the primary circuit. In this model Harvey ties in the production of the built environment with capital flows and the recurring crises of capitalism. The process of profit equalization, however, would seem to be a more appropriate explanation of shifts between the two circuits because this does not involve an *a priori* assumption of underconsumption or overaccumulation. This paper, with its emphasis on circuits of capital, considers issues that are more fully developed in Harvey's third book, *The Limits to Capital* (1982), an ambitious work whose aim is nothing less than to provide a re-exposition and extension of Marx's original analysis of capitalism. It is an attempt to rewrite Marx's *Capital*, with even the exposition closely mirroring Marx's work. Chapter 1, for example, begins with a discussion of commodities, use values, and exchange values, just as in Marx's original. A "first cut" theory of crisis is a basic model of capitalist economy using Marx's basic concepts. A "second cut" incorporates money, finance, and the concept of fixed capital. A "third cut" is more explicitly concerned with space and location. The book also extends and codifies the notion of circuits of capital (see figure 5.1). Rent theory, the differential mobilities of capital and labor, and notions of regional and international uneven development are also examined. The production of spatial configurations and the functioning of the space economy are now seen as central facets of a capitalist economy in crisis. Within this general framework Harvey (1982, 374) notes that we should view

location as a fundamental material attribute of human activity but recognize that location is socially produced. The production of spatial configurations can then be treated as an "active moment" within the overall temporal dynamic of accumulation and social reproduction.

Figure 5.1
The circuits of capital
Source: *Harvey (1982)*

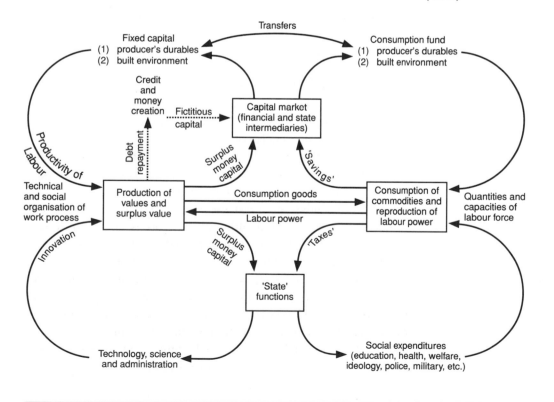

Two more books appeared in 1985 and one in 1989 that were essentially revisions to his papers written in the 1970s and early 1980s. A more radical departure was *The Condition of Postmodernity*, published in 1989. Harvey's goal was to anchor the condition of postmodernity back to what he saw as the material realities of capitalist organization. In particular, he argued that since the early 1970s new forms of capital accumulation could be identified; a more flexible, post-Fordist system that brought about changes in the dimensions and experience of time and space, which ultimately was the economic bedrock on which lay changing cultural forms. Postmodernism was the "culture clothing of flexible accumulation."

It is now fashionable to dismiss the work of David Harvey. One example is the book review by Dear (1992), who seeks to do a demolition job on Marxism and Harvey from the postmodern perspective. Feminist critiques of his work have also emerged that criticize his emphasis on class rather than on gender. In some quarters Harvey is now seen as overly deterministic, a remnant of the short-lived intellectual Marxist renaissance, a figure, like Marx himself, only of historical value. This is a mistake. Harvey's work *is* at times overly deterministic. Having read most of his papers and books I am conscious of the cliché, in all his post-1973 works, of heavy structural critique with only an emancipatory flourish about praxis and social agency on the last page in the final paragraph. Harvey is a theoretician. This is both his weakness and his strength. His commitment to (academic) Marxism means his work is like a story the punch line of which is known in advance. We know that things will be reduced ultimately to the (changing) mode of production. That is where his analyses leads us. Human agency, social change, resistance and contest from below are all weakly developed in his work. But given all that, Harvey is a theoretician of enormous subtlety, finesse, and genuinely creative thought. He explores the link between space and society with power and originality. While his theory is at times like a straitjacket, at others it has all the power and focus of a laser beam able to cut through some very dense material. His writings on the city should not be ignored and, although his work is capable of serious criticism (but whose work is immune from that?), it is always provocative, interesting, and stimulating. His is an authentic voice, a serious commitment to scholarship, and a searching intellect. While most writers on space, society, and the urban condition import theories from other areas, Harvey is one of the few writers to generate theories of society and economy that take space, the built environment, and the city as central components. To ignore Harvey is to avoid a unique and important intellectual contribution.

The socialist city

Marx's legacy was not only to a group of academic writers. He informed the political practice of the twentieth century and was an important intellectual element in the socialist challenge to the capitalist mode of production. This challenge took two main forms, and in each of them the city was an important element.

The first was the socialist revolutions that sought to transform capitalism into socialism. The Bolshevik Revolution, the rise of Communist China, and the adoption of a Marxist rhetoric around the world were some of the most momentous political changes of the twentieth century. These changes were recorded in and through the city. When a city changes from capitalist to socialist, city form becomes less the product of market forces and more the result of government planning. The city becomes an important part in the iconography of the new society.

The socialist cities of the twentieth century drew much of their inspiration from the Moscow Plan of 1935. This was a plan for the reconstruction of the capital city of the Soviet Union. It enunciated city planning according to contemporary principles. It proposed that cities should be limited in size, that city centers should be given over to ideological rather than business functions, and that the state should control housing allocation.

Beijing in China provides a good example (see Samuels and Samuels, 1989). The city was reshaped to produce an image of a modern socialist society. An area beside the Gate of Heavenly Peace was bulldozed to accommodate Tiananmen Square, completed in 1959. This is one of the largest squares in the world, covering 50 hectares. On the western edge of the square the authorities built the Great Hall of the People, on the eastern edge the Museum of the Chinese Revolution, and in the center a 37-meter-high granite obelisk as a monument to the Peoples' Heroes. The square, built as a symbol of the new socialist China, the setting for mass processions, also became the setting for mass protests. The student sit-in at Tiananmen Square in 1989 was a mark of social protest. The subsequent massacre became a symbol of a corrupt regime smashing popular protest.

Berlin provides an example of the divergent paths of the capitalist and socialist city. After 1945 the city was divided into east and west sectors. In the west, which had always been the wealthiest part of the city, the center was dominated by business and shopping, much as in other Western European cities, with a substantial group of Turkish migrants living in the shabbier, older housing areas. In the center of

East Berlin there were few shops or services. The streets were widened
to provide avenues for state processions and government buildings
were erected: the center as ideology rather than the center as business. A wall separated the two cities, until its fall in 1989 marked the
beginning of the end of the Iron Curtain, the Cold War, and a socialist Europe.

We can also see some of the changes by looking at cities before and
after revolutions. Garnier (1973) has recorded the history of Havana
before and after the revolution led by Fidel Castro. Before the
revolution a small elite, mainly living off the American exploitation
of sugar, lived in a salubrious sector of the city in a succession of villas stretching along the coast. There were periodic cycles in villa
construction as the price of sugar varied on the world market. The
rest of the population were located in two areas: those who lived in
the central city in dwellings previously occupied by the rich, and those
in peripheral shantytowns. After the revolution, the housing stock
was allocated more by need than by economic bidding power, with
a consequent mixing of social classes. This type of change and its
effects on segregation were also seen in Prague, where Musil (1968)
notes:

> *The influence of economic factors was replaced . . . by a housing policy*
> *which allocates new dwellings by preference to young families with*
> *children, to employees of key economic branches and to families living*
> *in very bad and unhealthy conditions.*

Since 1989 the reverse process has been in operation. The decline of
communism has also had its impact on the cities. There has been the
iconoclastic destruction of the communist legacy: the statues of Lenin
have been destroyed, the Communist Party headquarters have been
abandoned and the Berlin Wall has been torn down. The introduction of a capitalist economy will have major impacts on the
formerly socialist cities. The market will become the principal allo-
cator of land use rather than government planning, and the centers
will become dominated more by business than by politics. The greatest impact will be on the costs to the average citizen. In most
European socialist cities, the mass of the population lived in modern,
large housing complexes on the edge of the city. Housing was cheap,
utility costs were low, and mass transport was enormously subsidized.
A return to market rents and full-cost fares will have a dramatic effect
on the average costs of ordinary citizens just at a time when incomes
are static or declining. Much of the housing and transport costs were
enormously subsidized. The move from socialist city to capitalist city

contains enormous tensions and costs. In the short term the citizens of these cities have all the disadvantages of socialist bureaucracy and capitalist markets without the benefits of central planning or free markets.

The impact of socialist rhetoric and practice was not limited to those societies that underwent communist revolutions. In the capitalist world there was resistance. The capitalist mode of production did not go unchallenged. From critics to reformers, the voice of protest was raised and points of resistance were established. The cities were an important site of challenge as centers of the organized working class. In their institutions and cultural practices, from burial and building societies, to soccer teams and festivals, they provided a communal impulse which resonated in the life and form of the city. Cities were places of public space, and these spaces bore the imprint of tension and contest. Parks and recreation sites competed with factories and profitable enterprises, housing based on need as well as housing based on ability to pay was built, and public as well as private transport was available. Where the organized working class was an important political constituency in city politics we can see varying levels of what we may term municipal socialism. The context of national politics is also an important element. Cities in the Scandinavian countries, for example, are more concerned with quality social housing and the provision of public goods and items of collective consumption than in the United States, where a working-class consciousness is often vitiated or replaced by ethnic divisions, and the concern with rights rather than social needs leads to more privatized cities. Variations also occur within countries. In Britain cities such as Newcastle, Glasgow, and Manchester, with long traditions of Labour Party control, have greater public goods provision than the more middle-class towns and cities of the south-east of England. There has also been change over time. The provision of public goods and services was at its peak in the social democracies of Europe from after the Second World War until the 1970s. Then issues of funding and rising costs began to appear. Some countries, particularly the Scandinavian countries, maintained high levels of provision, whereas others, such as Britain, embarked on a process of recommodification and privatization that reached its ideological peak during the Thatcher regime of 1979–90, when social housing was sold off, subsidies were reduced, and the metropolitan, predominantly socialist, authorities were simply abolished.

CITIES AND MODES OF CONSUMPTION

To focus on the relationship between mode of production and city structure is a useful, if very general, first approximation. A major problem, however, is that it lumps together societies as varied as Brazil, United States, Zaire, and Japan, in all of which the capitalist mode of production is dominant. Rio, Detroit, Manchester, Kinshasa, Tokyo have many similarities, but they also have many differences. A focus on the mode of production means looking more closely at the former than at the latter. A distinction is sometimes made between rich and poor cities, referring to their location in so-called rich and poor countries. The United States would be considered rich and Brazil poorer. The problem with this division is that there are rich people in poor countries and cities and poor people in rich countries and cities: New York has some very poor people while Rio de Janeiro has some very rich people. The adjectives rich and poor when applied to either countries or cities fail to register these distinctions.

A more compelling method is to consider differences in the mode of consumption. We can make a distinction between those countries characterized by high mass consumption and those noted for much lower levels of consumption. This is a rough demarcation, but a useful one.

Cities of high mass consumption

Capitalism in the nineteenth century was based on the production of commodities. Personal consumption was limited to the rich and the affluent. The majority of people were relatively poor. This began to alter in some countries in the twentieth century as a capitalism of mass-produced, mass-consumed goods became important. In 1908 Henry Ford (1863–1947) designed his Model T car. By cutting production costs and creating an efficient assembly line Ford was able to build and sell a large number of cars at a relatively low price. Between 1908 and 1928 over 15 million cars were sold. A mass market had been created. At the heart of the system of mass consumption is

- relatively high wages with which people can afford to buy consumer goods;
- credit systems that enable people to acquire highly priced items and pay back the cost over a long period; and
- an ideology that sanctions and fosters continued consumption.

High wages result from capital–labor relations, in which labor has the ability to demand and maintain high wages. Once mass consumption becomes the norm the whole system is dependent on continued high incomes. While individual capitalists may want to keep wages as low as possible to maintain profit levels, they are dependent on the system as a whole to maintain purchasing power. Thus a company that makes cars may want to keep its labor costs down, but it needs workers to have enough money to buy cars.

If spending ability is limited to disposable income then a brake is put on consumption. People will be able to buy small-cost items but not expensive goods. Credit bridges the gap. High mass consumption is predicated on sophisticated credit arrangements. The system encourages personal indebtedness.

People also have to be encouraged to buy, and to keep on buying. The system of mass consumption is thus based on a whole set of social and political beliefs in which continued consumption is lauded. The agreed political need for continued growth or the more personal need to achieve status through particular forms of consumption are not inherent, universal needs; they are the "needs" of a particular economic system.

We can examine some of the tensions in the cities of this economic arrangement by considering the two icons of cities of high mass consumption: the *car* and the *suburb*. The car is the most personal form of transportation. It is individually owned and driven. It is an

The political economy of urbanization

Illustration 5.3
Fifth Avenue, New York, where the wealthy classes reside. A successful businessman poses beside his car, a symbol of conspicuous sustained consumption (© Format Photographers; photograph: Jacky Chapman)

113

expensive item, sometimes bought outright but more often through some credit arrangement. It uses up scarce materials and runs on a finite resource, petroleum. Car consumption has increased, until today cars constitute one of the most important means of transport in the developed world. And the result has been the transformation of the city to accommodate an increasing number of cars. Concrete roads swirl around the city, cutting off neighborhoods and generating noise and toxic fumes. To build more roads is to generate more traffic. The individual dream has become the collective nightmare.

The suburb of owner-occupied housing has been made possible by sophisticated credit arrangements, which allow people to take out large, long-term mortgages, and by relatively high purchasing power, which allows households to afford the mortgage repayments and transportation costs. Suburbs condense and reflect these trends. It is not too fanciful to suggest that suburbanization is both cause and effect of high incomes, personal indebtedness, and the nuclear family. However, the system is highly geared. Personal loans can be serviced if the economy is booming, but a decline in growth throws the whole system into turmoil as households refrain from taking on new debt, which in turn feeds the recessionary tendencies even more. Investment in the suburbs has been an important engine of economic growth, but it has also become the source of economic crisis.

Cities of peripheral capitalism

The world economy can be considered as having a small, rich core and an extended periphery. The core countries include the United States, Japan, and most of Western Europe. These are the societies of mass consumption. The peripheral parts of the world have their economies orientated toward the core and have less autocentric economic growth and lower levels of national income and wealth. The cities of the periphery differ in many regards, but they have a number of similarities. Two of the most obvious are the *informal economies* and the *shantytowns*.

There is a basic mismatch in many Third World cities between the number of employable people and the number of jobs in the formal economy. The formal economy provides jobs with steady wages, regular hours of work, and social security benefits. The severe lack of this type of employment in association with low or nonexistent levels of government support means that people have to make a living as best they can. Without formal employment or government income support they find money in the informal economy. Shoe-cleaning in Lima, small food stands in Caracas, prostitution, drugs, and theft are just some of the range of activities that can provide income in cities of high unemployment. These cities are highly bifurcated between the small minority of the very rich and the vast majority of the poor. The rich in many of these cities live in highly segregated compounds with lifestyles that the other citizens can only imagine in their wildest dreams. There is a chasm between the urban experience of the rich and the poor.

Shantytowns are the physical expression of both problems and solutions. They are found in all large cities in the capitalist Third World. They vary from the temporary shelters on the sidewalk to the stable communities of many years' standing. On the one hand they highlight the problem of poverty. Unlike the cities of high mass consumption, incomes are much lower and credit facilities are weakly developed. The state has too few funds to provide enough housing for those who need it. The end result is that people have no option but to build their own shelter, wherever and however they can: next to trash dumps, close to factories, underneath highways; wherever there is space and an accessible location, shelter is built. Sometimes the materials are flimsy, barely keeping out the rain, but sometimes they are sturdy, well-made examples of self-help housing. On the other hand, the shantytowns, at least the better-built ones, represent a solution to an endemic housing shortage. They show the power of individual action and the force of collective resolve in the face of

The political economy of urbanization

Illustration 5.4
Philippino immigrants; Eastern Malaysia: a makeshift shanty-town
(© Roger Scruton)

difficult conditions. With few resources and little official help, these shantytowns are also a symbol of hope.

CITIES AND MODES OF REGULATION

I have made a useful but very general distinction between cities in terms of the dominant mode of production. Another distinction was made between modes of consumption. But an even further sifting is required if we are to be sensitive to the differences between societies within the different types of consumption. There is, for example, a world of difference between the look, feel, and experience of cities in the United States compared to those in Sweden or the Netherlands or even Britain. The fact that they are all capitalist societies, marked by high mass consumption, does not allow us to note the differences; to handle these we have to be aware of the mode of regulation of the economic system.

There is no such thing as a free, unfettered capitalist market. Capitalism has always been regulated. Capitalist economies are embedded in specific societies with different traditions, belief systems, histories, and geographies. And all these characteristics are not incidental to the functioning of the market, they are central. In the rest of this chapter I will note how the mode of regulation varies over space and across time.

Variation over space

The important question is not whether markets are regulated or not regulated, because all markets are regulated, but in whose interests are they regulated? We can draw a rough distinction between markets that are more regulated in relation to maximizing social welfare and those that are more regulated in favor of maximizing private profits. Most of the Scandinavian countries, for example, have redistributional social programs based on a heavy and wide taxation load and a high degree of social consensus. This filters down to the city level and is apparent in the commitment to public transport systems, social housing, and the quality and extent of public spaces. A stark contrast can be drawn with the United States, where the emphasis on individual rights as opposed to collective goals is transmitted through a regressive taxation system and ultimately leads to cities distinguished, as Kenneth Galbraith (1958) described, by private affluence and public squalor: cities with marked inequalities in wealth, restricted social welfare programs, and, for such an enormously wealthy country, generally poor-quality public services, and few public spaces or any real quality of beauty.

Variation through time

The mode of regulation is not fixed. Things change. In the 1980s there was strong political pressure in many rich countries for de-regulation. The term is very misleading because it suggests less government intervention. A more appropriate term is reregulation because it implies a redirection of government involvement. It is not a question of less regulation but of who benefits from changes in the regulation. Commitments to social welfare also change over time. In many countries social welfare spending is predicated on a high taxation load. When and if enough people feel the weight is uneven, unfair or not worth it, then taxation revolts are possible. There are also moves in the opposite direction. In the United States, for example, the need for some form of universal health care became a major political issue in the 1990s, after decades during which politicians assumed that no form of socialized health care could be introduced.

A number of commentators have pointed to a major change in the mode of regulation of advanced capitalist countries (for example, Aglietta, 1979; Lipietz, 1986). Fordism was a regime of regulation as well as a system of production. It involved collective bargaining between big capital and organized labor to set the framework for wage levels and conditions of employment. The state was an integral part of this negotiation, setting the regulatory framework, providing a whole range of goods and services and, in some states, providing a welfare system that guaranteed minimum levels of incomes, education, and health provision. The system developed in North America and Western Europe after 1945 was based on a social contract between the state and its citizens and was underwritten by continued economic growth, which ensured rising incomes, state revenues, and the preconditions for an organized and effective working class.

After the mid-1970s increased competition, declining rates of economic growth, and less cohesive national communities effectively undermined the stability of the old system of regulation. Permanent unemployment varied between 5 and 10 percent in even the richest countries, and deindustrialization weakened the power of organized labor. Although the new post-Fordist system varied in its intent and extent there was a retreat from universal welfare provision, a decline of national wage agreements, a more entrepreneurial state, and the creation of a regulatory system that was more open to the needs of business. There was privatization of many state-run enterprises and less regulation of wage levels and working conditions. Lash and Urry (1987) refer to the change as a move from organized to disorganized capitalism. Although they correctly identify an important social change I am unhappy with their choice of terms. I feel that it is not a disorganized capitalism but a reorganized capitalism, a capitalism in which the balance has moved more toward the demands of capital than toward the needs of labor. To use the term "disorganized" is to imply that there is no order. There is an order that the term "reorganized" at least recognizes.

Some of the changes in the mode of operation of the state are shown in table 5.2 The changes outlined have a marked effect on the look and experience of cities. In Britain, for example, the local variant of the post-Fordist state was the Thatcherism of the 1980s, which saw the sale of public housing, the shift from social policies to those aiding economic growth, and a general decline in those urban public services that did not directly aid private profitability. In the United States Reaganomics stimulated private growth but ignored the social malaise in the inner-city areas. The rich got richer while the poor

TABLE 5.2 THE FORDIST AND POST-FORDIST STATE	
Fordist state	*Post-Fordist state*
Regulation	Reregulation
Rigidity	Flexibility
Collective bargaining	Local or firm-based negotiations
Socialization of welfare	Privatization of collective needs and security
Centralization	Decentralization and increase of interregional and intercity competition
"Subsidy" state	"Entrepreneurial" state
Indirect intervention in markets through income and price policies	Direct state intervention in markets through procurements
Industry-led innovation	State-led innovation
National regional policies	"Territorial" regional policies

Source: After Swyngedouw (1986) and Harvey (1989 a and b)

languished in the ghettos. Government policies are neither the source of all problems nor the fount of all solutions. They are, however, very important in setting the tone of economic and social change. The big shift has been from welfarism to post-Fordism. But there are signs of a reaction against the reregulation of the markets simply to aid business. In the 1990s there is an increased acceptance of the reality of the social costs of unequal growth, the corrosive effects of long-term poverty, and the recognition that the state has more than just a passive role in economic growth and quality of life. The 1980s marked the zenith of the postwar belief in the power of the market. The 1990s could be the period when a reappraisal suggests a renewed interest in the role of regulation to achieve social and economic goals. These broad-scale changes are more than just changes in political beliefs; their unfolding consequences have left a definite mark on the urban order.

GUIDE TO FURTHER READING

Marxist approaches to the city include:
Bassett, K.A. and Short, J.R. (1980) *Housing and Residential Structure*, London: Routledge.
Feagin, J. and Smith, M. (eds) (1987) *The Capitalist City*, Oxford: Blackwell.
Katznelson, I. (1992) *Marxism and the City*, New York: Oxford University Press.
Lefebvre, H. (1995) *Writings on Cities*, ed. and trans. E. Kofman and E. Lebas, Oxford: Blackwell.
Short, J.R. (1985) Human geography and Marxism. In Z. Baranski and J.R. Short (eds), *Developing Contemporary Marxism*, London: Macmillan.
Tabb, W.K. and Sawyers, L. (eds) (1984) *Marxism and the Metropolis*, New York: Oxford University Press.

On flows of investment in the city:
Gordon, D.M., Weisskopf, T.E. and Bowles S. (1983) Long swings and the non-reproductive cycle, *American Economic Review* 73, 152–7.
Massey, D. (1984) *Spatial Divisions of Labour*, London: Macmillan.
Wilson, D. (1991) Urban change, circuits of capital and uneven development, *Professional Geographer* 43, 403–15.

On class and class conflict:
Gordon, D.M. (1984) Capitalist development and the history of American cities. In W.K. Tabb, and L. Sawers (eds), *Marxism and the Metropolis*, New York: Oxford University Press.
Katznelson, I. (1979) *City Trenches: Urban Politics and the Patterning of Class in the United States*, New York: Pantheon.

Castells' work on the city as a place of crises and conflict is contained in two books:
Castells, M. (1977) *The Urban Question*, London: Edward Arnold.
Castells, M. (1983) *The City and the Grassroots*, London: Edward Arnold.

Harvey's major books:
Harvey, D. (1969) *Explanation in Geography*, London: Edward Arnold.
Harvey, D. (1973) *Social Justice and the City*, London: Edward Arnold.
Harvey, D. (1982) *The Limits to Capital*, Oxford: Blackwell.
Harvey, D. (1985a) *The Urbanization of Capital*, Oxford: Blackwell.
Harvey, D. (1985b) *Consciousness and the Urban Experience*, Oxford: Blackwell.
Harvey, D. (1989a) *The Condition of Postmodernity*, Oxford: Blackwell.
Harvey, D. (1989b) *The Urban Experience*, Oxford: Blackwell.

Examples of works on the socialist city include:
Garnier, J.P. (1973) *Une ville, une révolution: La Havane*, Paris: Maspero.
Harloe, M., Szelenyi, I. and Andrusz, G. (1996) *Cities after Socialism*, Oxford: Blackwell.
Musil, J. (1968) The development of Prague's ecological structure. In R.E. Pahl (ed.), *Readings in Urban Sociology*, Oxford: Oxford University Press.
Samuels, M.S. and Samuels, C. (1989) Beijing and the power of place in modern China. In J. Agnew and J.S. Duncan (eds), *The Power of Place*, London: Unwin Hyman.

For urban developments in peripheral capitalist societies, have a look at:
Gugler, J. (1988) *The Urbanization of the Third World*, Oxford and New York: Oxford University Press.
Roberts, B. (1995) *Cities of Peasants Re-viewed*, London: Edward Arnold.

On the new mode of regulation:
Aglietta, M. (1979) *A Theory of Regulation*, London: New Left Books.
Halal, W. (1986) *The New Capitalism*, New York: Basic Books.
Lash, S. and Urry, J. (1987) *The End of Organised Capitalism*, Oxford and Cambridge, Mass.: Blackwell.
Lipietz, A. (1986) New tendencies in the international division of labor: regimes of accumulation and modes of regulation. In A. Scott and M. Storper (eds), *Production, Work, Territory: The Geographical Anatomy of Industrial Capitalism*, London: Routledge.
Moulaert, F. and Swyngedouw, E. (1989) A regulation approach to the geography of flexible production systems, *Environment and Planning D: Society and Space* 7, 327–45.
Sayer, A. (1989) Postfordism in question, *International Journal of Urban and Regional Research* 13, 666–95.
Swyngedouw, E. (1986) *The socio-spatial implications of innovations in industrial organization*, Working Paper 20, Lille: Johns Hopkins European Center for Regional Planning and Research.

Other works cited in this chapter:
Baran, P. and Sweezy, P. (1966) *Monopoly Capital*, Harmondsworth, Middx: Penguin.
Clark, G.L. (1981) The employment relation and spatial division of labor: a hypothesis, *Annals of Association of American Geographers*, 71, 412–24.
Dear, M. (1992) Review of *The Condition of Postmodernity*, *Annals of the Association of American Geographers* 81, 533–9.
Galbraith, K. (1958) *The Affluent Society*, London: Hamish Hamilton.
Giddens, A. (1973) *The Class Structure of the Advanced Societies*, London: Hutchinson.
Harvey, D. (1974) Class monopoly rent, finance capital and the urban revolution, *Regional Studies*, 8, 239–55.

Harvey, D. (1975) Class structure in a capitalist society and the theory of residential differentiation. In R. Peel, P. Haggett, and M. Chisholm (eds), *Processes in Physical and Human Geography*, London: Heinemann.

Harvey, D. (1976) Labor, capital and class struggle around the built environment in advanced capitalist countries, *Politics and Society* 6, 265–94.

Harvey, D. (1978) The urban process under capitalism, *International Journal of Urban and Regional Research* 2, 101–31.

Scott, A.J. (1988) *Metropolis: From Division of Labor to Urban Form*, Berkeley and Los Angeles, Cal.: University of California Press.

Walker, R.A. (1981) The theory of suburbanization: capitalism and the construction of urban space in the United States. In M. Dear and A.J. Scott (eds), *Urbanization and Urban Planning in Capitalist Society*, London: Methuen.

Chapter 6

CAPITAL, LABOR, AND THE CITY:
CASE STUDY I, PART 1

[S YDNEY] IS PART SAN FRANCISCO. A BIT OF ENGLAND. THE FLAVOR OF NEW YORK.

AIRLINE ADVERTISEMENT (1980)

In 1971 in Sydney, Australia, there was a strange alliance between residents of an upper-income neighborhood, Hunters Hill, and a militant trade union, the New South Wales (NSW) Builders' Labourers Federation (BLF). They agreed to combine forces to stop residential development on the public open space known as Kelly's Bush. The BLF imposed a ban on the site. Here was a case of union power being exercised not over the traditional concerns of wages or conditions but over an environmental issue. This was the beginning of the Green Ban movement, which, centering on Sydney, involved the BLF stopping an estimated $A 3,000 million-worth of development. Green Bans were imposed on individual building projects (for example, the proposed car park outside the famous Sydney Opera House, because it involved the destruction of some fig trees, and the demolition plan for the Theatre Royal), and major redevelopment schemes (such as The Rocks, Woolloomooloo, and the plan to develop an Olympic stadium in Centennial Park).

Between 1971 and 1974, the New South Wales BLF was a major force in shaping Sydney. Their policy was to impose Green Bans only when local residents were against the redevelopment proposals. The BLF was vilified by the Liberal state government and widely criticized in the press. In 1974, after an application to the Australian Industrial Court from the Master Builders' Association, the BLF was deregistered. This meant it was banned from the Australian arbitration system, its members were not eligible for agreed wage increases, and other unions could poach members. Subsequently, the NSW branch was taken over by the federal BLF (based in Melbourne), whose secretary, Norman Gallagher, was opposed to the Green Bans and was influential in getting the leadership of the NSW BLF banned for life.

In 1985, Gallagher was found guilty in a Melbourne court of accepting bribes from major developers. The federal BLF was deregistered by a special act of federal government in 1986. In 1994 the BLF merged with the Construction, Forestry, Mining and Energy Union. The national secretary of the new union said: "the union was more responsible these days and would never use BLF tactics. It was more interested in developing training schemes for its members than industrial militancy" (Russell, 1994).

*Capital, labor, and
the city:
case study I:1*

In this chapter I want to tell the story of the BLF and its involvement in Sydney. The story is particular to one city at one period of time but is of wider significance; it condenses some of the issues discussed in the previous chapters, including:

- the conflict between capital and labor in an urban setting;
- the connection between local struggles and global economic trends;
- the role of social action in shaping the built environment;
- the tension between the city as a scene for capital investment and a place to live, a machine for making money as well as an arena of social life.

I want to tell the story in two ways. In this chapter I tell it in a wide context. The next chapter consists of an interview with one of the main protagonists of the drama. This chapter is theoretical and empirical, the next is anecdotal and personal. Both approaches have a legitimate place in a critical social science and a progressive urban geography.

THE CONTEXT

Capital–labor relations in the construction industry

The basic relationship in the private sector of a capitalist society is the employment of labor by capital. The negotiations between the two sides are conducted through the intermediaries of labor organizations (unions) and management. Capital is primarily concerned with maintaining and enhancing profitability through minimizing the production costs and controlling the labor process. Labor in contrast has a concern with maintaining and increasing rates of pay and improving the conditions of employment.

The type of construction sector found in the United Kingdom,

Australia, and parts of the United States differs from most other forms of commodity production:

- production takes place on specific sites over relatively small time periods; and
- it is a nomadic enterprise involving the movement of labor power and some of the means of production.

In the negotiation/conflict between the two sides each has a particular mix of strengths and weaknesses. For labor the nomadic nature of the sector and the relatively short life of any one site pose problems for union organization and mobilization. Compared to the typical factory, labor turnover is high and the duration of employment is short. The net result: organized labor is relatively weak. A contrast can be made, however, between the small sites and the very large sites that can involve hundreds of workers on longer-term contracts. Here unionization is easier. The same contrast is also apparent between the residential and nonresidential sectors of the construction industry. House-building usually involves at any one time smaller sites and smaller numbers of workers than the construction sites of commercial and industrial buildings. Levels of unionization are lower and levels of subcontracting are higher in the residential sector. In this study we will be concerned with only the nonresidential sector.

Ultimately, labor can withdraw its power and/or sabotage production. These actions have special potency in the construction sector with its heavy reliance on external financing and where contracts are often given on the cost-comparison basis of lowest bid; the firm giving the lowest bid may not always win the contracts but, except in price-fixing rings, the competition favors firms putting in low tenders. This can mean small margins between profit and loss, a situation reinforced by fixed-price contracts and heavy penalty clauses. The withdrawal of labor for even small periods of time can thus mean heavy financial penalties for construction capital.

In summary, then, organized labor exercises its power by withdrawing labor power from sites but has the problem of organizing a nomadic, high-turnover workforce. Construction capital has much power over a traditionally weakly organized labor force but can face severe financial difficulties if production times are delayed. These relative positions vary over time as they are affected by changes in the labor process, the general economic climate, and the position in the property cycle. It is this last feature that we will consider in some detail.

The 1968–74 property cycle

Sydney, like cities in Europe and North America, experienced a rapid growth of office development in the late 1960s and early 1970s. Some of the reasons include a steady fall in the rates of return afforded to capital investment in manufacturing industry in the developed world at the same time as there was an increase in the amount of liquid capital. The declining returns afforded to manufacturing were caused by labor shortages and consequent militancy, raw material cost increases, and competition from the newly industrializing countries, the precise mix of these factors varied in different countries. The growing pool of liquid capital was evident in the growth of financial institutions such as banks, pension funds, and insurance companies. At the international level, the collapse of the system of fixed exchange rates and the creation of an international financial market meant that capital could be shifted around the world. Dollars generated in Europe by US multinationals could be invested through London in commodity production in Asia or property development in Australia. Capital that required better returns was invested in urban commercial property because there was a growing demand for office accommodation from the expanding service and financial sectors, especially in the large international cities. Commercial property was a favored investment site because:

■ it took up large amounts of capital (an attraction for the big investment funds needing to place lots of investments;
■ there was a demand;
■ the investment was relatively trouble-free; and
■ scarcity value was maintained by the absolute nature of space, reinforced in many places by planning controls.

The property boom also involved public authorities. The late 1960s and early 1970s was a time of increasing state expenditure. Expanded education and health programs, for example, involved large building programs. The state in its many forms (local states, statutory authorities, and so on) not only provided the context for property development and was an element in the demand but was also actively involved. Especially where authorities held land, the state could become a player as well as a referee in the property game. In some cases, the entry of public authorities politicized urban development issues even more as questions of accountability and electoral liability were highlighted. State involvement brought into sharp focus the discussion about what types of cities were being produced. And for whom?

It was Kenneth Boulding who noted that you need to be an anthropologist, not an economist, to study banking. Once an investment is thought to be profitable, capital floods in. But what is rational for one can prove disastrous for the group. There was no check on expansion as more money was diverted to this expanding sector. The provision of office space went above the level of demand, and by 1973 the bubble was beginning to burst. Many building projects were speculative enterprises kept going by long lines of credit. When it became clear that demand was slackening, the result was empty office blocks and impatient creditors. By 1974, property companies found it difficult to let their properties and pay their creditors. By the mid-1970s, the property boom was over as the office blocks lay empty and some of the smaller property companies and property-oriented finance companies went bankrupt. Capital switched to more profitable enterprises, but, as an obvious legacy, the boom had transformed the built environment of the central cities and disrupted many communities along the fault line between the central business district (CBD) and the inner city. Cities and their citizens had been subject to what Ambrose and Colenutt (1975) referred to as the *property machine*.

The 1968–74 property cycle in Sydney

Some indication of the cycle in Sydney is given in figure 6.1. Notice how the boom gathers pace in the late 1960s, peaks in 1971–2 and falls away to a relative slump in 1977. Thereafter, there is evidence of another smaller cycle that peaks in the late 1970s and falls in the early 1980s. The data in figure 6.1 also show the overwhelming importance of offices.

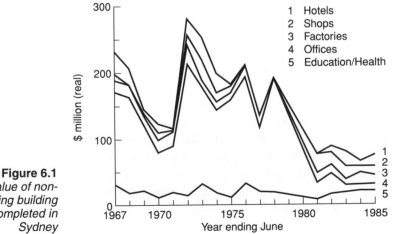

Figure 6.1
The value of non-dwelling building work completed in Sydney

This boom in offices was fueled by a number of factors. There was a growing need for offices from the expanding financial sector of banks, finance companies, and related businesses (Daly, 1982). The financial sector wanted offices in central locations, particularly in Sydney. The boom reflected and enhanced Sydney's pre-eminence over Melbourne as Australia's international city. There were also the requirements of a burgeoning public sector, which needed offices to house the expanding white-collar workforce and the specific buildings (for example, schools, universities, and hospitals) associated with its expanding functions. This period marked the coincidence of growth in both the private and public sectors.

The expansion of the commercial office sector was financed by both local and foreign capital. The boom was particularly large because of the relative openness of Australia to foreign investment. Traditionally, Australia, a dominion-capitalist country, was tied to British markets and linked with British capital, but during the 1970s investment came not only from Britain but from other countries in Europe, North America, and increasingly from Japan, Hong Kong, and South East Asia (Adrian 1984).

Successive postwar state governments in New South Wales (NSW) had encouraged commercial development. The Liberal government that ruled under Askin over much of the cycle from 1965 to 1975 was simply the latest in a long line of progrowth governments eager to attract capital investment (Sandercock, 1975). At the local level, Sydney City Council (SCC) was Labor-controlled between 1949 and 1967. The council made few attempts to halt development in the city, but the Liberal government which came to power in 1965 dismissed the council in 1967 and appointed three

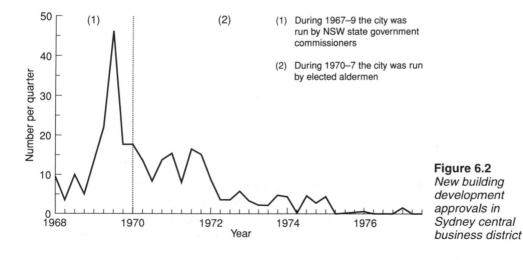

(1) During 1967–9 the city was run by NSW state government commissioners

(2) During 1970–7 the city was run by elected aldermen

Figure 6.2
New building development approvals in Sydney central business district

commissioners to define the boundaries. Between 1967 and 1969 the commissioners ran the city, allowing a flood of development approvals (figure 6.2).

To summarize, when the property boom reached its peak, there was a prodevelopment state government and a CBD controlled by a nonelected progrowth triumvirate. After 1970 the SCC was an elected one but dominated by the probusiness Civic Reform Association, which saw office development as a sign of metropolitan progress and, in some instances, a way of personal enrichment.

CAPITAL–LABOR RELATIONS IN THE SYDNEY PROPERTY CYCLE

The boom

The boom had two important features that affected capital–labor relations:

(a) Most construction activity in central Sydney occurred on large sites. The average size of development applications in the CBD of Sydney increased from 10,000 m² in 1967 to 14,490 m² in 1969 to 21,000 m² in 1972 to 27,000 m² in 1974. For labor, the large sites meant more workers, longer employment on the sites, and thus easier conditions for organizing building labor.

(b) Many of the building projects were speculative enterprises. In the public sector projects there was a specific client who would eventually be responsible for picking up the bill, but the private sector projects were built to meet a perceived demand, not the requirements of specific clients. Development companies needed to borrow money to finance their operations. Credit allowed the projects to be built but made the companies vulnerable. Credit lines could not be extended indefinitely.

In general, the building boom gave extra leverage to labor: their strength was enhanced by the low levels of unemployment, which between 1965 and 1975 did not go above 3 percent for Australia. In effect, the property boom meant a potential shift in the power relations between building capital and building labor.

Before the boom, conditions in the construction industry reflected the power of capital and the weakness of labor. There was no holiday pay, few changing or washing facilities in what was a dirty job, no job security, and dangerous working conditions. The onset of the boom meant labor was in demand and could be more easily organized.

Working conditions

Sections of labor sought to get wage increases and improved working conditions. They were able to do so because the building boom meant that there were more workers on more easily organized big sites. The Builders' Labourers Federation (BLF) increased its membership from 4,000 in 1968 to 10,000 by 1970. Previously, the smaller unions had been held in check by the penalty clauses of an arbitration act that imposed large fines, up to $1,000 a day. In 1969 an act of union solidarity involving almost a million workers (in support of a union official, Clarrie O'Shea, who had been jailed for nonpayment of fines) signaled the end of these repressive measures. The way was now clear for small unions to take effective strike action. The tremendous increase in days lost to strikes in the NSW construction industry at this period is shown in figure 6.3. I will discuss two of the strikes in Sydney.

In 1970, after the failure of negotiations with the Master Builders' Association (MBA), the BLF in New South Wales organized a five-week strike in support of increased wages and better conditions. It was called the 100:90 Strike because they wanted labourers' wages to be not less than 90 percent of the wages of craftsmen: a demand made relevant by the deskilling of crafts in the wake of mechanization. The BLF wanted an increase of $6 a week whereas the MBA offered between $1.50 and £2.50.

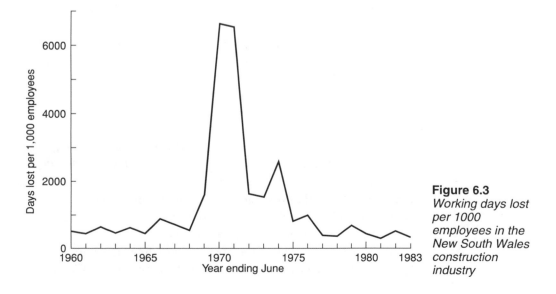

Figure 6.3
Working days lost per 1000 employees in the New South Wales construction industry

The strike began in April 1970. The secretary of the BLF noted:

From the beginning, we wanted to tie up Sydney's central business district. This was the most important step. We were hitting the big developers who had put out a lot of money on land, the price of which they themselves had driven out by outbidding each other. Much of this money they had borrowed from other sources, including various agencies of the state government. (Mundey, 1981, 56–7)

Pickets were sent out to as many sites as possible to enforce the ban on work, an action that received very bad publicity in the local (overwhelmingly conservative) press. The *Sydney Morning Herald* (May 28, 1970) described it as "mob lawlessness," "ugly and decidedly un-Australian tactics," suggesting that "a clear threat of industrial anarchy and hooliganism lies behind the BLF's attempt to blackmail employers." The *Daily Telegraph* editorial of May 29, 1970 referred to the strikers as a "gang of toughs who call themselves vigilantes of the builders' labourers."

The press coverage was overwhelmingly of this type. In comparison to the public sector strikes of bus drivers and teachers that were going on at the same time, coverage was small and vehemently anti-labor. There was no countervailing voice of sympathetic consumers as with the bus and teaching strikes. Few people knew what went on the other side of those pavement hoardings, and few cared.

In the third week of the strike, the BLF adopted a selective strategy. Companies which signed the agreement for improved wages and conditions would have the bans lifted. On May 29, 1970, five major firms signed the agreement. The BLF successfully exploited a major cleavage in the construction industry. Although all companies may benefit from group solidarity, individually it is more rational for them to meet workers' requests in order to finish the job. As the director of industrial relations of the Master Builders' Association of Australia noted in an interview with me in 1986:

If you're not working, it costs you between $30,000 and $50,000 in interest payments. So when unionists ask for more money amounting to say, $3,000, well, there is no comparison. $3,000 versus $50,000.

Two weeks later, the MBA agreed to go to arbitration. The BLF achieved its objectives. The strike had been successful, gains had been made and building workers' confidence was high.

The other major strike of the boom period drew upon this confidence and involved all the building unions in New South Wales. In

1970 and 1971 there was a growing campaign to improve accident pay and compensation. This was an important matter in a dangerous job made more dangerous by the drive to reduce construction times. In April 1971, members of the Building Workers' Industrial Union (BWIU) walked off the Sydney Opera House project. The campaign was extended by the BWIU and soon involved the other building unions. On May 3, 1971, over 38,000 building workers went on strike. The strike involved ten unions; for the first time since 1947 all building unions were involved in a single campaign. The union demanded $10 a week increased pay, full pay while on compensation, and long-service leave. The builders offered only $3.75 a week increase. The strike again concentrated on the large speculative sites in central Sydney. On 14 May, the Master Builders' Association decided not to negotiate, but individual developers were signing agreements, and by May 18 the unions went back to work with agreements from builders to pay $6 a week more, to pay 80 cents per person per week into an accident/compensation fund, and to pay a wage of $32.50 per week (plus $9 for the wife and $4 for each child) to any person injured on the job. The strike had successfully gouged out benefits from the profits of the building boom.

These strikes and others of the time shared two characteristics. First, they used leverage on the large speculative central-city sites, where developers were vulnerable to stoppages. Gains made from these large developers were used as a basis for industrywide settlements, which included the more weakly organized house-building industry. Second, the unions adopted selective strategies, closing down some sites through picketing. When the developers of these sites signed agreements, it was easier to persuade other developers.

Green Bans

Organized building labor, the BLF in particular, also extended their concern beyond the narrow range of wages and conditions of employment in what came to be known as Green Bans. These involved union actions to block developments, not for increased wages but for environmental or wider social considerations (Jakubowicz, 1984; Roddewig, 1978).

In the early 1960s, the BLF had been a right-wing union whose leadership seemed to have little concern with improving the lot of the workers. A radical rank-and-file group within the union sought to gain control and eventually was successful in the 1964 union election. For the next ten years, the unions followed a radical line dominated by notions of direct action, rank-and-file participation, regular elections for union office, and the fostering of community–labor links. The leaders, Joe Owens (secretary, 1973–4), Jack Mundey (secretary, 1968–73), and Bob Pringle (president, 1969–75), were committed to improving conditions in the industry as well as to wider political goals. Mundey was arrested in anti-Vietnam War demonstrations, and in 1971 Bob Pringle and another BLF member cut down the goalposts at a ground where the Springbok rugby team was to play. The leadership had the ideology and adopted the tactics of direct action of the New Left, then developing in Australia as well as in North America and Europe, particularly around the issue of the Vietnam War. Green Bans were part of a wider political struggle and a broader political philosophy.

The first Green Ban began in the upper/middle-income Sydney suburb of Hunters Hill. In 1970, a plan to build 57 townhouses on a piece of open space known as Kelly's Bush met with local resistance. The Battlers of Kelly's Bush were a group of local residents, all women, who sought to resist the development and to maintain the open space. The Battlers wrote to local and state governments but met with little success. In 1971 they were approached by the BLF leadership. The BLF pledged its support and put a ban on any construction work at Kelly's Bush. For the next few years, during the peak of the building boom, the BLF Green Ban policy was a major factor in shaping Sydney. Crude estimates by reporters of the *Sydney Morning Herald* put the value of work at $3,000 million. How this figure was arrived at is impossible to discover (was it construction costs, final selling price?) but it continues to be used in the literature (for example, Jakubowicz, 1984; Sandercock, 1975).

There were two types of bans. *Permanent bans* involved a resolute commitment to a particular action. Examples included the refusal to work on a proposed Olympic stadium in Centennial Park, the refusal to demolish the Theatre Royal, and the Green Ban put on the proposed underground car park opposite the Sydney Opera House because it involved the destruction of old fig trees. *Temporary bans* were used to give greater strength to groups (usually residents) in their negotiations with developers and state authorities. They were also used to aid nonresident groups. In 1973, for example, the BLF imposed a ban on work at Macquarie University because a homosexual student had been expelled from one of the residential colleges. In the same year, a ban was imposed on the University of Sydney because two women were not allowed to give a course on women's studies. In both cases, the BLF action led to further negotiations, and eventually the student was reinstated and the course was given.

The Green Bans involved local resident groups. There were good

Illustration 6.1
Sydney Opera House. A symbol of Sydney recognized around the world, it was part of the BLF struggle (© British Architectural Library, RIBA, London; photograph: A.C. Cooper Ltd)

reasons for resident-group activity. The building boom had affected the residents of inner Sydney: they faced incursions into their open space, the negative externalities of new building, increased traffic and, for the lower-income groups, reduction of housing opportunities as developers sought to build offices and expensive apartment blocks. The local planning system gave almost no voice to local residents; power was firmly held by the state government, whose power base did not lie in inner Sydney. Inner Sydney had a high proportion of owner-occupiers, young middle-income groups. In the analysis of changes in postwar Sydney up to 1971, Kendig (1979, 79) came to the conclusion:

> *By any of the established measures – subdivision of dwellings, over-crowding, conversion to rental occupancy, price and rent changes, new private residential investments, and socio-economic status of the residents – inner areas were "filtering up" rather than "down," both absolutely and relative to the rest of the metropolis.*

This social base provided much of the membership of inner-city resident action groups, though the groups were not exclusively middle income. In 1971, the Coalition of Resident Action Groups (CRAG) was established in Sydney with the aim of exchanging information, organizing joint action and engaging in general lobbying (Nittim, 1980). By 1972, CRAG and the BLF were in alliance, with advantages for both sides. For CRAG, an alliance with the BLF gave the power to stop developments; the BLF had the muscle to stop demolition and halt building projects. For the BLF, CRAG and its members gave legitimacy. Throughout the Green Ban period, the BLF faced heavy criticism from developers, the state authorities, and the press that their actions were undemocratic. The Sydney press was savage in its attack. The *Sydney Morning Herald* (August 14, 1972, 8) wrote about "delusions of grandeur" and "the highly comical spectacle of builders' laborers . . . setting themselves up as arbiters of taste and protectors of national heritage," and the *Australian*, in an editorial (September 5, 1972, 9), noted:

> *When the vocal leader (Mundey) of a tiny minority in one union begins to sway public and municipal decisions on multi-million dollar questions in which he has no expertise whatever, it is time to begin asking what has gone wrong with the process of government in this country?*

The press campaign personalized the issue, focusing on Mundey and his membership of the Communist Party of Australia. The assumption was that mere laborers had no role to play in city planning; they were communists, who were endangering big projects and frightening away foreign investors. The resident-group connection showed the BLF had wider support. The policy of imposing bans only when there was local resistance ensured and reflected popular support.

The slump

By 1973 the building boom was beginning to slow. In November 1973, the *Australian Financial Review* had a headline that read "Property Sales Bubble Bursts." In the same year, over a half million square meters of office space in Sydney's CBD lay vacant, a fifth of the total office space in the city. By 1976 the boom was over and unemployment was beginning to rise. Building workers were affected in terms of rising unemployment and reduced wages. The slump meant a decline in the demand for labor and a weakening in the bargaining power of the building unions. Figure 6.4 shows how wage fell relatively after 1974.

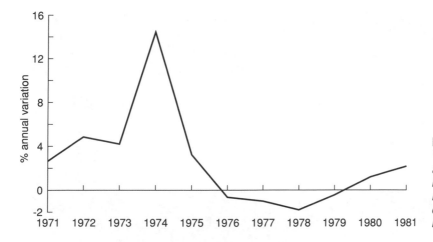

Capital, labor, and
the city:
case study I:1

Figure 6.4
Variation in wages
and earnings of
building workers,
net of the
consumer price
index

There had been two basic responses of building capital to the rise of the BLF and its Green Ban policy. One element saw the need for some recognition of environmental issues and sought some form of compromise with the BLF and the residents' groups. This fraction was represented by the Urban Development Institute of Australia. They wanted development through dialogue, and held a conference in March 1974 to which they invited Mundey and representatives of CRAG. (The discussion is contained in their journal the *Developer*, 12 (1), May 1974). These urban developers wanted to keep in business by placating the opposition. The other fraction, represented by the Master Builders' Association of New South Wales, wanted to emasculate the opposition. They were fearful of the power of the BLF, the Green Ban policy and, in particular, the emerging demand in 1973–4 for permanency of employment in the building trade, which questioned their power base of hiring and firing. They had a strange ally in the shape of Norman Gallagher, the federal secretary of the BLF based in Melbourne. There was little love lost between Gallagher and the NSW leadership of the BLF. Gallagher was a member of the Maoist Communist Party opposed to the Communist Party of Australia, which Mundey supported. Moreover, Gallagher had little sympathy with the tactics and goals of his NSW colleagues. In October 1973, he said: "We can't carry the whole conservation movement on our backs" (*Sydney Morning Herald*, October 27, 1973, 4).

The slump in building, for Gallagher at least, posed the question of jobs versus Green Bans. The Green Bans were simply a luxury of the boom, now to be discarded. Gallagher sought to get rid of the Pringle–Owens–Mundey leadership but in the NSW BLF elections of 1973 pro-Gallagher candidates were defeated. In the same month,

Illustration 6.2
Centennial Park, Sydney. This park was to be the site of an Olympic stadium until it was placed under a permanent green ban (© Australian Picture Library/ J. Carnemolla)

the Master Builders' Association attempted to lock out BLF members and were met with a work-in. In 1974, the Master Builders' Association applied to have the BLF deregistered and thus denied legal status in the centralized wage-fixing agreements of Australian industrial relations. On June 22, 1974 the BLF was deregistered by the Australian Industrial Court.

The deregistration meant Gallagher had control. In October 1974 he put his men in charge. The Green Ban policy was dropped as was the employment permanency issue. In April 1975, 24 members of the NSW BLF, including Mundey, Pringle and Owens, were expelled from the union. They appealed and the Federal Court of Australia ruled that the expulsions were illegal, but they were never allowed back into the union. Having rid themselves of the bothersome, radical leadership, the builders could now tolerate a weak union headed by Gallagher. In 1976, the BLF was reregistered *with the support of the Master Builders' Association*. As a postscript to this part of the story, it can be noted that, in 1985, Gallagher was convicted of accepting bribes from developers over the period from June 1976 to December 1981.

CONCLUSIONS

The 1968–74 property boom was an international phenomenon. Similar tales of capital investment, property development, and consequent social struggles could be recounted for many cities around the world. This chapter shows how the general story unfolded into a local drama. Capital investment into the built environment has social consequences. Property booms and slumps involve changing power relations between construction capital and labor. Property booms have very important effects, not only in terms of enabling labor to obtain benefits in the workplace but also in socializing the debate about the form and function of cities. In the case of Sydney, the particular power of organized labor led to Green Bans. The growth of the Green Ban movement can be seen against the background of the building boom. For the workers in the BLF, the boom meant secure continued employment. As one right-wing BLF member remarked to a journalist in 1972:

> *Our members tolerate Mundey's views because they really don't matter. Times are easy for us: there's plenty of work around. We get pretty good money and if Jack Mundey wants to sprout [sic] off about things, that's OK. But things would be different if things got hard in the industry.* (*Australian*, September 5, 1972, 4)

It is too easy, however, to see the Green Bans simply as a function of the building boom. There had been booms in the past without Green Bans and not all building unions at the time pursued a Green Ban policy. The BLF leadership made a successful connection between working conditions, rates of pay, and broader social and environmental issues. The radical leadership won the confidence of the rank and file through its pursuit of higher wages, its policy of limited tenure of office, and its openness to bottom-up policymaking. The radical BLF showed that alliances between labor and residence-based urban social movements are possible and that connections between production-based and consumption-based groups are feasible. The circumstances have to be right, but a crucial element is people with the vision to make the connections.

The demise of the radical BLF and the decline of the property boom meant a setback for oppositional movements in Sydney. The story is not one of increasing gloom. We can identify at least three enduring positive consequences of the 1968–74 boom period. First, not all the gains of construction labor were lost in the subsequent slump. The Green Bans were dropped, but the improvements in working conditions did not revert to the preboom position (see Frenkel and Coolican, 1980, 1984). The almost total unionization of big sites continued, and a closed shop of "no union ticket – no start" was effectively established for all large nonresidential sites. The issue of safety, once raised, refused to disappear. Most sites now have safety codes, and safety considerations have been incorporated into design criteria. All high-rise buildings in Sydney now have safety nets. The boom allowed organized labor to civilize much of the industry and put capital–labor relations on a new terrain of conflict and compromise. Current agreements, for example, include a 38-hour week, portable superannuation, long-service leave schemes, and a national safety code. There is a tension in this relationship. For the union representatives, especially of the larger unions, there is a danger of incorporation, of putting claims of particular sites into line with broader corporatist deals. As for the builders, they want to deal with a small number of union officials because this ensures easier negotiations; but this concentrates power in the hands of those few officials. Organized labor wants power without so much responsibility, whereas capital wants the unions to have responsibility without too much power.

Second, the struggles of the BLF and community groups such as CRAG sensitized a broader public to environmental issues. The Labour government of New South Wales that came to power in 1976 established a Land and Environment Court and a Heritage Council and in various environmental planning acts sought to incorporate public participation. The spirit of legislation, if not its practice, owes much to the Green Bans.

Third, the social struggles of the period have an enduring legacy in the landscape of Sydney. The fig trees still grow opposite the Opera House, Centennial Park does not have an Olympic stadium (yet), and many of the new developments are retaining the façades of buildings scheduled for demolition during the boom. These are not once and for all victories. Consider The Rocks, one of the oldest parts of Sydney adjacent to the CBD, saved in the 1970s from high-rise commercial development in a bitter struggle between the BLF and residents on the one hand and developers and the state government on the other. As demand for more office space continues, so the pressure builds up on The Rocks. Old terraces are being turned into offices, up-market and tastefully renovated, but *offices* all the same.

The old buildings are being retained, but there is a change in the social community if not in the physical façades. Parts of The Rocks are becoming tourist centers, the site of a commodified history. But it is not yet an outright loss. The Rocks continues to be an entertainment center for ordinary Sydneysiders. The streets, full of Japanese and American tourists during the day, at night resound to the extended vowel sounds of young Sydneysiders.

DATA SOURCES

Three data sources were used as part of the research. The newspaper quotes were taken from a survey of the Australian Newspaper Archives, Department of Political Science, Research School of Social Sciences, Australian National University.

Further information on the BLF was based on papers in the Joseph Owens Collection (Boxes 192–205) in the Archives of Business and Labour, Australian National University.

Last, personal interviews were conducted in the period April–September 1986 with Jack Mundey, former secretary of the BLF in New South Wales; Clive Bubb, currently industrial relations officer of the federal Master Builders' Federation; and Tom McDonald, national secretary of the Building Workers' Industrial Union.

GUIDE TO FURTHER READING

This chapter is based on a previously published paper:
Short, J.R. (1988) Construction workers and the city. 1: Analysis, *Environment and Planning A* 20, 719–32.

Other works cited in this chapter:
Adrian, C. (ed.) (1984) *Urban Impacts of Foreign and Local Investment in Australia*, Canberra: Australian Institute of Urban Studies.
Ambrose, P. and Colenutt, R. (1975) *The Property Machine*, Harmondsworth, Middx: Penguin Books.
Daly, M.T. (1982) *Sydney Boom, Sydney Bust*, Sydney: Allen & Unwin, 42–63.
Frenkel, S.J. and Coolican, A. (1980) Competition, instability and industrial struggle in the New South Wales construction industry. In S.J. Frenkel (ed.), *Industrial Action*, Sydney: Allen & Unwin.
Frenkel, S.J. and Coolican, A. (1984) *Unions against Capitalism*, Sydney: Allen & Unwin.
Jakubowicz, P. (1984) The Green Ban movement: urban struggle and class politics. In J. Halligan and C. Paris (eds), *Australian Urban Politics*, Melbourne: Longman, Cheshire, 149–66.

Kendig, H. (1979) *New Life for Old Suburbs*, Sydney: Allen & Unwin.

Mundey, J. (1981) *Green Bans and Beyond*, Sydney: Angus & Robertson.

Nittim, Z. (1980) The coalition of resident action groups. In J. Roe (ed.), *Twentieth Century Sydney*, Sydney: Hale & Iremonger, 231–47.

Roddewig, R.J. (1978) *Green Bans*, Sydney: Hale & Iremonger.

Russell, M. (1994) Merger ends colourful BLF history, *Sydney Morning Herald*, March 31.

Sandercock, L. (1975) *Cities for Sale*, Parkville, Victoria: Melbourne University Press.

Wooden, M. and Creigh, S. (1983) Strikes in post-war Australia: a review of research and statistics, WP-60, National Institute of Labour Studies, Flinders University of South Australia, Bedford Park, SA 5042.

Chapter 7

CAPITAL, LABOR, AND THE CITY:
CASE STUDY I, PART 2

[JACK MUNDEY IS] ONE OF THE MOST IMPRESSIVE AUSTRALIANS.
PATRICK WHITE, *FLAWS IN THE GLASS* (1980)

In the first part of this case study I considered the struggle between capital and labor during a property boom and slump in Sydney from a broad perspective. In this part I want to illuminate the story further by giving a voice to one of the main protagonists. Between 1968 and 1973 the secretary of the BLF was Jack Mundey. Born in far north Queensland, Mundey came to Sydney in 1951 to play professional rugby league. After leaving the game he worked on building sites, becoming a union delegate in 1956. He became involved in branch meetings, seeking to improve conditions and democratize the union. During his period of office, he was concerned with improving working conditions, with Green Bans, and with wider political issues; he demonstrated against the Vietnam War and was arrested for protesting against a South African rugby tour of Australia. He stepped down as union secretary in 1973 in line with the policy of limited tenure of office. In 1975, along with Joe Owens, Bob Pringle, and others, he was banned by the federal leadership from the BLF, which along with the big developers effectively blacklisted him from working in the construction industry. Throughout the 1970s, he was involved in various government commissions and United Nations projects concerned with conservation. In 1984 he was elected an alderman to Sydney City Council and he has continued to lecture throughout Australia.

This interview took place in Sydney Town Hall on May 2, 1986. Jack Mundey's enthusiasm, wit, articulateness, and commitment are not captured fully on the written page. He is, as the Nobel Prize winner Patrick White noted, "one of the most impressive Australians" (1980, 224).

Illustration 7.1
Jack Mundey, with microphone in hand: Australian activist and trade unionist
(© Australian Picture Library/ Oliver Strewe)

AN INTERVIEW WITH JACK MUNDEY

John Rennie Short: With the benefit of hindsight, how and why did the Green Ban movement get going?

Jack Mundey: The commencing point of the Green Ban movement was the climate of a reactionary state government under Askin. You had a period where developers had open-slather* and you had a developer-orientated government. The State Planning Authority was completely elitist and insensitive to ordinary citizens' views on planning, and there was virtually no public participation at all. It was this background that led the Builders' Labourers to become involved.

Short: Why was the NSW BLF involved?

Mundey: I think it's because the Builders' Labourers had had a big fight to cleanse itself. It was controlled by right-wing elements, and for a long time myself and other militants were blacklisted for years. When we cleaned the union up, we tried as best we could to ensure

*Carte blanche, free reign

that there wouldn't be any repetition of entrenched bureaucracy. We introduced very controversial issues to the union like limited term of office. To combat the idea that union officials stay there for too long, we introduced the idea of replenishing the leadership.

Short: You stepped down?

Mundey: Of course . . . as Judy my wife said, I stepped into oblivion. She claimed it was mad and elitist, as do a lot of other people. Maybe it would have been better to stay there, but then again, who's to say that had I stayed there for thirty or forty years I would be just the same as all the other bastards.

We were the first construction union in the world with women in the industry; we put the officials on the same wage as the workers on the job and limited tenure. As you probably know, everybody had to be elected and after two terms of three-year terms they had to relinquish though they could still be on the executive. That way you get the benefit of their experience. We were very involved in the struggle against the Vietnam War. I think we were the first union to really become involved in support of our blacks in a big way. It's true that other unions have carried resolutions in supporting blacks, but we actually brought blacks down from Northern Territory and Queensland and took them round the building sites so as they could firsthand explain to the building workers the plight of the aborigines; we are one of the unions that were also very involved against the Springbok tour here in 1971. So we've had this background of being really involved in social and political issues, and just two have come to mind that show we are different to most other unions. When Jerry Fisher, a twenty-year-old homosexual, got kicked out of Macquarie University, all the workers on that site stopped work and forced the authorities to put him back. In the following year when Elizabeth Jacka and Jean Cuthoys were running a course at Sydney University on women's social liberation, the authorities stepped in and stopped them, staff and students went on strike, and there were a lot of buildings on that campus; again, the workers stopped work and forced the authorities to allow these people to conduct their own women's social liberation course. I've just put those two things to show that when the women from Kelly's Bush came to us and said, "How about assisting us?" – well, most other unions, even left-wing unions, would have carried a resolution agreeing with them and sent a telegram to Askin and probably it would have stopped there. We said to these people, all women too, that if they could demonstrate that there was widespread local feeling and not just a few people who wanted to have

their own amenity, we would accede to their request, and if they made
a formal request to us to impose a ban, we would. Over 400 people
came to the meeting. They formally requested us to impose a ban,
and it was imposed. This was, I think, one of the strengths of the
Green Ban movement. It wasn't a question of union leaders flexing
their muscles or their egos and declaring, making judgemental value
on what should or should not be banned. Every ban was preceded by
a public meeting of people concerned to outline the issue or issues
involved and, then if requested, we imposed a ban. Some of the bans
were permanent such as Centennial Park, but other bans were temporary in the sense that they gave greater strength to the party or
parties who are arguing out with the government or developers, and
often compromises were reached and the bans were lifted, so they fall
into two categories.

So we came into the Green Ban movement through an open-
minded union at a time when the public were starting to rebel against
overdevelopment and the undemocratic way in which these developments were occurring. We reacted, because we were a fresh Union,
because we had come through a hard fight to cleanse the union. We
were in a position to respond, having the coverage both on the demolition of buildings and on the construction. We were the first on the
site. We were very strong; we had the industrial muscle to back up
our aesthetic considerations.

Short: The Green Ban movement coincided with a tremendous
building boom. This gave tremendous muscle to the BLF, and building workers in general; would Green Bans have been so successful
without the boom?

Mundey: That's the most regular question I get asked: I don't
believe so. It is often said that Green Bans were great, but you had
the "luxury" of a suitable economic climate. Well, I think to get
workers to stop work in any period is always difficult. So I reject that.
I think that the union had an advanced environmental understanding, and I believe that workers would respond in today's condition
as well if it was pointed out to them that we weren't for banning
buildings per se; we're for banning certain buildings – we want to
build socially useful buildings. That's the way we argued it, and so
while it's true that we had the enormous building boom at the time,
and that gave us extra strength, nevertheless, those workers when
they made decisions knew that they were denying themselves work
on that job.

Short: How did you get building workers to go on strike over environmental issues?

Mundey: It was, I think, in the first place, a belief in the leadership. I'm not painting a picture that all of the Builders' Labourers were spontaneously caught up with environmental awareness, but you see we'd been through some big fights. One in 1970 which we call the 100:90 dispute over the principle that labourers should not receive less than 90 percent of tradesmen's wages. This was a big five-and-a-half-week strike, and then the following year we had a fight over full pay when injured. Those two big struggles gave the workers a lot of confidence in their leadership, plus the other things I mentioned before, e.g. limited term of office, made many of the workers who normally look upon union officials as careerists say, "Well, look, these people are the same as us, they're fair dinkum."* That gave us a stronger rank-and-file connection than most unions enjoyed. In the beginning the executives voted for those, they then went to branch meetings and, on some occasions, the Green Bans were endorsed by strike meetings. In the beginning, it was a confidence in the leadership that allowed many of the workers to go along. They didn't understand fully the significance . . . I don't think we did either. I certainly didn't fully understand . . . I was much more aware than most of the membership because of my environmental actions and involvement, but they went along when we argued the matter out before meetings.

The right-wing unions and some of the left-wing unions were saying, "we're going too far." We argued that environmentalism is not a middle-class issue. Some of the more dogmatic on the left said: "Mundey, darling of the middle-class trendy; environmentalism is a middle-class issue, a Greenie issue," whereas of course we argued strongly, "Who have the worst housing? Who have the least leafy suburbs? Who are subjected to the most noise from big trucks? The less endowed, the working people, and of course their environment is every bit as important as the environment to say Kelly's Bush." Admittedly, there weren't too many builders' labourers at Hunters Hill, but we argued that there should be open land where people from Mt Druitt or anywhere else can enjoy. So we won the conviction of the workers. Likewise with historical buildings. A lot of our opponents, the developers and government, said, "Oh . . . it's Mundey, Pringle, and the leadership who are conducting this campaign and

*Genuine

145

not the membership." Like the Theatre Royal when they were going to destroy one of the last live theatres, we said it was impudent for them to say that builders' labourers were so ignorant that none of them go to the live theatre. Of course a lot of men are interested in the theatre and we demonstrated this by taking the theatre to the job. We argued we had every right to intervene on such things.

So the memberships were one. Did you see the *Rocking the Foundations?* It's a terrific film. You should see it. I think the film demonstrates that the rank and file were with the leadership, and I don't think they always fully understood, and I don't think that *we* fully understood the significance of what we were doing either.

Short: Looking back at the newspaper clippings of the time, it is clear that you faced tremendous opposition.

Mundey: On the one hand we had right-wing unions naturally opposed to us, and of course you had the Askin government and the developers. But we also had some of the more conservative left-wing unions querying whether we were going too far, whether we were becoming involved in issues that weren't really union issues. We argued that anything which concerned the worker and his or her family was of concern to the union. The union had a responsibility and an obligation to become involved in environmental issues, that they shouldn't be just swept under the carpet. Well, a lot of the unions saw that as a threat, in my opinion, as well as the limited tenure of office and our policy of democratization, of putting the union really under workers' control instead of having a tight hierarchy. Left or right, they're not much different in the way they conduct themselves in this or other countries for that matter.

On the other hand, you had people who are normally antiunion, certainly opposed to strikes, many of them Liberals who on issues like the Green Ban were on our side, and they found themselves very uncomfortable with a rough-hewn communist leader and a leadership of the union that was communist to labour and looked upon us as very militant. This polarization generated enormous discussions within the community at large. I think the Green Bans were the catalyst that brought about a greater consciousness of environmental issues generally, but certainly urban environmental issues – they had an impact on the environment movement the world over because most of the environment movement in other countries had experiences of hostility with unions over the jobs versus environmental issue, an issue carefully played and fuelled by corporate power, be it private or public.

Short: The deregistration of the NSW BLF in 1974 signalled the end of the Green Ban and the radical NSW BLF. How did it come about?

Mundey: The big developers. Gallagher was spawned by them when they couldn't bribe or coerce us. I was offered a $A20-million bribe if I could get the ban lifted on the Woolloomooloo site. When they couldn't bribe us, they tried to destabilize the union. When I stepped down as secretary [1973], the bloke that took over from me, Owens, was very capable, more capable than most of the other union officials, so I'm not for one moment saying that it was *the* extra position of Mundey. But when the changeover came, the developers thought now's the time to move. First of all they hoped that Gallagher's men would win the 1973 election, but they got licked. It was a re-endorsement of the Green Ban policy when Owens came in. Then they set about other ways of getting rid of us. Gallagher and the employers *agreed* to have the union deregistered. Gallagher used language like, "Now we've shaken the shackles off, we will fight outside the system," but it was by arrangement with J.C.W. Williamson.* When the Union was deregistered in June of '74, there were no longer branch meetings, no longer did the rank and file have control of their union.

Short: So it was more top-down than bottom-up?

Mundey: That's right. The union that we had was arguably the most democratic union in the history of this country for sure. It was so open. People were surprised, not only that the leadership was articulate (Pringle, Owens and myself and others), but you also had workers getting up and arguing good cases out, criticizing leadership. You go to most union offices and the secretary comes in: "Yes sir?" "I'd like to see Mr Mundey." And then she vanishes and closes the door. That sort of stuff, just like a business corporation. With us, workers used to come in and drink coffee, probably a bit too slack . . . holding up the work in the office and so on, but there was this terrific spirit; it was *their* union, and there wasn't any difference between the union bureaucracy and the rank and file and so, of course, the destruction of that was terrible.

*A theatrical agency.

When Gallagher moved against the NSW leadership and put in his own people and set them up, there was no recourse for the membership. He didn't want to be deregistered too long, because the BWIU* might move in on him and take members. So two years later after he expelled us on phoney charges, when he went for reregistration in 1976, who supported him? The Master Builders! They went along to court and supported Gallagher getting his reregistration back. When we went to court and got our union tickets for the right to work, who came along to say we're people of bad character? The Master Builders' Association. So Gallagher and the developers were in it together.

Short: What motivated Gallagher then?

Mundey: Gallagher? Well, look, he really is a dill,† but he has a lot of Collingwood†† cunning, a lot of rat-cunning. And it's like everybody else, I mean, how often have you seen mediocre people get power and hang on to it? And he got it. He got lots for himself; he got power, loved flexing his muscles and doing deals with big developers. He didn't have an ideology. The bloke that made the Builders' Labourers in Victoria back in the 1950s was an old Irishman called Paddy Malone, and he was a real old principled socialist, and he built the union up, and Gallagher was his successor. And then Gallagher came in at a time when we had the NSW branch burst forward, so he was the federal secretary when it became a very powerful union and a very influential union. And his ego went along with it. Gallagher was hardly a charismatic figure, but he had a certain presence nevertheless. He hung in there. It's a classical example of how people get power and hang on, but of course he had the support of those big developers all the time. And the Master Builders, they owed him something; Master Builders owed Gallagher. Gallagher did their bidding to get rid of us. The only reason that he lasted so long is that the developers spawned him.

Short: What happened to you after your connection with the NSW BLF was severed?

Mundey: Personally, I spent too much time after that being pretty subjective in trying to find ways to get back into the union movement. I went to England on a lecture tour and I went to the United

---

*   Building Workers' Industrial Union.
†   Idiot.
††   Working-class suburb of Melbourne.

*Capital, labor, and
the city:
case study I:2*

Nations Human Settlement and Habitat conferences. Being involved and seeing the potentiality . . . and then having that break was terrible. I vegetated a bit around that period. I kept some sanity by talking round unions and universities and trying to bring together the Red and the Green which has been my main thrust. Then my only son got killed as a passenger in a car, which flattened me still further in '82.

Short: You were elected an alderman in 1984?

Mundey: Yes. Naturally, everybody knows I am a Communist but people down at The Rocks,* because the union helped save The Rocks, asked me to stand against the right-wing Labour. The council is disgraceful and the Liberals are really bad, corporate Tories everywhere. I stood against two other resident action groups' people so I just got in. The more progressive the council had become, the usual story, the more the state government has taken away our planning powers.

Short: In Britain there is some discussion about local socialism through progressive local authorities. Any chance in Australia?

Mundey: Local independence can mean anything. After all in local government the world over, real-estate agents and developers show profound civic responsibilities. But we were lucky in the Sydney City Council with the independents all from community-based groups. We really rocked them. Each year they elect a new chairperson. I was chairman of planning. So last year, to get rid of us, the Libs and Labour did a deal and *voted together*, to omit us. And two Labour Party people got expelled because they wouldn't join a coalition with the Liberals. Unreal, isn't it? So that's the sort of thing you get with local government in Australia. You get the situation where the local government is looked upon as a poor relation, and when we demand public participation about what's going to be built, the state takes everything out of the council's hands. And they can sack a council at a whim and not give reasons. In fact, they sacked the Newcastle Council on the flimsy reason that their meetings were going too long.

Short: They'll be sacking most councils then . . .†

---

* An inner-city area of Sydney.
† Sydney City Council was sacked on March 26, 1987 by the New South Wales state government. One of the reasons given was their unnecessary delay of major developments.

Mundey: That's right. They can use any excuse, but I agree with you; I think that a socialist revival, if we can use that word, will most likely come through from below.

Short: Looking back, what were the longer-term effects of the Green Ban movement?

Mundey: I think the most important thing was the way in which we went beyond what I call hip-pocket nerve of economism and linked up with wider sections of society. And most unlikely alliances, middle- to upper-class aware people, together with the enlightened elite sections of the working class in common struggle in social and ecological issues. That's the lasting value of the Green Ban period. And it's unique anywhere in the world. People couldn't believe that we could weld together environmentalism and unionism. In answer to the fools on the extreme left saying it was just a middle-class issue, we argued for an alliance of the enlightened working class with the enlightened middle class. They should be natural allies. They shouldn't be opposed to each other. But I think the strength of the Green Ban movement is, it actually happened. I wasn't just theorizing about workers being involved in environmentalism, but it actually happened: The Rocks are there, Centennial Park isn't a sports stadium, it's there. And when the Labour Party came to office in New South Wales [1976], they introduced some of the most advanced or *the* most advanced environmental legislation, and that was also part of the aftermath of us. From going from the position where there was no public participation, the government was progressive on environmental issues and introduced good legislation, for example, the Environment Court with its first Chief Justice Jim McClelland. I think the [UK] Lucas Aerospace alternative corporate plan with their ideas of socially useful production were wider than ours, but against that, we actually achieved it. We did it. We didn't just theorize. And I think those two actions were the most exciting ones for the post-war years for the unions, because unions in the main are pretty conservative organizations.

Short: And the future?

Mundey: I believe that it has to come, that environmentalism has to become an integral part of progressive unionism. The same way as it's got to become an integral part of any decent political party. One of the greatest reasons I think in the demise of the left, and socialism generally, is the lack of a Green factor. I think the lack of an ecological factor is the biggest single weakness in holding back the refurbishing of socialism as a cause, and I think that had we lived longer, we would have impacted the unions much more and more permanently than we did. That's what I'm really sorry about, but I think it could come again. I don't say it will come again, but I think it could come again. There is *no doubt* that an urban Green mentality must come back into the socialist movement, otherwise I think the socialist movement will wane.

GUIDE TO FURTHER READING

This chapter was previously published as:
Short, J.R. (1988) Construction workers and the city, *Environment and Planning A* 20, 733–40.

For work on the Sydney property boom and Green Bans consider:
Daly, M.T. (1982) *Sydney Boom, Sydney Bust,* Sydney: Allen & Unwin.
Mundey, J. (1981) *Green Bans and Beyond,* Sydney: Angus & Robertson.
Roddewig, R.J. (1978) *Green Bans: The Birth of Australian Environmental Politics,* Sydney: Hale & Iremonger; Totowa, N.J.: Allanheld, Osmun.
Tarrant, D. (1993) Revolutionary veteran, *Sun-Herald,* May 23, 17.
White, P. (1980) *Flaws in the Glass,* London: Jonathan Cape.
Rocking the Foundations, 16-mm film and video, 92 min, 1985. Director and producer Pat Fiske. Produced by Bower Bird Films, PO Box 402, Bondi Beach, NSW 2026, Australia; distributed in the United Kingdom by the Workers' Film Association, 9 Lucy Street, Manchester M15 4BX; in the United States contact the Australian Film Commission, Suite 615, 9229 Sunset Boulevard, Los Angeles, CA 90069.

Chapter 8

YUPPIES, YUFFIES, AND THE NEW URBAN ORDER: CASE STUDY II

LONDON IS THE EPITOME OF OUR TIMES AND THE ROME OF TODAY.
R.W. EMERSON, *ENGLISH TRAITS* (1856)

DOWN BY THE DOCKS IS A REGION I WOULD CHOOSE AS ANY POINT OF EMBARKATION ABOARD SHIP IF I WERE AN EMIGRANT. IT WOULD PRESENT MY INTENTION TO ME IN SUCH A SENSIBLE LIGHT; IT WOULD SHOW ME SO MANY THINGS TO RUN AWAY FROM.
CHARLES DICKENS, *THE UNCOMMERCIAL TRAVELLER* (1861)

In chapters 2 and 5 I discussed some of the major economic changes affecting cities. These included:

- the global shift of manufacturing employment;
- the rise of service employment;
- the making of new social groups and classes;
- the emergence of a new urban order and its variation through the urban hierarchy.

In this chapter I want to consider how these trends are expressed and embodied in one part of one world city, London.

CHANGING SOCIAL RELATIONS

World cities are losing their status as manufacturing centers and are becoming centers for the tertiary and quaternary sectors of the economy. Since the mid-1960s a new international division of labor has emerged in which world cities have lost much of their manufacturing employment through closure, mechanization, suburbanization of industry, more efficient work practices, and what Peter Dicken (1986) refers to as the global shift of industrial employment from the core to the semiperipheral and peripheral countries of the world economy. New employment growth in world cities is dominated by service employment, especially in the producer services category. The biggest and fastest growth has occurred in financial services. The measurement, monitoring, moving, and managing of money is now a major growth industry. The changes have not been uniform across space. Selected countries in the semiperiphery, especially that subset known as newly industrializing countries including Brazil, Mexico and South Korea, have captured most of the industrial growth while in the core some countries have fared worse than others. Britain, because of its poor competitiveness, lack of investment, and a financial structure that easily allowed foreign investment, showed some of the biggest losses of industrial employment.

The decline of manufacturing employment in Britain was greatest in the big cities. Between 1971 and 1981, 1.8 million manufacturing jobs, over one-third of all manufacturing employment, were lost in the conurbations of Britain; in London alone 200,000 manufacturing jobs have been lost every five years since 1961 (Martin and Rowthorn, 1986). The net result was a form of deindustrialization with specific implications for gender and class relations. An examination of the figures in *Employment Gazette* reveals that between 1971 and 1981 the number of jobs done by men fell by 1.7 million; in contrast, female employment increased: over the period between 1961 and 1981 the number of women in paid jobs increased from 7 million to 8.5 million, from 35 percent of the total work force to 45 percent. The increase in part-time employment by 1 million jobs in the past 15 years has been almost entirely female labor. While cultural images of work and popular representatives of employment may still make a distinction between male workers and female housewives the new realities are very different. A majority of adult women have either part-time or full-time employment in addition to their domestic chores. As the male working class saw the closure of traditional avenues of employment, female members of the working class saw increased employment opportunities, albeit in routine jobs. Labor organizations have traditionally been forged from the experience of the male working class. Deindustrialization has meant a decline in the social and political power of the male working class.

Table 8.1 shows the general pattern of a decline in manufacturing employment over the period from 1971 to 1986 and the absolute and relative increase in service employment. The table also reveals that over 30 percent of this increase came from the financial services category. Both manufacturing loss and financial services gain have been urban-based. The predominant center is London, accounting for 60 percent of all financial and producer services employment.

TABLE 8.1 EMPLOYMENT IN THE UNITED KINGDOM, (MILLIONS) 1971–86		
Sector	*1971*	*1986*
Manufacturing	8.06	5.23
Services	11.62	14.49
Banking, finance, insurance & business services	1.33	2.20
All industries & services	22.13	21.59
Unemployed	0.75	3.28

Source: Social Trends, 1988, tables 4.9 and 4.19

In summary, there has been a loss of manufacturing employment and an increase in service employment, all against a background of rising unemployment. The social effects have been a reduction in the power of the traditional male working class, an increase in female employment and the emergence of a new middle class. These trends have been given popular recognition in the terms *yuppie* and *yuffie*, themselves part of a plethora of new words coined in the 1980s including *buppies, dinkies, swells* and (my favorite) *lombards*. A yuppie is a young upwardly mobile person though the *u* can also denote urban. Yuffies are young urban failures. If the yuffies are the successful new middle class, yuffies are the stranded and blocked working class.

The other terms? Buppie is the yuppie's black equivalent, dinkies are double income, no kids, and a swell is a single woman earning lots in London, a term that summarizes the rise of the female executive and perhaps the beginning of the end of male domination of senior and responsible positions. Lombard is lots of money but a right dickhead, a term of abuse whose real quality is only recognized if you know that one of the main streets in the City of London is Lombard Street.

There is always a problem in using very contemporary words. Nothing dates so much as the latest fashion. To use yuppies and yuffies in the chapter title of an academic book may be the equivalent of sporting bell-bottom trousers and a kipper tie to a 1970s party:

trendy at the time but if pictures are taken a source of embarrassment for the years ahead. The terms may have a very short shelf-life, but they ultimately refer to perennial questions of money, power, and class and allow us an entry into the dynamics of social relations. To consider the background of these terms is to grasp the tensions between the circumstances of social history and the agents of social geography.

There is another problem in using the terms; they defy simple empirical analysis. We do not know how many yuppies there are or the changing proportion of yuffies. They are as much myth as fact, points of popular debate as much as empirical realities. They are important as figures of contemporary urban folktales. Yuppie has become a term of abuse for profound reasons. Britain became the first industrialized economy but never became an industrial society. Wealth carried social obligations, and status was always as important as conspicuous consumption. The Thatcherite achievement was to introduce the bourgeois revolution Britain never had. But there has been popular resistance to this attempted rejection of the moral economy and its total replacement with a money economy. The critical use of the term yuppie is part of this distaste. The term yuffie, not so popular but becoming more so, expresses recognition of an underclass, a group of youths denied access to the fruits of economic growth. If the yuppies are the success story of Thatcher's Britain, then the yuffies are the failure; one the dream, the other the nightmare. In the rest of this chapter I shall use the terms in the double sense of empirical fact and urban myth; a use that straddles the ambiguity of cultural expression and social process, fact and fancy, myth and reality.

As myths, yuppies have become a powerful model, a peg for advertising campaigns and dedicated followers of fashion. Some developers have also built for the yuppies, and parts of cities have been yuppified. This has both an empirical and a symbolic element. Empirical in the sense that changes can be seen in the form of new housing stock, leisure facilities, and so on, and symbolic in the sense that the meaning of particular places has been transformed. As a fact yuppies were an emergent if short-lived social group with particular forms of employment and consumption. Their existence was due to the rise of nonmanual and especially managerial and professional categories of employment. Yuppies were the higher-paid members at the technical management levels of the control centers of international corporations, the expanding financial services sector, producer services, and the media industry. They were particularly found in London where these sectors are concentrated. The term yuppie was a loose one, suggestive of a new social group, not so much a class but more a constellation of groups whose emergence was noted if not fully identified. The term is useful as a shorthand, a generalization that stands in contrast to that other social grouping of contemporary society, the yuffie.

Yuffies are young urban failures. The "failure" is their inability to get a job. It does not imply personal failing or irresponsibility. The main problem of the yuffies is that they were born at the wrong time. Life chances of any social group vary through time; we know this from our experience as academics. Born in 1935, you managed to avoid serving in the war and if you followed an academic career you were at your most marketable when the higher education sector experienced its biggest expansion. Born in 1965 your chances of an academic career were severely limited by the financial restrictions on universities and colleges. Same occupation, contrasting opportunities for different cohorts. The same applies with broad social categories: a semiskilled worker in Britain had more opportunities when looking for a job in 1968 than in 1988. The yuffies are the unlucky cohort.

As a slump hit the world economy in the 1970s firms responded either by going out of business or by shedding labor. Labor was either sacked or "lost" through natural wastage. Young people coming into the job market for the first time bore the brunt of the recession because firms were not employing new labor. Their problems were exacerbated by the response of the British state from the mid-1970s to redirect public expenditure. The public sector was thus not able to soak up the unemployment produced by deindustrialization, and the net effect was an increase in unemployment in the United Kingdom. In 1988 over 3 million were out of work, almost 1 million of whom were under 25 (*Social Trends* 1988, table 4.23). In London a third of the population are aged under 26 and in 1988 one in eight were unemployed.

The young unemployed do not necessarily become yuffies. Inability to gain formal employment does not necessarily mean a complete reliance on government income support. Opportunities are available in the twilight world of the informal economy. Research in this area is difficult but the results we do have suggest that the amount of informal work done by the unemployed is very slight. The work of Ray Pahl (1984) suggests that those in employment or newly made redundant make greater use of the black economy because they have easier access to potential customers, materials, and networks of social communication. Young people with no, or limited, work experience are thus in a more difficult position than most. There is a distinction between individuals and households. A young person may be

*Yuppies and the
new urban order:
case study II*

unemployed but not necessarily poor if he or she is in a household
with a worker in paid employment (Pahl, 1988). Yuffies are not
simply the young unemployed, they are the alienated young unemployed. They are the people who rioted in 1980 and 1981. These
disturbances were not so much race riots as youth riots. They were,
in the words of Lord Justice Scarman (1981), a "burst of anger."
They indicated the street power of the yuffies.

Yuffies pose a problem for the state. Governments in liberal
democracies have the problem of providing income support that is
not too low to cause social unrest but not too high to discourage
recipients from looking for work. Yuffies also pose a threat in the
mythologies which circulate in town and cities. They are perceived as
the main source of crime, they threaten people and property, they are
the muggers and burglars, they have leading roles in the law-and-
order script which reads as follows: there was once a golden age where
cities had less crime, but now it is not safe to walk the streets because
these young hooligans threaten life and property. The nostalgic reference to the past and the calls for more policing is not new. Geoffrey
Pearson (1983) has shown it to be a recurring theme of urban Britain
at least from the Victorian period, an enduring fear which always fas-
tens onto the young male "lower orders." The latest folk devil is the
young black unemployed male, now a popular symbol of criminal
intent, social disorder, and moral disruption. Yuffies are the *id* of the
urban imagination.

The yuppie/yuffie theme captured a significant space in popular
culture. In film there was an identifiable genre of "yuppie in crisis;"
in 1988 BBC radio introduced a London-based serial, *Citizens*,
which provided a rich if short-lived contrast to the long-running,
rural world of *The Archers*; and the stable working-class community
of *Coronation Street* now has to compete with *Eastenders*. *Eastenders*
takes the yuppie/yuffie items as key points in its story line. The
making of City money in London was also the theme of the successful 1987 West End play *Serious Money*. There have also been
adaptations of the work of Dickens, including the Royal Shakespeare
Company's highly acclaimed *Nicholas Nickleby* and the 1987 movie
Little Dorrit. The revival of interest in Dickens is not accidental. He
was concerned with London, its social contrasts, the pace of social
change, the gaining and losing of money, property and position in
society. Dickens provides an imaginative encompassing of rapid
change in a world city. His rich and poor characters and dramatic light
and shade are the Victorian equivalent of our yuppies and yuffies. The
historical parallels are revealing. The opening scene of Caryl
Churchill's *Serious Money* is a quote from *The Stockjobbers*, a play by

Thomas Shadwell first performed in 1692. This reference and the
revival of Dickens are reminders that wealth and poverty have always
been the primary division of British society. The yuppie/yuffie
dichotomy may appear unusual from the perspective of 1958 and
1968 when economic growth was more equally shared and growing
state intervention was increasing the quality of life for the majority.
From 1698 or 1888 it comes as no surprise.

There is a basis of social experience for these cultural expressions.
In Britain there is a growing bifurcation of life chances. For those in
employment, income tax has been reduced. Since the Conservative
Party came to power in 1979 the basic rate of income tax has been
reduced from 33 percent to 25 percent, while the maximum rate has
been slashed from 83 percent to 40 percent. The wealthiest have
benefited most from these changes. The corollary is that those in low-
income employment face high marginal rates of taxation while the
unemployed are facing reductions in benefits. From April 1988 the
Social Security Act of 1986 came into effect, in which young people
were to receive no benefits if they refused a place or a youth-training
scheme. Under this new poor law arrangement a young, single,
unemployed person aged under 25 would receive £23.55 per week,
compared to £31.35 under the previous system. By contrast, the average weekly take-home pay of an accountant in the City of London in
April 1988 was £350. The net result is a growing gap between rich
and poor (table 8.2). The richest 10 percent of the population now
have more income than the bottom 50 percent. This is a reversal of
a 50–year trend towards greater equality of income. Not only is there
greater inequality it is becoming more visible. The term young in yuppie is not only a function of age but a position in the great divide in
attitudes to credit. The deferred gratification of the old middle class

TABLE 8.2 SHARE OF TOTAL INCOME AFTER TAX IN THE UNITED KINGDOM, 1975–6 AND 1984–5				
	Average income			
	1975–6		*1984–5*	
	% share	*£*	*% share*	*£*
Top 1%	3.9	9,010	4.9	31,060
Next 9%	19.2	4,910	21.6	15,240
Next 40%	50.3	2,900	48.6	7,640
Lowest 50%	26.6	1,230	24.9	3,160

Source: Social Trends, 1988, table 5.14

reared on ideas of sacrifice, saving, and waiting, gave way to the conspicuous consumption of the new middle class emerging in an era of credit cards, buy-now-pay later slogans and a banking system that encouraged personal indebtedness.

There is also a split in the labor market. It used to be assumed that high levels of unemployment would depress wages. This did occur in the 1970s and early 1980s, but since then those in middle- to upper-income employment have experienced real increases in disposable income not just through income tax changes but also through real increases in wages. The mechanism which links unemployment and wages seems to be the rate of increase of unemployment rather than the absolute level of unemployment. When people are losing their jobs this acts as a brake on wage claims. Labor is disciplined by the fear of unemployment. But when the rate of increase tails off, even at a high absolute level, as in the mid-1980s, then the fear of unemployment for those with jobs begins to lessen and wage claims begin to make their appearance. The large pool of the unemployed does not form a reserve army of labor, their existence depressing the wages of the employed; rather, there is a growing split between the incomes and life chances of those in and those out of employment, between those in low-income employment and those in middle- and upper-income employment. But even though there may be a bifurcation in the command over resources both groups continue to live in the same cities. Cities are shared spaces. In contemporary world cities there is a spatial as well as a social restructuring, and yuppies and yuffies are now living in the same social spaces.

RESTRUCTURING SPATIAL RELATIONS

A major cause of the spatial restructuring in world cities was the growth of the financial service industries and the associated increase in the demand for office space. There was a commercial office boom in the world cities in the mid- to late 1980s. Where the pressure cannot be met by intensification of existing spaces there is pressure for the extension of commercial space. The tight clustering of such industries means that the extensions cannot be too far away; firms renting space that is too distant lose credibility and vital contacts. In London the pressure has built up around the edges of the City.

Pressure has also come from new housing demands. The new middle class are more than end points of structural changes. As E.P. Thompson (1968) reminds us in the title and the text of his most famous work, classes make themselves. As part-fact, part-myth

yuppies made themselves in their lifestyles, especially in attitudes toward time and space. The filofax was the yuppie icon. It indicated the problem of time, yet its successful management. It suggested a life full of work, commitments, movement, and meetings. It represented a full life. The problem for the unemployed, in contrast, is how to fill time. The cruel paradox of modern life is that those with more resources have less time while those with most time have least resources. The attitude to time is matched by an assessment of space. Yuppies are inner-city dwellers. Their jobs are in the central areas. Not for them the trek to the suburbs made by their parents and dreamed of by their grandparents. A central location saves journey time to work, to entertainment, and for contact with friends and influences. It is also symbolic of wider attitudes. The suburbs are, in essence, places for children and indicate the willingness of people to lead their lives "for the children." Suburbs are places of sacrifice, sites for the reproduction of the family. The garden, the lower housing density, and the search for better schools are the essential ingredients of the suburban choice. Yuppie households, if they have children, are concerned as much with the wants of the adults as with the perceived needs of the children. The emergence of the yuppies was signaled by new forms of housing consumption. On the one hand, there is gentrification as middle-class groups move into low-income neighborhoods close to the city center. On the other hand, there are the new-build schemes. Aware of the market possibilities developers are now consciously meeting the demand for centrally located dwellings for young middle- and upper-income households with a mix of dwelling size designed to interest nonchild and single-person households.

This spatial restructuring involving the extension of commercial space and new forms of residential space is not just a demand-led phenomenon. It is also a result of the growing power and influence of financial institutions seeking long-term investment. It is as much investment as demand led. Much of urban research in the last two decades has been concerned with the relationship between the mode of production and urban structure. Too little attention has been paid to the importance of the mode of investment. Finance capital has had an enormous impact on the landscape and life of cities. Financial institutions, including insurance companies and pension funds, have been the recipients of the growth of personal savings. Money has flooded in as incomes increased, people were encouraged to invest in personal pension schemes and the number of people in occupational pension schemes quadrupled in 30 years. Recently in Britain there has been the move toward the privatization of old-age pensions whereby individuals have been encouraged to invest through a financial institution so that the state pension scheme currently available to all can be phased out. The result has been a huge increase in the savings pool available to investing institutions. Urban property is an attractive investment for those institutions because, as also noted in chapter 6,

- it takes up big chunks of money, a handy characteristic for hard-pressed investment managers seeking to make as few decisions as possible;
- it is a long-term investment which can be used to balance shorter-term investments in gilts, stocks and shares;
- its scarcity is assured by the nature of absolute space; in the urban context this is often reinforced by planning controls.

There is nothing an investment fund manager likes more than a tall office block on a prestige site in a favored location. Increasing asset value is assured. In the world cities property investment has been attracted to the commercial core and surrounding areas, particularly along the fault lines at the edge of the CBD. Here the conversion of residential use to commercial use and low-income housing to high-income housing provides the greatest returns. But while individual speculative ventures may give high returns, as in the case of one company that obtained permission for an office block in an adjacent residential area, such deals are risky and time-consuming. Pension fund managers are risk-averters rather than risk-takers. They seek high returns but on a very secure basis, as in the more orderly, organized extension of commercial space and residential renewal, such as the construction of Battery Park City on the southern tip of Manhattan, the commercialization of The Rocks area of Sydney and, the biggest of them all, the transformation of London Docklands.

London Docklands

Located just east of the capital's financial center, the 16 square miles of Docklands are the commercial water frontage of London (figure 8.1). It was also the home of working-class communities, almost 40,000 people initially based on dockwork. By the 1960s the docks were being closed because they were unable to cope with the bigger container ships. The port functions moved east to Tilbury, and in Docklands registered dock employment fell from 25,000 to 4,100 between 1960 and 1981 (Church, 1988).

London Docklands was well placed for spatial restructuring. Proximity to the City gave opportunities to developers for the recommodification of derelict land into offices and residences. There was an alignment of investment-rich institutions, a demand from a buoyant City for office property, and housing requirements of the growing new middle class, which all led to the recommodification and yuppification of the area. The recommodification required three things.

Incentives to private capital In the 1980 budget the Chancellor of the Exchequer announced the creation of enterprise zones to promote private redevelopment of inner-city areas. Under this scheme incentives were provided over the period 1981–91, which included exemption from rates and land taxes on site disposal, tax allowance for building construction, and relaxation of planning controls. Eleven zones were designated, one of them, the Isle of Dogs, in Docklands. This has been one of the most successful. For example, many newspaper offices have relocated from their traditional home on Fleet Street, and now the *Sun*, the *Daily Telegraph*, the *Guardian*, and the *Observer* are located in the zone. Incidentally, their move was part of a restructuring of labor relations involving a reduction of the labor force and the introduction of new technology.

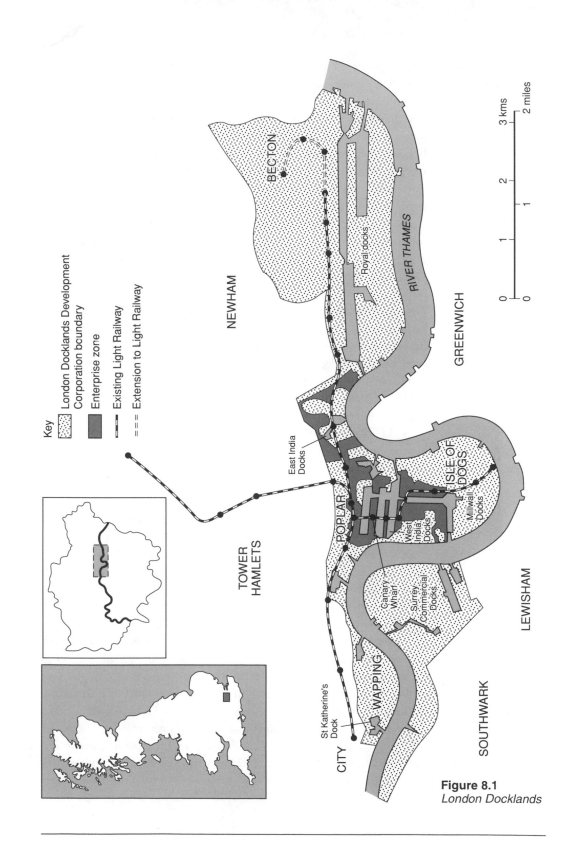

Figure 8.1
London Docklands

Political power   The commercial transformation of large areas will favor lucky landowners and astute developers, but it will not directly benefit the local people. Any truly democratic local representation will thus tend to resist such changes. For the developments to take place, power must be taken out of local hands. This is the rationale behind the creation of the London Docklands Development Corporation (LDDC). The LDDC was established by a Conservative government in 1981. It replaced the Docklands Joint Committee established in 1974 and is made up of representatives of five dock-lands boroughs. That committee was concerned with the needs of local residents. The nonelected, government-appointed LDDC has no need to court local political support. Its aim has been to "develop" Docklands for the private sector.

Central organization   Individual companies are unwilling and unable to undertake such large and speculative ventures. The LDDC has acted as a central organizer of the project – assembling land, making environmental improvements, and providing the vital initial infrastructure investment. The LDDC spent £130 million between 1981 and 1985, and almost £200 million from 1985 to 1987, including £35 million on a light railway system which links the area to the City, London's financial center. The area is now an attractive location for office users, it is now "closer" to the City and all central London, yet rents are only a quarter of what they are in the City.

The LDDC was successful in raising awareness of the commercial opportunities of Docklands. A barrage of publicity has changed the mental map of London. Previously the Docklands was "unknown" to the majority of middle-class Londoners. It was a spatially and socially self-contained segment of the capital. The LDDC campaign gave Docklands a higher profile and more "positive" image. Publicity photographs were carefully taken to show only the glitzy areas, and color enhancement changed the murky Thames into a sun-kissed, bright blue river, pollution-free, just waiting for you to windsurf.

Almost £2,200 million of private investment has been attracted. The whole area was transformed. Almost 500,000 square meters of office development are completed or under construction. By the year 2000, it is estimated that 2 million square meters will be constructed. Canary Wharf was the single largest project, a £3,000 million complex of office and shopping space which eventually will employ 72,000 people. The economic downturn and the fall in commercial rents hamstrung this venture, and the owners of the project went into bankruptcy in the early 1990s.

Housing has also been built: 13,000 dwellings were completed or

under construction by 1987, and the LDDC plan is to complete 25,000 dwellings by the end of the century. Selling points have been the water frontages and the relative cheapness considering the easy access to the City. — *for the people who need them?*

In effect there has been a transformation of the landscape of Docklands. The industrial buildings of the past are being recycled; in terms of both use and meaning. The Docklands as Victorian economic resource is giving way to Docklands as postmodern landscape of offices, from old working class to new middle class. Docklands has become a spectacle for the display of postindustrial employment and the (re)presentation of housing forms for the new middle class. The transformation of the Docklands is not only a change in use but a change in meaning.

Illustration 8.2
Acorn Walk, Rotherhithe, London. 1930s public housing was the dominant housing stock until the "redevelopment" of Docklands (© London Docklands Development Corporation)

A NEW URBAN ORDER

A new urban order is emerging from the contest for political power and social meaning in world cities. Commercial pressure for central locations, the growing power of the mode of investment, and the emergence of new social groups are taking place at the same time as deindustrialization pressure on the poor and the emergence of an underclass marginalized by economic change. I use my words precisely. "Taking place" is exactly what is happening as the two social forces are meeting in the same social spaces. Returning to Docklands again, Church and Ainley (1987) show how local unemployment, especially amongst the young, continued to persist despite the boom of Docklands. There was local resistance. The press releases of the Isle of Dogs' Neighbourhood Committee, for example, provided an antidote to the publicity machine of the LDDC. They pointed out that few of the jobs created went to local residents. When the average local income was £8,500 per household the average price of a two-bedroomed property in the area was £185,000. More radical has been the attitude of the group *Class War*. The East End has reached a point of no return; according to them, it's either resist or die. In their newspaper *Class War* and billposters they urged local people to mug a yuppie, scratch BMW cars, and make life as unpleasant as possible for the affluent incomers. Cast members of the TV soap *Eastenders* were attacked, and *Class War* accused them of being show-business sellouts; estate agents regularly had their hoardings daubed with graffiti, and September 10, 1988 was declared Anti-Yuppie Day. Class War has 1,000 members and a political philosophy. According to one spokesperson:

> *At first people thought we were just into violence. But we have our own political theory. We do not call ourselves anarchists any longer. Yes, we want to overthrow capitalism and if that has to be violent then so be it. We are interested in community politics for the working class to stick up for itself.* (Lashmar and Harris, 1988)

The threat is taken seriously by Scotland Yard, which assigned six officers full-time to monitor Class War.

Class War is unusual: perhaps the best (and only?) example of an urban social movement condensing the yuppie/yuffie bifurcation; more common are the unorganized random acts of resistance and vandalism. As a correspondent to the *East London Advertiser* wrote:

> *I was delighted the other day when sitting with my younger sister on the Isle of Dogs and saw some youngsters ripping up newly planted trees and using them to attack yuppie homes. Hopefully some young people locally will still have some fight in them and will repel these new Eastenders by making life unbearable for them.* (Kane, 1987)

As the letter suggests, young people constitute a point of resistance. They have energy and anger and have not yet learned to accept their fate. In Docklands, however, it looks as if this resistance will ultimately fail. The organized yuffies of Class War constitute a nuisance and a threat but not a permanent block to the changes. The power

of finance capital in alliance with a central government committed to private enterprise and big business is too large an opponent for a small working-class community with few political friends and limited resources.

But the yuffies still have power. Their very existence in the collective urban imagination has produced effects. First, there is the fear of crime; "colonization" of space involves the invasion of someone else's place. In the imperial past overseas colonization was underwritten by the British Army and Navy. Now it is the police who defend the urban colonizers. It is not that crime is any more prevalent in gentrified areas, although the contrast between rich and poor does provide greater opportunities. It is more a case of the new middle classes having the right language and the necessary confidence to demand better policing. Demands for more effective policing are greatest in areas undergoing gentrification. Second, the fear of the yuffies is apparent in the new built forms. There is a contemporary urban enclosure movement that is blocking off and minimizing public open space. Riverside frontages are being alienated, walls are being constructed, and barriers are being created to keep out the urban folk devils. The security arrangements of residential blocks are a major selling point, and commercial properties are so designed that their frontages ward off rather than invite. The attraction of water frontages is only partly the scenic views: on one side, at least, they can be easily defended against the yuffies. This bunker architecture is concerned more with security than display, personal safety more than show, and the exclusion of indigenous communities rather than their incorporation.

The fear of the underclass has always been a major element in the life of London, as in all world cities. In the past this has been managed by segregation, people knowing and keeping (in) their place. When different groups are in the same place the emphasis switches to the architectural design of the buildings, the location of buildings, and the construction of defensible spaces. In London Docklands and selected areas of other world cities economic restructuring is causing a change of use, a change of meaning, and a contest for the social control of urban spaces. The new urban order of disorganized capitalism will arise from this struggle; its eventual shape a function of conflict and compromise; its evolving form a mark of victory. And of defeat.

GUIDE TO FURTHER READING

This chapter was based on my previous paper:

Short, J.R. (1989) Yuppies, yuffies and the new urban order, *Transactions of Institute of British Geographers*, New Series 14, 173–88.

Other works cited:
Church, A. (1988) Urban regeneration in London Docklands: a five-year policy review, *Environmental Planning C: Government and Policy* 6, 187–208.
Church, A. and Ainley, P. (1987) Inner city decline and regeneration: young people and the labour market in London's Docklands. In P. Brown and D.N. Ashton (eds), *Education, Unemployment and Labour Markets*, London: Falmer Press.
Dicken, P. (1986) *Global Shift*, London: Harper & Row.
Kane, F. (1987) The new eastenders, *Independent*, September 26.
Lashmar, P. and Harris, A. (1988) Anarchists step up class war in cities, *Observer*, April 10, 9.
Martin, R. and Rowthorn, B. (eds) (1986) *The Geography of Deindustrialization*, London: Macmillan.
Pahl, R.E. (1984) *Divisions of Labour*, Oxford: Blackwell.
Pahl, R.E. (1988) Some remarks on informal work, social polarization and the social structure, *International Journal of Urban Regional Research* 12, 247–67.
Pearson, G. (1983) *Hooligan: A History of Respectable Fears*, London: Macmillan.
Scarman, Lord Justice (1981) *The Brixton Disorders, April 10–12, 1981*, Cmnd 8427, London: Her Majesty's Stationery Office.
Social Trends (1988) *Statistical Tables*, Office of Population Census and Surveys, London: Her Majesty's Stationery Office.
Thompson, E.P. (1968) *The Making of the English Working Class*, 2nd edn, Harmondsworth, Mddx: Penguin.

PART II
THE CITY AND SOCIETY

IN THIS PART I WANT TO SHIFT ATTENTION AWAY FROM THE STRICTLY ECO-NOMIC TOWARDS A GREATER CONSIDERATION OF THE CITY AS A SOCIAL ARENA. MY STARTING POINT IS AN ANALYSIS OF THE HOUSING MARKET IN CHAPTER 9. IN CHAPTER 10 I EXAMINE SOME OF THE LINKS BETWEEN SOCIAL AND SPATIAL DIFFERENTIATION WITH PARTICULAR EMPHASIS ON CLASS, ETHNICITY, GENDER AND SEXUAL IDENTITY. IN CHAPTER 11 I LOOK AT THE CITY AS A SET-TING FOR HOUSEHOLD AND INDIVIDUAL COPING STRATEGIES. CHAPTER 12 DISCUSSES THE CITY AS THE POLITICAL ARENA FOR FORMAL POLITICS.

THE CASE STUDIES CONSIST OF AN EMPIRICAL STUDY OF RESIDENTIAL MOBILITY (CHAPTER 13), A REVIEW OF WRITINGS ON GENDER, SPACE, AND POWER (CHAPTER 14), AND AN ANALYSIS OF THE SOCIAL CONSTRUCTION OF ETHNICITY IN US CITIES (CHAPTER 15). THEY PROVIDE SOME ILLUSTRATIVE MATERIAL AND TOGETHER ELABORATE ON SOME OF THE THEMES RAISED IN THE PREVIOUS CHAPTERS.

Chapter 9
THE HOUSING MARKET

A ND YET THEY THINK THAT THEIR HOUSE SHALL CONTINUE FOR EVER: AND
THAT THEIR DWELLING HOUSE SHALL ENDURE FROM ONE GENERATION TO
ANOTHER.

PSALM 49

U NE MAISON EST UNE MACHINE-À-HABITER.
LE CORBUSIER, *VERS UNE ARCHITECTURE* (1923)

One of the most important attributes of the city is as residence. People
live in cities. Where they live, how they live plays an important role in
the social order. Who we are is a function of where we are. And where
we are is an indicator of how we are. To understand how certain
groups are allocated to certain parts of the city it is important to understand the housing market. This is the most important mechanism in
the social sifting of the city. In this chapter I will examine the housing stock and the most important factors of housing demand and
supply, and conclude with a discussion of the residential mosaic.

THE HOUSING STOCK

Characteristics

The total supply of housing constitutes the housing stock. Housing
is an important commodity with a number of special characteristics,
including durability, space specificity, and relative cost.

Housing is one of the most durable of goods. It lasts a long time
because the costs of production are so much higher than the costs of
repair and maintenance. The average dwelling may have a "life" of
over 50 years. The notion of average is slightly misleading. The
poorer-quality housing does not last so long as the better-quality
housing. This leads to an historical selectivity. In the city there is an
historical weathering that tends to destroy the housing of the poor
and marginal yet retains and to some extent celebrates the housing
of the rich and powerful.

The durability of housing means that older housing is an important element in any city's total stock of housing. This legacy imparts the particular "feel," "look," and "character" of individual cities. Part of the charm of the New Town of Edinburgh, for example, is the pleasing symmetry of Georgian domestic architecture, whereas an important element in the "modernity" of Los Angeles is the contemporary nature of its housing stock. The housing stock of a city constitutes more than just accommodation; it is a link with the past, a record of history, a mute testimony to the periods of city growth and decline.

Land is an important precondition of housing production. This means that housing production is a function and reflection of the nature of real property rights and the nature of land-use legislation. In capitalist societies, the nature of landownership affects the type, scale, and cost of housing. Housing production is also a function and embodiment of the changing nature of land-use planning legislation.

Housing is, for all intents and purposes, immobile. Unlike other commodities that can be produced in factories, housing has to be produced on specific sites. On large projects, off-site mass production techniques will be important, but there are limits set by organizational and transport constraints. Productivity in house-building is thus lower than other types of commodity production. And this is part of the reason behind the high cost of housing.

Housing is expensive. For the average household, housing costs constitute a significant proportion of total income. The cost of housing is thus a crucial determinant of household living standards. Moreover, the immediate purchase of a dwelling is beyond the reach of all but the wealthiest, and this, as I shall discuss later in this chapter, has important consequences for the financing of housing consumption.

Change in the housing stock

At any one time the housing stock of any one city is in the process of change. There is loss through demolition and gain through new building. Growing cities build more than they demolish, while the reverse is true in declining cities. The housing stock is the physical expression of the vitality of the city.

Housing deteriorates. Weather, time, the action of the elements as well as constant usage lead to a deterioration. Regular maintenance is required; the older the dwelling the greater the need for maintenance. There are also more subtle changes in the perceived quality of the housing stock. There is the declining quality brought about by changed expectations: what was good enough for our grandparents is no longer acceptable to us. An apartment without its own bathroom and cooking facilities is seen as substandard, whereas 50 years ago more people shared bathrooms. In general, there has been, in the richer world at least, a steady improvement in housing quality. Figure 9.1 shows for the period from 1951 to 1976 the pattern in Britain for three indicators of housing quality: shared dwellings, dwellings declared unfit by the local authorities, and the number of households with a density of more than 1.5 persons per room. The general trend shows a vast improvement. This has been due to private and public investment. Against this rising tide of improvement and expectations there have been stubborn pockets of continual deterioration and decay. Poor housing is a symptom, as well as one of the saddest manifestations, of poverty. In the better-off neighborhoods housing is continually maintained and improved. In most areas there may be a slow though almost imperceptible decline in quality. And in the worst cases a downward spiral of decline, disinvestment, and further decline may send neighborhoods into a free-fall of rapid housing deterioration and rising community despair.

Changes in the total housing stock occur through the processes of demolition and new building. Piecemeal demolitions occur when individual owners make an economic decision to knock down the existing dwelling and either rebuild it or leave the site vacant. This decision is usually made when the income stream from the existing

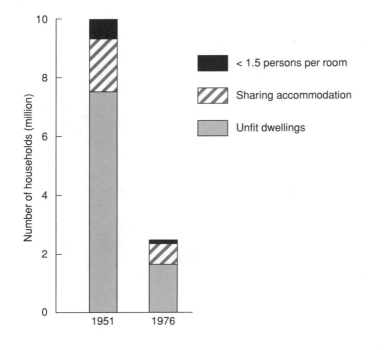

Figure 9.1
Housing quality in Britain, 1951–76

dwelling is less than the maintenance and repayment costs and the asset value of the dwelling is falling. This is the case in some inner-city areas of the United States, where there has been an effective abandonment of much of the dwelling stock as owners find more profit from fire insurance than from existing use. This is demolition by arson. The downward spiral of housing deterioration can become a self-fulfilling prophecy. As other houses are burned out, existing owners find it makes less and less economic sense to hang onto their property. Urban blight can settle over a neighborhood, casting a shadow over the entire housing stock.

Demolition as an organized phenomenon is generally the result of actions by the state. In these cases material interests in association with governmental policies shape the pace and extent of the subsequent reconstruction of the city. Let us look at two examples.

Between 1850 and 1870 the city of Paris was transformed. By 1850 the city had become a major metropolitan area, a center for

Figure 9.2
The modernization of Paris, c. 1850–70

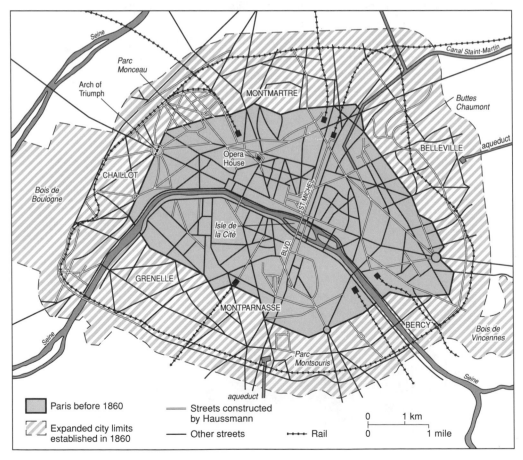

manufacturing and finance, and a seat of state power. Under the absolute power of Napoleon III from 1848 to 1870 and the direction of the authoritarian planner Georges Haussmann the urban landscape of Paris was transformed by massive clearance of low-income housing in the central-city area. Figure 9.2 shows the broad-scale nature of the changes. In effect, the scheme consisted of the clearance of the older and high-density housing of the poor and moderate-income population and in their place the construction of broad boulevards, public parks, public buildings, and new shopping areas. The winners were the moneylenders, who made profit from extending credit to the government, the state itself, which pushed broad, easily policed streets through pockets of working-class resistance, and the bourgeoisie of Paris, who saw the city written in their own image and in their own interest. The losers were the poorer groups and especially the emerging working class who were marginalized to the periphery of the city.

If we look at the urban renewal schemes of US cities from the 1950s to the 1960s a similar pattern of gainers and losers can be identified. The renewal consisted in the main of the clearance of low-income housing and replacement by middle- and upper-income housing and/or commercial developments that aided local business leaders. In his 1964 article, "The Federal Bulldozer", Martin Anderson estimates that almost a million people were evicted in US cities from 1949 to the mid-1960s. Four dwellings were demolished for every new dwelling built. Anderson sums up the effects:

- more homes were destroyed than were built;
- those destroyed were predominantly low-rent homes;
- those built were predominantly high-rent homes;
- housing conditions were made worse for those whose housing conditions were worst;
- housing conditions were improved for those whose housing conditions were best.

Postwar renewal schemes were not always so regressive. In Britain the urban renewal schemes of the 1950s and 1960s also involved the demolition of low-income housing in central urban areas. However, the vast majority of new building was public housing specifically designed for lower-income groups. Although the demolition programs destroyed existing communities, the rebuilding programs were not so markedly regressive as they were in US cities. The reason lies in the Labour Party's control of urban local government and its concern with redistributional consequences, as in meeting the needs of business.

Illustration 9.1
Paris demolitions: removal of a portion of the Quartier Latin. Old housing is destroyed in urban "renewal" (from a drawing by M. Thorigny © Mansell Collection, London)

Models of the housing stock

There are three models that seek to link the different parts of the housing stock with different segments of the population. These models were developed at different times with varying theoretical underpinnings. Thus an analysis of these models provides a discussion of the diverse processes at work in the city, an historical cross-section of dominant processes at different times, and a glimpse of the alternative ways to conceptualize the city.

The Burgess model

This model was developed by the sociologist E.W. Burgess, who worked in Chicago in the first third of the twentieth century. At that time the city was experiencing massive in-migration from other parts of the country and from Europe. Burgess was part of what became known as the Chicago School, a group of researchers including Robert Park and H.W. Zorbaugh who looked at the city as a labora- tory. For them, the city was a kind of social organism that could be

Illustration 9.2
Chicago immigrant tenements. Poor immigrants to the city could afford only cheap rented accommodation (© Hulton Picture Company)

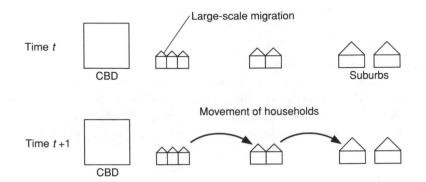

Figure 9.3
Invasion and succession: a simplified model
Source: *Short (1978)*

studied using biological analogies. To this social Darwinism they added detailed studies of particular urban types, for example, hoboes, and specific urban neighborhoods, such as the slum and the rooming-house district. Their work provides a rich source of historical material on a rapidly expanding city that was experiencing a huge surge of population growth.

Most of the migrants to the city had little money and limited resources. Their first move was to the inner city, where the cheapest housing could be found. As they gained a firmer foothold in the urban economy they moved further out to the more expensive housing. In his famous paper Burgess (1925) conceptualized the process as invasion and succession, as different groups moved out from the central city to invade the next neighborhood out. The result was a series of zones. A great deal of subsequent work has gone into identifying Burgess zones in cities around the world. Most of this work is of very limited value. Burgess' zones are a product of a particular time in a specific city. To be sure, there are factory zones and residential zones, but beyond these very general types nothing much can be gained from the search to rediscover 1920s Chicago in contemporary cities. The driving force behind this zonal structure was the population movement shown in figure 9.3. Notice how there is an implied relationship between housing type and social group. The older-established residential groups lived further out while the more recent arrivals have the poorest housing in the inner city. This is still a useful generalization through which to understand the relationship between housing and length of residence by social group for many cities in the world. It is not a universal model. It applies to cities with poor migrant groups and a private housing market in which housing quality is a function of income.

The Hoyt model

The second model that we consider was developed by the urban land economist Homer Hoyt. It is very similar to the Burgess model though the underpinnings and the political "message" are slightly different. In a 1939 monograph based on the analysis of 25 US cities Hoyt disputed the notion of a zonal structure. He argued that residential areas could be more properly understood as a pattern of sectors rather than as a series of zones. Hoyt identified a sectoral pattern of high-rent areas and suggested that the high-status sectors could be found along routes radiating out from the central area towards the homes of community leaders. Underlying the model was a process of filtering. The process is initiated by the construction of new dwellings for the high-income groups (figure 9.4). Their move into this new housing leaves vacancies, which are filled by the next income group. The housing stock, over time, filters down the social hierarchy. Hoyt's model is again based on a private market. Indeed Hoyt was a vigorous free-marketeer who saw any interference to the filtering mechanism, such as public housing, as creeping socialism. Hoyt's model was appropriate to a specific time and place: an urban United States where house purchase was beyond the reach of many and no compensatory social welfare policies existed. There has been

Figure 9.4
The filtering process
Source: *Short (1978)*

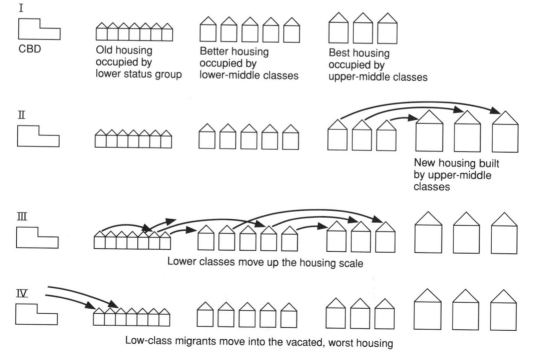

I

CBD

Old housing occupied by lower status group

Better housing occupied by lower-middle classes

Best housing occupied by upper-middle classes

II

New housing built by upper-middle classes

III

Lower classes move up the housing scale

IV

Low-class migrants move into the vacated, worst housing

a critique of the basic model. In a now-classic work, Walter Firey (1945) disputed the notion of an elite constantly on the move. His research on Boston's Beacon Hill suggested that sentimental attachment to certain areas could maintain the elite's residence. In effect Firey points to the power of place, the importance of sentiment, and the enduring connection between certain social groups and specific neighborhoods. He highlights the mediating role of culture in the stark model of rational economic behavior.

The rent gap theory

This theory emerged in the 1980s. It sought to explain the underlying reasons behind *gentrification*. This is the process whereby housing filters up instead of down. It is most commonly associated with selected inner urban areas of some big cities. In one sense it is the opposite of Hoyt's idea of filtering; rather than higher-income groups moving out and the housing filtering down, these groups are said to be moving back into the city and forcing out lower-income groups. This move back to the cities has been explained by many factors: the persistence of high-income jobs in the central-city service sector; new patterns of household formation with an increasing number of single person and nonchildren households; new patterns of consumption and new housing preferences amongst younger, affluent households. These are, in effect, demand-side arguments.

In contrast, one of the most supply-oriented commentators is Neil Smith. A former graduate student of David Harvey, he has been keen to identify structural factors. And, like his mentor, he is eager to find the hand of capital or, to be more accurate, the lack of capital. Smith's basic argument is that there has been an effective disinvestment from many inner-city neighborhoods. Capital has been invested in suburban locations. This creates a *rent gap*, the difference between the land value and the potential land value of an accessible inner-city location. The rent gap creates the conditions for new forms of investment. Gentrification is one of the net effects of this new reinvestment. In an interesting study, Smith (1991) sought to identify the gentrification frontier in New York's Lower East Side by examining tax arrears data by census ward. When these were plotted by time for each census ward Smith detected a turning point when reinvestment replaced disinvestment. Figure 9.5 shows the pattern for two wards, 34 and 38. When he plotted the turning-point data as a contour an interesting map was produced. Figure 9.6 shows the changing pattern of the falling-off in disinvestment over time and through space.

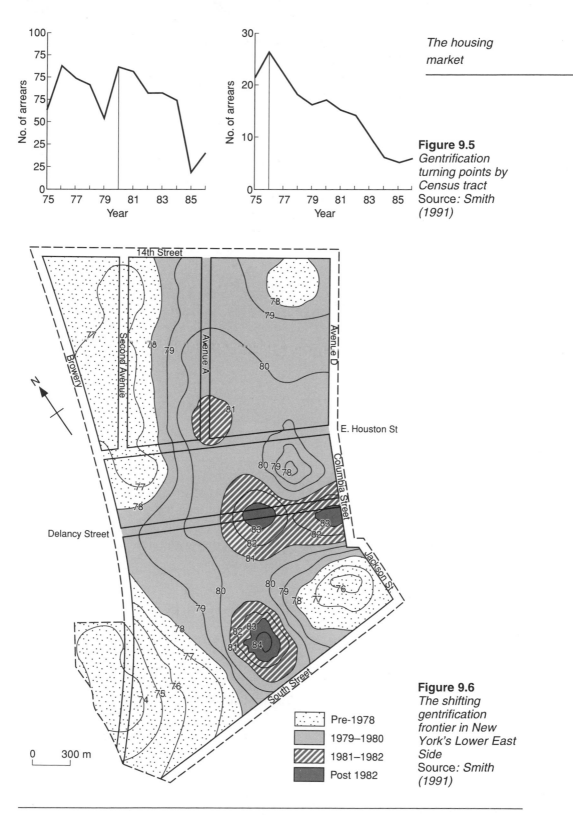

Figure 9.5
*Gentrification
turning points by
Census tract
Source: Smith
(1991)*

Figure 9.6
*The shifting
gentrification
frontier in New
York's Lower East
Side
Source: Smith
(1991)*

The rent gap theory, as enunciated by Smith, is an interesting hypothesis that counterbalances the sole reliance on demand-side explanations of gentrification. It has been subject to some criticism. David Ley claims to have found no evidence of the rent gap in the largest Canadian cities. The resulting debate (see Smith, 1987; Ley, 1986), while creating more heat than light, suggests an intriguing conclusion. The rent gap theory may be appropriate for big cities in the United States, especially given their patterns of investment and disinvestment, but it may have less relevance where there has been less capital withdrawal from the central city, as is the case in Canada and most of Western Europe. Moreover, the reliance on structural factors ignores local variations and cultural differences. These can be seen not as deviations from some ideal (New York's Lower East Side!) but as integral parts of the local urban structure. The rent gap is more an interesting hypothesis than a theory and should not go uncontested. It assumes that central-city accessibility creates an underlying real value to which present land values can be compared. But do we need such a model? Why not just see the surface patterns as the main variables, important in themselves, rather than as shadows or echoes of some greater reality that lies just below the surface?

All three models were developed in the United States at specific times and in specific cities: Chicago and New York. They address particular events: rapid in-migration and suburbanization; gentrification and the selective move back to some inner-city areas. The models generalize from these particular circumstances, but they never escape from them. It is important to remember the context of their generation when seeking to use them at other times and in other places. Rather than functioning as general theories, they are more usefully seen as intermediate theories derived from particular circumstances and capable of wider applicability only with careful consideration and acknowledgement of their particularities.

THE HOUSING MARKET

We can usefully picture the urban housing market in terms of three interrelated elements: production, supply, and demand.

The production of housing

Housing is produced in a variety of ways; four modes can be identified (figure 9.7).

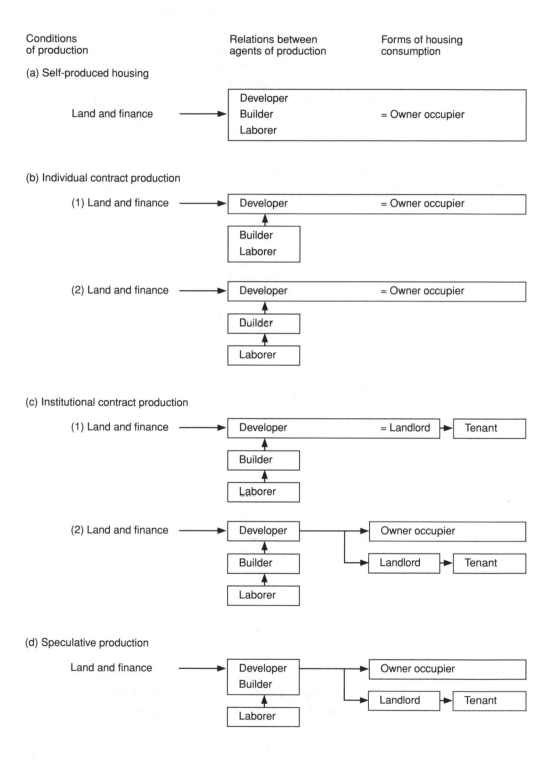

Figure 9.7 *Forms of housing production*
Source: *Cardoso and Short (1983)*

Self-produced housing

This is produced by the immediate consumers. Over the course of human history it has been the predominant form of housing provision. It is found throughout the world and includes a variety of housing types, quality and cost. To this day it is still one of the most important modes in the poorer parts of the world. It is sometimes given the name self-help housing. Whatever the precise term used, it involves people building their own shelter, using simple materials and relatively simple techniques of construction. In some places the building of a dwelling is a ritual process with precise rules for size, structure, and orientation. In the large cities of the poor world it tends to be the result of necessity, because neither the private market nor the state is able or willing to provide accommodation.

Markets respond to fiscal power, governments to political power. Housing need without power does not become effective demand; instead it remains at the level of need to be satisfied by finding space, material and willing hands. In some writings, self-produced housing is a sign of despair, because it marks the failure of the market to meet the essential demands of ordinary people. In another sense, however, it is a symbol of hope, a participatory form of self-designed shelter using recycled goods to construct homes in the face of urban poverty and government neglect.

Individual contract production

This mode involves relatively rich consumers hiring builders to construct accommodation. It was and continues to remain the prerogative of the wealthy. The large mansions, the imposing villas, and the grand residences bespeak a confident class of people eager to express their power and status in built form. These dwellings are more than just forms of accommodation, they are recorders of wealth, encoded with messages of status, confidence, breeding, and "good" taste. Although few in total number, this mode of production has been pivotal to changes in fashion and taste. Individual contract housing has been an important element in the expression and arbitration of aesthetic sensibility. When the rich Gamble family commissioned the architects Greene and Greene to build their summer home in Pasadena, California, or when Adolf Loos built a house for Gustav Scheu, or when Charles Rennie Mackintosh constructed Hill House near Glasgow for the publisher Walter Blackie, or when Frank Lloyd Wright designed houses for W.J. Winslow and Isidore Heller, they were more than just houses, they were important

statements of architectural expression, pivotal points in architectural development as well as major aesthetic statements in brick and stone.

Illustration 9.3
Falling Water, Pennsylvania; architect: Frank Lloyd Wright. Not just a house: an architectural statement (© British Architectural Library, RIBA, London)

Large-scale contract production

This occurs when individuals or institutions hire builders to construct a number of dwellings. It is found in the construction of early company towns such as New Lanark, built by the mill owner Robert Owen on the banks of the Lanark River in Scotland in the late eighteenth and very early nineteenth centuries. The more enlightened capitalists, like Owen, realized that a well-housed labor force was a healthy labor force and hence a more productive labor force. From Pullman, Illinois, to Bourneville in England company towns were constructed by industrial capitalists as a way of maintaining and controlling a productive labor force.

Large-scale production implies a sophisticated market system. In the nineteenth century it was found in some of the bigger cities in the capitalist world as housing demand, at least for the relatively affluent, was expressed in the construction of apartment blocks and other forms of mass housing.

In the twentieth century in the liberal democratic countries the state began to have an increased role. In some countries it became directly involved in the production of housing. In these cases the relatively large contracts allowed industrial techniques of mass construction to be used. Much of the mass-produced forms of high-rise housing were developed when the state was undertaking large-scale contract production. Public-sector housing is particularly suited to industrialized forms of housing production. In Britain, for example, high-rise tower blocks of industrialized production are almost all the direct result of public-sector housing initiatives of the 1960s and early 1970s. It was not a happy story. Tenants were often unwilling to live in tower blocks but were given little choice. Listen to the voice of despair:

Illustration 9.4
House-building on a massive scale in Seoul, South Korea (photograph: author)

I have lived in a damp flat on a council estate for two years and have grown cynical of its dwellings and people . . . large gardenless estates drably situated away and apart from the town . . . And here we sit like birds in the wilderness, three flats to a floor, four storeys high, separated by dim concrete corridors and icy stairs . . . it is easy to walk

into the wrong block. All are functionally square like slabs of dirty cake with windows. My low-ceiling walls are wet and mould thrives on them. Puddles collect on window-sills. Clothes in the wardrobe rot.

(Revell, 1982)

Speculative production

Such production involves the construction of housing by private developers to meet general demand. The dwellings are speculative because they are often constructed before any particular person buys them. For the builder, the production costs of a single unit of production are very high in relation to the capital invested. Builders thus need to sell their housing, but since immediate house purchase is beyond the reach of all but the wealthiest, this mode needs a sophisticated financial system. It is very dependent on external sources of finance both at the point of production, as builders have to lay out money before selling the dwelling, and at the point of consumption. Landlords and consumers need to pay the builders. Because housing is very expensive in relation to income, consumers need to find loans to purchase housing and landlords need to pay for the dwellings before collecting rents or selling the houses. Speculative housing not only needs sophisticated finance, it helps to create it.

The creation of capitalist economies of mass consumption is closely tied to the creation of the fiscal preconditions for the speculative mode of housing production. Governments have come to realize that stimulating housing production is an important way to stimulate the overall economy. Speculative mass housing has such large multiplier effects that it has become an important element in government economic policy. If the national economy is in recession, then governments can choose to lower interest rates, which generates more demand for new housing, and the subsequent production becomes an important stimulant to aggregate demand. If the economy is overheating, in contrast, choking off the demand for housing through increasing interest rates dampens inflationary pressures. Interest rates are important: they affect the real cost of housing because most of the money is borrowed, both by the producers and the consumers. The speculative form of housing production is an integral part of rich capitalist economies.

These different modes of housing production are not mutually exclusive. In any one city all four may be found at any one time. The precise mix will vary across the world. In the cities of the rich capitalist countries speculative production will be more important, whereas individual contract production will be the preserve of the wealthiest. In the cities of the capitalist periphery self-produced housing may be the dominant form of housing production, with the rich elite able to pay for individual contract production. With a small middle class and limited form of credit speculative housing is less important.

The mix of modes will also vary over time. A move from self-produced to speculative is a progression from precapitalist to capitalist, a shift that marks the commodification of housing provision and the enthronement of a capitalist economy.

The supply of housing

Housing in the last three modes of housing production has one important characteristic: it is very expensive in relation to income. This is the so-called *realization problem*: immediate house purchase is beyond the reach of all but the wealthiest. The different tenure types can be seen as different solutions to this problem. We can make a broad distinction between the private and public sectors. The private sector can be broken down further into private renting and owner-occupation.

Private renting In the case of private renting a tenant purchases accommodation from a landlord who owns the building. Privately rented accommodation caters to some of the richest as well as some of the poorest city dwellers. The amount of private renting is a function of the demand and the relative rate of return afforded to landlords. With low rates of return the more profit-conscious landlords will reinvest their capital for more lucrative returns.

There is a basic conflict in private renting. On one hand, the landlords want to maximize rents and minimize maintenance expenditure. On the other hand, tenants want to keep rents low and ensure that landlord maintenance levels are high. Landlords can reduce maintenance levels while tenants can withhold rents, at least until they are evicted. The conflict is exacerbated in tight housing markets. The history of private renting is the history of the unfolding conflicts. One example from Britain: in 1915 the city of Glasgow was a center of munitions and ship manufacturing. With increasing demand for housing and limited supply the landlords raised the rents by almost 25 percent. The response was quick and dramatic. Residents called a rent strike, industrial workers went on strike, and 15,000 workers threatened further strike action. The government, fearful of a rupture to wartime arms production, rushed a bill through Parliament which limited rent increases. This legislation laid the basis for subsequent government limitations on rent levels and rent increases. Tenants, if they are numerous and powerful enough, can force governments to legislate to control rent levels. This has happened at the national level in Britain and at the local level in various US cities, such as Santa Monica and New York. Tenants can use political power and influence to offset their weak bargaining position with landlords. Landlords, on the other hand, can respond by selling off their properties, disinvesting, and reducing maintenance expenditure. In some inner-city areas the process of disinvestment in association with overcrowding can lead to a marked deterioration of neighborhoods. Ultimately, landlords can abandon their properties.

Over the course of this century the main trend has been a decline in private renting in the richer countries of the world. While renting is still significant in the very large cities, especially as the tenure of last resort for the poor and as an important first stage in a housing career, it has been eclipsed by owner-occupation as the main tenure form.

Owner-occupation With owner-occupation households purchase ownership as well as accommodation. Since immediate house purchase is rare, mass owner-occupation relies on an extensive system of credit for both the producers and the consumers. Throughout this century most governments in the rich countries have encouraged owner-occupation through various fiscal and social policies. The creation of a property-owning democracy has been the goal of many governments eager to encourage a housing tenure system which chimes so well with the ideology of capitalism. In Britain, for example, in 1900 only 10 percent of the households were owner-occupied, but by 1990 this figure had increased to almost 60 percent; a direct result of growing affluence as well as direct government involvement, from enabling local authorities to provide mortgages to creating fiscal subsidies in the form of income tax relief on mortgage interest payments. However, the creation of a debt-encumbered section of the society whose standard of living is dependent on rates of interest puts a limit on the political feasibility of government fiscal policy. Once created, a majority of owner-occupiers becomes a powerful force, which puts limitations on interest rate increases. Important at the national level in this regard, owner-occupiers also become an important source of political activity at the local level. A dwelling is likely to be most households' single biggest purchase as well as its biggest single asset. An owner-occupied home is more than a dwelling: it is property, a source of future income and a means of wealth creation. Owner-occupiers are thus very sensitive to any changes in the local environment which affect the value of their property. Much local political activity is a way of maintaining or increasing property values and of fighting against things which depress local property values.

When owner-occupation is an important part of the housing market then the financial institutions that lend the finance for house purchase have an important role in structuring household choice and in controlling the fiscal lubricant to the market. Differential patterns of lending to households, dwellings, and residential areas structure the housing market. Let us consider briefly the notion of *redlining*. In the 1970s researchers in the United States discovered that many institutions did not lend in inner-city neighborhoods. The term "redlining" arises from the story of one bank in Boston that had a map with a red line around the area where it did not lend mortgages. This was both a cause and an effect of inner-city decline. The bank's actions, by not lending, meant that people who wished to buy housing had to raise loans at higher rates of interest which put pressure on maintenance and upkeep costs, made landlords pack in even more tenants, and in general created the financial context for disinvestment and decline. Not only were the institutions responding to inner-city decline, they were helping to cause a downward spiral of lack of investment leading to housing deterioration which lead to lack of investment . . . and so on. Redlining is one of the more obvious effects of financial institutions on the housing market. These institutions, by the amount they lend, the way they lend, and to whom and where they lend, are important agents in the structuring of the housing market and important factors in the allocation of housing opportunities and housing constraints.

Public housing   In the case of public housing, the realization problem is overcome by the state purchasing and/or building housing and then renting out to tenants. Systems of rent-pooling or direct subsidization allow for relatively cheap rents to be charged. Public housing is a result of market failure and popular pressure. Markets respond to economic power, not social need. Private housing markets do not respond well to the needs of the poorest, but yet the poorest have political power that can be transformed into public policies. Public housing results from bottom-up political pressure.

The size of the public housing sector is a function of political pressure. In the United States public housing has always been a small proportion of the total housing stock (less than 8 percent); it accommodates the very poorest and has a very bad reputation. "The projects," as this housing is commonly known, are seen as reservoirs for the poor, the black, the marginalized; the place of and for the underclass. In Britain, in contrast, public housing was constructed on a large scale after the Second World War as part of the social contract between the government and the people for wartime sacrifices, a cement of social bonding, and a function of the inability of the private sector to meet the housing demands of most of the population. By the late 1970s public housing constituted almost 35 percent of the total housing stock, with larger proportions in some regions and metropolitan centers. After 1979 the Conservative government undertook a widespread policy of privatizing the public housing sector, selling off housing to sitting tenants at vastly discounted prices. The policy was very popular because it gave tenants not only accommodation but an opportunity for wealth creation. There was selectivity in the process: it was the better-quality housing, the single-family dwellings in the more desirable neighborhoods that sold rather than the high-rise apartments in unsafe neighborhoods. By this process public housing was further stigmatized in the popular imagination.

In other European countries, especially in Scandinavia, public housing continues to be an important and valued part of the total housing stock. The changing size and function of the public housing sector is a direct function of broad-scale political changes. Throughout most of the rich world the extension of owner-occupation has reduced both the need and the political acceptability of public housing. The changes in Britain are the exemplar case of the recommodification of housing.

The urban sociologist Ray Pahl (1975) raised the important questions in cities: Who gets the scare resources? Who decides how to distribute or allocate these resources? Who decides who decides? The answers to these questions constitute a body of work sometimes referred to as *urban managerialism*. Housing has been one of the most studied of the scarce resources. A large body of work has examined the role of such housing managers as public housing officials, realtors, planners, local state officials, bureaucrats, banks and lending institutions (see Bassett and Short, 1980, 50–2). The rules and procedures of these managers structure the housing choices and constraints of households. We have already discussed the practice of redlining operated by some banks. This practice limited the housing opportunities of low-income households in the inner city. The papers in Goening (1986), for example, highlight the role of realtors in influencing the racial mix of neighborhoods in US cities. A study of public housing in the English city of Hull looks at how public housing managers assessed applicants (Gray, 1976). The study found that the assessment of the applicants was reflected in the quality of the housing received. Applicants who were rated highly received better-quality housing. This study and many others highlight the fact that bureaucratic procedures have an important role in translating housing demands into housing market consequences.

The demand for housing

We can make a distinction between need and effective demand for housing. We all have a need for shelter of some kind, a place to keep out the elements and conduct a private life. But need is not demand. The homeless have a need for housing but not enough market power. Although we all have a need we vary in our effective demand for housing. Need is a human attribute but demand is a function of economic and political power. Let us consider three of the principal sources of variation in demand.

Income In a purely private housing market, housing is allocated entirely on the basis of ability to pay. Households vary in the amount of money they can spend on housing. The best housing therefore goes to those who can afford it. Residential districts differ in the cost of their housing and the income of their residents. Every big city has its very rich areas where big houses pose in manicured gardens and expensive cars sit impressively in the expansive driveways. Every city also has its very poor districts where low-income households live in poor-quality, high-density housing, often in the least attractive parts of the city close to industry. In between these two extremes can be found a wide variety of middle-income districts. Not all housing is allocated simply on the basis of the ability to pay and hence on income. Many countries, particularly in Western Europe, have social housing programs in which housing is allocated on the basis of need rather than income. In these circumstances there is not the same simple linear relationship between housing quality and income. Government intervention can allow low-income households to live in very pleasant housing. The amount of social housing varies. It is very small in the United States and limited to the very poorest, whereas in Scandinavian countries it constitutes a significant proportion of the total housing stock. It becomes a target for attack whenever there is a crisis in government finances.

Stage in the life-cycle Through its life-cycle the typical household has a variety of space requirements. In Western cities young people typically leave their parents' homes. Assume a woman has just left college and lives on her own. She does not require much space, perhaps a room in a rented flat in the central city. She gets married, and now the new two-person household can afford a better place, still central but more up-market. If or when children come on the scene more space is required. A bigger house is needed, maybe even a garden; the household moves to the suburbs where more space is available. Eventually the children leave home, and the household size is reduced. The now-retired couple may decide to move into a smaller, specially designed dwelling. Table 9.1 shows one set of life-cycle changes and associated space requirements.

TABLE 9.1 HOUSING NEEDS ASSOCIATED WITH DIFFERENT STAGES OF THE LIFE-CYCLE	
Stage in life-cycle	*Housing needs/aspirations*
1 Pre-child stage	Relatively cheap, central-city apartment
2 Child-bearing	Renting of single-family dwelling close to apartment zone
3 Child-rearing	Ownership of relatively new suburban home
4 Child-launching	Same areas as (3) or perhaps move to higher-status area
5 Post-child	Marked by residential stability
6 Later life	Institution/apartment/live with children

Source: Short (1978)

This is not a universal model. It takes child-rearing and launching as the pivotal points of household change. But increasingly there are households without children. Almost 35 percent of households in the United States consist of a single person or households with no children. Moreover, the pattern outlined is culturally specific. In societies with a stronger extended family system, the atomistic pattern of separate households may not occur to the same extent. In these cases when people marry they may continue to live with their parents. In much of the developing world extended family systems are more important. In China the eldest son commonly brings his wife to live with his parents, and sometimes several brothers may set up a joint household that includes their wives, children, and parents.

However, the model is useful as an entry point into understanding the role of stage in the life-cycle. These stages are important in two respects. First, they provide us with a major mechanism to explain the pattern of residential mobility, the movement of households within urban areas. Almost two-thirds of all this movement is the result of changing space requirements associated with changing stages in the life-cycle. Second, a stage in the life-cycle is an important dimension of residential differentiation. Where there are sophisticated housing markets with a sensitive variation to housing demand then different housing types and residential areas will contain households at different stage in the life-cycle. There are some districts, especially in the inner city, dominated by single-person and no-children households. Then there are others, typically in the suburbs, dominated by households with children. Increasingly, as the population ages, there are also districts where elderly citizens predominate.

Ethnic status   Households vary in their ethnic identity. This can influence where they want to live and where they can live. Where there are significant differences between a majority culture and a minority culture this difference is often expressed in the residential mosaic. Ethnic clusters of the minority culture can be identified, such as the cases of Asians in British cities, Vietnamese in US cities, North Africans in French cities, and Turks in German cities. This ethnic clustering results from both choice and constraint factors. In terms of choice, minority groups sometimes prefer to cluster together. It provides safety in a potentially threatening society, a link with the home country, and a platform of shared culture and shared language in an alien society. Ethnic neighborhoods provide a basis for defense, support, and advancement for immigrants into a new society. Ethnic clustering may also arise from the practice of discrimination. In formal discrimination, specific ethnic groups may be prevented from living in certain areas. This policy was part of the South African system of apartheid. With the demise of white supremacist rule, there has been what Saff (1994) refers to as the deracialization of space but not desegregation. While official policies of apartheid have been overturned and the black middle class can move into formerly all-white neighborhoods, income polarization and the segregation of poor blacks continues to exist.

In the United States, although there was no official apartheid policy, there was and still is extreme segregation between white and black households. This is partly a function of income and life chances but also the result of discriminatory practices in mortgage lending and in the practices of estate agents/realtors who direct black households to predominantly black areas. Although such discrimination is illegal, informal practices of discrimination continue to be practiced. The work of Douglas Massey highlights the existence of what he terms *hypersegregation*: in 1990 one-third of black residents lived in neighborhoods that were at least 90 percent black; at least 70 percent of blacks in the 30 largest metropolitan regions would have to move neighborhoods to achieve true integration (Massey and Denton, 1993).

The consumption of housing

I began this chapter with a quote from the architect Le Corbusier to the effect that a house is a machine for living in. It is often quoted, its implication of functional, brutal simplicity an attractive possibility to some, distasteful to others. Although provocative it is not accurate. A house is of greater significance than just a shelter from the elements. Housing has many other attributes. The purchase or renting of accommodation is one of the biggest items of household expenditure. The cost of housing affects household budgets, and changes in housing costs impact on households, especially those with lower incomes. But housing is also more than just a cost; it is a setting, an arena. Primary dwellings are where we spend much of our spare time, and its quality and size have important consequences on our health, physical and social (see Smith et al., 1991). Our dwellings are also of crucial significance in early socialization – the family home is the setting for social interaction across generations and between genders. As children we are socialized into the world initially and perhaps most profoundly in our homes. In our dwellings we learn of the world from our families. The very notion and construction of the family takes place in the family home. Indeed, the very idea of home is of profound social and cultural significance. The home is a pivotal area in important polarities: refuge/journey; safety/danger; inside/outside; private/public; family/community. As the modern world fractures traditional communities, the home takes on a supercharged significance, for some a retreat from the public world. But the home is also a site of tension, the primary stage for the enactment of our family dramas, family conflicts, and family histories. Power struggles between generations, between genders, between differing conceptions of self and immediate others have a profundity and significance in the home. The home is a social construct whose changing meaning and significance tells us much about the nature of society. It is also a site in its own right of important developments. In an interesting article Lynn Spigel (1992) examines the importance of television in postwar suburban homes in the United States and its effects on gender relations, community bonding, and "family" values.

In a fascinating study Donald Katz (1992) chronicles the story of one middle-class family in the USA in the postwar era. He details significant events year by year from the return of the father from the war in 1945 to 1987. Housing is important in this story. The family's move to the suburbs in 1952 was seen as an escape from the city; they even changed their name from Goldenberg to Gordon at the same time. By 1955 cracks were found in the house; a metaphor Katz develops for the growing unease in the family: between the parents and their four adolescent children. Things did not turn out well. One child became a heroin addict, another married and divorced several times, while the only son's experience was the sad one of a gay man watching many of his friends dying from AIDS. Only the youngest daughter lived a quiet life with husband and children. The book chronicles postwar USA through the lens of one family. And in this story the houses they occupy are more than just physical places, they are full of emotional meaning.

Housing is not just a reflection of our social life, it can become an important variable. Educational attainment, to take just one example, is partly a function of income and official schooling but also, and especially in the early years, a function of teaching inside the family home. The presence and use of books in a home is one of the best indicators of successful educational attainment. Educational attainment, social and mental health, notions of gender roles and responsibilities are all forged in the crucible of daily living in the home. A house is more than a machine for living in.

THE RESIDENTIAL MOSAIC

The operation of the supply and the demand for housing allocates different groups to different types of housing in different parts of the city. The result is to produce a rich residential mosaic.

A general model

Figure 9.8 is a general model of the residential mosaic. Let us look at it in some detail. It identifies three dimensions of social space: income, ethnicity, and stage in the life-cycle. These dimensions reflect the main factors of housing demand, and they have a distinct spatial pattern; income tends to have a sectoral pattern, ethnicity has a clumpy pattern, while stage in the life-cycle has a ringlike structure. These dimensions of social space are superimposed one upon another through the physical fabric of the city. This model pertains most effectively to cities in North America and Western Europe. In cities in peripheral capitalist societies the three dimensions may not be so distinct. It must be remembered that figure 9.8 is a model, useful for

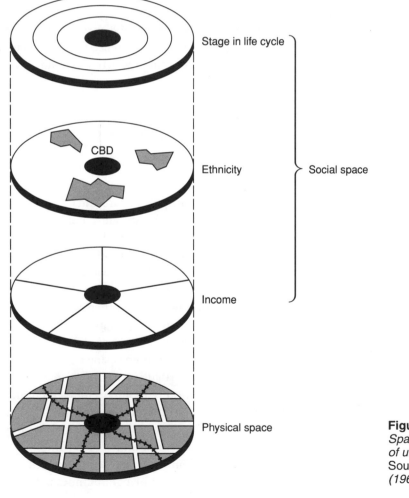

Figure 9.8
*Spatial dimensions
of urban structure*
Source: *Murdie
(1969)*

providing a provisional understanding but not a solid predictor of what will be found in cities around the world.

The residential mosaic is not a static phenomenon. Changes are occurring all the time:

- some neighborhoods deteriorate while others are gentrified. This has been particularly noticeable in residential districts close to the centers of very large cities in Western Europe and North America;
- the boundaries of ethnic neighborhoods expand and contract as the diverse communities grow and decay;
- the spatial patterns may be changed, as in the case of the construction of condominiums in suburban districts, which means that there will be single-person households in the suburbs as well as in the central city, and thus distort the ringlike pattern (figure 9.8).

We can picture the different slices of figure 9.8 as static snapshots of a constantly evolving picture, the whole as a freeze-frame of constant action. At certain times and in some cities the action is rapid; at other times, in other cities, change is slow.

Neighborhood typologies

There are distinct neighborhoods in a city. The bigger the city the greater the variety of neighborhoods. The precise number and range of neighborhoods depends upon the purpose at hand. If you are traveling alone at night you might want to distinguish between safe and unsafe neighborhoods. And this definition will vary for different members of the city population. What may be safe for a female member of the white middle-class may be full of dangers for a young, African-American male. If you are looking for a good time certain places will be seen as dull and boring whereas others will be perceived as exciting. Different purposes, different typology.

We can identify different purposes and hence different methods and resulting classifications. Advertising companies have identified lifestyle communities which have particular patterns of consumption. Their identification and demarcation is an important element in targeting the selling of specific goods and services to the most appropriate groups of people. The Claritas Corporation, for example, has identified 40 different lifestyle communities. Paul Knox (1993) has mapped the distribution of nine of these communities in the Washington metropolitan area. These nine communities account for

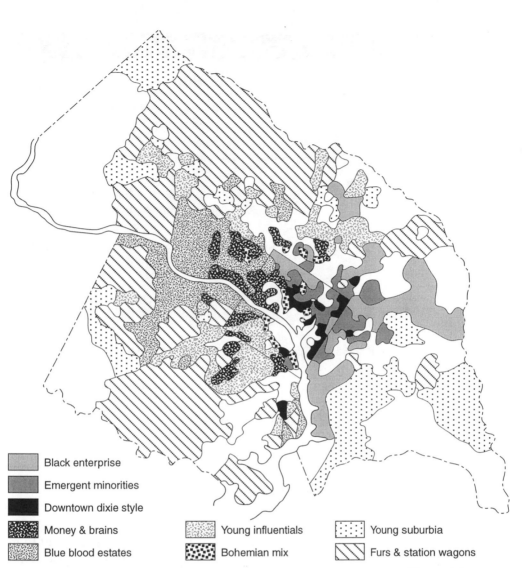

	Black enterprise
	Emergent minorities
	Downtown dixie style

| | Money & brains | | Young influentials | | Young suburbia |
| | Blue blood estates | | Bohemian mix | | Furs & station wagons |

Figure 9.9
Communities in Washington, D.C.
Source: *Knox (1993) and Weiss (1988)*

almost 80 percent of the total metropolitan population. The distribution is shown in figure 9.9, and a brief description of the typology is given in table 9.2. A broader, more personal classification is given by Reyner Banham (1971) in his classic study of Los Angeles. Banham was as concerned with urban form and architectural style as he was with social distributions. He identified four major ecologies:

- surfurbia;
- foothills;
- plains of id;
- autopia.

TABLE 9.2 TYPOLOGY OF RESIDENTIAL AREA	
Type	*Description*
Money and brains	High-income, white-collar, professional
Blue-blood estates	Very wealthy
Young influentials	Young, single or dual-career households with high incomes
Fur and station wagons	Couples in thirties and forties with teenage children
Young suburbia	Younger households with young children
Bohemian mix	Gentrifying areas
Black enterprise	Affluent black, middle-class
Emergent minorities	Black, working-class households
Downtown dixie style	Very low-income, black areas

Source: After Knox (1993) and Weiss (1988)

Surfurbia consists of the beach communities that hug the coast from Malibu to Balboa. The foothill communities include Beverley Hills and Pasadena, and the plains of id stretch throughout the flat land of the central basin of the metropolitan region. Autopia refers to the landscape of the freeway, the endless miles of concrete lanes taking a seemingly endless amount of traffic around and around. The typology is neat, clever, and very informative. It has the benefits of parsimony and profundity.

A more general typology for US cities has been suggested by Peter Marcuse (1989). In response to the focus on the simple dichotomy of the dual city Marcuse proposed a fivefold division:

■ luxury city, housing the very rich;
■ gentrified city, into which the young professionals are moving;

- suburban city, the main location of the middle class;
- tenement city, housing lower-paid urban workers and their families;
- ghetto, the location of the very poor.

This is a simple model but an effective one. There is a rich variety of possible neighborhood typologies. The smaller the number of categories the greater the variation within the categories. There is a trade-off between the number of categories and ease of comprehension. A small number of categories is easier to take in, but comprehension is achieved at the expense of detail. The choice depends on the methods used, the purpose of the exercise, and ultimately the position of the observer.

Residential areas and social life

Residential areas are more than just outcomes of housing supply and demand. They have an important, though rather underresearched, role in the construction of communities. The connection between residential areas and social life is most apparent in the shaping of attitudes and the politics of place.

Residential areas can be important in shaping a variety of attitudes. In a now-classic study, Brian Robson (1969) looked at the relationship between residential areas, social status, and attitudes to educational attainment. He found that people of similar status but living in different areas had differing attitudes. People with differing status but living in the same area held similar attitudes. In other words, the study showed that the local area had an important role in influencing attitude. The residential area provides the locale for a community of shared attitudes. A similar finding has been reported in the geography of voting and the so-called neighborhood effect. This effect has been identified in a number of studies which showed that political disposition was affected by the local area; people of similar social status tended to vote differently depending on where they lived (Johnston et al. 1990; Taylor and Johnston, 1979). There is also a politics of place in which residents get involved in issues and debates affecting their local area. This is a topic I will consider more fully in chapter 12.

There are a number of factors which strengthen the ties within a local area. If there are shared occupational experiences then work and home can become more of a seamless web of shared attitudes. Neighborhoods of similar groups of workers have stronger bonds than areas where people have varied work experiences. Family structure is also important. In areas where childrearing is important, households tend to have a similar concern with protecting the local safety of their children. The more the area is isolated from the rest of society the greater the internal cohesion. This isolation can be in the form of geographic separation or social isolation. While small mining communities may be far away from metropolitan society, the isolated world of the ghetto may be separated from the rest of the society through very different life experiences and expectations to produce residential communities with widely different dominant values and shared beliefs. The work of Elijah Anderson (1990), for example, points to the difference between the dominant street code of the ghetto with its emphasis on obtaining respect through reputation and specific material goods, and the values of more affluent, mainstream, suburban areas.

The importance of the residential area varies throughout the population. For people whose status and self-esteem are tied to more distant workplaces, the dwelling may be a machine for living in. But for those who are more tied to the home – homemakers, the retired, and the young – the residential area is of greater importance. Youth gangs, for example, are based on the territoriality of residence amongst young people whose status and identity are defined with reference to their peers rather than to their family or the wider society.

The residential mosaic is fracturing the city into distinct areas. At certain times and in some places where conditions are favorable, these areas are the basis for identifiable communities of shared attitudes and common interests in which broad value systems are shaped to local needs. The identification of these communities and their creation and restructuring is one of the more important topics of a renewed urban geography, combining as it does the important issues of place and space, economy and culture, global and local.

GUIDE TO FURTHER READING

Traditional models of the housing stock:
Burgess, E.W. (1925) The growth of the city. In R. Park and E.W. Burgess and R.D. McKenzie (eds), *The City,* Chicago, Ill.: University of Chicago Press.
Hoyt, H. (1939) *The Structure and Growth of Residential Neighborhoods in American Cities,* Washington, D.C.: Federal Housing Administration.

On gentrification and the rent gap hypothesis consider:
Clark, E. (1987) *The Rent Gap and Urban Change,* Lund: Lund University Press.
Ley, D. (1986) Alternative explanations for inner city gentrification, *Annals of the Association of American Geographers* 76, 521–35.

Smith, N. (1987) Gentrification and the rent gap, *Annals of the Association of American Geographers* 77, 462–5.

Smith, N. (1991) Mapping the gentrification frontier. In M. Keith and A. Rodgers (eds), *Rhetoric and Reality in the Inner City*, London: Mansell.

Wessep, J. (1994) Gentrification as a research frontier, *Progress in Human Geography* 18, 74–83.

Much of the material on the housing market is drawn from my previous work, including:

Bassett, K. and Short, J.R. (1980) *Housing and Residential Structure: Alternative Approaches*, London: Routledge & Kegan Paul.

Cardoso, A. and Short. J.R. (1983) Forms of housing production, *Environment and Planning* A 15, 917–28.

Short, J.R. (1978) Residential mobility, *Progress in Human Geography* 2, 419–47.

Short, J.R. (1982) *Housing in Britain: The Postwar Experience*, London: Methuen.

Short, J.R. (1984) Housing in Britain. In J.R. Short and A. Kirby (eds), *The Human Geography of Contemporary Britain*, London: Macmillan.

Short, J.R., Fleming, S. and Witt, S. (1985) *Housebuilding, Planning and Community Action*, London: Routledge.

Various aspects of the residential mosaic are covered by:

Banham, R. (1971) *Los Angeles*, Harmondsworth, Mddx: Penguin.

Knox, P. (1993) The postmodern urban matrix. In P. Knox (ed.), *The Restless Urban Landscape*, Englewood Cliffs, N.J.: Prentice-Hall.

Marcuse, P. (1989) Dual city: a muddy metaphor for a quartered city, *International Journal of Urban and Regional Research* 13, 697–708.

Murdie, R.A. (1969) *Factorial Ecology of Metropolitan Toronto, 1951–1961*, Research Paper 116, Department of Geography, University of Chicago, Chicago.

Robson, B.T. (1969) *Urban Analysis*, Cambridge: Cambridge University Press.

Weiss, M.J. (1988) *The Clustering of America*, New York: Harper and Row.

Other works cited:

Anderson, E. (1990) *Streetwise: Race, Class and Change in an Urban Community*, Chicago, Ill.: University of Chicago Press.

Anderson, M. (1964) The federal bulldozer. In J.Q. Wilson (ed.), *Urban Renewal*, Cambridge, Mass.: MIT Press.

Firey, W. (1945) Sentiment and symbolism as ecological variables, *American Sociological Review* 10, 140–8.

Gray, F. (1976) Selection and allocation in council housing, *Transactions of Institute of British Geographers*, NS 1, 34–46.

Johnston, R.J., Shelley, M. and Taylor, P. (eds) (1990) *Developments in Electoral Geography*, London: Routledge.

Katz, D. (1992) *Home Fires: An Intimate Portrait of One Middle Class Family in Postwar America*, New York: Random House.

Massey, D. and Denton, M. (1993) *American Apartheid: Segregation and the Making of the Underclass*, Cambridge, Mass.: Harvard University Press.

Pahl, R. (1975) *Whose City?*, Harmondsworth, Mddx: Penguin.

Revell, D. (1982) Who ordered their estate? *Guardian*, May 14.

Saff, G. (1994) The changing face of the South African city: from urban apartheid to the deracialization of space, *International Journal of Urban and Regional Research* 18, 377–91.

Smith, S.J., McGukin, A. and R. Knill-Jones (eds) (1991) *Housing for Health*, London: Longman.

Spigel, L. (1992) The suburban home companion: television and the neighborhood ideal in postwar America. In B. Colomina (ed.), *Sexuality and Space*, New York: Princeton Architectural Press.

Taylor, P. and Johnston R.J. (1979) *Geography of Elections*, Harmondsworth, Mddx: Penguin.

Chapter 10

THE SOCIAL ARENA

ALL HUMAN BEINGS HAVE A DEEP PSYCHOLOGICAL NEED FOR A SENSE OF SECURITY WHICH COMES FROM KNOWING WHERE YOU ARE. BUT "KNOWING WHERE YOU ARE" IS A MATTER OF RECOGNISING SOCIAL AS WELL AS TERRITORIAL POSITION.

EDMUND LEACH, *CULTURE AND COMMUNICATION* (1976)

The divisions of society are embodied in space and place. The city separates out different types of people; it also acts to bring certain types of people together. Part of the differences between people is in the spaces they occupy, the places they inhabit. Part of the similarities between people is in their shared spaces and common places. In this chapter I will examine some of the relationships between urban space and the social order. I will consider the relationship between the city and

- class;
- ethnicity;
- gender;
- sexual identity.

THE CITY AND CLASS

In English the term "class," as a description of different groups in society, emerged most fully, according to Williams (1976), during the industrial revolution. It was then that the terms "middle class," "working class" and "upper class' began to be used on a regular basis. The industrial revolution involved a spatial reorganization as well as an economic reorganization of society. Urbanization went hand in hand with industrialization. The new industrial order was also the new urban order in which social classes replaced social rank and modernity replaced tradition. The industrial cities were the crucible in which classes and class identity were shaped and formed. For Marx and Engels the creation of an urban working class was the creation of an agent of social change. They believed that the economic system of capitalism created the class, while the urban experience gave the class

an ability to see itself as a class; the urban working class was to be the
gravedigger of the bourgeois social order.

An alternative perspective is provided by the historian Patrick Joyce
(1980). In examining the culture of factory cities in the north of
England after 1850 Joyce points to the practice of deference.
Employers exerted control inside and outside the factory, their power
permeating the locale. There was an inculcation of subordination
through the dependence on work opportunities. But subordination
was also created by the workers themselves. Work was a source of
pride and meaning, there was

> *a commitment to work which was more than mere rational calcu-
> lation. Work got under the skin of everyday life . . . These attachments
> amounted to something like the tyranny of work over life.*
> (Joyce, 1980, 97)

The domination of work over people's lives led to the acceptance of
the authority that governed the routines of work.

To compare Marx and Joyce is to contrast the extremes of rejection and deference, revolution with acceptance. But the comparison
also draws attention to the role of mediating effects in the articulation
of class relations. Joyce's work shows how a relationship of basic
antagonism can, through the interweaving of work, religion, politics,
and daily life, lead to a relationship of accommodation. These
relationships do not remain fixed. A change in the world economy,
the introduction of new practices, or a change in the community can
all lead to a change in class relations.

For Marx the basic division is between capital and labor, between
those who own/do not own the means of production. This is an
enormously simple yet powerful division. It is an analytical device that
can unlock general patterns, broad themes, and wide sweeps of social
theorizing. It is less useful in an understanding of classes in a particular city. The capital–labor cleavage is expressed in the dynamics of the
economy and articulated more in the authority relations between
management and unions than in the local community. And there is
a reason for this. The factory culture that Joyce identified has been
changing over the last 150 years. The tight nexus between employers, employees, and the local community, in which authority relations
existed both inside and outside the factory, has broken down. There
are still some factory towns in which a single employer dominates the
labor market as well as the social, political, and cultural life of local
communities, but these are the diminishing exceptions. Much more
common, and especially in bigger cities, is the disconnection between

capital and place. The resident capitalist with an interest in a particular community is being replaced by a multinational corporation with
interests in global markets and general accounts rather than in particular communities. Space has replaced place as the arena of capitalist
calculations. The post-Fordist revolution is not only a change in production, it also signifies a transformation in the relationship between
capital, labor, and community.

Capital

The capital–labor distinction is an analytical device of a high order of
generality. We can make further distinctions. There are different types
of capital. The Ford Motor Company and the family restaurant
employing two nonfamily members can both be considered as capital, but there are as many differences as there are similarities. Capital
varies in size, from big organized capital to small capitalists.
Government policy, for example, responds more to the needs of big
capital than to those of small capital. Big motor companies are bailed
out by the government, small restaurants are allowed to go to the
wall. Alliances between big capital and organized labor can often
undermine the position of small capital. The costs of labor market
policy regulation and implementation fall more heavily on small
capital. If all businesses have to fill in forms, big companies have
whole departments devoted to this task, whereas very small entrepreneurs have to do it themselves along with numerous other things.

A distinction can also be made between mobile capital and less-
mobile capital. The distinction is more gradual than precise. Mobile
capital has the ability to move easily and quickly. Capital–labor
relations are thus skewed towards capital because it has the ability to
move. Capital is much more mobile than labor. Less-mobile capital,
in the short to medium term at least, has to find some form of accommodation with the power of labor. Thus in the 1920s and 1930s the
auto industries of the United States were racked with labor disputes
as each side, tied to the existing locations, sought to reach an advantage. By the 1980s and 1990s the companies were less restricted to
specific locations. Labor had less bargaining power, and this was
reflected in the increasing intensity of work and the relative reductions in wages in comparison with other sectors of the labor market.

We can also identify place-specific capital whose interests are
bound up with the fortunes of a particular place. This is a declining
though still significant fraction of capital. It includes local real-estate
companies, local companies, and banks and financial institutions
whose profitability is specifically tied to a local place and the health

of its economy. In the United States it is associated with the forces behind civic boosterism. In urban systems where a primate city does not siphon off economic growth there are more opportunities for cities to move up or down the urban hierarchy. In the case of the United States, the sheer size of the country and the variety of economic opportunities in a mature and expanding economy reinforce the possibility of this movement. The ability and opportunity for movement up the urban hierarchy helps explain the persistence and strength of civic boosterism, which has been a common feature of municipal affairs in the United States. Small town boosterism in the early part of this century was given dramatic documentation in Sinclair Lewis's 1922 novel *Babbitt*. The "hero" of the novel is the realtor George F. Babbitt, a prosperous citizen of Zenith, a classic booster talking up his town, selling it as a place of expansion, a possible Chicago of the future. Boosterism continues to be an important element of urban politics. Gottdiener (1987) suggests that there has been a decline in the 'politics' of urban politics in the contemporary United States because of the power of corporations and the failure of cities to generate sufficient revenue. In effect, the need to attract business underscores the actions of boosters and suggests a strong link between business leaders and civic authorities. Contemporary urban boosterism has been placed in a broader political economy context by Logan and Molotch (1987), who document the economic growth lobby formed by the leading players in US cities; a consensus on stimulating investment and economic growth while limiting the redistributional function of the state. Realtors, local banks, influential politicians, corporate chairpersons, and chambers of commerce all seek to define the city as an economic growth machine. They are all eager to promote a probusiness agenda for their particular city against the background of competing cities and alternative investment opportunities. The net effect, argue Logan and Molotch, is the domination of business interests in the urban politics of the United States.

Labor

Different fractions of labor can be identified, but not with ease or a large measure of confidence. The rate of economic change has seriously undermined the ability to speak with any certainty about the labor market. With this very important qualification in mind two very general categories can be identified. First, there is the working class. In the first instance it is the creation of the industrial revolution, although, as E.P. Thompson reminds us, classes made themselves as much as they were the product of general economic forces. The exemplar working class is associated with urban manufacturing, male employment, and a culture of the collective. If this definition holds, then what we have witnessed in the last 150 years is the rise and fall of the working class. In the richer countries manufacturing employment has declined, and the power of organized labor has been diminished by the mobility of capital, technological changes, and the decline of the corporate compromise between capital, labor and the state. While the loss of manufacturing in the core countries has led to the decline of the working class, the growth of manufacturing employment in the periphery has not led to the growth of the working class there. Manufacturing employment is different in the contemporary Third World compared to manufacturing in late nineteenth-century and early twentieth-century Europe and North America. More women are employed, and flexible production does not lead to the same culture of the factory. In the large manufacturing cities of the rich countries we are effectively waving farewell to the working class.

Second, there is the middle class. Even its very name suggests an ambiguous position between the capitalists and the workers, some penumbral position between the light and the dark. The one constant of the last 150 years, if not much longer, has been the rise of the middle class. The growth of corporate and government bureaucracies and the need for managerial and high-level technical labor have all led to the growth of a labor fraction that falls between the capitalists and the workers. There is now a significant group whose material interests are ambiguous; they may side with capital or with organized labor, depending on the stakes and the issues.

There are, of course, various fractions within these two broad groupings. A labor aristocracy has been identified with relatively high incomes and good working conditions. This labor aristocracy of the rich countries has been seen as the leading power in organized labor and by some as the reason why there has not been social revolution as predicted by Marx and Engels. The labor aristocracy had an interest in turning social revolutionary movements into social democratic movements. It is one of the paradoxes of the twentieth century that the "workers' movements" were most successful not in the advanced capitalist countries but in the more peripheral countries of the world economy. In terms of the middle class, two opposing trends have been identified. On the one hand, commentators like Braverman (1974) have pointed to the deskilling of the middle classes, while on the other, observers such as Abercrombie and Urry (1983) point to a professional-managerial class with a contradictory class location that has given rise to a new form of politics. Both trends may be occurring. We can imagine the deskilling of some sectors; much of the traditional management and documentation skills in the industry have been undermined by technological changes; while in other sectors, such as the so-called producer services, there are new centers of middle-class growth and influence.

Problems with class

There are a number of difficulties in using the term "class." Let me mention two: class consciousness and limitation of coverage.

Class consciousness   Such terms as working class and middle class are broad brush, general and hazy. Part of the difficulty lies in the difference between class position and class consciousness. A distinction has been made between *class in itself* and *class for itself.* A class in itself is an objective fact; a class for itself is a self-conscious class able to see its position in the scheme of things. The division is useful but care needs to be exercised. Class as an objective fact depends on the perspective of the observer and an *a priori* set of assumptions. Class for itself is dependent on the emergence of a class consciousness. There are a number of conditions that promote such an emergence:

- perception of contradiction. When there is widespread perception of conflict and contradiction in society then class consciousness in some form is more likely to occur. This is, however, inhibited by the ideological state apparatus, including the education system, mass media, and government information systems. News coverage in the United States, for example, has been described by Noam Chomsky as the manufacture of consent, through which there is the explicit minimization in the coverage of social conflict and the projection of a society in basic harmony;
- communication distance between members. When members of a class are close together either in geographical or communicational proximity then class consciousness is more likely to develop. Isolated mining communities, for example, where work, community, and locale are closely intertwined, produce some of the strongest areas of working-class consciousness. Although urbanization brings workers together it also separates them into different residential areas. The small one-class mining community is the exception rather than the rule. In big cities with a varied residential mosaic, the pattern of

residential differentiation acts to inhibit class consciousness. The precise spatial articulation of community has an important part to play in the creation or inhibition of a general class consciousness;

■ turnover of members. When there is low turnover in a class then class consciousness has the necessary time and stability to develop. One of the most important changes of flexible production is the inhibition of long-term occupation groups with shared experiences and common practices. The net effect is to further inhibit class consciousness.

Writings on class in recent years have followed a distinct pattern. In the 1960s and 1970s the resuscitation of Marxist scholarship sought to explain why class consciousness was not more prevalent and why there was not more social conflict. It was assumed that capitalist societies necessarily produced class consciousness. The United States, for example, was thus seen as an "exception" and Europe as more "normal." The aim was therefore to explain the exception. More recently, class has been ignored, replaced by gender, race, and ethnicity as topics of hot interest. However, we need not junk the concept of class. We should not be explaining why it fails to appear. This is a sterile topic. Given the enormous barriers previously outlined, the really interesting thing is why it occurred at all. An analysis of its appearance, disappearance, and residual existence allows us to uncover some of the more important linkages between economy and society, community and locale, work and identity. Rather than bemoan that in many cities fashion consciousness has replaced class consciousness, we need to understand the shift, plot its trajectory, and explain its dynamic.

Limitation of coverage   Class is concerned with the world of work, the realm of production, people as workers. This is an important area of social life, but it is all-encompassing. It ignores the role of people outside the workforce and important nonwork differences between men and women, young and old, black and white. Class gets us only partly along the road. It is not so useful in understanding conflict based in consumption issues or the city as an arena for cultural identity or the city as a place of social reproduction. The city is many things. A place to work but also a place to share identity, raise a family, adopt a posture. Class is a useful concept, one that would repay a more serious evaluation, but one that is partial and selective.

With all the qualifiers just made, is there anything to say about the relationship between class and the city? I think there is. Even with all the provisos about the partial nature of the concept and the "problem" of class consciousness there are still a number of themes which deserve closer analysis. Let me examine some of these in broad outline.

The wealthy

It was the novelist F. Scott Fitzgerald who wrote, "Let me tell you about the very rich. They are different from you and me." Ernest Hemingway is supposed to have replied, "Yes, they have more money."

We could make a distinction between the rich, the very rich, and the superwealthy, but the important point to make is that all of them inhabit a different world. The difference varies by country and city. The poorer the country the more different the rich are. In richer countries the rich are different but share much of the public culture. In poorer countries the rich move in a different universe; they have access to goods and services that are denied the vast majority of the population. There are some places that have become the watering holes of the global rich: the exclusive ski lodges of Vail, Colorado, or Gstaad, Switzerland, the exclusivity of Bermuda or Monaco, the penthouse apartments of Fifth Avenue in New York City, the rococo palaces of Beverley Hills, the country estates of rural England. All these are some of the culturally sanctioned forms of consumption for the rich.

The rich have not figured in social analyses as much as the poor. Urban studies are full of the life of the poor, with urban geography often telling the story of the homeless and the dispossessed. This gives a voice to the voiceless. But there are more subtle reasons behind the bias. Academic observers feel more comfortable observing people of a similar or lower status. Academic observation of the poor, especially the foreign poor, has power relationships and authority roles built into the very fabric of the encounter that make it easier to obtain information while also being socially confirmed. The rich provide no such luxury. The academic observer is discomforted by the affluent, their lack of deference, their confidence, their unwillingness to play the role of willing participant.

The rich have also withdrawn from view. In 1899 Thorstein Veblen's masterful book *The Theory of the Leisure Class* was first published. Veblen pointed to the conspicuous consumption of the rich. He was writing in the United States when the robber barons such as Vanderbilt were building huge mansions and wealth was displayed in opulent and extravagant displays of building, socializing, and consumption. Since then the wealthy have moved from conspicuous to inconspicuous consumption. There are exceptions. These include the nouveau riche pop stars with their Rolls Royces and the commodity dealers with their huge estates and high-profile "charitable" contributions. But these are the exceptions. The rich are able to keep a lower profile. This is expressed in where they live and how they live. The robber barons built huge mansions so that the population could see their wealth; they built to impress. Now the dominant form of housing is secluded, hidden from public view. The rich in many Third World cities live behind walls patrolled by armed guards. Even in the supposedly more stable democracies of the West the rich are protecting themselves from public view. One of the chapters in Mike Davis's book, *City of Quartz* (1990), is concerned with the creation and maintenance of gated communities, so called because they have gates to keep out the rest of the population. This trend is creeping down the income scales so that much of even middle-income Los Angeles consists of a patchwork of gated enclaves. The city is fragmenting.

For the rich in most countries there are still certain places to live, certain places to go on holiday, certain schools to send the children, certain colleges to attend, certain favored occupations. Wealth and place are interwoven. More work is needed to show the changing connections between the rich and the places they inhabit.

The middle class

The term "middle class' is loaded with both meaning and ambiguity. Its very usage reveals much. In Britain the term is often reserved for white-collar workers and members of the various professions such as education, law, and medicine. In the United States most factory workers would describe themselves as middle class; in the United Kingdom this would be seen as an act of social pretension.

The emergence of the middle class is bound up with new forms of urbanization. Situated between the two great divisions of the nineteenth century, the growth of the middle class in the twentieth century has been embodied in economies of high mass consumption. The automobile and the suburb condense the patterns of economic consumption and cultural reproduction of middle-class life.

There are a number of political questions concerning the middle class. The first is: To whom do they ally themselves? In the UK the question was seen in terms of the affluent worker. What happens to those manual workers who are relatively well paid? With their extra income, more consumer durables, and owner-occupied suburban lifestyle, do they become more conservative? The implicit assumption is that low wages are associated with political radicalism. The work of Goldthorpe et al. (1969) showed that these changes had relatively little effect on traditional working-class attitudes. This study was taken at a particular time. A follow-up study would be of great comparative value.

In the United States, where a majority of the population would define themselves as middle class, the pressing political question has been: Who can capture the hearts and minds of the middle class? The history of recent US politics is essentially one of the struggle for the middle class. The emergence of Reagan Democrats in the 1980s was the capturing of the middle ground by the Republican Party, at least in terms of presidential elections. Political debates were centered on meeting the aspirations of the middle class. If the question of the 1980s in the United States was capturing the middle class, the issue of the 1990s has become saving the middle class. One of the most astute commentators, Kevin Phillips, published a widely read book that detailed the erosion of the middle-class lifestyle (Phillips, 1993). Given the majority classification, this was an important peg on which to hang a more general discussion of the decline of the United States. The middle class had become an icon of the United States, and its growth and decline had become an important gauge of the strength and vitality of the whole country.

Attention has also focused on the new middle class. These are the white-collar workers of the tertiary and quaternary sectors, the baby boomers employed in public and private sectors, the symbolic analysts, the aging yuppies (see chapter 8). David Ley (1994) has suggested that this new class has a distinct geographical identity, essentially inner-area metropolitan, and there is a relationship between place and identity that is mutually reinforcing. In three Canadian cities he tested the extent to which gentrification by this new middle class was associated with changes in political attitudes. In Montreal, Toronto, and Vancouver he found no relationship between what he termed social 'upgrading' and the rise of conservative politics. To what extent this is a temporary phenomenon and applies at the individual level rather than at the cruder ecological level he examined is something that only time and more detailed work will provide.

The middle class is important. Its size, expansion and contraction,

changing composition and allegiances tell us much about a society;
its forms of consumption structure much of twentieth-century urbanization; and to understand the middle class is to understand one of
the most important and powerful agents of social evolution and urban
change in the twentieth century.

The underclass

The underclass has always been seen as a problem. As a group marginalized by society and the economy they have figured as a source
of social disruption. In the nineteenth century terms like "mob,"
"crowd," "the great unwashed," "the other half" were used, and in
the twentieth century the "underclass," or sometimes the place-
names were used, such as "inner city" or "ghetto." Whatever the term
used it always had the same tone of fear and apprehension.

Marx used the term "reserve army of labor." He connected the
underclass to the fluctuations in the capitalist economy. During
boom periods more labor was required, but during downturns unemployment increased. The poor were like a reserve army called into
economic service during the boom but dismissed back into poverty
during the slumps. In many of the poorer countries of the world the
underclass continues to perform this same function. In the richer
countries the fluctuations of the private market have been offset, to
varying degrees, by the welfare state. Welfare payments provide
recipients with the means to live. Since the nineteenth century welfare payments have been a cause for concern. The Victorians sought
to distinguish between the deserving and undeserving poor. The
former were eligible for public assistance, the latter were not. The
spectre of the undeserving poor obtaining public benefits continues
to haunt the popular imagination.

The level of welfare payments is set by two opposing forces. On
the one hand, they must be high enough so that people do not fall
into abject poverty. If they are set too low then people will not benefit
and social peace could be threatened. On the other hand, if they are
set too high then, it is argued, the recipients may lack the necessary
incentive to rejoin the labor force and will continue to be a drain on
the taxpayer. During a fiscal crisis of the state or when taxation levels
are deemed to be high the latter argument is heard more frequently.
One current argument in the United States is over the existence of a
permanent underclass. Benefits are so high, argue critics of the welfare system, that many recipients lack the necessary incentive to work
and eventually a culture of dependence is established. These debates
are not independent of race, because it is commonly perceived that

African Americans constitute a significant proportion of welfare recipients. The permanent underclass is seen as a major source of crime, social disorder, and disease. The contemporary debates mirror the arguments of the last century.

The home of the underclass is the inner city, sometimes called the ghetto. In popular imagination this is the setting for social breakdown, the place where normal rules of society do not apply and cannot be enforced. It is the id of the urban imagination.

The underclass has been an important part of social debates in contemporary United States. A number of causal arguments can be noted. In *The Truly Disadvantaged* (1987), the sociologist William Julius Wilson focused on the exodus of working-class and middle-class blacks from the ghetto. This movement was caused by large-scale job losses as inner-city factories closed, jobs were exported to the suburbs and sometimes overseas, and deindustrialization meant a loss of the semiskilled and unskilled jobs that had initially attracted black migrants from the South. The more affluent moved out, and this differential outmovement magnified social isolation from mainstream values and behavioral patterns within the ghetto. The easy distinction between respectable middle class and the black lumpenproletariat denied a moral base has been criticized by Duneier (1992), who argues that the debate is riddled with folk images of an underclass dominated by hustlers and criminals. His own book sought to show, in a very detailed ethnographic study, the moral universe and respectability of ghetto dwellers in Chicago. An alternative view was propounded by Charles Murray (1984), who argued the conservative line that social welfare payments reduced the incentive to work and encouraged illegitimacy; educational standards had dropped in schools, and "liberal" values had led to the decline of the family. The underclass, in this argument, was caused by social welfare and liberal ideas. His answer was to abolish welfare. The arguments have raged, sometimes informed by data, often not. For example, it does not seem that welfare drives illegitimacy; rates have continued to increase even as welfare payments have fallen in real terms.

The underclass is created and maintained by a number of factors. Structural changes in the economy have rendered many unskilled people surplus to requirements. Isolation in the ghetto limits mobility. But cultural factors are also important. When dominant community values eschew paid employment, when crime and violence kick the heart out of a caring community, then it becomes difficult for people to escape. It is a difficult issue because the arguments are associated with politically partisan viewpoints. "Liberals" have found it difficult to speak about individual responsibilities and community pathologies while conservatives seem uncomfortable with the structural context and the effects of social marginalization. And yet, it is in these spaces between the easy political rhetoric that more convincing explanations can be found.

In an interesting book Robert Reich (1991) draws attention to the loss of community, not in a vague sociological sense but connected to the creation of a global web of economic transactions. He argues that there is a disconnection between different members of the same spatial community. We may live in the same city, but if my job is in a dynamic sector and yours is in a declining sector then our life experiences are very different. To some extent this difference is off-set by the public sector. You may have less money than me, but our children still attend the same school, we take books out of the same library, and we use the same public park. But if there is a cutback in the public sector or if the public sector contribution is limited (and remember that Reich is writing from a US perspective) then the inequalities between groups will heighten. We may inhabit the same city but the differences between us will grow. And they will be exac-erbated by the opting out of the rich: sending their children to private schools, hiring private security guards to police their gated commu-nities, buying recreation at private country clubs. During rapid economic change and a reduction in the role of the public sector, inequalities will be exaggerated. Class position rather than shared location will be the determining factor in quality of life. The shared space of cities will become more segregated, increasingly a mosaic of impermeable boundaries as the shared space of community is replaced by the divisions of class and wealth.

THE CITY AND ETHNICITY

Ethnicity is a complex word. It has been used to refer to religious denomination, racial category, and nationality. This slipping usage is part of its nature, there is no simple definition because it is a pro-visional, historically conditioned, socially constructed term. Ethnicity is a social construction, not a biological fact. People are not born with an ethnic identity as much as they are given one, socialized into one. Groups are racialized.

Ethnicity has two attributes. On the one hand it is an imposed identity. Ethnicity is imposed on certain groups in the discourses of othering. Kay Anderson (1987, 1991), for example, shows in her analysis of Vancouver's Chinatown that the three levels of govern-ment (federal, provincial, and municipal) played an important role in constructing the category of Chineseness. The government, through territorial arrangements, sponsored and reinforced racial concepts that sustained and reproduced the ideas and practices of ethnic difference and racial separation. The distinction made in the United States between blacks and whites meant that in the United States blacks were created as a separate group and, given the overlay of power, black was associated with all kinds of negative connotations, from the patronizing "childlike" to the more fearful "violent."

On the other hand, ethnic identities are constructed between individuals into some collective identity, experience (real or imagined), and history. Thus blacks in the United States have created a culture of resistance, an identity forged in suffering and redemption that ranges from the Civil Rights Movement and Black Pride to Nation of Islam. More generally, as Keith and Cross (1993, 21–2) note, "in the process of race formation, this tension between the voluntarism of specific forms of racial mobilization and the choiceless confines of racist discourse echoes through the formation of all racialized collective identities."

The role of space and place is crucial to ethnic identity; indeed, to the whole notion of ethnicity. In this section I want to consider two aspects:

■ ethnicity and territoriality; and
■ ethnicity and conflict.

Ethnicity and territoriality

The extent to which the urban areas of multiethnic societies are associated with certain ethnic groups depends on a number of factors. Table 10.1 lists 14 variables that affect the internal cohesion of ethnic groups relative to the wider society. The more the characteristics of an ethnic group share a similarity with the variables of the left-hand column rather than those of the right, the more separate they will be from the host society. When the ethnic group speaks a different language then internal group cohesion will be stronger. Thus English-speaking migrants to the United States are more dispersed in US society than non-English-speaking groups. The variables are not independent one from another. Non-English-speaking groups tend to experience more discrimination, have lower levels of education, and often come from a different "race." A whole set of interdependent variables cluster around the general notion of "difference" or "otherness' between a group and the host society.

most not
prominance

TABLE 10.1	VARIABLES THAT AFFECT THE SALIENCE OF GROUP MEMBERSHIP	
Tend to increase salience	*Tend to decrease salience*
1 Large group (relative to total)	Small group
2 Residentially concentrated by region and community	Residentially scattered
3 Short-term residents (high proportion of newcomers)	Long-term residents (low proportion of newcomers)
4 Return to homeland easy and frequent	Difficult and infrequent
5 Speak a different language	Speak the dominant language
6 Different religion from majority	Share majority religion
7 Different race	Same race
8 Entered the society by forced migration or conquest	Entered voluntarily
9 Come from culturally different society	Come from culturally similar society
10 Attracted to political and economic developments in land of origin	Repelled by those developments
11 Homogeneous in class and occupation	Diverse in class and occupation
12 Low average level of education	High average level of education
13 Experience a great deal of discrimination	Experience little discrimination
14 Resident in a society with little social mobility	Resident in open-class society

Source: After Yinger (1986)

Illustration 10.1
Ethnic pride in Reading, UK (photograph: author)

The greater the degree of otherness of an ethnic group the more spatially segregated they are. Spatial segregation both reflects and embodies otherness. The exemplar case is the ghetto. This is an Italian word that was used to refer to the Jewish neighborhoods in medieval cities, a segregation enforced by custom and law. The ghetto both encapsulated and reinforced the otherness of the Jews. Living in separate communities their identity was maintained but so was their difference, and thus arose the opportunity for anti-Semitic rhetoric. The Jewish ghetto was the place of the non-Christian other, the unbelievers, the people who spoke a different language and worshiped a different God. Denied access to most occupations, money-lending was one of the few opportunities legally open to them since it was proscribed to Christians by medieval doctrine. This only increased the Jews' otherness and the contempt in which they were held and gave a strong financial basis for anti-Semitism. If you owed someone a great deal of money it was much easier to take part in or organize a pogrom. The story of the original ghettos and the twentieth-century experience of European Jewry reveals the social costs and human tragedies of being the other.

Enforced segregation was also part of the constitutional makeup of the 1948–93 white regime in South Africa. Under the Group Areas Acts of 1950 and 1966 whites, coloureds (mixed race), and Indians were restricted to specific neighborhoods. Blacks were assigned to "homelands" and thus were seen not as citizens of South Africa but as temporary visitors restricted to the peripheral shantytowns; their movement was controlled and restricted by pass laws. There were differences between the cities. The entry of a black middle class into the formerly all-white neighborhoods of Johannesburg made that city the most racially integrated city in the country. The smaller and less economically dynamic city of Pietermaritzburg kept its apartheid lines of segregation less permeable. The urban divisions of race and color will last in all South African cities long after the fall of the white regime and the dismantling of the system of apartheid.

Spatial segregation is also apparent in the distribution of African-Americans in the United States. Within living memory in many parts of the country African Americans were not allowed into specific neighborhoods. Special allowances were made in Miami, Florida, up to the early 1960s for "black" entertainers to travel to work in the "white" areas of the city. There now is no formal system of apartheid. What maintains the system is the legacy of the past and the operation of present inequalities. African-Americans are in a weaker economic position than whites, their average family income is two-thirds the national average, and rates of unemployment are almost twice as high. There are also more subtle forces at work. When African-Americans move into white neighborhoods there is what has been referred to as white flight. When the proportion of blacks passes beyond about 8 percent, a "tipping point" is reached and the outmovement of white households begins. There is also evidence that blacks are segregated out of certain neighborhoods by lending institutions and realtors. The net result is a separation between blacks and whites, with blacks being concentrated into overwhelmingly black neighborhoods. This residential segregation reflects and enhances racial attitudes, practices, and beliefs. The otherness of the African-American community is embodied in the marked spatial segregation.

Ethnicity is a social construction. Zucchi (1988), for example, shows how individuals left Italy, but a collective identity as "Italians" only really developed once they settled in Toronto, Canada. Ethnicity is not something inherent, it is created. And when people share a similar background in a foreign city the bonds between them are forged and enhanced; the links of these chains are elements of "ethnic" identity.

Ethnicity is never fixed. As a social construction, rather than a biological constant, it is subject to change, revision, and restructuring. The process of change is tied to territory. We can imagine a simple three-stage model. When people come to a city, especially a city in a foreign country, their social needs and spatial segregation help in the construction of a shared definite ethnicity. A process of assimilation intimately related to suburbanization marks the second stage of a weakening of the original ethnic identity. The so-called melting-pot notion for American cities was that the varied "ethnic" groups would melt into one whole. It never really happened. The third stage is not a homogeneous whole, but fragments of ethnic identity. In the United States, for example, the term "American" often has a prefix: African-American, Italian-American, Chinese-American. Ethnic identity is celebrated rather than denied.

Ethnicity is always in flux. What constitutes "home" is never fixed. John Western (1992), for example, examined the experience of black families moving from the island of Barbados in the West Indies to London, England. The people discovered that they were strangers, blacks in a white country, but through time they forged an identity, a new geography, and a new family history in which the notion of home became more problematic. As they made a life and had children, where exactly was home? Barbados? London? Who exactly were they? Who were their children? Barbadians? English? Londoners? Black British? The study is all the more interesting because the author, John Western, is in a very different power position: a white academic using his social skills to examine the lives of the black other; but he also shares a similar type of ambiguity: an Englishman living in the United States, an American citizen with an "Oxford" English accent. His book examines the inherent ambiguities and uncertainties in the maintenance of "ethnic" identity.

Ethnicity and conflict

Ethnicity binds together by distinguishing members of a group, but in the process it also creates nonmembers. Ethnicity separates as well as brings together. Inclusion also implies exclusion. We can see this most clearly when competing groups share the same space. Let us consider two examples.

In the city of Belfast social difference and togetherness are defined primarily with reference neither to skin color nor to race but to religious affiliation. Religion is the rhetoric of difference. Protestant and Catholic are two poles around which cluster a whole set of national identifications (British versus Irish), history, geography, and mythology. How do the two communities share the same space? The social geographer Frederick Boal focused on the inner-city areas of Shankill and Clonard (sometimes called Falls Road). Shankill was 99 percent Protestant while Clonard was 98 percent Catholic. Figure 10.1 shows

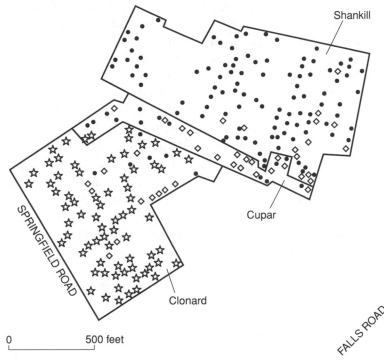

SHANKILL ROAD

☆ Springfield Road

◇ Falls Road

● Shankill Road

Shankill

Cupar

SPRINGFIELD ROAD

Clonard

FALLS ROAD

0   500 feet

Figure 10.1
*Bus stops used in
Belfast*
Source: *Boal
(1968)*

the sharp divide between the Catholic and Protestant communities
in terms of the bus stop used to travel to the city center. Notice how
people in the two different communities tended to go to different bus
stops. This was not just a simple exercise in distance minimization.
Boal interviewed 33 people in Shankill who lived closer to the Falls
Road bus stop. Of these, 79 percent went to the further bus stop.
(Boal, 1968). This study was undertaken in 1967–8. Only months
later sectarian conflict increased dramatically. In a subsequent paper
Boal (1972) speaks about the segregation in space more in terms of
conflict. The informal polarization of the two communities became
increasingly rigid, marked by walls, barricades and the exit/forcing
out of Protestants from Catholic areas and of Catholics from
Protestant areas. Security became one of the prime requirements of
physical planning in Belfast. Security walls were constructed between
the two communities. The shared space of the city became a divided
community as sectarian conflict increased. The separation of the communities was an attempt to minimize conflict, yet paradoxically it

helped to reinforce it. The walls and barricades polarized the two communities still further, and segregation increased, as did completely separate spatial activity patterns. The two communities became alienated from each other, strangers in a shared city.

Jerusalem is another example of a city shaped by competing ethnic groups. Jews and Arabs inhabit this ancient town. In the recent past, prior to 1967, the city was clearly divided into Jewish West Jerusalem and Arab East Jerusalem (figure 10.2). There were even two distinct central business districts. In effect, there were two cities. However, with the Israeli annexation of the West Bank from Jordan, East Jerusalem came under Israeli control. (Here I draw heavily upon the excellent study by Romann and Weingrod, 1991). One consequence was Jewish settlement into East Jerusalem. These "settlers" created a more patchwork pattern. They also increased tension. Urban space in both an economic and a symbolic sense became the setting and source of conflict between the Arabs and the Jews with, at least until 1993, Jewish settlers having the force of the Israeli state behind them. East Jerusalem became more Jewish. At the local scale high levels of segregation were maintained and reinforced. There were in effect no mixed neighborhoods: separate worlds in the same urban space. Parallel services were created. There were, for example, separate Arab and Jewish bus routes. They sometimes served different locations, but their main function was to serve the two different communities. The conditions and constraints were asymmetrical. Given the uneven distribution of economic activity, Arabs are obliged to travel into Jewish areas while Jews have more choice. Moreover, the whole setting is asymmetrical given the brute fact of Israeli control. The setting, timing, and nature of community interactions were set by Jewish control and power.

In their study Romann and Weingrod show the pattern of conflict and accommodation that characterizes such a deep cleavage. The title of their book, *Living Together Separately*, signals the ambiguity of confrontation and cooperation involved in the daily negotiation of living in a contested city. The division marks the very fabric of urban life:

> *Ethnic spatial divisions are also expressed in other ways: Hebrew versus Arab shop signs, different contents and styles in displaying merchandise, cafés occupied by the two sexes (in the Jewish sector) or by men only (in the Arab sections of the city), differently colored local buses. . . . The time dimension is also highly indicative, particularly with respect to the weekly Sabbath and annual round of holidays observed by Jews and Arabs. Friday noon dramatically illustrates the*

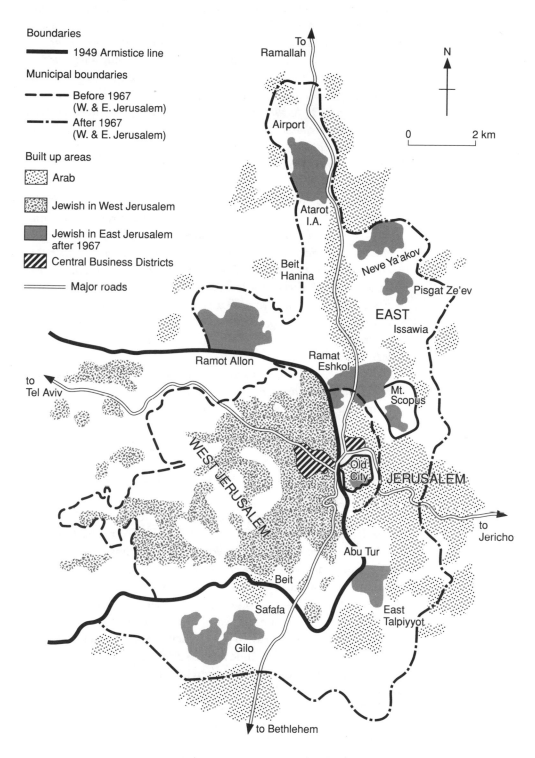

Figure 10.2 *Boundaries and ethnic areas in Jerusalem in 1990*
Source: *Romann and Weingrod (1991)*

coexistence of Jerusalem's two distinct worlds. Whereas in the commercial center of Jewish West Jerusalem streets, shops and cafés are at that moment packed with customers concluding their weekly activities on the verge of the Jewish Sabbath, less than a mile away the Old City alleys overflow with streams of traditional Muslims pouring out from the great mosque on the Temple Mount following the Friday noon prayer. On Saturdays and Jewish holidays when stores in West Jerusalem are closed and its commercial center is practically abandoned, bazaars and business districts in Arab East Jerusalem experience their peak activity and are crowded with Arabs, Jews and tourists . . .

Crossing the ethnic boundary is, for both Arabs and Jews, a highly conscious act that is normally done under specific circumstances and for well-defined purposes. Indeed, because of the deep spatial segregation of residential and business areas, interaction between members of the two communities necessarily involves crossing over to the other side. However, the practice of "open bridges" between the two city sections is complemented by the principle of "closed gates:" the substantial intermingling of the Arab–Jewish daytime population is followed by the general retreat and segregation of the same population at night . . .

. . . members of both communities have little information or knowledge regarding daily affairs and events on the "other side." Ethnic boundaries and barriers of estrangement are reflected in this division of perceptions, attitudes and behaviors: Jews and Arabs continue to live in different social worlds, each sharing life experiences largely ignored by, or unknown, to the other.

(Romann and Weingrod, 1991, 47, 49, 221–2)

Ethnic conflict is sometimes expressive of more general relations of power. In 1969–70 Belfast was a scene of social unrest. This was more than "ethnic" conflict between two opposing groups, it was a struggle for equal access to power by a Catholic minority who saw themselves as marginalized by a foreign power. In 1987 the *intifada* shook the grip of Israeli power on East Jerusalem as well as the other occupied territories. Again this was the expressed grievance of a population rendered powerless by what they saw as a foreign power. Ethnicity is tied to power. Indeed the social construction of ethnicity is an expression of both the exercise of power and the lack of power.

Illustration 10.2
*Jerusalem: street
scene in the Old
City (© Topham)*

THE CITY AND GENDER

Gender is a social construct as well as a biological fact. People are
born either as males or females; this is the biological fact. But the roles
that men and women perform and what it "means" to be a man or
a woman are social constructions. Space is crucial to these
constructions.

Feminist research

There has been an explosion of writings, debates, and arguments over
the past fifty years centering around an emerging feminist discourse.
A number of important themes can be identified. First, there has been
a large body of work concerned with making women's lives more
visible. It is the feminist equivalent of, and unique contribution to,
an alternative history and progressive geography that seeks to tell the
story of the powerless. A number of studies have pointed to the
underrepresentation of women's experience in the standard urban
geography literature. For example, one of the chapters in the book

Geography and Gender: An Introduction to Feminist Geography (Women and Geography Study Group, 1984) was explicitly concerned with the role of women in urban spatial structure. Much of this work raises themes previously ignored by (male) geographers, such as issues of domestic labor, work–home separation, and the living and working experience of women. I will give three brief examples.

- Traditional debates on the process of suburbanization failed to consider the gender bias at work, at least in middle-class suburbs, where the work–home separation had a distinct gender bias, with many women restricted to the domestic sphere.
- The bulk of domestic labor is performed by women, who also have primary responsibility for childrearing and childcare. This imposes considerable burdens on women who work both at home and in paid employment.
- Women are paid less than men and are overrepresented in the low-paid, part-time sectors of advanced economies. In the United States, for example, there has been a feminization of poverty.

Much of previous work focused on the public world; it concentrated on men's activities and ignored the role of women. This was partly a function of the male bias of the observers. In academia as in many other professions women are underrepresented.

There has been not just an empirical concern to address the male bias. The second theme has been a theoretical elaboration of the concept of patriarchy, which can be defined as a system of interrelated social structures, practices and ideologies through which men subordinate women. We can identify a number of ways in which the city in advanced capitalist countries embodies the operation of patriarchal power:

- gender-biased, work–home place separations both reflect and reinforce the linkage of femininity to domesticity. Women's responsibilities for domestic labor restrict their mobility and affect their access to employment opportunities, services, and facilities. The work of Hanson and Pratt (1988, 1991), for example, shows some of the links between domestic ties, locational restrictions, and the occupational segregation of women;
- the design and organization of urban space reinforces the sexual division of labor. The term "man-made city" is indicative of the

social construction of urban space, the male domination of the
design and planning professions, and in the very designs that
reinforce gender bias. In a broad historical sweep, Elizabeth
Wilson (1991) argues that what is wrong in the design of cities
is the masculine desire to control disorder and especially men's
need to control the "place" of women;

■ there are significant differences in the way women and men
experience the city. Women's use of urban space, for example, is
more constrained than men's because of the fear of male
violence. Women are more sensitive to the fear of sexual
violence, and this structures their behavior in many cities.
Strategies of individual safety include avoiding certain places at
certain times, going to certain places only when accompanied,
or not participating in an entire repertoire of activity, especially
at night. Gill Valentine (1989, 386), for example, contends that
"women are pressurised into a restricted use and occupation of
public space."

Feminist research has illuminated our view of the city. It has opened
up the discourse and uncovered ignored lives and muted voices. The
debate is ongoing: a number of points can be noted.

First, the notion of patriarchy is being refined. Crude notions of
patriarchy see its operation in all social structures, behaviors and attitudes that in turn are read off simply from the *a priori* existence of
patriarchy. This is a short circuit to intellectual advancement. It gives
the same ideological straitjacket as structural Marxism, incidentally
sharing the same certainty, all-encompassing theory, and messianic
vision. It focuses on grand structure and the role of women as passive
victims. More flexible positions focus on process and struggle and see
gender as a site of resistance and contestation as well as a setting for
subordination and oppression.

Second, the singular notion of feminism is being replaced by the
concept of feminisms. Subtle and not-so-subtle differences are
emerging. Theoretically there are those who link issues of patriarchy
to those of class conflict and racial struggle, while there are others
who see patriarchy as the primary object of study and as the political
adversary. These two sets of coordinates provide a very large graph
where current work is widely scattered: postmodern feminisms,
Marxist feminisms, libertarian feminisms. The categories are many.

Third, the simple, undifferentiated notion of "women" is being
revised. Women's experience of the city, for example, is different from
men's. This is a useful "first cut." But to look in more detail suggests that women of different ages, classes, and races have as many

differences as similarities. As with their male colleagues the class and race bias of feminist researchers, predominantly affluent, white, and middle-class, was and continues to be reflected in their work. Less naive conceptions of women that are now being operationalized are much more sensitive to differences in age, race, and class (see Katz and Monk, 1993; Peake, 1992). Some of the more interesting work in the future will highlight the tensions, connections and intersections between race, class, ethnicity, age, and gender.

Fourth, what strikes most observers of advanced capitalist cities is the changing and unstable nature of gender divisions. More women not only are in paid employment but are also moving up the corporate hierarchy. The so-called glass ceiling may exist, but the trajectories of some women, at least, seem to be upward. This is in stark contrast to the declining employment opportunities of manual workers in the manufacturing sectors. Gender and class are intersecting in some places and diverging in others to produce interesting and new forms of social differentiation. Liz Bondi (1992, 164–5), for example, writes with reference to gentrification:

> *In a UK context, the interconnections between class, gender and sexuality are nicely illustrated by the contrasting connotations of the wine bar and the pub: the former is metropolitan, middle-class, sexually integrated and more likely to be tolerant of, or at least not openly hostile towards, "alternative" expressions of sexuality; the latter is more likely to be local, working-class, sexually segregated and overtly sexist and heterosexist.*

Bondi argues that urban social change, such as gentrification, is both a reflection and an embodiment of changing gender and class relations. Deindustrialization, gentrification, impoverishment, the creation of a dual labor market, and the decline of urban public services, to name just a few, all have an effect on various ethnic, gender, and class groups. Indeed they help to determine the changing definition and demarcation of these groups.

Finally, the feminist critique will produce, albeit delayed and halting, a masculine response. Feminism has put gender on the agenda. The bulk of feminist writing, however, has been done by and for women with an explicit or implicit political agenda. It has been tied to the "women's movement." The great silence of the gender and geography debate is any full discussion of masculinities. This is a topic that will develop in the future only when men begin to probe their individual and collective identities. The emerging "men's movement," once it moves beyond the narrow and comforting niche of self-help and group encounter, will provide a major intellectual stimulus to our understanding of the world. Many questions await this perspective. The city as male space has been assumed rather than demonstrated, and what exactly is the male bias in urban planning? Does it exist? Does it represent only certain forms of maleness? These are questions that will be fully articulated only when men *qua* men begin to respond to the feminist critique with a wide-ranging discussion of masculinities. The discussion of gender has been biased toward women, whereas the position of men has been taken for granted or subsumed under uncritical and naive notions of male, men, and masculinity. The nuances, depth, and coloration of a full understanding of gender will come about only when men take a more critical and reflective view of their own social (re)construction and representation. This is a topic that will be discussed more fully in chapter 14.

THE CITY AND SEXUAL IDENTITY

Gender and sexuality are intertwined. Simple gender divisions differentiate between men and women. But this does not capture all the possible sexual orientations. There are also the sexualities of gay men, lesbians, and bisexuals. As with minority ethnic groups, communities of sexual dissidents can often be found in an urban setting, both as a form of defense and as a form of cultural expression.

Attitudes towards different sexualities vary enormously. In predominantly Judeo-Christian societies homosexuality is frowned upon and in some cases is illegal. There is a wide spectrum of heterosexual response, from gay bashing to acceptance to support. Where and when homosexuality is disowned, homosexuals either have to live hidden lives, their sexuality not openly practiced or only admitted in the form of communities of resistance. These communities vary from the small spaces of escape, which include the one gay bar in the small heterosexual town, to the gay neighborhood in the metropolitan city. One tends to be furtive and marginalized, the other a more open celebration of sexual difference. In his book *States of Desire: Travels in Gay America* (1980) the writer Edmund White gives a marvellous descriptive account of the variety of gay communities around the United States. In some places gay communities are part of the rich mosaic of social difference, in others they are sporadic sites of resistance.

Three strands can be identified in the concern with sexuality and space. First, there is a large body of literature that describes lesbian and gay spaces, ranging from the single sites (such as gay bars), to gay neighborhoods and "gay" cities such as San Francisco and West Hollywood where homosexuality has almost become the sexual norm rather than the sexual other (see Adler and Brenner, 1992). Second, particular attention has been paid to the relationship between gays and gentrification. For good reason. In some major cities there was a substantial involvement of the gay community in gentrification. In Sydney's Paddington district, for example, small houses close to the city center were progressively abandoned by nuclear families as they moved to the suburbs. Gay households tended to be smaller in size and put more emphasis on accessibility to the range of urban services. It became possible to create a neighborhood of tolerance away from the more judgemental heterosexual suburban communities. Lauria and Knopp (1985, 161) suggest:

> *Gays, in essence, have seized an opportunity to combat oppression by creating neighborhoods over which they have maximum control and which meet long neglected needs.*

Finally, there has been a small but growing literature on the city as a setting for sexual encounters. Cities are places where people congregate, interact, meet, and touch each other. For a variety of reasons, including repression, prudery, and embarrassment, urban scholars have rarely accorded this element its true importance. With the more open discussion of sexual matters, however, the link between sexual desire and the city will become much more central. Topics may include an examination of the spaces for different sexual expression, the link between private and public sex, the city as pleasure machine. For example, in an interesting paper David Bell (1993) considers the spaces and politics of sexually dissident male homosexuality. The link between geography and sex is a fascinating topic and one that is sure to attract further attention. The group of papers assembled by Bell and Valentine (1995) suggests the richness to be added to our knowledge of the city by considering the connections between space, sex, identities, and communities.

SETTINGS FOR EXPLOITATION, SITES OF RESISTANCE

In this chapter I have considered four sources of social differentiation: class, ethnicity, gender, and sexual preference. They are some of the most important, though not the only, dimensions of difference. I have, for example, said nothing about age, health, or physical and mental abilities and characteristics.

The terms themselves are not simple, or easy, to use. The problem cannot be solved by a linguistic analysis. The fuzziness of their meaning is an important part of their character; they are textual chameleons, constantly changing, always transforming, suffused with ambiguity and imprecision.

They are not only sources of differentiation, they are also sources of exploitation. Class, ethnicity, gender, and sexual orientation mark people out from one another. But these distinctions are not innocent. To be black in a white city, or working class in a capitalist city, or a woman in a man-made city, or a gay in a predominantly straight town, is to be in a subordinate position that affects your life chances. It is also to be located in a set of cultural values in which some experiences are seen as more important, are used as the standard against which others are measured and evaluated, and are taken as the norm to define deviancy and difference.

Some fruitless discussions have been pursued to find the primary source of exploitation. Marxists tend to focus on class, feminists on gender, minority scholars on ethnicity, and gays and lesbians on sexuality. There is no one answer, it depends on the observer. For white working-class males it is class, for middle-class white women it is gender, for many middle-class black males it is race, and for white gays it is sexual orientation. There is no one compelling

The social arena

Illustration 10.3
Castro street fair in San Francisco. Castro is a predominantly gay neighborhood in a city known for its tolerance of various sexual orientations (© Sunil Gupta/Network)

Illustration 10.4
Squatters in Groningen, the Netherlands, resist gentrification. An artistic call to arms in this Dutch city seeks the destruction of the yuppie city (photograph: author)

answer for everyone. What is more interesting is how the various sources of differentiation intersect and connect to produce a variety of communities.

These differences are not just settings for exploitation, they are also sites of resistance. Throughout this chapter I have sought to show how these sources of difference produce communities of resistance in which the other becomes the norm, where differences become a source of celebration as well as of cultural expression. Class, ethnicity, gender, and sexual preference provide sources of resistance that contest the prevailing norms. Such communities can be seen as a lens of refraction through which the periphery is focused to become the center.

GUIDE TO FURTHER READING

On the city and class, see:

Abercrombie, N. and Urry, J. (1983) *Capital, Labour and the Middle Classes*, London: Allen & Unwin.

Braverman, H. (1974) *Labor and Monopoly Capital*, New York: Monthly Review Press.

Davis, M. (1990) *City of Quartz*, London: Verso.

Goldthorpe, J., Lockwood, D., Bechofer, F. and Platt, J. (1969) *The Affluent Worker in the Class Structure*, Cambridge: Cambridge University Press.

Gottdiener, M. (1987) *The Decline of Urban Politics*, Beverly Hills, Cal.: Sage.

Joyce, P. (1980) *Work, Society and Politics: The Culture of the Factory in Late Victorian England*, London: Methuen.

Leeds, A. (1994) *City, Classes and the Social Order*, Ithaca, N.Y.: Cornell University Press.

Ley, D. (1994) Gentrification and the politics of the new middle class, *Environment and Planning D: Society and Space* 12, 53–74.

Logan, J.R. and Molotch, H.L. (1987) *Urban Fortunes: The Political Economy of Place*, Los Angeles, Cal.: University of California Press.

Phillips, K. (1993) *Boiling Point: Democrats, Republicans, and the Decline of Middle-class Prosperity*, New York: Random House.

Reich, R. (1991) *The Work of Nations*, New York: Alfred A. Knopf.

Williams, R. (1976) *Keywords*, Glasgow: Fontana.

On the underclass, consider:

Duneier, M. (1992) *Slim's Table: Race, Respectability and Masculinity*, Chicago, Ill.: University of Chicago Press.

Jencks, C. and Peterson, P. (eds) (1991) *The Urban Underclass*, Washington, D.C.: Brookings Institution.

Lemann, N. (1991) *The Promised Land: The Great Black Migration and How It Changed America*, New York: Alfred A. Knopf.

Murray, C. (1984) *Losing Ground*, New York: Basic Books.

Wilson, W.J. (1987) *The Truly Disadvantaged: The Inner City, the Underclass and Public Policy*, Chicago, Ill.: University of Chicago Press.

The following studies look at different aspects of the city and ethnicity:

Anderson, K.J. (1987) The idea of Chinatown: the power of place and institutional practice in the making of a racial category, *Annals of the Association of American Geographers* 77, 580–98.

Anderson, K. (1991) *Vancouver's Chinatown: Racial Discourse in Canada, 1875–1980*, Montreal: McGill-Queens University Press.

Boal, F.W. (1968) Territoriality on the Shankill–Falls divide, Belfast, *Irish Geography* 6, 30–50.

Boal, F.W. (1972) The urban residential sub-community: a conflict interpretation, *Area* 4, 164–8.

Keith, M. and Cross, M. (1993) Racism and the postmodern city. In M. Keith and M. Cross (eds) *Racism and the City*, London: Routledge.

Lemon, A. (ed.) (1991) *Homes Apart: South Africa's Segregated Cities*, London: Chapman & Hall.

Romann, M. and Weingrod, A. (1991) *Living Together Separately*, Princeton, N.J.: Princeton University Press.

Western, J. (1981) *Outcast Cape Town*, Minneapolis: University of Minnesota Press.

Western, J. (1992) *A Passage to England*, Minneapolis: University of Minnesota Press.

Yinger, J.M. (1986) Intersecting strands in the theorization of race and ethnic relations. In J. Rex and D. Mason (eds), *Theories of Race and Ethnic Relations*, Cambridge: Cambridge University Press.

Zucchi, J. (1988) *Italians in Toronto: Development of a National Community*, Kingston, Ontario: McGill-Queens University Press.

In the section on the city and patriarchy I have drawn heavily upon:

Peake, L. (1992) Challenging the patriarchal structuring of urban social space? Gender, "race," class and sexuality. Seminar delivered to Geography Department, Syracuse University, February 14.

For only a small sample of the material on gender and the city, consider:

Bondi, L. (1992) Gender symbols and urban landscapes, *Progress in Human Geography* 16(2), 157–70.

Hanson, S. (1992) Geography and feminism: worlds in collision, *Annals of the Association of American Geographers* 82(4), 569–86.

Hanson, S. and Pratt, G. (1988) Reconceptualizing the link between home and work in human geography, *Economic Geography* 64(4), 300–21.

Hanson, S. and Pratt, G. (1991) Job search and the occupational segregation of women, *Annals of the Association of American Geographers* 81(2), 229–53.

Katz, C. and Monk, J. (eds) (1993) *Full Circles: Geographies of Women over the Life Cycle*, London: Routledge.

Kobayashi, A. (ed.) (1994) *Women, Work and Place*, Toronto: McGill-Queens University Press.

Massey, D. (1994) *Space, Place and Gender*, London: Verso.

Matrix (1984) *Making Space: Women and the Man-made Environment*, London: Pluto.

Valentine, G. (1989) The geography of women's fear, *Area* 21(4), 385–90.

Wilson, E. (1991) *The Sphinx in the City*, London: Virago.

Women and Geography Study Group (1984) *Geography and Gender: An Introduction to Feminist Geography*, London: Hutchinson.

On the relationship between sexual desire and space, consider:

Adler, S. and Brenner, J. (1992) Gender and space: lesbians and gay men in the city, *International Journal of Urban and Regional Research* 16(1), 24–34.

Bell, D. (1991) Insignificant others: lesbian and gay geographies, *Area* 23, 323–9.

Bell, D. (1993) Citizenship and the politics of pleasure. Paper presented to the Institute of British Geographers Annual Conference, University of London, January 7.

Bell, D. and Valentine, G. (eds) (1995) *Mapping Desire: Geographies of Desire*, London: Routledge.

Lauria, M. and Knopp, L. (1985) Toward an analysis of the role of gay communities in the urban renaissance, *Urban Geography* 6(2), 152–69.

White, E. (1980) *States of Desire: Travels in Gay America*, New York: E.P. Dutton.

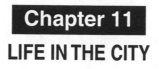

Chapter 11
LIFE IN THE CITY

LIVING IN THE CITY, ONE FINDS ONESELF UNCONSCIOUSLY SLIPPING INTO MAGICAL HABITS OF MIND.

JONATHAN RABAN, *SOFT CITY* (1974)

THE SOUL OF THE CITY WAS ALWAYS MY SUBJECT AND IT WAS ROILING SOUL, TWISTING AND TURNING OVER ON ITSELF, FORMING AND REFORMING, GATHERING INTO ITSELF AND OPENING OUT LIKE BLOWN WIND.

E.L. DOCTOROW, *THE WATERWORKS* (1994)

In the previous chapters we looked at the city with an impersonal eye. In this chapter I want to look at the city as a place where ordinary people lead their lives and make their way. Three themes will be considered:

■ getting by;
■ the city as stage;
■ citizens as space–time travelers.

GETTING BY

One of the brute facts of life is that, apart from a lucky few, most people or, more accurately, households, need to make an income in order to live. Income can come from inherited money, investment sources and, for the majority of people, employment. With regard to employment, we can make a distinction between the formal and the informal economy.

Formal employment

Who we are is a function of what we do. It is one of the first questions asked of people: What do you do? Formal employment connects our private and public selves.

Employment in the formal sector involves the sale of labor in the marketplace, formally recorded in government and official statistics.

This employment provides income, status, and identity. Unless you are fortunate enough to have inherited large amounts of money, then, like most people, you will need a job to provide an income. The income from employment pays for both the necessities and the luxuries of life. The more money you have the better housing you can afford, the bigger the car you can drive, and the more expensive the clothes you can wear. Differences in income are expressed in modes of life and forms of consumption.

Differences in employment income are related to the supply and demand for different types of labor. When and where there is a large demand and limited supply, the price of labor increases. Conversely, when there is limited demand and a big supply then the bargaining power of labor is decreased and the resultant income is less. To this simple model has to be added a number of intervening factors: the state of the general economy, the rate of technological change, which creates new forms of supply and demand, and the ability of labor to control the supply of labor and the work process. Labor that lacks skills has a weaker position than labor with skills. The more valuable the skills for employers then the greater the bargaining power of labor. These differences are expressed in the greater income of skilled workers compared with nonskilled workers.

The skills required in the marketplace are constantly changing. The most important shift in recent years has been the deskilling of much manual employment. The skills of a manual workforce in an advanced economy are no longer the trade secrets of the boilermaker, the welder, or the metalcraft worker. These have been replaced by automation, robotics, and standardized industrial production techniques. Flexible production involves a reduction in the demand and hence in the bargaining power of skilled manual workers. More recently, there has also been a reduction in the need for many of the skills of the white-collar workers. Office automation, the greater use of computers, the shift in management practices, and the streamlining of the executive hierarchy have all produced a decline in the need for white-collar labor. The net effect has been to create a distinct core-periphery structure in the contemporary labor market (figure 11.1). The core consists of well-paid workers enjoying employment security, training, and generous fringe benefits. This is the world of the business lunch, the seat in the business section of the aircraft, the keys to the executive suite; this is the world of affluence. There are two kinds of semiperiphery. The first consists of full-time workers with less status, permanence, and prestige. The second group are people on short-term or part-time contracts. The periphery consists of those in self-employment, subcontractors, and those who work from home or

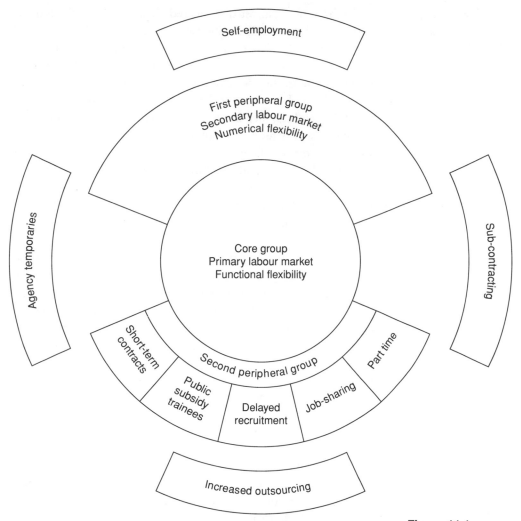

Self-employment

First peripheral group
Secondary labour market
Numerical flexibility

Agency temporaries

Sub-contracting

Core group
Primary labour market
Functional flexibility

Short-term contracts

Public subsidy trainees

Second peripheral group

Delayed recruitment

Job-sharing

Part time

Increased outsourcing

Figure 11.1
Labor market structures under conditions of flexible accumulation
Source: After *Institute of Personnel Management (1986)*

through employment agencies. The rise of the semiperiphery and periphery has many implications for the bargaining power of labor and the very experience of work. On the one hand, flexible systems allow people to spend more time in the home and with the family. This is in contrast to core workers whose life, especially family life, may be subordinate to their work. On the other, workers in the periphery and semiperiphery are often separated one from another. David Harvey (1989), for example, points to the vitiation of class consciousness and collective experience by the increase in the more atomized, individualized forms of work.

Labor needs skills to have more power in the marketplace, but a reliance on too-specific skills will allow technological changes to render certain skills redundant. The skills of the bootmaker and the hatmaker have now almost disappeared. It is also advantageous for labor to control the supply of labor and, indeed, as many of the work practices as possible. One of the most successful fractions of labor is the medical profession. Doctors claim a monopoly over debates about health and healing; they control the entry of new recruits, and have insinuated themselves into a position of power and prestige which is reflected in their high income. Few other skilled nonmanual workers have been so successful in controlling their area of work and remuneration. Doctors are the exception. Teachers, in contrast, have less control over the supply and entry into the profession. The result has been a steady shift in the supply–demand relationship and a corresponding deterioration in comparative living standards between doctors and teachers over the past 30 years in most advanced countries.

Employment is more than just a source of income. It provides meaning and identity. People are defined by the job they perform. Occupations vary in their status and remuneration: some jobs have both high status and high remuneration, for example medical specialists; while others have high remuneration but less prestige, for example manual workers earning lots of money through long hours and high performance; while yet others have better status but less money, for example teachers. Occupations provide more than just the means of life; they represent success and failure, prestige, relative rank, power, and influence.

Who fills which positions in the occupational structure is not a random process. Social patterns of differentiation are created and maintained through employment. Gender differences are embodied in patterns of employment: women are overrepresented in the part-time, low-paid sector, and even when in the same employment women are paid less than two-thirds of the male rate. Ethnic differences are also reflected in occupational structure. Recent migrants to a city often fill the role of a reserve army of labor, performing the low-paid jobs that no one else wants. In a fascinating book a journalist exposed the appalling working conditions of Turkish immigrants in Germany (Wallraff, 1988). It is a sad story of racism and exploitation. There is also the existence of so-called ethnic entrepreneurs. This term is used with reference to such groups as Koreans in the United States and Indians and Pakistanis in Canada and the United Kingdom. These groups are overrepresented in the small, family business sector. For ambitious households with strong family ties and obligations, a family business allows sweat equity to be used in a new society in a work environment that maintains and reinforces extended family structures.

Social differences are also expressed in employment patterns. This observation can lead to a circular form of reasoning. Poor people are poor because they are in low-paid jobs. Wealthy people have highly paid jobs. These are truisms that do not provide any causal mechanism. It is much more important to look at how certain groups both get and maintain certain jobs. Entry into formal employment is controlled by systemic requirements such as educational qualifications, which in turn reflect and reinforce the existing bases of inequality. To become a doctor, for example, it is necessary to go to college, to forgo income in the short to medium term. Some groups, especially the wealthier segments of society, are much more able than others to pursue such a strategy for themselves and their children. There is also a controlling culture that decides who is appropriate for certain types of jobs. Racial, social, and gender discrimination act as barriers to certain groups and allow easy entry for others. In an interesting study the British sociologist Paul Willis (1978) posed the question: Why do working-class kids get working-class jobs? Part of the answer, he showed, was in their culture of resistance to the formal education system. By rejecting the ladder of educational attainment as a dominant force in their life they doomed themselves to educational mediocrity and hence to limited job opportunities. By their rejection they were accepting a limited horizon of employment opportunity.

Employment is one of the central experiences of our public life. It provides us with money, meaning, identity, social relationships, and a major intersection of shared and private experiences. Because employment is so important the lack of employment can be a devastating blow; not only as loss of income but also as loss of meaning. Jeremy Seabrook (1981) looked at the experience of long-term unemployment in Britain in the late 1970s and early 1980s, a time when unemployment was fast approaching 3 million people. His book records the destruction of a sense of purpose and meaning, the loss of a sense of indispensability. Seabrook was at pains to draw a contrast between the contemporary experience of unemployment and the previous time of mass unemployment in Britain during the 1930s. He noted that, while people are now materially better off than in the 1930s, their position was still dire. Unemployment was a profoundly corrosive experience in the modern period because it was experienced individually; it was not a shared predicament but a private grief. An addictive dependency on affluence meant the private inability to purchase consumer durables and created a state of captive dependency rather than the basis for group mobilization. To an extent Seabrook idealizes the experience of unemployment in the 1930s and has a naive view of working-class culture. He looks back to a golden age of shared community values that owes more to nostalgia than careful analysis. His book, however, manages to convey the tragedy of unemployment, especially when experienced as a private failing rather than the basis for social mobilization.

Informal economy

The informal economy is the unrecorded sector where few, if any, taxes are paid. This sector is just as complex as the formal sector. Based on his work in Latin American cities, Ray Bromley (1988), for example, identifies nine different sectors. These include retail distribution, small-scale transport, personal services, security services, gambling services, recycling enterprises, prostitution, begging, and property crimes involving illegal appropriation through stealth (theft), the threat or use of violence (robbery) or deception (conning). Work conditions vary from short-term wage-work to precarious self-employment. The workers in this sector may be disguised wage-workers (that is, they are paid a wage but it is not recorded), workers on short-term wage-work, dependent workers (who may lease a personal transport vehicle from an employer), and the self-employed. In his work in the city of Cali, Bromley found that 40 to 45 percent of people who worked in the street were in precarious self-employment, 39 to 43 percent were disguised wage-workers, 12 to 15 percent were dependent workers, and only 3 percent were short-term wage-workers.

A great deal has been written about the informal sector. Cheng and Gereffi (1994) identify three different approaches to this sector in the last 25 years (table 11.1). While the emphasis has varied over the years, there has been a consistent concern with the dynamics of the sector. The informal sector can be seen as a sophisticated response to the lack of formal employment opportunities. Nici Nelson (1988), for example, provides a discussion on the sexual division of labor in the informal sector of the squatter settlement Mathare in the city of Nairobi. She shows that maize beer brewing and prostitution, although illegal, are rational choices for many women in the area. There is a demand for them and few other employment opportunities. Moreover, the work is done in the home, which enables the women to care for their children. Nelson (1988, 188) notes, "Women manipulate the various kinds of sexual relationships to maximize their economic security in the urban area."

The divisions between the formal and informal sectors fluctuate according to circumstance. When the formal economy provides many employment opportunities that provide a good living, then the

TABLE 11.1 THREE APPROACHES TO THE INFORMAL ECONOMY

	Social marginality	*State regulation*	*Small firms*
Chronology	1970s	1980s	Late 1980s and 1990s
Disciplinary approach	Economic demography	Political economy	Social economy
Analytical focus	Urban poverty	Legality of economic activities	Social embeddedness of economic activities
Level of analysis	Demographic shifts, uneven industrialization, and their consequences for social marginality	Legal regulation of production with reference to class politics and economic restructuring	Interaction between local social networks and the resource environment of small firms
Key concepts	Social reproduction imperative; job creation; demographic mobility; income opportunities; overurbanization; collective consumption	Bureaucratization; class politics; labor control; industrial structure; sectoral linkages; capital movement; economic restructuring	Entrepreneurship; domestic subcontracting; social reciprocity; resource mobilization; opportunity structure
Terminological preference	"Informal sector"	"Informal economy"	"Informalization"

Source: After Cheng and Gereffi (1994)

informal sector becomes less significant. However, if the formal sector provides few jobs or only jobs with low wages then the informal sector can be seen as a sophisticated coping strategy. Even when someone in the household is working, as Alan Gilbert (1992, 85) notes with reference to employment in many South American cities:

hours are long and exacting, and most jobs are very badly paid. Such workers cannot afford health care for their families, diet is inadequate, most struggle to survive. With men unable to increase their wages, despite working longer and longer hours, wives and children contrive to augment family incomes in a variety of ways. They sell chewing gum on street corners, they clean shoes, they wash cars, they recycle all kinds of scrap. The informal sector is very often highly organized. Dealers employ whole teams of young boys to scour garbage dumps for anything of value, and street vendors jealously guard the best pitches.

Illustration 11.1
*Street hawkers,
Solelo, Guatemala.
People use a
variety of tactics to
make a living
(© Environmental
Picture Library/Sue
Ford)*

Illegal informal economy The informal economy involves transactions which are not recorded: sometimes, because they are illegal. This is the shadowy world of prostitution, selling illegal drugs, racketeering and the like. It is difficult to estimate its full extent. We can note, however, parallels with the formal economy. There is a similar size distribution of enterprises, with the Mafia and organized-crime syndicates comparable with IBM and General Motors in economic strength and market share, tailing off to the small, one-person independents struggling to maintain a market niche. There is also the same cyclical nature, with good years and bad years, and a similar pattern of investment and disinvestment that one finds in the formal sector: prohibition in the United States, for example, inflated the demand for alcohol by limiting its supply, and the result was that alcohol production and distribution became a source of huge profits and attracted the interest and business practices of organized crime.

Much of the informal illegal sector consists of the production and distribution of goods and services of which there is a demand but which have been made illegal. The demarcation of legal–illegal varies: alcohol is not illegal in the United States but cocaine is; prostitution is legal and regulated in both Germany and the Netherlands but is illegal in the United States; one can buy marijuana in Amsterdam without breaking the law, but the same transaction in New York would be considered criminal. The "economy" of the illegal informal economy arises because there is a demand for certain goods and services; the "illegal" comes from the matrix of cultural values and political rhetoric which makes some things legal and others illegal.

There is no hard and fast line between the formal and illegal sector. The line between legal and illegal is constantly being crossed: police who take bribes; chemical companies that illegally dump waste; corporations that form illegal cartels to charge high prices to the federal government. The distinction between the three sectors, formal, informal, and illegal, is at times fuzzy. Rather than look at the differences, a more stimulating strategy may be to look at how transactions criss and cross the arbitrary lines. I have already noted the investigative work by Wallraff. In his exposé of immigrant work practices in what was then West Germany he showed at one point how a chemical company used Turkish workers in an unrecorded transaction to undertake illegal waste disposal: formal, informal, and illegal intersecting in the one transaction.

The communal economy   This economy involves the cashless exchange of goods and services. It is common in neighborhoods and extended family systems. I can illustrate with an example. If a couple wants a baby-sitter for an evening they have a number of possibilities: they can hire someone and record the transaction and pay taxes (the formal economy); they can hire a teenager and pay them an agreed sum without informing the authorities (the informal sector); or they can ask a neighbor, giving the clear understanding that they will return the favor. The last, and often the most common, response is an example of the communal economy in action. It can range from reciprocal favors, such as baby-sitting, grass-cutting and garbage removal, to a host of household chores from building maintenance to car pooling.

The extent of the communal economy can change over time and will vary by context. A classic study undertaken by Michael Young and Peter Wilmott (1957) examined a working-class neighborhood in East London. They found that the strong, extended family system, the overlapping connection of many of the families, in association with a precarious employment situation, led to a very subtle and complex communal economy. They did a follow-up study of similar households that had moved to a new town in the country. The break-up of the extended family, the better employment opportunities, and the rising level of individual household affluence led to a decline in the communal economy. Young and Wilmott describe this change as one from a people-centered to a house-centered existence.

Two competing trends are at work in the communal economy. On

Illustration 11.2
(a) São Paulo, Brazil; (b) Shanty houses built over the sea.

the one hand there is the decline in the traditional communal economy associated with the breakdown of the extended family system in many societies. On the other hand there is an increase in newer models of the communal economy as many households, especially child-oriented households, are so stretched for time that certain forms of community adaptation have taken place, from informal baby-sitting circles to car pools. This communal economy links households with shared needs and constraints, albeit belonging to different families.

The communal economy both condenses and reflects the strength of community ties. These tend to be strongest when there is a distinct sense of shared identity (and this could be based on family ties, ethnicity, gender, status, or income). The communal economy allows

informal obligations and rights to be spread in a net of mutual ties and benefits.

The domestic economy   Return to the baby-sitting example cited in the previous section: if the couple get an older sibling to look after a younger child then this is an example of the domestic economy. The domestic economy is the amount, type, and division of labor within the home.

In the affluent world, and throughout much of the rest, a dominant trend has been the commodification of the household economy.

More and more goods and services previously undertaken by households themselves are not part of the formal economy. Where households used to preserve their produce they now increasingly buy it from stores. Where households used to decorate their own homes they employ a professional decorator, and where they used to sit round a fire and sing songs or tell stories they now cluster around the television screen or the computer game.

This commodification involves a trade-off. It is much easier to use a washing machine than to wash by hand. Domestic appliances "save" time in one sense. However, they have to be paid for, time has to be spent at work to pay for them. Time is spent in order to save time.

The division of labor within the household economy has also changed over the years. A hundred years ago there was much greater use of paid domestic labor. The increasing cost of labor has meant the decline of mass domestic labor though it still persists amongst the wealthy, and in the rich countries a high proportion of such work is done by foreign, vulnerable, and illegal workers.

Within the household the division of labor is a source of change, conflict, and negotiation. As more women have joined the formal labor force they feel the double demand of work and home because they carry much of the domestic load. It is not too fanciful to link the contemporary feminist movement with the rising resentment against two workloads. The division of domestic labor is not simply an apportionment of necessary work. It involves questions and representations of femininity, masculinity, and the family.

Household resources and strategies

There is a range of resources available to households. The sociologist Enzo Mingione (1987) provides a classification (table 11.2). Income from the formal economy is just one of the resources. The mix of resources varies. For households with good formal employment there will be less need for the others. In countries with generous state subsidies the quality of household life will not just be a function of private income. Households with few formal opportunities either from the market or the state have to rely on the informal economy.

The strategies available to a household will depend on the resources. A household with a large income from the formal economy will not have to sell cigarettes on the street corner. A household with few formal opportunities, in contrast, thus has to look at alternative sources. To get by, households will adopt a variety of coping strategies in order to extend the range of resources available to them.

	Internal: produced by the households themselves	External: contributed by the state, extended family, friends, self-help networks
TABLE 11.2 CLASSIFICATION OF SURVIVAL RESOURCES ENTERING THE REPRODUCTION MIX OF HOUSEHOLDS		
Formal market monetary resources	Income deriving from various forms of formal employment	State income subsidies Inheritances Formal donations & gifts Other formal subsidies
Monetary resources deriving from outside the formal market	Income deriving from various forms of informal or traditional employment activities	Informal donations, loans, subsidies Gifts Exchange of work
Nonmonetary resources	Domestic activities Work for self-consumption & do-it-yourself Self Service	State services Donations in work for direct consumption or in kind directly produced by the donors Free communal assistance

Source: After Mingione (1987)

THE CITY AS STAGE

There is a variety of metaphors to characterize life in the city. We can see it as a journey, a dance, an odyssey and, using the title of a novel by Franz Kafka, we can see it as a trial. If you have ever been stuck in traffic in hot, humid weather after a frustrating, exasperating day then Kafka's title always seems the most appropriate. In the next section I will examine how we can use the idea of a journey. In this section I want to develop just one theme, and that is the city as stage. I draw heavily upon the work of Erving Goffman. In his book *The Presentation of Self in Everyday Life* (1959) Goffman develops the notion of social activity as a performance. The messages we give about ourselves vary by the performances we enact. Goffman develops spatial metaphors of front stage and back stage. Front stage is where performances are enacted, back stage is where the props are stored. performances vary with setting. Front stage we are keen to give a good impression, back stage we can relax. Goffman uses the example of waiters and waitresses in a restaurant. In public they are deferential and considerate to the customers and move with an unhurried grace. In the kitchen there is frenzied activity, criticism of their customers, and general backbiting.

To see social interaction as a drama unlocks a rich vein of metaphors: image, theme, plot, script, roles, back-stage, protagonist, and audience. These can all be utilized to describe and explain social interactions. To be more precise, these interactions are sociospatial. They all *take place*. They occur in a spatial setting. Space is not just backdrop. Space and place are crucial to what performances are given and how they are received. Edward Hall (1959) speaks about space as the silent language, a crucial element in our communication of messages. In a fascinating book, Joshua Meyrowitz (1985) argues that the widespread use of electronic media has distorted the traditional relationship between space and communication. He argues, for example, that status and authority consist, in part, in hiding back-stage behavior. The media allow us to see the back-stage behavior of those in positions of power. The results are rarely flattering. When Richard Nixon released his tapes of private discussions in the White House in early 1972 many people were appalled at the language. The difference between back-stage and front-stage behavior is most marked for those in greatest authority. Back-stage visibility can lead to decline of authority.

We can picture the city as a variety of settings all with differences in appropriate behavior. We move from shop to subway, from work environment to one of recreation and leisure. As we move through these different places we enact new performances, we play a variety of roles from consumer to commuter, and from worker to player.

Goffman's work has been used in many urban ethnographies that focus on behavior and social interaction. In his book *Streetwise* (1990), Elijah Anderson discusses two neighborhoods in Philadelphia where he lived from 1975 until 1989: the Village, an area of gentrification, and Northton, a predominantly black area badly affected by job losses and rising drug use. Their proximity leads to the sharing of the public space of the streets by very different groups. Anderson looks at the negotiation of public spaces by the different communities. For the middle-class whites and blacks

the central strategy in maintaining safety on the streets is to avoid strange black males. The public awareness is color-coded: white skin denotes civility, law-abidingness, and trustworthiness, while black skin is strongly associated with poverty, crime, incivility, and distrust.

Thus an unknown young black male is readily deferred to. If he asks for anything, he must be handled quickly and summarily. If he is persistent, help must be summoned. (Anderson, 1990, 208)

The different groups, when passing through the public space of the streets, learn different cues, scripts, and performances. The street is a stage and the goal is to ensure a happy ending. Anderson consciously draws upon Goffman to inform his detailed study of how class and race interact and intersect in the streets.

Sociospatial interaction is dynamic, constantly changing, subject to ephemeral contingencies. Susan Smith, using the concepts of plot, script, and performance in her work, describes one encounter in the inner city of Birmingham, England:

The police officers seemed to stiffen their walk and move closer together. One twitched his hand towards what might have been a radio, and both fixed their eyes on the oncoming group with the consequence that their subsequent conversation spilled melodramatically from the sides of their mouths. The effect was to reframe a leisurely stroll into a display of professionalism. The young, in turn, exaggerated their usual bounce into what could have been construed as a swagger. They talked more loudly and gesticulated more often. A frame orientated towards fun slipped into one characterized by ritual demonstration . . . as the groups moved closer and one officer's request for a chip was laughingly answered with the flash of an empty packet, a friendly shrug of the shoulders was sufficient to dispel the atmosphere of confrontation and replace it with one of amiable sparring. (Smith, 1988, 31–2)

Urban ethnographies of this kind can do much to illuminate our understanding of social interaction; they extend our understanding of the subtle links between communication and space. However, there seems to be a bias toward the poor, the marginalized, and the inner city. I have already made comments about this bias reflecting and reinforcing the power relationship between the observer and the observed. Let me note again that we have rather fewer studies of the rich, the powerful, and those in authority. The techniques of ethnography and Goffman's overall structure are powerful conceptual tools, but they are not being fully developed if they are only used on the poor.

The city as journey

The city can also be seen as the setting for a journey. From Homer's *Odyssey* to Bunyan's *Pilgrim's Progress* and Saul Bellow's *Adventures of Augie March*, the notion of the journey as a metaphor of life's progress has been a continual theme in creative renderings of the human condition. The modern detective story, for example, is an important genre which provides a transect through the social landscape of the city and indicates the connections between high and low life, wealth and poverty, light and dark, good and evil.

CITIZENS AS SPACE–TIME TRAVELERS

In this section, however, I want to take the notion of journey more literally. We can begin by looking at the notation devised by the Swedish geographer Torsten Hagerstrand (1970) in association with his colleagues at the University of Lund. They started off from the basic position that people move through time and space. Space is timed and time is spaced. Figure 11.2 shows how the two coordinates of space and time can be used to plot space–time paths. Figure 11.2(b) notes the co-location in time and space as four schoolchildren come together in school. The case of (c) shows co-location in

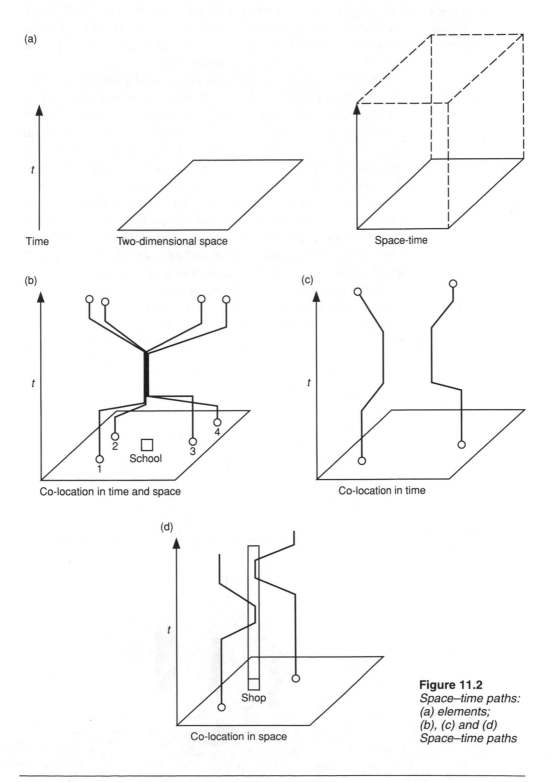

Figure 11.2
Space–time paths:
(a) elements;
(b), (c) and (d)
Space–time paths

(a)

t

Time

Two-dimensional space

Space-time

(b)

t

1

2

School

3

4

Co-location in time and space

(c)

t

Co-location in time

(d)

t

Shop

Co-location in space

255

time, an example being two people who have the same work hours but different work places. Space–time paths of individuals and places can also be recorded. In (d) we can see the pattern of two people shopping at the same store at different times.

Our activities in the city are anchored around a number of recurring activities. Every weekday most people have to go to work or school. These are the *pegs* on which we hang our journey through time and space. At any one time we have a range of available space in which we can travel. These are termed *prisms*. They are shown diagrammatically in figure 11.3 with reference to the lunch hour of two office workers. B has access to a car while A does not. B can travel further in the available time and thus has a larger prism. Pegs and prisms are the constraints under which we operate. Figure 11.4 shows the prism of one person and three available jobs. The three solid blocks A, B and C are the times of available jobs. In this case jobs A and C are outside the person's prism and thus unavailable.

We can put together the pegs and prisms of one person's journey through one urban day. Figure 11.5 shows the space–time path of one person, let us call her Josephine Doe. She wakes up at 7 a.m. She does not start work until 9 a.m. so this gives her some time and space. Between 9 a.m. and 5 p.m. she has to be at work so she is fixed in both time and space, with a small opportunity over her lunch break. She returns home by 7 p.m. and has a limited prism before going to

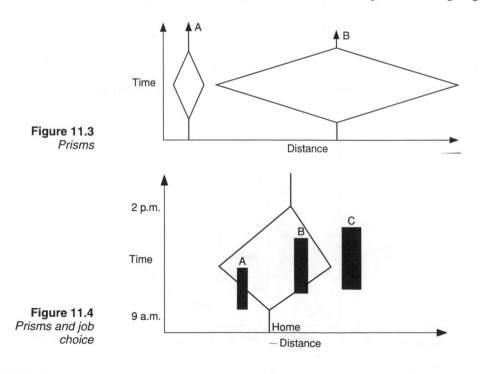

Figure 11.3
Prisms

Figure 11.4
Prisms and job choice

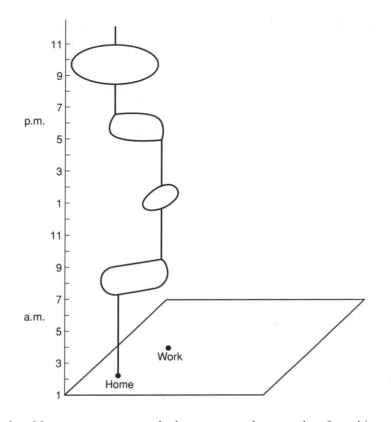

Figure 11.5
Pegs and prisms

bed at 11 p.m., to get enough sleep to start the next day. Stated in these terms the space–time paths we follow have a repetitious feel to them and a severe limitation. Some people are more limited tha. others, and one point of the notation is to highlight the different constraints on different types of people and different types of activities.

The important point to draw from this brief introduction is that space and time are interconnected. Space is time and time is space. Much of our urban analysis has been too concerned with space. There are few studies which recognize the interconnection between the two (Parkes and Thrift, 1980, is a notable exception). However, if we view the people of the city as space–time travelers we begin to incorporate the temporal dimension into our understanding. The basic fact of our existence is that we occupy and move through both time and space. An understanding of both is vital to our understanding of life in the city. The notation of space–time paths is very flexible and allows a rich variety of different themes to be pursued. Fashions come and go, and the postmodern turn in urban studies and human geography has shifted focus away from empirical studies. However, this notation deserves more attention and further refinement because it affords us a useful framework for understanding and recording how the city both embodies and reflects the space–time paths of different groups and individuals as they make their way in the urban arena.

Street people and air people

The journeys that we weave through time and over space reflect many things: age, ethnicity, class, income, and all those other factors that distinguish us one from another. Sometimes the divisions are subtle, sometimes stark; an understanding of them is vital to a broader understanding of the structure and functioning of society. Let me elaborate with an example. The writer Jonathan Raban makes a distinction in New York City between street people and air people. Let me quote from him at some length:

> *There were the Street People and there were the Air People. Air People levitated like fakirs. Large portions of their day were spent waiting for, and travelling in, the elevators that were as fundamental to the middle-class culture of New York as gondolas had been to Venice in the Renaissance. It was the big distinction – to be able to press a button and take wing to your apartment. It didn't matter that you lived on the sixth, the 16th or 60th floor: access to the elevator was proof that your life had the buoyancy that was needed to stay afloat in a city where the ground was seen as the realm of failure and menace . . . Their New York consisted of a series of high-altitude interiors, each one guarded, triple-locked, electronically surveilled. They kept in touch by flying from one interior to the next, like sociable gulls swooping from cliff to cliff. For them, the old New York of streets, squares, neighbourhoods, was rapidly turning into a vague and distant memory. It was the place where TV thrillers were filmed. It was where the Street People lived . . . places like Brooklyn and the Bronx were as remote as Beirut and Teheran. Nobody went there. The subway system was an ugly rumour. At present the two cities were held together, one on top of the other, by the slender umbilical of the elevator.* (Raban, 1990, 80–4)

Raban's discussions of the different urban paths in the city tell us much about the broader divisions of the city. Social differences are reflected and condensed in the separate social worlds in which we live and work and move.

One of the great works of Western literature is Homer's *Odyssey*. It tells the story of the homeward voyage of Odysseus. He has fought in the Trojan wars, but because he has offended the sea god Poseidon he is forced to wander for nine years before he can return to house and family. During these years he has a variety of adventures: he encounters ferocious monsters, giants, sirens who try to lure him from his homeward journey. It is a great adventure story, the template of many subsequent tales as varied as *Pilgrim's Progress* and *ET*. It can also be read as a metaphor. Counterposed to the journey of life is the refuge, the home, the place where we are trying to get to. In a fascinating study, Witold Rybczynski (1986) looks at the emergence of the home in Western society and the variety of themes that have dominated, from intimacy and privacy to efficiency and austerity and to the enduring concerns with comfort and well-being. There is a variety of "homes." While the domestic home has been represented as the primary refuge, this notion ignores the domestic drudgery, domestic violence, and domestic dangers faced by some of the more vulnerable people in the home.

We are making our way to different "homes." The places that provide us with comfort and well-being may be the nostalgic past, our favorite restaurant, neighborhood bar, sports field, friend's place, our parents' places, the holiday place. If we conceptualize life in the city as a journey, then the necessary counterpoint is the idea of the refuge, the place(s) where we feel "at home." Like Odysseus, it sometimes takes a long time with many distractions and obstacles, but we always seem to be on that journey.

Timed spaces and spaced times

I arrived well before dawn at King's Cross Station in London in an overnight sleeper train from Aberdeen. I was going to a job interview. To be honest, I had no intention of taking the job. It was March 1973. I was in my final year at university and knew I wanted to go to graduate school. But just in case things did not work out I had applied for a couple of jobs in advertising. One firm was so keen to hire they offered me an interview at their head office. That is why I was in London at such an early hour. The station was deserted. A few people were moving around and the streets were quiet, the shops still closed up, and the bustle of the giant city had yet to begin. Only a few cars and some early-morning workers broke the calm of the huge but sleeping city. It was a bright, fresh morning so I decided to walk the

Illustration 11.4
Wealth and poverty: Ascot, UK, June 1981. Street people and rich people share the same peace but inhabit different worlds (© John Sturrock/Network)

four miles to my interview. I took my time. I stopped at a café for breakfast. The customers were leisurely, taking their time. As I lingered over my third coffee, the pace picked up. More people were coming in and the atmosphere was changing: from a quiet community to a rushed crowd. Outside, as I continued my journey, the city woke up. There was more traffic, more noise. Shops were opening, stalls were being set up. I eventually arrived at the headquarters in the business district. It was an all-day interview. At 5.30 p.m. I joined the flood of commuters making their way from work. I stopped off at a restaurant and experienced the boredom of a very quiet place. But by the time I was finishing my dessert, a lively, animated crowd had filled the waiting space. The "muzak" which had appeared so loud was now subdued by the voices of the customers. On my walk back to the station the crowd in the streets was of younger people, seeking entertainment and excitement. The city was now a setting for the pursuit of pleasure rather than for the workings of commerce. They still interconnected: I was accosted twice by prostitutes close to the station. I waited for my late-evening train. The station slowly emptied as the last trains to the suburbs took home revelers and people who had worked late. It was almost empty except for my fellow travelers. We got on the train as it sat in the almost silent station and headed north, through the night, back to Scotland.

I tell this story because it encapsulates two more general themes: the timing of space and the spacing of times. The city exists in time as well as space. The café, the business district, and the restaurant were all timed spaces; they had rhythm and cadence. The population of the business district, for example, ebbed and flowed as commuters came in the morning and left in the evening. At lunchtime the streets were packed with people, at midnight the streets were empty and threatening.

At both the micro- and macro-level the city pulses with the flows of people and events. A much more dynamic view of the city would incorporate the movement over time and through space of events, people, and activities. A greater sensitivity to the spatiotemporal dimension can only enliven our understanding of the city.

GUIDE TO FURTHER READING

On getting by in the city, see:
Bromley, R. (1988) Working in the streets: survival strategy, necessity or unavoidable evil. In J. Gugler (ed.), *The Urbanization of the Third World*, New York: Oxford University Press.
Cheng, L. and Gereffi, G. (1994) The informal economy in East Asian

development. *International Journal of Urban and Regional Research* 18, 194–219.

Gilbert, A. (1992) An urban explosion. In J.R. Short (ed.), *Human Settlement*, New York: Oxford University Press.

Harvey, D. (1989) *The Condition of Postmodernity*, Oxford: Blackwell.

Institute of Personnel Management (1986) *Flexible Patterns of Work*, London: IPM.

Mingione, E. (1987) Urban survival strategies, family structure and informal practices. In M.P. Smith and J.R. Feagin (eds), *The Capitalist City*, Oxford: Blackwell. ·

Nelson, N. (1988) How women and men get by: the sexual division of labour in the informal sector of a Nairobi squatter settlement. In J. Gugler, (ed.), *The Urbanization of the Third World*, New York: Oxford University Press.

Seabrook, J. (1981) *Unemployment*, London: Quartet.

Wallraff, G. (1988) *The Lowest of the Low*, London: Methuen.

Willis, P. (1978) *Learning to Labour*, London: Gower.

Young, M. and Wilmott, P. (1957) *Family and Kinship in East London*, London: Routledge & Kegan Paul.

On the city as stage:

Anderson, E. (1990) *Streetwise: Race, Class and Change in an Urban Community*, Chicago and London: University of Chicago Press.

Goffman, E. (1959) *The Presentation of Self in Everyday Life*, New York: Anchor.

Hall, E.T. (1959) *The Silent Language*, New York: Doubleday.

Meyrowitz, J. (1985) *No Sense of Place*, New York: Oxford University Press.

Smith, S.J. (1988) Constructing local knowledge: the analysis of self in everyday life. In J. Eyles and D.M. Smith, (eds.), *Qualitative Methods in Human Geography*, Oxford: Polity Press.

On the city as journey:

Hagerstrand, T. et al. (1970) What about people in regional science? *Papers of the Regional Science Association* 24, 7–21.

Parkes, D.N. and Thrift, N.J. (1980) *Times, Spaces and Places,* London: John Wiley.

Raban, J. (1990) *Hunting Mister Heartbreak*, London: Collins Harvill.

Rybczynski, W. (1986) *Home: A Short History of an Idea*, New York: Viking.

Chapter 12

THE POLITICAL ARENA

Oᴜʀ ʜᴏᴘᴇ ᴀɴᴅ ʙᴇᴛ ɪs ᴛʜᴀᴛ, ɴᴏᴛᴡɪᴛʜsᴛᴀɴᴅɪɴɢ ᴛʜᴇ ᴛʜʀᴇᴀᴛᴇɴɪɴɢ sᴛᴀᴛᴜs ᴏꜰ ᴛʜᴇ ᴄᴜʀʀᴇɴᴛ ʜɪsᴛᴏʀɪᴄᴀʟ ᴄᴏɴꜰʟɪᴄᴛs, ʜᴜᴍᴀɴᴋɪɴᴅ ɪs ᴏɴ ᴛʜᴇ ᴇᴅɢᴇ ᴏꜰ ᴍᴀsᴛᴇʀɪɴɢ ɪᴛs ᴏᴡɴ ꜰᴜᴛᴜʀᴇ, ᴀɴᴅ ᴛʜᴇʀᴇꜰᴏʀᴇ ᴏꜰ ᴅᴇsɪɢɴɪɴɢ ɪᴛs ɢᴏᴏᴅ ᴄɪᴛʏ. Aᴛ ʟᴀsᴛ, ᴄɪᴛɪᴢᴇɴs ᴡɪʟʟ ᴍᴀᴋᴇ ᴄɪᴛɪᴇs.

Mᴀɴᴜᴇʟ Cᴀsᴛᴇʟʟs, *Tʜᴇ Cɪᴛʏ ᴀɴᴅ ᴛʜᴇ Gʀᴀssʀᴏᴏᴛs* (1983)

Political interaction takes place. In a variety of settings, including the home, the work place, spheres of production, consumption, and representation. In this chapter I will be concerned with the practice of a more formal politics in the arena of the city. The city is both an arena for the struggle of power and the outcome of such struggles. I will consider three of the most important "players" in the arena: households, business, and the state.

HOUSEHOLDS

Households use the city in a variety of ways. Three general elements can be identified: these are households as

- taxpayers;
- users of services;
- residents.

Taxpayers

Many households are taxpayers. They pay both federal (national) and local taxes. Like all taxpayers around the world they want to pay the minimum and get the maximum. Below this broad consideration there are a number of other factors. Levels of taxpaying and attitudes to taxpaying vary significantly. In much of Europe, Scandinavian countries in particular, there are much higher levels of taxation than in the United States. In the Netherlands, for example, people seem willing to shoulder a comparatively higher tax burden to sustain the quality of public services than do households in the United States. The results are clear in the different levels of urban public spaces.

Households in some countries have a much higher level of taxation tolerance. In all countries, however, there are limits to the taxation load. Households are particularly sensitive to rates of increase and issues of equity. Taxation increases that are small and gradual are noticed less than sudden hikes. Taxes that are considered unfair are also unpopular. For example, the Conservative government elected in Britain in 1987 sought to replace local property taxes with a poll tax where every adult, irrespective of income, was required to pay the same amount. The tax led to very sudden hikes and obvious anomalies. Resistance to the tax was the background to the overthrow in 1990 of Prime Minister Margaret Thatcher who had committed her government and her reputation to the imposition of the new tax. Less-dramatic examples of taxpayers' revolts can also be found. In California the passing of Proposition 13 in 1977 on the state ballot was the result of taxpayers' resistance to continual tax increases. The result was a severe reduction in public spending with generally regressive results.

City taxes are often based on property. They are more visible, more direct than taxes based on general consumption (such as sales taxes) or on income tax. City taxes seem more arbitrary, more susceptible to change because they are more local. Moreover, they impinge more directly on the wealthiest members. The net result is that city property taxes are more often fought against because they seem arbitrary and they affect the better organized, the more articulate, the more politically connected. Income tax is a national affair, you cannot escape the net, but local taxes are just that, local, and hence people can move to a nearby location if it is accessible and has a lower tax burden. The net result is that in many countries there are limits placed on city taxes.

Users of services

Households use a variety of public goods and services. There is a whole range of goods and services that are provided for and by, directly and indirectly, the state. The precise form may vary; in the case of public housing, for example, the government provides a public good which is consumed by individual households. Then there are such public goods as roads and highways that are consumed collectively. We can make a further distinction between goods and services that are allocated on the basis of need or merit and those that are universally available. We have to be careful when we use the term "public goods and services" that we specify which type. Those that are collectively consumed, for example, transport, education, policing, tend to generate more public awareness because they involve the majority of households and especially the wealthier, more articulate groups. Those goods and services that are allocated on the basis of need and generally go to the poorest groups, such as public housing in the United States, tend to figure lower on local and national political agendas. There is often an implied distinction between welfare goods and services and nonwelfare goods and services. The former tends to go to the poorer. There is a politics of naming with associated undercurrents of charity and benefits, whereas the public goods and services consumed by the wealthier are rarely seen or discussed as "welfare" benefits. Both food stamps for the poor and tax concessions to the wealthy are benefits; the difference between them is that one goes to the poor and one goes to the rich. How they are portrayed and described says more about power than about fiscal reality.

Over the long term, the range of public goods and services has been growing, both in cities with a history of social welfarism and in those that are marked by a commitment to privatism. If we look at cities around the world today and a hundred years ago one of the most distinctive changes is the scale and provision of public goods and services, whether it be in public housing, public education, public transport, provision of infrastructure, transfer payments or social welfare, the scale of government intervention has been increasing. The quality of private life is in some measure a function of the quality of the public city. And here we come to a possible paradox. Although households as taxpayers may want taxes to be kept as low as possible, the same households as users may want a high level of public provision. The paradox is partially avoided by the direction of criticism to bloated bureaucracies and government inefficiencies. Cut out waste, say the critics, because taxes can be reduced without reducing services. They have a point. All bureaucracies have a tendency to expand, and in governments the possibility of deficit financing allows the expansion to occur beyond the limits of direct funding. The result is an increase in public bureaucracies. But there is also the uncomfortable fact that it may not be possible to get high-quality public goods and services without paying for them.

Residents

Households are also residents of particular places. This makes them sensitive to the politics of location. The quality of a location is dependent on what is happening around it. The value of a house, for example, partially depends on the area in which it is located. We can picture the city as a huge externality surface. Imagine that a new park has been opened in a neighborhood. The easy access to this green space is a positive benefit. Imagine that a strip club has been opened in the same neighborhood. It attracts a late-night crowd that parks on the streets. Most residents would see this as having a deleterious effect on the area; in other words, a negative externality. Sometimes the same thing can have both positive and negative externalities. The public park may, at night, attract rowdy teenagers or provide the setting for drug dealers. The city can be seen as a constantly changing externality surface.

Households will try to maximize public goods and repel public bads. They will attempt to get those goods and services that generate positive externalities and to resist those that generate negative externalities. Especially if they are homeowners. The steady increase in owner-occupation throughout North America and much of Western Europe has created a tenure group that is very sensitive to changes in house prices. The purchase of a house is most households' biggest single outlay, their biggest asset, and one of their main sources of wealth and collateral to borrow money. Owner-occupiers are thus very sensitive to those factors they can influence that affect the price of their home. Most changes in house prices are large secular trends, but there are also local effects. In a neighborhood thought to deteriorating, for whatever reason, house prices will fall. Owner-occupiers will resist negative externalities that impinge on house prices. The politics of location is, in essence, the struggle to reinforce positive externalities and repel negative externalities.

Although we have used the term "household," not everyone in the household is equally concerned with the politics of location. In households with a traditional gender division of labor, for example, wives and women are those most sensitive to changes in the local environment because they are the ones who have shouldered much of the responsibilities of the home and childrearing. They therefore have a much more direct experience of such community matters as schooling, levels of traffic flows, quality of local public services, and the intrusion of negative externalities. In the past 30 years we can see a relationship between feminism and community involvement. Much of the strength and vitality of community action has come from women, while some of the confidence of the women's movement has come through successful community action.

If things deteriorate (for example, taxes rise, the quality of the public city worsens, or a negative externality affects the neighborhood) households have a choice. The decision is often summarized as exit/voice. It takes a lot, however, before this stark choice is reached. Households vary in their propensity to move. More likely to move are younger households, renters, and those of recent residence. The longer a household stays in a dwelling and a particular neighborhood, the less likely they are to move. This principle of cumulative inertia means that, especially in stable neighborhoods, households do not make the decision lightly. Generally, a rather dramatic shift needs to occur before households consider this choice. One of the most dramatic examples of exit was in metropolitan United States where white middle-class flight to the suburbs since the 1960s has created chocolate cities and vanilla suburbs. The "tipping point" was when and where African-American households constituted more than about 10 percent of the area population. This was enough to set off the outmovement of white middle-class residents. Fear of crime, fear of declining educational standards, and falling house prices are all embodied, for many white households, in the presence of black households. As Andrew Hacker (1992, 38) has noted:

> *If you are black, these white reactions brand you as a carrier of contaminations. No matter what your talents or attainments, you are seen as infecting a neighborhood simply because of your race. This is the ultimate insult of segregation. It opens wounds that never really heal and leaves scars to remind you how far you stand from full citizenship.*

If households do not move but they still feel aggrieved, then they may articulate their concern. This is the voice strategy. Households, if they are very wealthy, well-connected and powerful, can influence events. The power of individuals should not be overlooked in shaping the nature of urban society. The ability of rich families to shape cities to maximize favorable outcomes is a fact of life. Generally, the less democratic the society and the smaller the city, the greater the power wielded by individuals. However, most individual households have limited influence. They achieve more power to influence outcomes by joining together in groups. These are called resident groups, neighborhood groups, urban protest movements, and sometimes urban social movements. We can identify three general aspects of such group activity: the context, the voicing of concern, and outcomes.

The context We have already discussed some of the reasons for protest: taxes, services, and externalities. If taxes are seen to be high, if public goods and services are seen to deteriorate, an if negative externalities are perceived, then there is the context for household discontent and possible group action.

TABLE 12.1 MAJOR CLEVAGES			
Goal of the urban movement	The city as use value	Identity, cultural autonomy and communication	Territorially based self-management
Ideological themes and historical demands included in this goal	Social wage; quality of life; conservation of history & nature	Neighborhood life; ethnic cultures, historical traditions	Local autonomy; neighborhood decentralization; citizen participation
Name of the adversary	Capital	Technocracy	State
Goal of the adversary	The city as exchange value	Monopoly of messages and one-way information flows	Centralization of power; rationalization of bureaucracy; insulation of the apparatus
Conflicts over the historical meaning of city	City as a spatial support for life	City as a communication network and a source of cultural innovation	City as a self-governing entity
	versus City as a commodity or a support of commodity production and circulation	*versus* Despatialization programmed one-way information flows	*versus* City as a subject of the central state at the service of worldwide empires

Source: After Castells (1983)

In a broad-ranging historical survey of grassroots action in the city Manuel Castells (1983) identifies three major sources of protest, centering on the demand for goods and services, cultural identity, and political power (see table 12.1). Castells' book is an ambitious attempt at a cross-cultural, transhistorical survey of urban struggles and is a major source of information, ideas, and insights into the city as the site of struggle and social change.

The voicing of concern   Protest groups are formed by people who perceive that important issues can be addressed by collective action. This implies that there are people with the time, commitment, and belief to mobilize and organize the local community. Such people are few and far between. Most people have neither the time nor the energy. This may explain why urban protest groups are the exception rather than the rule. Most groups are established by the actions of a few individuals, and in the early stages most groups have a very definite core–periphery structure, with a smaller, active core doing most of the work and a wider, less-active peripheral membership. Groups often wax and wane as the more active individuals enter and leave.

Groups, once formed, have a variety of strategies. Let us consider two: *service strategies* and *influence strategies*. Service strategies use and mobilize the community's own resources in different ways:

- complementary strategies to augment existing services. Examples include the self-build groups found in many big cities in poor countries where there is limited state provision of housing. The groups may lack market demand but they take over land and build their own housing;
- alternative strategies to demonstrate new ways of meeting a need and providing an alternative. Residents who fight against traffic use in their neighborhood may suggest alternative routes for heavy traffic;

Illustration 12.1
Protest march, 24 February 1990, against a planned urban motorway to run from Kings Cross to Archway in north London (© Format Partners; photograph: Maggie Murray)

■ substitute strategies to replace existing forms of service provision. Some religious groups opt out of public education and provide their own form of education.

Influence strategies involve the deflection of externalities and the allocation and reallocation of resource provision. Three influence strategies are noted in table 12.2:

TABLE 12.2 A REPERTOIRE OF COLLECTIVE ACTION	
Action	*Category*
Surveys, collection and presentation of evidence Petitions	Persuasive
Lobbying of local government offices, councilors, ministers, government departments, and other decision-makers	Collaborative
Fighting individual cases Deputations Rallies Marches Refusal to pay Civil disobedience	Confrontational

■ persuasive strategies involve bringing the issue to the attention of the authorities;
■ collaborative strategies are a notch above persuasive for a more open encounter with the authorities;
■ confrontational strategies can take the form of deputations, rallies, and marches, up to and including acts of civil disobedience.

Together, all these strategies constitute a repertoire of collective action. The type of action may vary over time. A group may move from persuasive through to confrontational if conditions perceptively worsen and there is no sign of government response. The type of action will also depend on the general and local political culture. In repressive regimes protest may be banned and thus grievances are either unstated or may rupture into confrontation. Political regimes more receptive to public opinion are likelier to contain protest at the persuasive and collaborative levels.

The type of action used by a group will also depend on the relationship between the group and the political elite. Three forms of this relationship can be noted. *Political partnership* occurs when the group shares the same interests as the elite and can therefore adopt a more conciliatory approach. *Political communion* describes the case when the group need not be involved in overt action because its interest are shared by the political elite. In many US cities business leaders are not involved directly in civic affairs. In many cases they do not need to be because business interests are built into the worldview and regular practice of municipal government. *Political exclusion* occurs when certain groups are so marginalized that their interests are not represented. Many groups are excluded from the political agenda. People who are poor and powerless remain poor and powerless because their interests are rarely given much attention. Their grievances may not be formulated, or articulated, and even if they become a political issue the decision may consistently go against some groups. Martin Luther King, Jr described a riot as the language of the unheard. Business leaders do not riot because they do not have or

Illustration 12.2
Early Sunday morning in Toxteth, as youths and police face-off in the Liverpool inner-city suburb, 1981 (© Hulton Deutsch Collection Ltd)

need to, their interests are secured. A marginalized group may move
from political exclusion to rioting for, as the English politician
Charles Fox noted in 1777, people "who have no hope and nothing
to lose will always be dangerous."

Outcomes   The outcomes of collective action form a continuum from
success, through partial success to failure. The result will depend on
a variety of factors, but of prime importance is the relative degree of
power wielded by the group compared with the authorities. Although
the group may have limited resources and power, if it shares the same
interests as the authorities then some measure of success may be
expected. Success is most likely when a group has effective power and
a congruence of interest with the relevant authorities. Success is least
likely when weak groups are pitted against authorities who do not
share the groups' interests or concerns. Let me elaborate with an
example. The political scientist Patrick Dunleavy (1977) looked at

TABLE 12.3 AN UNEQUAL STRUGGLE	
Power resources	*Constraints*
Local authorities	Reference public opinion
Monopoly of information, decision and timing	
reduction or withdrawal of services	
blight creation: neglect of repairs	
witholding of payments related to compulsory purchase orders	
creation of neighborhood conflicts	
control of jobs (of employees of council and businesses displaced by clearance)	
unfavorable typing of residents	
unfavorable housing allocations	
withdrawal of housing rights	
eviction	
Clearance area residents	
access to councilors	Uncertainty, lack of information
access to local media	Poor conditions (therefore high costs of delay)
access to reference publics	Dispersion (in many cases)
direct action	Virtually complete housing vulnerability
	Job vulnerability (of local authority employees and employees of business displaced by clearance)

Source: After Dunleavy (1977)

272

the experience of comprehensive redevelopment in Britain. This involved the demolition of old housing and the construction of high-rise public housing. Dunleavy looked at the area of Beckton in the London borough of Newham. He paints a picture of a weakly organized, poorly resourced community group failing to achieve any influence with the local authority, which did not accept the legitimacy of the group. The vast disparity in power resources is shown in table 12.3. The local authority had the monopoly of information and real powers in terms of eviction and access to housing opportunities, while the residents in the clearance area had only access to local politicians. The local authority had few constraints while the residents were very vulnerable in their jobs and housing opportunities.

Three general types of outcomes are identified in figure 12.1. In the case of (a), the outcome is regressive as more benefits go to the rich. Urban renewal in metropolitan United States in the 1960s, for example, led to a loss of low-income housing and increased investment opportunities for investors. In (b) the outcome is redistributional because most benefits go to the poor. Programs which reduce basic living costs, such as introducing cheap mass-transit schemes or cheap public housing, will benefit those on low incomes proportionately more than those on higher incomes. In the case of (c) benefits are skewed toward the middle-income groups. Universal benefits, such as free health or education, tend to be of benefit more to the middle-income groups because the rich often opt out and use

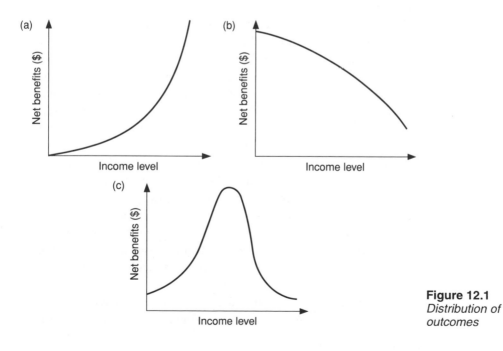

Figure 12.1
Distribution of outcomes

273

private services and the lower-income groups often have to compete against the middle-income groups, which have the social skills and resources to take better advantage of universal systems of provision.

BUSINESS

Business interests vary, in size, type, location, and long-term strategy. There is a big difference between General Motors and the mom-and-pop corner store. There is also a big difference between General Motors, Dow Chemical, and Microsoft. The term "business," therefore, is a loose general expression covering a variety of different interests. However, a number of general points can be noted in the capitalist world. In the city as political arena business interests are primarily concerned with reducing costs, making profits, retaining and increasing market share. These are the key elements of business strategy. Businesses, especially big business, have advantages. They provide employment for the population and revenue for city and state governments. Their interests are built into the dominant ideologies of capitalist societies.

Business interests can either be politically represented by specific parties and individuals or indirectly, through the interconnections between business and political elites and in the fiscal realities imposed on local communities and city governments. Over the years, business leaders have become less involved directly in local urban politics. They rarely need to be, because their interests are already at the top of the agenda. A sound local economy is essential for good employment opportunities and a solid taxation base. In an interesting study Roger Clements (1969) looked at the changing role of local business leaders in the government of the English city of Bristol. He discovered a steady withdrawal over the years from direct representation. The stated reason, lack of time, was shown not to be accurate. Clements demonstrated how most of the business leaders were involved in voluntary activity. The main reason was that urban politics became part of national political representation with career politicians and the rough and tumble of political elections. The subculture of senior business people reinforced the active role of leadership, authority, and hierarchy. This experience clashed with the more face-to-face confrontation and discussion of the democratic political process. It became increasingly difficult to reconcile the expectations and privileges of this subculture with the assumptions and practices of democratic debate. Business leaders were less involved because they did not need to get involved to ensure their interests. Their interests were part of the taken-for-granted view of what was in the "general interest." In many cities the "general interest" is very often the politically acceptable form of business interests.

Business, although one of the most important players in the urban arena, does have certain constraints. Although business has economic clout it does not have votes. It can buy votes, directly and indirectly, legally and illegally, formally and informally, but politicians need to be responsive to public opinion to get re-elected. When there is win–win situation politicians can appease both business and the electorate, but when conflicts between community and business arise then politicians have to decide. So although business does have power it does not have unlimited power. In some localities the political culture may even be embodied in political representation that responds as much to labor as to capital. There are many socialist and reformist municipal governments throughout Europe, and the contemporary business orientation of municipal governments in the United States is in contrast to the more radical posture of cities in the 1930s.

While business lacks direct political representation it nevertheless wields political power. Business ideology permeates through many areas of civic culture and political practice. One example is shown in the work of Crenson (1971) and what he terms the unpolitics of air pollution. He looked at air pollution in major US cities in the 1960s and noted how it was not a political issue. The large companies responsible for the pollution had enough clout to dispute scientific findings, and ultimately appealed to the fact that the economic base of the city was tied to the industrial processes that created the pollution. Business power was effective in making sure that air pollution did not appear on the political agenda. Another example is the study by Lisa Benton (1992), which looked at how industrial pollution in the city of Syracuse appeared on the public agenda very late in the day only because of the power of business to link its interests with the general interest. Despite the reality of pollution there was nonrecognition of pollution as a major issue of political importance because of the political and economic power of local industries.

In their book *Urban Fortunes: The Political Economy of Place* (1987) Logan and Molotch document the economic-growth lobby formed by the leading players in US cities: a consensus on stimulating investment and economic growth while limiting he redistributional function of the state. Realtors, local banks, influential politicians, corporate chairs, and chambers of commerce all help to define the city's goal and main function as an economic growth machine. They are all eager to promote a probusiness agenda for their particular city against the background of competing cities and

alternative investment opportunities. The net effect is for the domination of business interests in the urban politics of the United States.

Business wields power directly in a number of ways. I shall consider two:

- investment flows; and
- lobbying.

Investment flows

Business affects the economic and political life of cities by its patterns
of investment and disinvestment. Investment flows into areas of
greatest profit and seeps away from sectors, industries, and places
where profits are low and declining. This pulsing of capital invest-
ment/disinvestment affects the nature of cities. With disinvestment
come the politics of decline, the fight over scarce resources, and enormous pressure on localities and city governments to replace a
shrinking employment and tax base. With rapid investment come the
politics of growth, the need to balance economic growth, and pressures for expansion with social equity and environmental
sustainability. The politics of place are bound up with the patterns of
investment and disinvestment.

Bigger businesses with larger investments wield more power than
smaller businesses do. And the more mobile businesses, companies
that can and do carry on business in a variety of different places, have
more leverage because they can and do relocate. The broad economic
changes which I discussed in Part I have all led to the greater mobility of capital compared to labor. The internationalization of the
economy gives business a greater range of locational choice. Flexible
production systems and the globalization of economic activities have
strengthened business in its dealings with organized labor and individual cities. Over the past 20 years there has been a shift in the
balance of power throughout the rich capitalist world as a growing
number of businesses become disconnected from their need to locate
in particular places. General economic space has replaced specific
place as a major locational requirement, and the result has been a
steady downward shift in the wages and conditions of organized labor
in the rich capitalist world. Many businesses, and especially manufacturing businesses, can shift to low-cost areas, either within
countries or between countries. This gives them the ability either to
move or effectively threaten to move. Threats are only powerful if
they can be enforced. This power, in turn, can be used by businesses
which remain *in situ* to reduce labor costs and taxation loads.

Business also acts directly to influence governments. The more powerful the business the more effective the lobbying, just as the bigger the business, the more resources can be devoted to influencing political outcomes. Businesses lobby for a variety of things; let us consider three general cases:

- redirecting government taxation and expenditure;
- influencing the climate of industrial relations;
- creating more space for business.

Redirecting taxation and spending   All businesses want to pay less in taxes and to get more government services. Ideological arguments used to buttress this position include the need for fiscal incentives to aid economic growth and the assertion that high taxes will stifle business confidence. But here business can be caught in a paradox. They want to minimize their taxes yet still benefit from public expenditure that aids their business dealings. The paradox is partially resolved by the attack on unproductive forms of public expenditure. But even here problems can arise. Public expenditure, even transfer payments to the poor, may be necessary to stimulate overall purchasing power in the economy. Conflict may occur between different sectors of the business world. Defense industries, for example, will do all they can to maintain defense expenditure whereas other sectors may want less spending on defense and more on other sectors. As a rule of thumb, we may note that business will lobby for government expenditure which helps their dealings, but when this expenditure does not aid their efforts, or only helps other business, all manner of fiscal and political reasons will be mounted to show the deleterious effects of government spending.

Industrial relations   Business wants a legislative framework that allows it to have control over labor. This enable it to keep costs down and profits up. Business is not always successful. In Britain between 1974 and 1979 a Labour government signed a social contract with the trade unions that, in return for limiting wage increases, changed the framework of industrial relations. In Acts of 1974 and 1976 workers were given protection against dismissal, increased redundancy payments, paid maternity leave, and union immunity from common-law action. With the election victory of a right-wing Conservative Party in 1979 the balance of power shifted and business was in a much stronger position to lobby government effectively. The result was the

1980 and 1982 Employment Acts that reduced union picketing pow-ers, made unions liable for damages, and effectively destroyed the closed shop which had required all workers to be in the union. The legislation weakened the power of organized labor.

The relationship between business and the state is ambivalent. As one commentator notes:

> *In general employers want a government which keeps out of industry (but bails out, on industry's terms, firms which get into difficulties); which does not allow the level of unemployment to get too low (but keeps the economy buoyant); which keeps control of unions and income growth (but does not get in employers' way when doing so).*
>
> (Crouch, 1979, 147–8).

Creating space Business wants government to help it secure and increase its profitability; it will lobby government to create space for this to occur. Let us consider an example taken from a detailed study (Short et al., 1986). House-builders operate a business in which the role of government is crucial. In Britain builders need planning per-mission from local authorities to build houses. Central government has an important role to play in setting the context for local author-ity actions, especially through the circulars issued by the central government, and in particular by the Department of the Environment (DOE). As the amount of house production increased from the mid-1960s onward, builders lobbied both central and local government in order to effect changes to their advantage. One important issue was the case of land availability. Builders wanted a constant supply of cheap, available land; they did not want delays in the planning process; this would reduce the supply and increase the cost of land. To this end they lobbied central government. Their suc-cess can be seen in the tenor of circulars about land availability issued by the DOE from 1970 onward. These were issued by both Labour (1974–9) and Conservative (1970–4 and 1979–) governments. A reading of them shows a steady increase in the incorporation of the needs and demands of builders into the principles and practice of land-use planning. The Conservative government of 1979 was par-ticularly probuilder, partly on shared ideological grounds and partly because builders are traditionally one of the single largest contribu-tors to Conservative Party funds. The Secretary of State for the Environment actively encouraged house-builders. In 1981 he was quoted in the house-builders' trade journal:

I do happen to believe that your industry is now becoming organized effectively to do many of the things that I wish industry at large had organized itself to do twenty years ago . . . You are now showing a willingness to get involved in the real nuts and bolts dialogue with local authorities and central government . . . I don't say you will get results immediately but democracy is about pressure. People like me are a focal point of pressure.

(*Housebuilders' Federation Annual* 1981, 21–2)

The circulars produced by the Conservative government reflected the pressure from builders. Circular 22/80 noted, "the Government wants to make sure that the planning system is as positive and helpful as it can be to investment of industry and commerce and to the development industry." In effect, the builders were successful in shifting the land-use planning system to reflect their needs and demands.

When private businesses struggle they sometimes cast their eyes to the privileged position of state-run enterprises. Businesses lobby to break the monopoly of what they see as unfair competition. They face difficulties. Government bureaucracies are large and powerful and jealously guard their domain. However, the ideological movements of Reagonomics and Thatcherism, which saw business as more efficient than government, allowed business to lobby successfully for more business space. Let us consider one example. In the United Kingdom most local governments had their own building departments, called Direct Labour Organizations (DLOs). In the early and mid-1970s the DLOs did more than just maintenance, they were involved in construction on local authority housing and other projects. From the mid-1970s onward, as a building recession deepened, private builders wanted more business and they sought to lobby government. The builders were successful with the Thatcher government, which came to power in 1979. Immediately, the Department of the Environment advised local authorities to put more of their maintenance work out to contract and required DLOs to make a 5 percent return on capital, a return which building firms had not achieved in the previous eight years. The action did not just create more space for private business, it unfairly disadvantaged the DLOs.

The privatization schemes of the Thatcher government have been copied by many countries as governments seek to make public companies more efficient and as businesses successfully lobby for more space.

Businesses lobby to achieve specific ends. These will vary according to the type and size of the business. Success depends, much as for community groups, on the amount of power and the connections with relevant decision-making bodies.

THE STATE

The state, in its various forms, is both a player and a referee in the urban arena. The state regulates the interaction between community and business as well as acting as an agent in this interaction.

General comments

One of the most important characteristics of the state has been its steady growth. Whether measured in terms of employees, levels of taxation and spending, or sheer amount of legislation, one of the most significant worldwide changes in the twentieth century has been the inexorable increase in the size of the state. In both rich and poor, capitalist and socialist, stable and unstable societies the trend has been the same.

In capitalist societies the state is an arena for competing interests. Some are more powerful than others, and particularly important is big business. In the longterm the state reflects the interests of big business more than those of small business or organized labor. This does not mean that the state does not respond to popular pressure; especially in liberal democracies, it is subject to popular pressure. In less-democratic systems the state, at least in the short to medium term, can suppress popular demands. At any one time, therefore, state policy and action will reflect the balance of power between competing groups. This balance also reflects the broader economic climate. During economic growth, when labor is scarce and government revenues are increasing, the state will be much more responsive to programs of social welfare than when unemployment is high and government revenues are tight. Government policy is a function of the balance of social forces and the general economic climate.

The boundaries of state involvement are constantly changing. Social pressure and the fear of social instability have all prompted involvement in things as varied as public housing, the regulation of specific transactions, and levels of unemployment benefits. The degree of involvement reflects the amount of social pressure, which in turn sets the political context for subsequent government involvement. For example, after the Second World War there was more pressure for social reform in Britain than there was in the United States. The result in Britain was the establishment of universal healthcare and the building of public housing, which, at its peak, constituted almost a third of the total housing stock. Subsequent debates in Britain did not question the need for universal healthcare but argued only about the amount of its budget. Things were very different in the United States, where universal healthcare has yet to be achieved. The case of public housing in Britain also shows the reverse trend. Public housing grew in absolute and relative terms throughout the 1950s, 1960s and early 1970s. However, the Conservative government of 1979 embarked on a policy of selling off public housing. This privatization of a public good was a selective process. It was the very best public housing that was sold, leaving a poorer-quality residual core that led to a stigmatization of public housing. This recommodification of housing was a retreat from government involvement.

The state is subject to various kinds of pressure. Elsewhere I have described these as a series of crises (Short, 1984, 1993). The term "crisis" is used in the double sense that it has in Chinese, where the two ideograms used to describe it respectively represent danger and opportunity. An *economic crisis* occurs when the economy fails to meet popular expectations. Lack of jobs, decline in living standards, and reductions in purchasing power are all perceived in a negative manner, and if they affect more than a permanent underclass they create the conditions for a *legitimation crisis,* in which the state loses its ability to reflect the popular will of the country. *Rationality crises* result from the failure to make the necessary amount of correct decisions. Two subtypes can be noted. Type 1 occurs when economic policies are incorrect, and type 2 occurs when the state fails to provide the necessary education programs and the like. *Fiscal crises* occur when expenditures exceed revenues.

Urban governments

I will consider three aspects of urban government:

■ central–urban relations;
■ forms of urban government;
■ urban regimes.

Central–urban relations   Urban governments are not the primary source of state power. In all but a few countries, such as Switzerland, the power to tax and spend ultimately lies with federal and state authorities. Urban governments, however, are more than just neutral transmission belts taking the policies of higher levels of government

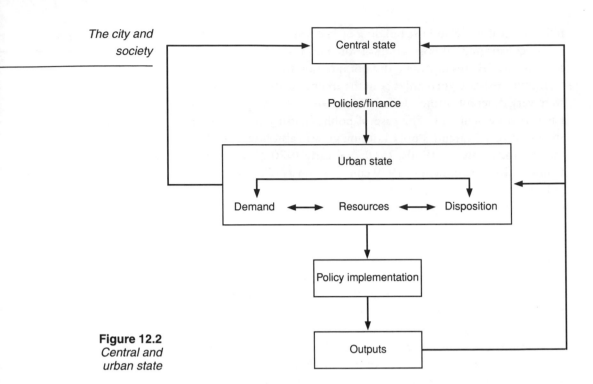

Figure 12.2
Central and urban state

to the urban citizenry. Figure 12.2 indicates three sources of difference between cities: demand, resources, and disposition.

Cities vary in the range and type of inhabitants. In poorer cities there will be greater demand for welfare programs provided by central government but administered by the municipal authority. In cities with a higher proportion of elderly, such as retirement communities in Florida and Arizona, healthcare provision will be skewed toward the demands of the elderly.

Cities also differ in the resources at their disposal. The tax base will vary significantly between growing cities and contracting cities, between those with a buoyant economy and those with a sinking economy. If there is no equalization mechanism, either by state or federal authorities, then these differences will be reflected in the ability of cities to meet the demands of the population.

Cities also may have different political cultures. Some are more radical than others, some are willing to spend more than others. Fiscally conservative city governments will tend to spend less than liberal cities do. Political disposition affects the destination as well as the amount of city government spending.

Crises are expressed in different ways at the different levels of government. This is most evident in the case of fiscal crises. There is often a distinction between government taxation and spending. Central government takes the bulk of revenues, but much of the spending is undertaken by city governments. One strong tendency is for central governments to pass some of the responsibilities for spending onto city governments while keeping to themselves a large proportion of tax revenue. The effect is to shift the burden of the fiscal crisis onto the cities, especially the poorer cities where there are more demands for types of welfare spending. Popular protest against spending cuts are thus more often than not directed at city officials who have fiscal responsibility but lack fiscal power.

Forms of urban government Imagine a continuum of autonomy for urban governments. At one end urban governments have responsibility for both defining policy goals and achieving these goals. At the other end the city authorities have little or no say in these formulations and objectives. There are national differences. In state systems where power is more decentralized, such as Switzerland, municipal governments have greater autonomy. In centrally ruled systems urban governments have little independence. The city of Paris in France, for example, is very much under the control of central government to a much greater extent than exists between the central powers in the United States and Britain and respectively New York and London. The arrangement ensures that a large proportion of government expenditure is directed at the French capital. The results are obvious. Compared to either London or New York, Paris has an impressive public transport system, its roads are cleaner, its recent public building is much more striking and, in general, the quality of the public city is much higher.

The most significant trend has been a long-term shift from one end to the other. The rise of the state has been the rise to power of the central state. There have been countervailing tendencies, as when central governments give city governments more responsibility. But when we look closely at these shifts we invariably note that while central government may shift responsibility it tends to hang on to real power, whether fiscal, legislative, or legal.

Different types of governmental organization can be identified. These vary by country and reflect broader political and historical differences. There are also differences over time. Government reform, though prompted by a crisis of legitimation, often takes the shape of administrative reorganization. Urban governments in Britain, for example, have been subject to many changes. Metropolitan counties were created in 1974 and then abolished by the Conservative government in 1986, partly because these counties were predominantly Labour Party controlled and thus the political enemies of a right-wing

Illustration 12.3
Tokyo City Hall. With revenues from local business Tokyo City government could afford a magnificent new headquarters (photograph: author)

government. There are also differences within the same country. Figure 12.3, for example, shows the different city government forms in the United States. The mayor–council form is found in the older cities of the north-east and mid-west. In this form the council is the main decision-making body, and the council members are elected to represent different wards of the city. In the strong mayor system the mayor can appoint the chief administrators of the various

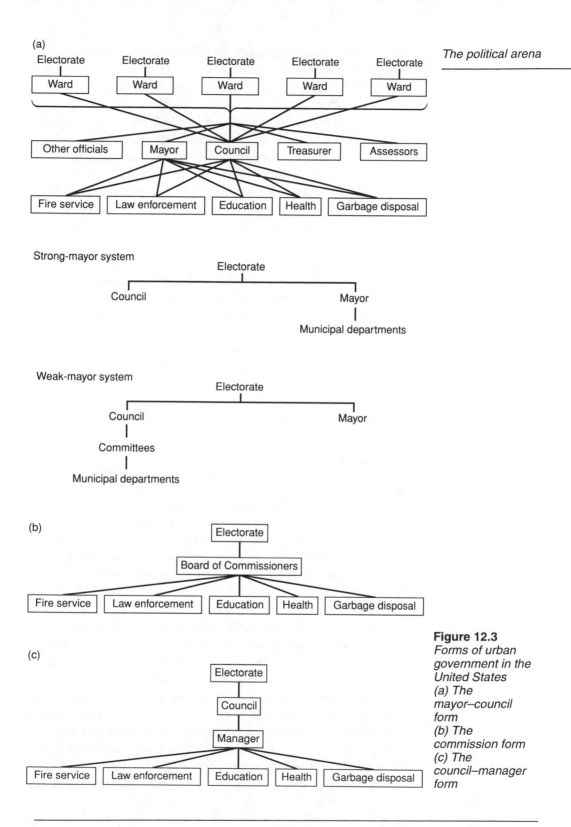

Figure 12.3
*Forms of urban
government in the
United States
(a) The
mayor–council
form
(b) The
commission form
(c) The
council–manager
form*

departments. In the commission form of government political power resides with an elected commission from three to seven members who run city government for up to four years. In the council–manager form an elected council sets taxes, determines the budget, and appoints a manager who is directly responsible for the everyday running of city hall. Each of the systems reflects different political pressures. The mayor–council form should be more responsive to the electorate, which directly elects council men and women. The mayor–council system is more responsive to the politics of place. Under the council–manager system, in contrast, the political discourse is dominated by the claims of efficiency and rationality rather than those of redistribution or social justice. Forms of urban government are not politically neutral.

Metropolitan fragmentation occurs when numerous administrative-political boundaries overlie a single metropolitan region. New York metropolitan region, for example, has over 1,500 different political units. Severe fragmentation makes it more difficult to run and administer public services. If this is so, why does it occur? Inertia is one reason. Urban growth outstrips the slow nature of administrative-political change. Moreover, political units rarely vote themselves out of office, even for the greater public good. There are also powerful forces which resist incorporation into metropolitan government. Fear of higher taxes and contact, especially in the school districts, with low income minorities give backbone to the suburban resistance to metropolitan incorporation. In some cases fragmentation is fostered by central government. Between 1974 and 1986 some of the public services in London was administered by the greater London Council (GLC). The Conservative government that came to power in 1979 in Britain soon became obsessed with the desire to abolish the GLC. The role of place and personality was crucial. The headquarters of the GLC was beside the River Thames and visible from the Houses of Parliament. The leader of the GLC was Ken Livingstone, an impressive media performer who constantly criticized the Conservative government and, in particular, the Prime Minister, Margaret Thatcher. The central government passed legislation which simply abolished the GLC in 1986. Politics and personality had overridden efficiency and rational planning. But then, they always do.

Metropolitan fragmentation is often overlain with differences in needs, resources, and disposition. Let us consider resources. If municipal revenues are based on property taxes, then, in a city with a large number of small units, the tax base will vary significantly. There will be rich and poor areas. Some of these differences will be made up by some form of central government equalization process, a process very susceptible to political manipulation and control. But when this process is unfair or limited in size or subject to fluctuation, the disparities will not be overcome. And then we come to a possible paradox: the poorer the area the greater its needs. In other words, with metropolitan fragmentation there can be an inverse relationship between needs and resources. This paradox is most apparent in the United States where there is a central–city–suburban fiscal disparity problem. This is a cumbersome, yet accurate, term which identifies the fact that central cities with the poorest populations and the greatest needs have some of the lowest resources. Their tax base has fled to the suburbs, which have more affluent populations and thus lower demands yet more resources. These disparities are overlain by ethnic segregation. Compared to the suburbs, a greater proportion of central-city residents are low-income, African-American households. Metropolitan fragmentation is maintained by the power of suburban municipalities to resist incorporation and their fear that such incorporation will lead to increased taxes, declining public services, and poor-quality schooling. Metropolitan fragmentation in the United States is both a cause and effect of racial inequality.

Urban regimes   Two questions recur when people look at city government. Who rules? How do they rule?

The question of who rules has long been a source of interest. The *elitist* position states that a self-conscious, business elite effectively runs the city. The *pluralist* sees power dispersed among a large number of competing interests. The dissimilarity between the two refers to broad differences not only in understanding society but also in approach. The elitist position tends to identify power-holders by reputation. Researchers, in this approach, will often ask a preselected group of citizens in the city the question: Who wields effective power? The recurrence of specific names helps identify the elite. The pluralist position focuses on identifying the range of interests involved in specific decisions. The attention to reputations highlights a cohesive power elite while the emphasis on decisions highlights a range of different interests. A *neo-elitist* position, while extending the cruder forms of the elitist position, points to power as lying not so much in the fight over particular decisions but in influencing which decisions come onto the political agenda for discussion. The differences between the pluralist and neo-elitist position have been summarized by Lukes (1974), who also proposes a three-dimensional view of power which incorporates behavior, decision-making and non-decision-making, issues and potential issues, observable as well as latent conflict, and subjective as well as real interests (table 12.4).

	TABLE 12.4 PERSPECTIVES ON POWER	
Pluralist	*Neo-elitist*	*Three-dimensional view*
Behavior	Behavior	Behavior
Decision-making	Decision-making and non-decision making	Decision-making, non-decision-making and control of political agenda
Issues	Issues and potential issues	Issues and potential issues
Observable conflict	Observable conflict	Observable conflict and latent conflict
Subjective interests	Subjective interests	Subjective and real interests

The questions of who rules and how they rule have been informed in recent years by the debate on urban regimes. In his work on Atlanta, Clarence Stone (1989) developed the notion of urban regimes to refer to the informal partnership between city hall and downtown business elites. City hall is dominated by political questions of maintaining and extending political support and leadership, while the business elites are concerned with economic issues of profit and loss. The combination of political and economic logic, with all the ensuing tensions, conflicts and ambiguities, constitutes the local urban regime. The options and concerns of urban regimes vary over time and space; they may be inclusionary or exclusionary and will vary throughout the metropolitan regions; suburban regimes, for example, are more concerned with preserving property values. Judd and Kantor (1992) identify four cycles of regime politics in the United States. In the *entrepreneurial cities* up to the 1870s merchant elites controlled the city. Then with industrialization and large-scale immigration business interests had to work with political representatives of the newly organized immigrants. The result was the *city of machine politics*. From the 1930s to the 1970s a *New Deal coalition* was instituted in which federal policies were used to stimulate urban economies and maintain the Democratic power base. This regime collapsed with the internal revolt of the ethnic minorities, who numerically and politically became more important. In the contemporary cycle the regime is dominated by promoting *economic growth and a political inclusiveness*. The ambiguities between these political

TABLE 12.5 A TYPOLOGY OF URBAN REGIMES			
	Regime types		
Defining characteristics	*Organic*	*Instrumental*	*Symbolic*
Purpose	Maintenance of status quo	Project realization	Redirection of ideology or range
Main motivation of participants	Local dependency	Tangible results	Expressive politics
Basis for sense of common purpose	Tradition and social cohesion	Selective incentives	Strategic use of symbols
Quality of coalition (congruence of interests)	Political communion	Political partnership	Competitive agreement
Examples	Saunders (1980)	Stone (1989)	Boyle (1990)
Relationship with environment: local nonlocal	Exclusive orientation Independent	Exclusive orientation Dependent	Inclusive orientation Dependent

Source: After Stoker and Mossberger (1994)

and economic logics constitute the tension of contemporary urban United States.

Stoker and Mossberger (1994) identify three regime types: organic, instrumental, and symbolic (table 12.5). *Organic regimes* occur in small towns and suburban districts with a homogeneous population and a strong sense of place; their main aim is maintain the status quo. *Instrumental regimes* are concerned with specific targets identified in the political partnership between urban governments and business interests. *Symbolic regimes* occur in cities undergoing rapid changes, including large-scale revitalization, major political change, and image campaigns that try to shift the wider public perception of the city. We should see these three categories as ideal types, with any one city regime exhibiting characteristics, albeit in different proportions, of each type.

The concept of urban regimes focuses our attention on the linkage between business and politics and the tensions, compromises, and deals necessary for democratic politics to work in a capitalist society.

GUIDE TO FURTHER READING

I have drawn heavily on my previous work:
Short, J.R. (1984) *The Urban Arena*, London: Macmillan.
Short, J.R. (1993) *An Introduction to Political Geography*, London: Routledge.

On households in the urban arena:
Castells, M. (1983) *The City and the Grassroots*, London: Edward Arnold.
Dunleavy, P. (1977) Protest and quiescence in urban politics: a critique of some pluralist and structuralist myths, *International Journal of Urban and Regional Research* 1, 193–218.
Hacker, A. (1992) *Two Nations*, New York: Ballantine.
Saunders, P. (1979) *Urban Politics: A sociological Interpretation*, London: Hutchinson.

On business:
Benton, L.M. (1992) A witches brew: a history of pollution in Onondaga Lake. Unpublished MA thesis, Department of Geography, Syracuse University.
Clements, R. (1969) *Local Notables and City Council*, London: Macmillan.
Crenson, M. (1971) *The Unpolitics of Air Pollution*, Baltimore, Md: Johns Hopkins University Press.
Crouch, C. (1979) *The Politics of Industrial Relations*, London: Fontana.
Logan, J. and Molotch, H. (1987) *Urban Fortunes: The Political Economy of Place*, Berkeley, Cal.: University of California Press
Short, J.R., Fleming, S. and Witt, S. (1986) *Housebuilding, Planning and Community Action: The Production and Negotiation of the Built Environment*, London: Routledge & Kegan Paul.

On urban government and the state:
Boyle, R. (1990) Glasgow: urban leadership and regeneration. In M. Parkinson and D. Judd (eds), *Leadership and Urban Regeneration*, London: Sage.
Judd, D. and Kantor, P. (eds) (1992) *Enduring Tensions in Urban Politics*, New York: Macmillan.
Lukes, S. (1974) *Power*, London: Macmillan.
Stoker, G. and Mossberger, K. (1994) Urban regime theory in comparative perspective, *Environment and Planning C: Government and Policy* 12, 195–212.
Stone, C.N. (1989) *Regime Politics: Governing Atlanta* Lawrence, Kan.: University of Kansas Press.

Chapter 13

RESIDENTIAL MOBILITY IN THE CITY: CASE STUDY III

T<small>HE GREATEST INCONVENIENCES OF</small> B<small>RISTOL, ARE ITS SITUATION, AND THE</small>
<small>TENACIOUS FOLLY OF ITS INHABITANTS.</small>

D<small>ANIEL</small> D<small>EFOE,</small> A T<small>OUR THROUGH THE</small> W<small>HOLE</small> I<small>SLAND</small>
<small>OF</small> G<small>REAT</small> B<small>RITAIN</small> (1724)

In chapters 9, 10 and 11 I examined the operation of the housing market, the construction of residential areas, and the role of individual households in structuring their urban experience. In this chapter I will highlight, through the use of case study, just some of the connections between these broad themes. In particular I will show:

- how the housing market both reflects and structures household actions;
- how the actions of individual households reflect and modify the residential mosaic;
- how residential structure and housing markets are connected through the exercise of housing constraints and choices on different types of households.

These connections will be demonstrated by exploring the reasons for and consequences of residential mobility. Residential mobility, defined as the movement of households within urban areas, is now the predominant form of population movement in Europe and North America. Two-thirds of all moves in both the United States and Britain are intraurban. The actual amount of movement is considerable. Each year 10 percent of British households and 20 percent of North American households move. This chapter will present results from a study of mobility in a British city to discover who moves, why they move, and where they move from.

If residential mobility is viewed as one expression of the supply–demand relationship operating in the housing market, then previous research has undoubtedly emphasized the demand element. Two stands can be identified. The first is represented by the neoclassical, microeconomic models of the city (Alonso, 1964; Muth, 1969; Evans, 1973), which implicitly consider residential movement in terms of households moving to balance changing space requirements against the cost of the journey to work. Put simply, the trade-off model predicts movement away from the city center as household size and/or space requirements increase. Second, residential movement has been analyzed from the standpoint of the decision-making process of households. The seminal papers of Wolpert (1965) and Brown and Moore (1970) focused attention on the factors affecting the household decision to move, the evaluation of alternative vacancies, the search for vacancies, and the choice of a specific dwelling. In this approach great emphasis is placed on consumer tastes and preferences in the explanation of movement patterns. These demand-oriented approaches have limited explanatory as opposed to descriptive power. Their analysis, embedded within the ideology of consumer sovereignty, considers households as autonomous decision-making units and ignores the processes that structure the decision-making environment. Housing consumption patterns are not merely the reflection of household preferences but relate to the nature of housing finance sources and ultimately to the character of the socioeconomic structure. The second aim of this chapter will therefore be to use this perspective as a framework for discussing residential mobility, with emphasis on the effect and importance of housing supply and allocation in structuring mobility patterns.

THE APPROACH

The approach adopted in this chapter is to study a group of movers into different areas of the city of Bristol. This is a medium-sized city, approximately 90 miles west of London. It is the unofficial regional capital of the south-west of England.

A consideration of the range of destination areas allows the examination of similarities and contrasts in the movement patterns of households of different socioeconomic, age, and status categories, and consequently an analysis of the effects on mobility of differential access to housing. Because of time and cost constraints, only movement into or within the private sector will be considered. This selectivity obviously affects the general conclusions that can be drawn from this study, and the specific effects of this exclusion on the public sector will be noted in the appropriate places.

The primary data source used was the 1971 census, which gives a

*Residential
mobility in the city:
case study III*

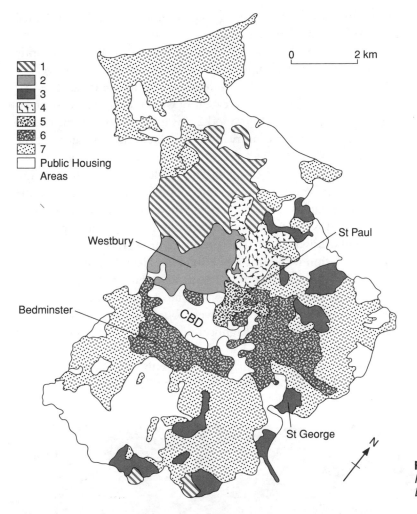

0   2 km

Legend:
1
2
3
4
5
6
7
Public Housing Areas

Westbury

St Paul

Bedminster

CBD

St George

N

Figure 13.1
*Neighborhoods in
Bristol*

range of information including socioeconomic status, housing,
demographics, and household structure for different area units. The
smallest available unit is the enumeration district (ED), which
includes on average between 200 and 300 households. In Bristol
there were 821 districts. Of these 219 were excluded because they
contained more than 60 percent of households renting from the
council (figure 13.1). As a preliminary to identifying residential areas
of the city, a principal component analysis with varimax rotation was
performed on ten variables for the 602 EDs within Bristol. The component scores of each ED were used in a nonhierarchic grouping
program that produces optimum groupings on the basis of approxi-
mating a local minimum for the sum of squared distances between
the observation and the group center. More details on the statistical
procedures are available in two of my earlier works (Short, 1976,

1978). The result was a seven-group classification of the residential mosaic of the city (figure 13.1).

Neighborhood 1 was a high-status residential area predominantly composed of owner-occupiers. The majority of households were at the childrearing and childlaunching stages of the life-cycle. The two outliers of this neighborhood category were recent high-cost housing developments. Neighborhood 2 was located close to the central city. In the nineteenth century it was the elite residential area but the large houses were subdivided into flats and bed-sitters for students and young professional couples. The residents of the third neighborhood were mainly low-income nonmanual and high-income manual households at the childrearing stage in the life-cycle. Owner-occupation was the predominant form of tenure. The distribution of this neighborhood reflected the patchy nature of recent private housing construction within the city boundary. Neighborhood 4 was an area of demographic diversity. It was in a state of transition from being an area of owner-occupation to one of multioccupation. In this area old persons in large houses were found adjacent to subdivided flats for young couples. Neighborhood 5, the most multiracial of Bristol's neighborhoods, had a majority of manual-occupation households and a tenure distribution evenly split between private renting and owner-occupation. It had the usual problems of poor

Illustration 13.1
*St Paul's, Bristol:
inner-city housing
(© Bristol City
Council)*

housing and overcrowding generally associated with run-down inner-city areas. Forming a girdle around the central city, neighborhood 6 had nineteenth-century terrace dwellings, mainly occupied by manual-occupation households in owner-occupation. There was a high proportion of elderly households. It was best described as a stable, inner-city, working-class area. Neighborhood 7 consisted of interwar and immediate postwar private housing. The residents were mainly in the low-income nonmanual and high-income manual categories.

The seven neighborhoods and the public housing areas constituted the residential mosaic of Bristol. To study movement into a range of residential areas all the neighborhoods should be sampled, but, given the constraints of time and money, this was not feasible. To give a range of coverage, neighborhoods 1, 3, 5, and 6 were selected. The selection was a balance between the search for diversity and the dictates of obvious constraints. Contiguous EDs within these four neighborhoods were selected as sample areas (figure 13.1).

Recent movers into these sample areas were identified from the electoral register. This list of persons over eighteen years of age is compiled by the local authority and, after amendments, is published every February. Although it is the only sampling frame giving universal coverage, it tends to underestimate movement in areas of multiple occupancy and obviously ignores the most recent movers. Generally only one form is delivered to each dwelling, and in areas of multiple occupation many households are not recorded. This means that the sample of households moving into neighborhood 5 is likely to underestimate households moving into multioccupied dwellings. Households that moved into dwellings after the compilation stage in late November are obviously excluded, which means that only those households that had moved within a three- to eighteen-month period from the date of the survey were identified. All households in the sample areas were checked in the 1974 and 1975 main electoral lists, and all households that appeared in the latter register but not in the former were identified. After an introductory letter interviewers went to these "new" households to conduct the questionnaire with the head of the household in early March 1975. Most of the required information was easily obtained through the questionnaire, and heads of households found little difficulty in answering questions related to previous address, sources of finance, and so on. In terms of why households move, respondents were asked, "What made you decide to leave the last place you lived in?" After the first response all respondents were asked if there were any other reasons. When no further responses were forthcoming they were asked to rank the reasons they had given according to importance.

Households identified from the electoral registers but excluded from the questionnaire included those that had moved from outside the city, those now in public housing, and those that had not moved within an eighteen-month period from the date of the interview.

THE RESULTS

The data generated by the responses to the questionnaire survey of recent movers generated answers to the question: Who moved? Why did they move? Where did they move from? What sources of housing finance did they use? The results are shown in figure 13.2 and tables 13.1–13.4.

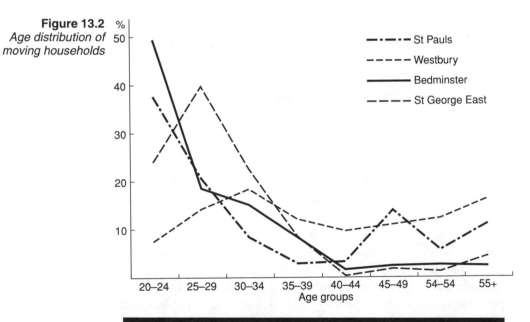

Figure 13.2
Age distribution of moving households

TABLE 13.1 SOCIOECONOMIC STATUS OF MOVERS INTO SAMPLE AREAS

	High income, nonmanual (socioeconomic groups 1, 2, 3, 4)	Low-income nonmanual (socioeconomic groups 5, 6)	High-income manual (socioeconomic groups 8, 9, 12, 14)	Low-income manual (socioeconomic groups 7, 10, 11, 15	Students
Bedminster	2.8	25.0	55.0	15.8	1.4
St George	15.3	30.7	48.0	6.0	—
Westbury	69.2	27.1	3.7	—	—
St Pauls	7.8	7.8	13.1	44.7	26.6

*Residential
mobility in the city:
case study III*

	Percentage of households in each sample	Reason given
Bedminister	70	Marriage/to own a house
	13	Change in household size
St George	66	Marriage/to own a house
	12	Change in household size
	12	Troublesome neighbors
Westbury	28	Change in household size
	23	To own a house
	10	Previous residence was only temporary
St Pauls	21	Force to move
	21	Setting up new household
	20	Changing space requirement
	12	Last place too expensive
	10	Poor physical condition of previous dwelling

TABLE 13.2   MAIN REASONS FOR MOVEMENT[a]

Note: [a]Reasons accounting for less than 5% of responses are not included.

Four main conclusions emerged from these results. First, the predominant reason for movement was the changing space demands associated with changes in the life-cycle. The formation and growth of the household provided the driving force for the majority of residential movement in the private housing market. Particularly important in the owner-occupier sector was the stage of household formation linked with the desire to own a house. For some households the movement into owner-occupation was prefaced by a temporary stay in private renting; for all households in this sample that were moving within the owner-occupier sector the average length of stay in the previous residence was five years two months. The corresponding figure for households moving from private renting into owner-occupation was two months. In this respect private renting provided a temporary form of accommodation, a stepping-stone to owner-occupancy. Second, in contrast to the majority of

TABLE 13.3   PRESENT AND PREVIOUS TABLES OF HOUSEHOLDS MOVING

	Present tenure	Previous tenure (as % of continuing households)				
	(% of all households)	Owner occupation	Council housing	Renting unfurnished	Renting furnished	Other
(A) To Bedminster						
Owner-occupation	84.7	42.0	4.0	8.0	26.0	2.0
Council housing	—	—	—	—	—	—
Renting unfurnished	9.4	4.0	—	—	2.0	—
Renting furnished	5.9	2.0	—	2.0	6.0	2.0
Other	—	—	—	—	—	—
	100.0					

Note: New-households, where the present head of household was previously living with parents or in-laws, constitute 42.5% or this sample. Of these new households almost 90% moved into owner-occupation.

	Present tenure	Previous tenure (as % of continuing households)				
	(% of all households)	Owner occupation	Council housing	Renting unfurnished	Renting furnished	Other
(B) To St George						
Owner-occupation	82.3	47.0	3.5	10.5	28.5	—
Council housing	—	—	—	—	—	—
Renting unfurnished	10.0	4.0	—	—	7.0	—
Renting furnished	5.8	—	—	—	3.5	—
Other	1.9	—	—	—	3.5	—
	100.0					

Note: New households constitute 44.9% of this sample and of these 70% moved into owner-occupation

	Present tenure	Previous tenure (as % of continuing households)				
	(% of all households)	Owner occupation	Council housing	Renting unfurnished	Renting furnished	Other
(C) To Westbury						
Owner-occupation	84.0	60.0	—	8.6	11.5	5.7
Council housing	—	—	—	—	—	—
Renting unfurnished	7.7	—	—	1.4	4.3	—
Renting furnished	5.5	—	—	—	5.7	—
Other	2.8	1.4	—	—	—	—
	100.0					

Note: New households constitute 11.5% of this sample, 90% of whom moved into owner-occupation.

	Present tenure	Previous tenure (as % of continuing households)				
	(% of all households)	Owner occupation	Council housing	Renting unfurnished	Renting furnished	Other
(D) To St Pauls						
Owner-occupation	42.5	13.8	—	10.6	16.2	—
Council housing	—	—	—	—	—	—
Renting unfurnished	25.0	5.4	—	8.1	—	—
Renting furnished	32.5	2.7	—	2.7	24.3	16.2
Other	—	—	—	—	—	—
	100.0					

Note: New households constitute 10% of this sample. Of these 50% moved into owner-occupation, 25% into unfurnished accommodation and 25% into furnished accommodation.

movers, there was a specific group; who moved not because of changing space requirements but because they had no other option. These very low-income households, elderly couples, single-parent families, and some service workers moved in the twilight world of poorly maintained rented accommodation in the inner city. This type of household was underrepresented in this survey because the sampling frame was biased against households living in multiple-occupation

Residential
mobility in the city:
case study III

Destination	Public housing areas	Neighborhood origin							Total
		1	*2*	*3*	*4*	*5*	*6*	*7*	
Bedminster (area in neighborhood 6)	16.2	0.0	5.4	4.0	6.7	1.3	38.8	27.6	100
St George (area in neighborhood 3)	4.6	0.0	11.9	14.6	0.0	2.3	33.3	33.3	100
Westbury (area in neighborhood 1)	3.4	42.5	33.3	1.7	8.7	0.0	1.7	8.7	100
St Pauls (area in neighborhood 5)	5.2	2.8	25.7	0.0	2.8	27.9	5.6	20.0	100

TABLE 13.4   NEIGHBORHOOD ORIGIN OF MOVERS TO SAMPLE AREAS (%)

dwellings and because the exclusion of the public sector ignored those households that had been rehoused by the local authority. Third, as a generalization, moving households had younger heads of household than the average for the total population. Intraurban migration in the private sector is an age-selective process. Fourth, movement generally took place within the same neighborhood or between neighborhoods of similar socioeconomic status. If, for the sake of argument, it is assumed that movement from the neighborhoods was in proportion to the respective populations of the

Illustration 13.2
*Bedminster,
Bristol: terraced
housing (from
Hebron House)
(© Bristol City
Council)*

neighborhoods, then the neighborhoods listed in table 13.5 send more households than predicted by the neighborhood population. From the table and the previous results it is clear that distinct channels of movement can be identified. These channels can be considered as streams of households of particular socioeconomic status into particular areas of the city. Three such channels can be identified: a high-status channel consisting of neighborhoods 1 and 2, a low socioeconomic status channel comprising neighborhood 5 and the student movers from neighborhood 2, and a medium socioeconomic status channel including neighborhoods 3 and 6. This latter channel can be subdivided in terms of the varying proportion of nonmanual workers, which is larger in the case of neighborhood 3. These channels can be seen as the process by which socioeconomic status segregation in the city is maintained.

TABLE 13.5 NEIGHBORHOODS SENDING MORE HOUSEHOLDS TO SAMPLE AREAS THAN PREDICTED BY RELATIVE POPULATION SIZE OF NEIGHBORHOOD

Neighborhood	*Origin neighborhoods*	*Percentage greater than predicted*
Bedminster	6	21.3
St George	6	16.0
	3	10.5
	7	5.4
Westbury	1	37.6
	2	23.0
St Pauls	5	35.0
	2	15.4

THE STRUCTURING OF MOBILITY PATTERNS

Entry rules and patterns of mobility

Entry into owner-occupation is defined by the ability to pay the initial deposit and to satisfy the housing finance sources of ability to make long-term repayments. Buying a house also entails a large commitment, given the necessary legal requirements and the need to find a

Illustration 13.3
*Durdham Down,
Bristol: expensive,
detached housing
(© Bristol City
Council)*

buyer prior to moving. Both of these requirements can take up to several months to complete. In contrast, entry into the private rented sector is defined primarily by the ability to pay the required rent and entails a minimum commitment, because movement into and out of this tenure category is comparatively easy.

The entry rules into the various tenure types affected mobility patterns in three ways. First, for households with no large commitment to accommodation, for example young professional mobile couples and student households that need accommodation for short periods of time, private renting provides a suitable form of temporary residence. When these households form and break up (following the pattern of the academic year in the case of student households), mobility occurs within the private rented sector. In Bristol some of these transient households are moving to neighborhood 5 in response to the changing patterns of supply of private rented accommodation. Second, for potential owner-occupiers there is the problem of raising the initial deposit and actually finding a suitable dwelling. If the formation of the household predates either of these two requirements, then temporary accommodation is required. This may account for the brief residence in private renting of subsequent owner-occupiers identified in this sample. Third, for those households that cannot meet the entry requirements of owner-occupation

– the very low-income households – alternative accommodation has to be found. Since public housing cannot meet all demands (Bristol had 5,000 households on the waiting list for public housing in 1975), these households are effectively trapped in the private rented sector. When they move, it is within the relatively cheap renting areas of the city. This is the case for some movers identified in neighborhood 5 who had little choice in their form of housing consumption.

Allocation procedures and patterns of mobility

The dominant form of movement for this sample of movers was into and within owner-occupation. For newly formed households the desire to become owner-occupiers was a considerable stimulus to movement. This wish is understandable, given the ability to choose between various forms of tenure. There were obvious financial incentives in owner-occupation at this time, which included tax relief and the possibility of securing a profit in the event of subsequent sale. Owner-occupation had obvious use value to households and the real possibility of exchange value.

The two most important sources of housing finance for those in the sample were the building societies and the local authority. Two criteria used by these institutions, related to their policy of minimizing risk, affect patterns of mobility. They both operate on a 25-year, or in some cases shorter, repayment period, which biases mortgages away from more elderly applicants. This tendency to grant funds to

Illustration 13.4
St George, Bristol: new box-type housing (© Bristol City Council)

younger households has the effect of filtering out the more elderly households from the process of moving, and partly explains the distinct age bias of the movers identified in this study. The age bias is less marked for the high-income households in Westbury because purchase of their present dwelling was often heavily assisted by the sale of their previous dwelling. The pattern of mortgage allocation only partly explains the evident age bias, because increased age and length of residence in one dwelling leads to greater ties with the dwelling and greater emotional links with the surrounding neighborhood. The propensity to move declines with increasing age and length of residence.

The second criterion used by these finance institutions in allocating mortgages is an income:mortgage ratio. In a previous survey of Bristol house owners, Ball and Kirwan (1975) found that the mortgage loan was between two and a half and three times the head of household's annual income. Given the unequal distribution of income between socioeconomic groups, especially between manual and nonmanual workers, different socioeconomic groups have differential house-buying powers. The different incomes and resultant mortgages explain, in part, the migration channels that were identified. Lower-income households that were able to obtain a mortgage were restricted to house purchase in the cheaper housing areas of Bedminster and St Pauls, whereas the higher-income households could successfully bid for the more expensive housing in Westbury (table 13.6). The general argument that we can draw from this is that households of different incomes and resultant mortgages have differential house-bidding functions, and when households move these differences are broadly reflected in migration channels. And, as noted earlier, these channels can be seen as one factor in the maintenance

TABLE 13.6 PURCHASE PRICE OF HOUSES IN THE SAMPLE AREAS (%)

Price	Bedminster	St George	Westbury	St Pauls
Less than £2,000	—	—	—	6.2
£2,000–£3,999	1.4	2.4	—	17.6
£4,000–£7,999	69.7	24.3	—	58.7
£8,000—£11,999	28.9	73.3	8.0	11.7
£122,000—£19,999	—	—	58.2	5.8
> £20,000	—	—	33.8	—
Total	100.0	100.0	100.0	100.0

of socioeconomic status within the city. Of course, this argument does not explain why higher-income households do not pre-empt the cheaper housing. To explain this in full it is necessary to consider the financial benefits of a mortgage commensurate with income and the role of housing consumption as a status symbol for higher-income households.

The differences in the mortgage allocation policies of the local authority and building societies have effects on mobility patterns and more general implications for the chances of some households to become owner-occupiers. The local authority, in comparison with the building societies, tends to advance a higher proportion of mortgages for lower-income households and for the purchase of older property in the inner city. Building societies, on the other hand, prefer to advance mortgages for the purchase of relatively new suburban housing. In Bristol, Szaroleta (1976) found that society managers operated a minimum lending policy in St Pauls and surrounding areas. These differences between finance sources are clearly reflected in the fact that 88 percent of households in this study that moved into owner-occupation and were classified as low-income, manual households received their mortgage from the local authority. Table 13.7 highlights the relative importance of building societies in St George and St Pauls. Although this table shows that the societies did invest in Bedminster, the majority of low-income, manual households moving into this area had received local authority mortgages. The intervention of the local authority had thus made possible the movement of low-income households into owner-occupation in the inner city. The building societies, by more readily granting mortgages for such new suburban estates as St George, have fostered movement to the suburbs.

TABLE 13.7 SOURCES OF FINANCE FOR HOUSE PURCHASE (%)				
Source	*Bedminster*	*St George*	*Westbury*	*St Pauls*
Building society	63.5	83.5	42.5	23.0
Local authority mortgage	22.5	7.1	—	61.1
Life insurance policy	2.8	—	3.7	—
Own funds	11.2	4.7	47.5	4.2
Loan from employer	—	4.7	6.3	—
Other	—	—	—	11.7
Total	100.0	100.0	100.0	100.0

CONCLUSIONS

In this chapter I have offered some results from a study of mobility in Bristol and discussed the relationship between this movement and aspects of housing supply and allocation in the private housing market. Before drawing general conclusions it seems pertinent to examine two deficiencies of this study. First, it was based on four areas of one city at one point in time. Changes in housing policy and changes in building society mortgage allocation in response to its relative position in the capital market will obviously influence the patterns of residential mobility. Second, this study discussed factors of housing supply and allocation couched in general terms and related them to local patterns of mobility. For example, data on the specific lending patterns of building societies in Bristol were not available, and this meant that their policy had to be inferred from national data, from information culled from other studies and from the responses to the questionnaires. Unless the societies in Bristol adopt a radically different posture from societies in the rest of the country this does not appear to be a major drawback. The results from other specifically Bristol-based studies (Ball and Kirwan, 1975; Szaroleta, 1976) suggest that it is not an inferential leap in the dark.

On the basis of the results presented, it would seem that residential mobility in the private housing market can generally be described as a response to changes in the family life-cycle. The formation of a new household and the arrival, growth, and eventual departure of children all cause changes in household space requirements, and residential mobility can be seen as the process whereby households move to obtain housing in conformity with their new space requirements. Yet there is a significant proportion of households that have little option but to move and that have little choice in their housing consumption. The expression of the response to changed space requirements does, however, reflect more than the preferences of individual households. The differentially priced housing market, the unequal distribution of income, and the policies of the housing finance institutions all affect the response of households to new housing needs. These factors structure the decision-making framework of households and broadly outline the type and location of housing available to different households. The decisions of individual households are more adequately explained as a form of adaptive behavior in relation to the nature of the housing system, which in turn is shaped by the nature of the wider society.

GUIDE TO FURTHER READING

This chapter was based on the following:

Short, J.R. (1976) Aspects of residential mobility in Bristol. PhD thesis, University of Bristol.

Short, J.R. (1978) Residential mobility in the private housing market of Bristol, *Transactions of the Institute of British Geographers*, New Series 4 533–47.

Other works cited include:

Alonso, W. (1964) *Location and Land Use*, Cambridge, Mass.: Harvard University Press.

Ball, M. and Kirwan, R. (1975) The economics of an urban housing market, Bristol area study, *Centre for Environmental Studies Research Paper 15*.

Brown, L.A. and Moore, E.G. (1970) The intra-urban migration process: a perspective, *Geografiska Annler* 52B, 1–13.

Evans, A.W. (1973) *The Economics of Residential Location*, Edinburgh: Bell.

Muth, R.F. (1969) *Cities and Housing*, Chicago, Ill.: University of Chicago Press.

Szaroleta, S.W. (1976) *Building Society Policy in Bristol*, Internal Housing Report, Bristol: Avon County Council, Planning Department.

Wolpert, J. (1965) Behavioural aspects of the decision to migrate, *Regional Science Association Papers* 15, 159–72.

Chapter 14

GENDER, SPACE, AND POWER: CASE STUDY IV

T HE PROBLEM OF POWER, LIKE SPACE, IS LEARNING HOW TO SHARE IT.
ANDREA SPURLING, *MEN AND WOMEN: THE USE AND*
ABUSE OF MUTUAL SPACE (1992)

Gender issues have been alluded to throughout this book and were given particular focus in part of chapter 10 under the section entitled "The City and Gender." In this chapter I want to give even more time and space to these issues because they are of such importance. This case study chapter, like the others, focuses on a particular area, but, unlike the other case studies, the area in question is not a particular city but a body of literature. The geography and gender literature is reviewed with a particular point in mind: the development of the idea of masculinity as a contested site of contradictory representations and practices. In this chapter I develop a number of themes raised in previous chapters:

- the social construction and reconstruction of gender identities;
- the role of space and place in these shifting identities.

I will consider the broad outlines of feminist critique on the practice and subject matter of geography before going on to discuss the growth of writings on men and masculinities. I will then draw attention to the importance of place in a full discussion of gender and power.

FEMINIST CRITIQUES

One of the most important social movements in recent years has been the development of feminism and feminist critiques of social structures and relationships. Feminism is a single term for what in reality is a broad set of multilayered positions and practices. Here I will focus on selected feminist writings as they inform the debates in geography.

Illustration 14.1
TUC Women's Right to Work march, 1982: the women's movement and a broader political struggle (photograph: Brenda Price)

Compartmentalizing is invariably problematic; nevertheless, a threefold distinction to classify feminist works is rewarding in that not only does it suggest a development and expansion of feminist debates over time but also it helps to contextualize the geographic writings of women, gender, and space within a wider feminist project.

Harding (1991), Di Stefano (1990) and McDowell (1991) have all adopted similar threefold divisions:

■ feminist empiricism or rationalism supplies investigation;
■ feminist standpoint theory examines the social construction of gendered identities;
■ postmodern feminism explores pluraled, gendered identities.

Feminist empiricism involves an alternative approach to social inquiry that challenges traditional androcentric research methods (Millman and Moss Kanter 1975). It criticizes existing methods of inquiry as being incomplete in their methods of analysis and structurally flawed, but it calls less for the disbanding of existing paradigms and more for a change in methodological inquiry. For this reason feminist empiricism has been accused of simply adding women to pre-existing science without addressing the central reasons for women's initial exclusion. Feminist empiricism, however, allows feminist research to enter existing bodies of knowledge with less resistance than revolutionary research methods and causes an immediate and inevitable transformation of the subject.

Feminist standpoint theory, as opposed to feminist empiricism, seeks not to dislodge male authority but rather to place female knowledge alongside it (McDowell, 1993b, 320). It celebrates difference and seeks to validate the female perspective by recognizing the distinct position of women in society. Feminism is therefore seen as able to produce more accurate and varied analyses than traditional research. Haraway, as a prominent contributor to feminist standpoint theory, argues on eight material "grounds" that women's experience is actually more inclusive than that of men. The perspective of the dominant system will invariably be both partial and perverse: "there is good reason to believe vision is better from below the brilliant space platforms of the powerful" (Haraway, 1991, 190–1).

In *postmodern feminisms*, a number of writers have drawn attention to the ethnocentric bias of much feminist writing. "Once again. Who is *we*?" (Rich, 1984, 231). Adrienne Rich addresses ethnocentric ideas of the homogeneity of women's experience as she locates her ethnicity within a feminist movement. Chandra Talpade Mohanty (1991) similarly acknowledges the need for a variety of women's voices rather than a totalizing feminist movement. She criticizes Momsen and Townsend (1987) for having a Eurocentric view of "development" that displaces women's differing concerns and aspirations in "third world" countries from those in the West. Other authors discussing the issues of decolonizing feminism include Jane

Parpart (1993) and Gloria Anzaldua (1990). bell hooks has also been a key discussant on women's differing cultural reactions to oppression; she notes that feminist debates in academia are not the only sites of resistance – by introducing the idea that for some unarticulated black women homeplace is a site of resistance and liberation struggle (hooks, 1990). Postmodern feminisms recognize the "significance of understanding and struggling against the *collective*, but not *uniform*, oppression of women" (McDowell, 1991, 131).

We can also identify the more recent emergence of a feminist backlash. There are the general commentators like Camille Paglia (1992, 1994) who provide a wide-ranging criticism of contemporary feminists as well as the more focused criticisms: Christina Hoff Sommers (1994) laments the ascendancy of gender feminism over equity feminism; Sherry Henry (1994) indicates the deep divide between the articulation of the women's movement and the hopes and fears of the majority of women; and Kate Roiphe (1993) questions the construction of "women as victim" in much feminist writing. The book edited by Koertge and Patai (1994) criticizes what they see as many of the "mistakes" of women's studies in the academy. Feminism has now matured, at least in the writings of the intelligentsia, to have spawned a growing literature of auto-critique and anti-orthodoxy.

Feminism and geography

The term "feminist geography" is often used, perhaps misleadingly, as an overarching title that refers to any area of geography and women. An important distinction should be made between *geography of women, feminist geography* and *analysis of women and space*. Johnson (1989) concludes that a geography of women used existing geographical paradigms to explore women's lives, whereas feminist geography stems from an emancipatory project to change the discipline from within. Analysis of women and space accounts for contemporary projects that lie uneasily between the two, not claiming to be part of a women's radical emancipatory project yet providing a more critical critique of existing methods of social inquiry than simply mapping women's lives.

Geographic dimensions of feminist empiricism are evident in the mapping of women's unfair subordination to men and spatial difference in access to resources between the two sexes. Such mappings occur at a variety of spatial levels. Differing international experiences are discussed by Seager and Olson (1986), Katz and Monk (1993) and Momsen and Townsend (1987). Such works provide a detailed mapping of the economic conditions of women in comparison with men on an international basis. For some this confirmed an international conspiracy to subjugate women in all societies; for others it provided empirical examples of the lack of women's access to economic power in countries outside the West. The national level of analysis includes Holcomb and Jones (1990) in the United States and Duncan (1989) in Britain. The microlevel of the urban environment and the home itself is also part of empiricist analyses, providing a source for a host of studies looking at women's urban spatial restrictions (Castells, 1977) and the gendering of space and appropriation of "public" areas by men through the built environment (Matrix, 1986).

Until the 1970s women remained invisible in many analyses of social space: geography was deemed guilty of being solely (hu)man geography. Most leading geographic journals had few contributions by women, while geography departments were conspicuously lacking women faculty. (This is not to suggest that there has been satisfactory progress on this issue either.) The early association of geography with men (and only men) stemmed from biological determinist ideas that boys possess innately superior spatial abilities to girls, as well as from the ideological foundation of societies (the Royal Geographic Society among them) that women should be excluded from positions of influence (Rose, 1993, 1). Zelinsky (1973b) was one of the first to address the masculinization of geography by providing empirical evidence exposing women's underrepresentation in all academic positions in geography departments beyond the undergraduate level, as well as the consequences of gender stereotypes in the discipline (Zelinsky, 1973a).

Origins of a distinct field labeled feminist geography are harder to pinpoint, however. Burnett's 1973 article in the radical journal *Antipode* is regarded as one of the first to formally highlight the invisibility of gender and the assumption that the male experience was the norm. A greater awareness of gender within the discipline was beginning to be formed with the first undergraduate text to raise issues of feminism and geography: it was published in 1984 by the Women and Geography Study Group of the Institute of British Geographers entitled *Geography and Gender*. Useful reviews of the history of feminist geography include McDowell (1993a, 1993b), Bondi (1990) and Bowlby et al. (1989).

Postmodernism and deconstruction theory challenge the simplicities of regarding patriarchal power as the ability to inscribe the public sphere with masculine images while feminine attributes are merely reflected in the private world of the home. Indeed, the very notion of "public" and "private" are contested to be academic inventions rather than reflections of real life. Bowlby et al. (1986) propose that the three spheres of home, workplace, and community "should not be seen as separate [but] the interrelationships between them should be recognized as reciprocal" and that the construction of gender identity is constructed in each of these spheres. (For other discussions on the relations between feminism and postmodernism, see Bondi and Domosh, 1992; Fincher, 1989; Probyn, 1990; and Mascia-Lees 1989).

Feminist geography challenged the implicit masculinity of the subject. It has been challenged not only to make women visible within the subject but actually to cause a revolution by challenging many of its basic epistemological foundations. Indeed, a persistent tension between assimilation and ghettoization (Bondi, 1990) is of particular current concern for many feminist geographers. McDowell's conclusion about whether this revolution in geography has actually occurred is not entirely optimistic as she debates on the image of "spoiling the cut or reshaping the garment": "Geography is, as yet, too little influenced by feminist scholarship, despite a decade, and more of exciting and innovative work" (McDowell, 1993b, 329).

THE DEBATES ON MASCULINITIES

"Years ago," notes the American writer Garrison Keillor, "manhood was an opportunity for achievement, and now it is a problem to be overcome" (1993, 11). It has also become a subject of intense debate. In recent years there has been a huge amount of writing on masculinity: there are readers (Thompson, 1991; Firestone, 1992); textbooks (such as Doyle, 1989; Franklin, 1984; Kimmel and Messner, 1989); journals, such as *Achilles Heel*, first published in 1978 (Seidler, 1991a), and *Masculinities: Journal of the Men's Studies Association*, first published in 1993; book series, such as Routledge's *Critical Studies on Men and Masculinities*, edited by Jeff Hearn, and *Male Orders*, edited by Victor Seidler; and a rapidly exploding body of literature that includes academic books as well as articles in popular journals. In the early weeks of 1994 alone *Business Week's* cover had the headline "White, Male and Worried" (Galen, 1994), *The Economist* had an article entitled "White Male Fear" (Lexington, 1994), and the cover of *Time* had a picture of a pig in a suit, collar and tie with the title "Are Men Really That Bad?" (Morrow, 1994).

Writings in social science have centered on men and yet at the same time have ignored their existence. Michael Kimmel (1990) refers to this as the paradox of the invisibility of men. This paradox is well captured by Jonathan Rutherford (1988, 23): "Today the masculine myth is being sufficiently questioned to drag it into view. Like the Invisible Man of H.G. Wells, whose death is signified by its return to visibility, the weakening of particular masculine identities has pushed them into the spotlight of greater public scrutiny."

There is a contemporary crisis of masculinity. Feminist critiques of sexism, masculinity, and patriarchy have made masculinity, for some if not all, a source of shame, a cause of guilt, and a subject of some scrutiny. Many males feel threatened by the underlying critique and the changing culture that questions continued male dominance in many fields of human endeavor. The male grip on public power is being questioned, challenged, and resisted. Traditional masculinity is subject to criticism by men as well as women (Abbott, 1987; Brittan, 1989; Brod, 1987). There is a sense of anxiety underpinning much of the reassessment and discussion of masculinity. Much of the work has been referred to as men's studies and covers a large area of interest; of the many let us consider three:

- masculinities and social change;
- the variety of masculinities;
- representations of masculinities.

Masculinities and social change

An important theme is the notion that masculinity, like femininity, is a social construct rather than a biological fact. As such it is subject to change and transformation. Changes in conception of masculinity reveal and embody wider social changes (Connell, 1987; Franklin, 1988). The changing expression of masculinity has been the subject of historical analyses. Rotundo (1993), for example, looks at the transformation in US masculinity from the revolution to the contemporary period. In focusing upon middle-class men in the north-east, he argues for radical changes; in colonial America "communal manhood" was stressed, emphasizing social bonds in the wider community and position at the head of the household. In the nineteenth century "self-made manhood" emerged, which stressed competition and tied men's primary identity to the workplace. In the twentieth century there's a "passionate manhood" that stresses aggression and sexual desire. Similar fundamental changes are shown in Roper and Tosh (1991) with reference to Britain. Lynn Segal (1990) looks at the evolution of masculine identities from the nineteenth century to the present day. She ties in modern images of macho masculinity to the period of colonial expansion, 1870 to 1914, when there was greater stigma associated with men's physical weakness. Segal concentrates her gaze on the postwar period and shows the evolution from family man and wartime hero to the Angry Young Men of the 1950s and on to the neo-macho gay men of today. She notes the multiplicities of masculinity and what we may term their neo-plasticity.

Sensitive historical analyses have shown that masculinity is less a function of biology and more a product of culture and history; less an eternal model and more a contested site of contradictory and ambiguous social forces.

Varieties of masculinities

A unitary concept of masculinity ignores its contradictory impulses and fails to make connections with other sources of social differentiation. The exploration of the variety of masculinities has been a focus of men's studies of recent years. A number of different elements can be identified.

First, there has been a critique of traditional male role models. The notion of the uncaring, insensitive man has been subject to scrutiny and criticism. The analyses range from the general (Kimmel, 1987; Morgan, 1992) to the psychoanalytical (Rutherford, 1992) and the more openly autobiographical (Jackson, 1990; Cohen, 1990). At this juncture men's studies merges with the nascent men's movement. The movement, or movements to be more precise, consists of a number of strands. Three can be noted. There are the *mytho-poetics*, who provide a critique of traditional models of masculinity and attempt to break through into fuller forms of manhood through group encounters, men-only meetings and rituals, and through resurrecting alternative male identities locked in myths and fairy tales (see Harding, 1992). One of the most influential is Robert Bly. A poet and translator, Bly is best known for his book *Iron John*, first published in 1990. The subtitle is *A Book about Men*. In this book Bly (1990a) provides a reading of the Grimm Brothers' fairy tale of Iron John, that connects with wider notions of male initiation and the need for mentoring. Elsewhere Bly (1990b) has said that the father–son link has been broken by the work patterns and domestic arrangements dominant in Western societies since the industrial revolution. There is a father-shaped hole in the heart of modern man. Bly urges men to get in touch with their inner warrior, their wild man that is hidden by conformity to contemporary society. Moore and Gillette (1990), much influenced by Bly, identify four archetypes of the mature masculine: king, warrior, magician, and lover.

There are also the more explicitly *profeminists*, whose position is a development of a positive response to the feminist critique (see Jardin and Smith, 1987; Kimmell and Mosmiller, 1992; Seidler, 1989, 1991b, 1994). This strand is more political and sometimes critical of the mytho-poetics. The importance of personal political action was summarized by Kimmel (1993) when he noted that "what we need is less Iron Johns and more ironing Johns." The articulation and development of this position has also produced a vigorous debate involving women responding to the men's movement and subsequent rounds of debate between men and women (Hagan, 1992; Porter, 1992). Questions arising from the debate include: Is there such a thing as a feminist man? The discontinuity between men and feminism has traditionally been large, with most men feeling left behind by feminist developments. And yet many are suspicious of the greater inclusion of men into the feminist project. Steinem raises the question: Is the men's movement "a movement towards a society of mutual respect and safety for all, or just propaganda for a kinder, gentler patriarchy or both?" (1992, v). And Susan Harding captures some of the ambiguity: "A kind of monster lurks in the logic of white feminist discourse: he is white, economically privileged, Western heterosexual man – and he is a feminist too" (Harding, 1991, 274).

Then there is what we may term the *new men* position as evidenced from such varied writers as Aaron Kipnis (1991) and Sam Keen (1991). Kipnis seeks to define a position beyond what he terms a heroic hypermasculinity and a feminized hypomasculinity, a position he defines as authentic, integrated masculinity in which physical characteristics are neither hard nor soft but flexible, neither controlling or controlled but vigilant, and emotional characteristics are neither close nor unprotected but receptive, neither aggressive nor passive but assertive, and neither defensive or wounded but one of deep feeling. Sam Keen in his book *Fire in the Belly: On Being a Man* attempts to find a similar kind of position for the new man, beyond the warrior myth, informed but not dominated by the feminist project of the past 25 years. The new man, according to Keen, is a site of paradoxes and some difficulty. He writes of moving from sunny pragmatism to dark wisdom, from having the answers to living the questions, from cocksureness to potent doubt, from numbness to manly grief, from artificial toughness to virile fear, from isolation to the awareness of loneliness, and from false optimism to honest despair.

A second element in the exploration of the varieties of masculinities has been a concern to identify the diverse characteristics behind the notion of man. This approach extends masculinity beyond a narrow, singular, undifferentiated entity. There are three powerful sources of differentiation. The first refers to the different male roles in personal relations: sons, brothers, lovers, husbands, and fathers. Each involves a different facet of the male experience (Firestone, 1992). The second source of difference is the varied social role that men perform: men at work, men at play, men together, and men with women (Thompson, 1991). The differences exhibited in each of these social settings suggest that the rigid concept of man needs to be replaced by a more flexible concept of man and masculinities. The third source of difference is with reference to the broader dimensions of social differentiation. These include stage in the life-cycle, race and ethnicity, nationality, and sexual orientation. Levinson et al. (1978) conducted one of the first major studies of the changing patterns of adult development. Their life-cycle changes of the novice phase of early adulthood, the settling-down period, the midlife transition, and middle and late adulthood may be applicable to women as well as to men and their biographical material is richly illuminating of the social consequences of personal psychological changes. In his very detailed ethnographic study of a small group of men who habitually eat at one restaurant in Chicago, Mitchell Duneier (1992) manages to highlight the connections between masculinity, race, and stage in the life-cycle. His analysis of the moral order of elderly, working-class, black men shows the various dimensions of difference that intersect with masculinity. In a similar way Anne Allison's (1994) study of a Tokyo hostess club reveals much about the construction of masculinity and national identity. The issue of sexual orientation is a complex one. A subtle difference can be noted. Whereas the women's movement has been informed somewhat by the writings and political positioning of gay women, the men's movement and men's studies have had less explicit contact with gay men. In the academy gay studies now include both men and women. However, men's studies have been denied the full creative contact with the male gay experience. But with an emerging concern with sexuality, the body, and pleasure perhaps this lacuna can be filled and a fuller notion of male sexuality can be explored.

The unitary concept of male and the single notion of masculinity ignores internal divisions between men and the connections with other sources of social differentiation. There is a variety of male identities and these crisscross with other sources of differentiation, including (along with some stereotypes in parentheses) age (from bright young thing to boring old fart), race (male blacks and their traditional association with virile male energy), national identities (such as the Australian notion of mateship), sexual identity (gay versus straight), and class and occupation (often associated with

Illustration 14.2
*Different types of
men. Men come in
all shapes, sizes,
styles and types.
Be wary of using
the term "men" with
a cavalier
disregard of such
differences (© Mike
Abrahams/
Network)*

competing body imagery and levels of male bonding to produce continuums such as from computer nerd to sleek executive to beefy dockworker). The resulting "cells" produce a rich mosaic from young, Scots, working-class, gay, to black, middle-class, American, cross-dresser. Even this small range should warn us of the great difficulty in speaking about either men or masculinity except in the very broadest terms.

Representations of masculinities

An important area of work has been on the representation of masculinity in a variety of texts. This has been one of the hot topics, combining, as it does, issues of gender and representation (Cohen, 1993; Craig, 1992; Hearn, 1992; Jackson, 1991; Roper and Tosh, 1991). This body of literature reminds us that masculinity has been portrayed in a variety of different ways at different times in order to achieve different purposes. These studies reinforce the notion that masculinity is not a single, homogeneous, unchanging fact but a construct "specific to historical time and place, continually being forged, contested, reworked and reaffirmed' (Jackson, 1991, 210).

As with women, the ways that men are represented are not neutral. There are dominant forms of representation. In a study of how men are represented in television Fejes (1992) shows that TV man is more likely to be employed, married, and dominant. TV man fits into the traditional patriarchal notion of man that so many of the men's studies literature tells us is not the true and only presentation of men. Fejes suggests that TV man can influence men who watch TV. Pecora (1992) discusses the way that comic-book heroes show a very stereotypical view of men and masculinity. The superheroes of comics, as in many other representations of men, remain silent to the changing notion of masculinities found elsewhere, as in the construction of the new man (see Chapman and Rutherford, 1988).

Different cultural forms have been used to depict masculinity. Visual culture, in particular, has played an important, often celebratory role in circulating images of male power and the norms of manliness. A selection of paintings in a special exhibition at the Tate Gallery showed a concern with sexual power and the depiction of the male body by such varied artists as David Hockney, Jacob Epstein, Jackson Pollock, and John Singer Sargent (Stephenson, 1992). Other paintings across a historical period, including John Everett Millais's 1852 *The Order of Release* and Stanley Spencer's 1937 *Double Nude Portrait*, also "signal a crisis of faith in the conventional premises of masculinity across a wide historical period. They show up the fragile nature of male social power and also question its related myth of sexual dominance" (Stephenson, 1992, 4).

Certain types of males are represented in certain ways. Black males, from the photographs of Robert Mapplethorpe to the popular street movies, are move often seen as embodiments of raw male energy, potent sexuality, and brute strength. Even in the supposedly more liberal realms of academic sociology Mitchell Duneier has suggested that with a heavy reliance on male ghetto-dwellers and hustlers "one should not rely too greatly upon ethnography for an enlightened image for these works concomitantly foster many of the same inaccurate images of blacks" (1992, 142). He writes of "the unconsciously demeaning image of blacks that emerges from much American sociological work" (1992, 147).

Representations are neither socially neutral nor politically innocent. Between the complex realities of multiple masculinities and the simple, more partial views depicted in various cultural forms lies the mark of power/lack of power, exclusion/inclusion, and a dominant/subordinate position in society. Representations reveal much about the operation of power in society.

Five conclusions can be drawn from this brief review of writing on men and masculinities.

First, masculinity is not a biological category as much as a social construct subject to change, revision, and multiple representations. Masculinity is not a fixed, coherent, or singular identity. This suggests a number of avenues of further work, including the mapping of different dominant masculinities over time and across space and the identification of the variety of male roles and their shifting nature as they are tied to broader processes. Some examples of possible connections include: the development of the male as lone hero and of what Macpherson (1962) identified in the capitalist-liberal ethos as possessive individualism; collective bonding arising from shared work experiences in the growth and development of male working-class occupations and working-class consciousness (Cockburn, 1983); the development of the so-called new man in shared work and domestic arrangements (Segal, 1990).

Second, masculinity is not fixed. it is a relational, constantly shifting attribute defined in relation to the feminine. Changing notions of femininity have caused a reassessment of masculinity. The move from women as dependent to women as partners has caused a shift in the perception of men and male roles in the family; from patriarch to partner may be glib but may have some accuracy. There are also material changes: in the United States in the 1950s an average middle-class family could maintain a house and children with just one breadwinner. To maintain the same style of living now more people in the household need to work. There is no one-to-one neat correspondence, but this economic pressure is part of the shift in perception and role from patriarch to partner.

Third, masculinity is a site of interconnection and tension with other sources of social differentiation, including class, sexual orientation, race and ethnicity, nationality, and stage in the life-cycle. The interconnection of these social differences produces a complex mosaic of identity and difference.

Fourth, masculinity is both lived experience and imagined desires. Social studies need to connect more with psychoanalytic theory to understand the role of fantasy in self-identification and social constructions of masculinity. The role and scope of male desire has not been given enough consideration in social analyses of masculinity.

Finally, masculinity is not only socially constructed and reconstructed, it is spatially grounded. Sallie Westwood's 1990 paper gives us just one example of a careful examination of one form of masculinity and its attendant spatial grounding and embodiment. She deconstructed "young black masculinity" in the public spaces of the street and football field. Police harassment and the hostile nature of the streets requires streetwise knowledge and the ability to act and react to confrontations with other men. Similarly, the football pitch is an "arena of contested terrain and an area of struggle in which masculinities are called up as part of the fight against racism" (Westwood, 1990, 59).

GENDER, SPACE, AND POWER

There is now a large body of work on feminism and feminist geography and a smaller, though growing interest in masculinities. The debates on geography and gender could and probably will take a variety of directions. In the remainder of this chapter I want to focus on the links between a relational view of gender, an appreciation of power, and an explicit awareness of the importance of space and place in the social construction and reconstruction of femininities and masculinities. What follows is more fragmentary and suggestive than coherent and definitive.

There are two points that define the terms of debate in this section of the chapter:

- gender as relational;
- the interconnections between gender, space and power.

Gender relations

Gender roles vary through time and over space and are constantly changing as dominant feminine and masculine roles shift and turn in relation to each other. There has been a great deal of work that considers the importance of time. Part of the feminist project has been the rewriting of (his)story, locating women within historical texts by rewriting existent stories, and unearthing previously unwritten subjects. In this sense feminism has served as a re-examination of a gendered history and a reappraisal of existing hegemonic methods of inquiry. (For a survey of work in what we may term historical geography consider Rose and Ogborne, 1988; Miller, 1983; Davidoff and Hall, 1987; and Nead, 1988.) The relational format of gender and time is also recognized within texts on masculinities. As mentioned earlier in this chapter, the works of Rotundo (1993), Roper and Tosh (1991) and Segal (1990) give historical narrative to the idea of constant shifts in both perceptions and presentations of maleness and patriarchy. They provide a critical analysis of gender relations and the social elasticity of masculine identities over time.

Gender and its social construction, I argue, varies not only over time and through history but between space and place. The character of gender construction is therefore both a reflector *and* an influencer of the spatial structure and temporal nature of our environment. Gender relations – the complex interplay of sex caste roles that each of us are assigned to any one time – therefore mirror our surroundings while at the same time influencing the structure of them (England, 1991, 135). The interplay of gender and space is at the center of a geography of gender. 'Geography in its various guises influences the cultural formation of particular genders and gender relations [while] gender has been deeply influential in the production of 'the geographical'" (Massey, 1994, 177). Spatial variability, therefore, not only implies a difference in the construction of gendered identities but proposes location as an integral part of their formation.

Investigation into the interplay of gender and space has been a central focus of feminist inquiry within geography. Women's varied experiences according to location and subsequent reactions to patriarchy provide a host of recent studies (Bowlby et al., 1986; Duncan, 1991; England, 1991; Fincher, 1989; Spain, 1992). Nevertheless, despite some implications that feminist geography should be just as much about men as women (Massey, 1994, 189), the other half of the gender equation – men – seems to be a neglected concern within most feminist geographic texts. And while there has been much work on the spatial nature of male sexuality (Bell, 1992), it is only recently that geographers have addressed a geography of gender inclusive of men and the spatial construction of masculinity (Jackson, 1991; Spain, 1992).

Gender relations are not static relationships. The variations can be captured by considering the differing types of patriarchal power (Ramazanoglu, 1988). Foord and Gregson (1986) highlight four forms of relations in patriarchy: biological reproduction, heterosexuality, marriage, and the nuclear family. Walby (1989), in turn, shows six sites with "dimensions" or elements of patriarchy: capitalist work, the family, the state, violence, sexuality, and culture. Hearn (1987) distinguishes four forms of reproduction – sexual, biological, generative, and physical/violence – that are organized through four dominant institutions of patriarchy – hierarchic heterosexuality, fatherhood, the professions, and the state – and two forms – paid work and ideology – that are not organized through specifically patriarchal institutions. These analyses assist in a compounded, pluralized view of patriarchal power and the diversity of masculinities (Hearn, 1992, 49, 237).

Linda McDowell and Doreen Massey's (1984) insightful discussion of the intersections of gender, capitalism, and situation serves to illustrate the heterogeneous nature of patriarchy and the fluid pattern of relations between men and women. Four distinct locations in nine-teenth-century Britain, from the rural Fens to urban Hackney and from the coal mines of the north-east to the central Lancashire cotton towns, provided examples of how capitalism and patriarchy were articulated together in the workplace. Relations between women and men varied as "contrasting forms of economic development in different parts of the country presented distinct conditions for the maintenance of male dominance . . ., capitalism presented patriarchy with different challenges in different parts of the country" (McDowell and Massey, 1984, 128). Simon Duncan (1991) also explores gender divisions of labor and the spatial variation in the degree to which women are engaged in paid work. His work also points to the complex pluralities of femininities and their reciprocal relationship with masculinities.

A near-contemporary example of the malleability of masculinities is provided by the example of the "machoization" of the male gay movement in the 1970s. Stereotypical masculine traits of physical strength and promiscuous sex, "machismo and muscles," are salient characteristics of hegemonic maleness, while gay maleness has been perceived as effeminate and weak, "queer and limp-wristed." Clone culture – the construction of a uniform identity related to traditionally "masculine" occupations such as the construction worker, leather biker, or cowboy – sought to affirm that gay men were, not just simply in appearance, "real" men too. Here gay life does not simply mimic hegemonic straight life but is a conscious appropriation and resistance to such masculine codes (Edwards, 1990, 114–15; 1994).

Space and power

The interplay between space, power, and gender is discussed by Leslie Weisman (1992) and Gill Valentine (1990). Public and private spaces are experienced differently according to race, gender, and class. What is "private" for some may be "public" for others, and what should be "public" for all often remains "private" for the few. The disempowered "street-walker" and the "street-dweller" have their private lives in full public view, while, conversely, "men can turn allegedly public city streets into a private male jungle where women are excluded" (Weisman, 1992, 67). Commodification of the female body through billboard advertising and the porn strip remind women of potential surveillance by the silent male gaze: "the 'respectable' male pastime known as 'girl watching'" (Weisman, 1992, 68). Women's inhibited use of public space is, Valentine (1990) argues, a spatial expression of patriarchy. Lovely open spaces such as heaths and woods and enclosed areas such as car parks and alleyways become gendered male spaces as a product of women's fear of confrontation. Patriarchal power is inscribed into the landscape through women's fear of violence. However, while some areas are perceived as safe during the day, fear of *all* areas predominates at night. (For different perceptions of crime between men and women, see Stanko, 1990.)

An important element in gender roles is the spatial dimension of

Illustration 14.3
Men and women in the same workplace: London rag-trade sweatshop (© Collections/ Geoff Howard)

power relations between the sexes. The most comprehensive example of such a work is that of Daphnie Spain (1992). Her book *Gendered Spaces* gives examples of how geographic and architectural spatial conditions have reinforced status and power differences between men and women. The exclusion of women from men's ceremonial huts is an instance of how limited access to the site of social knowledge and decision-making is relational to women's social power. Spain also looks at how education in the United States was distinguished, until relatively recently, by the spatial segregation of men and women. Women's increased access to educational establishments – from total exclusion, through separate classrooms to today's institutional acceptance – has again been met with an increase in women's status and power (Hansot, 1993). Gender, space, and power are linked. And unraveling, examining, and theorizing the links is one of the most important tasks of an inclusive geography of gender.

Andrea Spurling (1992), addressing sites of gender conflict and power relations, examines the spaces of education. Space in this context refers to the domination by men of university seminars and how women are silenced during and squeezed out of discussions. Seminars reward students not solely on their educational merit but rather on how well they react under patriarchally constructed assessments. Like Spain and Weisman, Spurling calls for an emasculating of existing conventions and a degendering of space, concluding, rather optimistically, that "the problem of power, like space is learning how to share it" (1992, 54).

Whatever the question, remarked Lenin, the answer is always power. Power is important to producing, maintaining, resisting, and changing gender relations. And the use and demarcation of space is integral to the exercise of power. There are connections between power and gendered spaces and space and power relations that can be uncovered by careful analysis of particular sites, such as the home, office, workplace, school, and university. In many of these places new gender roles are emerging. Our understanding of the dynamics of gender, space, and power can be advanced only by specific histories and particular geographies of individual places and characteristic spaces.

This chapter is based on a joint paper:

Short, J.R. and Fitzpatrick, A. (1994) Gender, space and power. Department of Geography, Syracuse University, mimeo.

The following bibliography is a vital part of the chapter, providing an important resource for further reading:

Abbott, F. (1987) *New Men, New Minds: Breaking Male Tradition*, Freedom, Cal.: Crossing Press.

Allison, A. (1994) *Nightwork: Sexuality, Pleasure and Corporate Masculinity in a Tokyo Hostess Club*, Chicago and London: University of Chicago Press.

Anzaldua, G. (ed.) (1990) *Making Face, Making Soul – Hacienda Caras: Creative and Critical Perspectives by Feminists of Color*, San Francisco, Cal.: Aunt Lute Books.

Bell, D. (1992) *Sexuality and Space Network Bulletin*, available from Department of Geography, Birmingham University, PO Box 363, Birmingham B15 2TT, UK.

Bly, R. (1990a) *Iron John: A Book about Men*, Reading, Mass.: Addison-Wesley.

Bly, R. (1990b) Robert Bly, Poet. In Bill Moyers (ed.) *A World of Ideas*, New York: Doubleday.

Bondi, L. (1990) Progress in geography and gender: feminism and difference, *Progress in Human Geography* 14, 438–45.

Bondi, L. and Domosh, M. (1992) Other figures in other places: on feminism, postmodernism and geography, *Environment and Planning D: Society and Space* 10, 199–213.

Bowlby, S., Foord, J. and McDowell, L. (1986) The place of gender in locality studies, *Area* 18, 327–31.

Bowlby, S., Lewis, J., McDowell, L. and Foord, J. (1989) The geography of gender. In R. Peet and N. Thrift (eds), *New Models in Geography: The Political-Economy Perspective*, London: Unwin Hyman, 157–75.

Brittan, A. (1989) *Masculinity and Power*, Oxford: Blackwell.

Brod, H. (ed.) (1987) *The Making of Masculinities: The New Men's Studies*, Boston, Mass.: Unwin Hyman.

Burnett, P. (1973) Social change, the status of women and models of city form and development, *Antipode* 5, 57–61.

Castells, M. (1977) *The Urban Question*, London: Edward Arnold.

Chapman, R. and Rutherford, J. (eds) (1988) *Male Order: Unwrapping Masculinity*, London: Lawrence & Wishart.

Cockburn, C. (1983) *Brothers: Male Dominance and Technological Change*, London: Pluto.

Cohen, D. (1990) *Being a Man*, London: Routledge.

Cohen, E. (1993) *Talk on the Wild Side: Towards a Genealogy of a Discourse on Male Sexualities*, London: Routledge.

Connell, R.W. (1987) *Gender and Power: Society, the Person and Sexual Politics* Stanford, Cal.: Stanford University Press.

Craig, S. (ed.) (1992) *Men, Masculinity and the Media*, Newbury Park, Cal. and London: Sage.

Davidoff, L. and Hall, C. (1987) *Family Fortunes: Men and Women of the English Middle Class, 1780–1850*, London: Hutchinson.

Di Stefano, C. (1990) Dilemmas of difference: feminism, modernity and postmodernism. In L. Nicholson (ed.), *Feminism/Postmodernism*, London: Routledge, 63–82.

Doyle, J. (1989) *The Male Experience*, Dubuque, Iowa: W.C. Brown.

Duncan, S. (1989) Gender divisions of labour in Greater London, *Urban
and Regional Studies, University of Sussex Working Paper 73*, Brighton,
Sussex.

Duncan, S. (1991) The geography of gender divisions of labour in Britain,
Transactions, Institute of British Geographers 16, 420–39.

Duneier, M. (1992) *Slim's Table: Race, Respectability and Masculinity*,
Chicago, Ill.: University of Chicago Press.

Edwards, T. (1990) Beyond sex and gender: masculinity, homosexuality and
social theory. In J. Hearn and D. Morgan (eds), *Men, Masculinity and
Social Theory*, London: Routledge, 114–25.

Edwards, T. (1994) *Erotics and Politics: Gay Male Sexuality, Masculinity and
Feminism*, London: Routledge.

England, K. (1991) Gender relations and the spatial structure of the city,
Geoforum 22, 135–47.

Fejes, F.J. (1992) Masculinity as fact: a review of empirical mass communication research on masculinity. In S. Craig (ed.), *Men, Masculinity and
the Media*, Newbury Park, Cal.: Sage, 9–23.

Fincher, R. (1989) Class and gender relations in the local labor market and
the local state. In J. Wolch and M. Dear (eds), *The Power of Geography:
How Territory Shapes Social Life*, London: Unwin Hyman, 91–117.

Firestone, R. (ed.) (1992) *The Man in Me: Versions of the Male Experience*,
New York: HarperCollins.

Foord, J. and Gregson, N. (1986) Patriarchy: towards reconceptualization,
Antipode 18, 181–211.

Foucault, M. (1977) *Discipline and Punish: The Birth of the Prison*, New
York: Pantheon Books.

Franklin, C.W. ɪɪ (1984) *The Changing Definition of Masculinity*, New York:
Plenum Press.

Franklin, C.W. ɪɪ (1988) *Men and Society*, Chicago, Ill.: Nelson Hall.

Galen, M. (1994) White, male and worried, *Business Week* January 31, 50–5.

Hagan, K.L. (ed.) (1992) *Women Respond to the Men's Movement*, San
Francisco, Cal.: Pandora.

Hansot, E. (1993) Historical and contemporary views of gender and education. In S.K. Bicklen and D. Pollard (eds), *Gender and Education*,
Chicago, Ill.: University of Chicago Press, 12–42.

Haraway, D. (1991) *Simians, Cyborgs and Women: The Reinvention of
Nature*, London: Free Association Books.

Harding, C. (ed.) (1992) *Wingspan: Inside the men's Movement*, New York:
St Martin's Press.

Harding, S. (1991) *Whose Science? Whose Knowledge? Thinking from Women's
Lives*, Ithaca, N.Y.: Cornell University Press.

Hearn, J. (1987) *The Gender of Oppression: Men, Masculinity and the
Critique of Marxism*, Brighton. Wheatsheaf; New York: St Martin's
Press.

Hearn, J. (1992) *Men in the Public Eye: The Construction and Deconstruction
of Public Men and Public Patriarchies*, London: Routledge.

Henry, S. (1994) *The Deep Divide: Why American Women Resist Equality*,
New York: Macmillan.

Holcomb, B. and Jones, J.P. (eds) (1990) *Geographic Dimensions of United
States Social Policy*, London: Edward Arnold.

hooks, bell (1990) *Yearning: Race, Gender and Cultural Politics*, Boston,
Mass.: South End Press.

Jackson, D. (1990) *Unmasking Masculinity: A Critical Autobiography*,
London: Unwin Hyman.

Jackson, P. (1991) The cultural politics of masculinity: towards a social geography, *Transactions, Institute of British Geographers* N.S. 16 199–213.

Jardin, A. and Smith, P. (eds) (1987) *Men in Feminism*, New York: Methuen.

Johnson, L.C. (1989) Feminist or gender geography in Australia?, *Journal of Geographic Higher Education* 13, 85–8.

Katz, C. and Monk, J. (eds) (1993) *Full Circles: Geographies of Women over the Life Course*, London: Routledge.

Keen, S. (1991) *Fire in the Belly: On Being a Man*, New York: Bantam.

Keillor, G. (1993) *The Book of Guys*, New York: Viking.

Kimmel, M. (1990) The masculinity of sociology. In J. Hearn, and D. Morgan (eds), *Men, Masculinity and Social Theory*, London: Unwin Hyman, 93–109.

Kimmel, M. (1993) Weekend warriors: the gender politics of the men's movement. Talk given as part of a day-long program entitled "Men, Gender and Social Change" at the Maxwell School of Citizenship and Public Affairs, Syracuse University, New York, September 23.

Kimmel, M. (ed.) (1987) *Changing Men: New Directions in Research on Men and Masculinity*, Newbury Park, Cal.: Sage.

Kimmel, M. and Messner, M. (eds) (1989) *Men's Lives*, New York: Macmillan.

Kimmel, M. and Mosmiller, T. (eds) (1992) *Against the Tide: Pro-feminist Men in the United States, 1776–1990*, Boston, Mass.: Beacon Press.

Kipnis, A. (1991) *Knights without Armor: A Practical Guide for Men in Quest of Masculine Soul*, New York: Putnam.

Koertge, D.N. and Patai, D. (eds) (1994) *Professing Feminism: Continuing Tales from the Strange World of Women's Studies*, New York: Basic Books.

Levinson, D., Darrow, C., Klein, E., Levinson, M. and McKee, B. (1978) *The Seasons of a Man's Life*, New York: Ballantine.

Lexington, D. (1994) White male fear, *The Economist*, January 29, 34.

Macpherson, C.B. (1962) *The Political Theory of Possessive Individualism*, Oxford: Oxford University Press.

Mascia-Lees, F. (1989) The postmodern turn in anthropology: cautions from a feminist perspective, *Signs: Journal of Women in Culture and Society* 15, 7–23.

Massey, D. (1994) *Space, Place and Gender*, Minneapolis: University of Minnesota Press.

Matrix (1986) *Making Space: Women and the Man-made Environment*, London: Pluto Press.

McDowell, L. (1991) The baby and the bath water, *Geoforum* 22, 123–33.

McDowell, L. (1993a) Space, place and gender relations. Part I: Feminist empiricism and the geography of social relations, *Progress in Human Geography* 17, 157–79.

McDowell, L. (1993b) Space, place and gender relations. Part II: Identity, difference, feminist geometries and geographies, *Progress in Human Geography* 17, 319–32.

McDowell, L. and Massey, D. (1984) A woman's place. In D. Massey, J. Allen et al., *Geography Matters! A Reader* Cambridge: Cambridge University Press, 128–47.

Miller, R. (1983) The Hoover in the garden: middle class women and suburbanization, 1850–1920, *Environment and Planning D: Society and Space* 1, 73–87.

Millman, M. and Moss Kanter, R. (eds) (1975) *Another Voice: Feminist Perspectives on Social Life and Social Science*, New York: Anchor Books.

Mohanty, C. (1991) Under Western eyes: feminist scholarship and colonial discourses. In C. Mohanty, A. Russo and L. Torres, (eds), *Third World Women and the Politics of Feminism*, Bloomington, Ind.: University of Indiana Press.

Momsen, J. and Townsend, J.G. (1987) *Geography and Gender in the Third World*, London: Hutchinson.

Moore, R. and Gillette, D. (1990) *King, Warrior, Magician, Lover*, New York: Harper.

Morgan, D. (1991) *Discovering Men*, London: Routledge.

Morrow, L. (1994) Are men really that bad?, *Time* February 14, 53–9.

Nead, L. (1988) *Myths of Sexuality: Representations of Women in Victorian Britain*, Oxford: Blackwell.

Paglia, C. (1992) *Sex, Art and American Culture*, New York: Vintage.

Paglia, C. (1994) *Vamps and Tramps*, New York: Vintage.

Parpart, J. (1993) Who is the Other? A postmodern feminist critique of women and development theory and practice, *Development and Change* 24, 439–64.

Pecora, N. (1992) Superman/superboys/supermen: the comic book hero as socializing agent. In S. Craig, (ed.), *Men, Masculinity and the Media* Newbury Park, Cal.: Sage, 61–78.

Porter, D. (ed.) (1992) *Between Men and Feminism*, London: Routledge.

Probyn, E. (1990) Travels in the postmodern: making sense of the local. In L. Nicholson (ed.) *Feminism/Postmodernism*, London: Routledge, 176–89.

Ramazanoglu, C. (1988) *Feminism and the Contradictions of Oppression*, London: Routledge.

Rich, A. (1984) Notes towards a politics of location. In *Blood, Bread and Poetry*, London: Virago Press, 210–31.

Roiphe, K. (1993) *The Morning After: Sex, Fear and Feminism on Campus*, Boston, Mass.: Little, Brown.

Roper, M. and Tosh, J. (eds) (1991) *Manful Assertions: Masculinities in Britain since 1800*, London: Routledge.

Rose, G. (1993) *Feminism and Geography: The Limits of Geographical Knowledge*, Minneapolis: University of Minnesota Press.

Rose, G. and Ogborne, M. (1988) Feminism and historical geography, *Journal of Historical Geography*, 14, 405–9.

Rotundo, A. (1993) *American Manhood: Transformations in Masculinity from the Revolution to the Modern Era*, New York: Basic Books.

Rutherford, J. (1988) Who's that man? In R. Chapman and J. Rutherford (eds), *Male Order: Unwrapping Masculinity*, London: Lawrence & Wishart, 21–68.

Rutherford, J. (1992) *Men's Silences: Predicaments in Masculinity*, London: Routledge.

Seager, J. and Olson, A. (1986) *Women in the World: An International Atlas*, London: Pluto.

Segal, L. (1990) *Slow Motion: Changing Masculinities, Changing Men*, New Brunswick, N.J.: Rutgers University Press.

Seidler, V. (1989) *Rediscovering Masculinity: Reason, Language and Sexuality*, London: Routledge.

Seidler, V. (ed.) (1991a) *The Achilles Heel Reader: Men, Sexual Politics and Socialism* London: Routledge.

Seidler, V. (1991b) *Recreating Sexual Politics: Men, Feminism and Politics*, London: Routledge.

Seidler, V. (1994) *Unreasonable Men: Masculinity and Social Theory*, London: Routledge.

Sommers, C.H. (1994) *Who Stole Feminism? How Women Have Betrayed Women*, New York: Simon & Schuster.

Spain, D. (1992) *Gendered Spaces*, Chapel Hill, N.C.: University of North
Carolina Press.

Spurling, A. (1992) Men and women: the use and abuse of mutual space. In
D. Porter (ed.) *Between Men and Feminism*, London: Routledge.

Stanko, E.A. (1990) *Everyday Violence: How Women and Men Experience
Sexual and Physical Danger*, London: Pandora.

Steinem, G. (1992) Introduction. In K.L. Hagan (ed.), *Women Respond to
the Men's Movement*, San Francisco, Cal.: Pandora.

Stephenson, A. (1992) *Visualising Masculinities*, London: Tate Gallery.

Thompson, K. (ed.) (1991) *To Be a Man: In Search of the Deep Masculine*,
New York: St Martin's Press.

Valentine, G. (1990) The geography of women's fear, *Area* 21, 385–90.

Walby, S. (1989) Theorizing patriarchy, *Sociology* 23, 213–34.

Weisman, L. (1992) *Discrimination by Design: A Feminist Critique of the
Man-made Environment*, Chicago, Ill.: University of Illinois Press.

Westwood, S. (1990) Racism, black masculinity and the politics of space. In
J. Hearn and D. Morgan (eds), *Men, Masculinity and Social Theory*,
London: Unwin Hyman, 55–71.

Women and Geography Study Group of the Institute of British Geographers
(1984) *Geography and Gender*, London: Hutchinson.

Zelinsky, W. (1973a) The strange case of the missing female geographer,
Professional Geographer 25, 101–5.

Zelinsky, W. (1973b) Women in geography: A brief factual account,
Professional Geographer 25, 151–65.

Chapter 15

RACE, ETHNICITY, AND THE CITY: CASE STUDY V

I N THE PROCESS OF RACE FORMATION, THIS TENSION BETWEEN THE VOLUN-
TARISM OF SPECIFIC FORMS OF RACIAL MOBILIZATION AND THE CHOICELESS
CONFINES OF RACIST DISCOURSE ECHOES THROUGH THE FORMATION OF ALL
RACIALIZED COLLECTIVE IDENTITIES.

MICHAEL KEITH AND MALCOLM CROSS, *RACISM AND THE*
POSTMODERN CITY (1993)

In chapter 10 I examined some of the relationships between ethnicity
and the city. In this chapter I want to explore these relationships by
looking in detail at the construction and maintenance of ethnicity in
one particular city, Syracuse, USA. The chapter extends ideas discussed in the previous chapter and in particular:

■ the idea that ethnicity is socially constructed and maintained;
■ the notion of ethnicity as an imposed identity;
■ the importance of space and place to these processes.

THE SOCIAL CONSTRUCTION OF ETHNICITY

The Latin motto of the United States, *E pluribus unum*, contains an
implicit observation and an explicit hope. The observation is that
there are many; the hope is that the many will be forged into one.
One of the most important and sustained sources of "the many" has
been race and ethnicity. Throughout the life of the Republic these
two interrelated dimensions have stood at the heart of social difference, social conflict, and social organization; they have been
particularly important in the larger cities where the ethnic mix has
been substantial and varied. Ethnicity serves as a vital ingredient of
metropolitan America. Katznelson (1979), for example, argues that
class consciousness in the cities of the United States was vitiated by
the strength of residential segregation along ethnic lines.

An important debate concerning race and ethnicity and the

American city can be summarized under the general heading of *melting-pot* (Hirschman, 1983). For over a hundred years the melting-pot hypothesis has been propounded and argued over. In essence, a simplistic model assumes that the various ethnic groups, while exhibiting differences when they first come to the city, will eventually be assimilated over generations through schooling,

Illustration 15.1
St Patrick's Day parade, New York, March 17 1992. More than 100,000 people marched through the city and almost two million took part in the city's celebrations (© Popperfoto; photograph: Don Emmert)

socialization, and contact with the wider society so that a more homogeneous American citizenry will be created. Behind the simple model
lies the assimilationist hopes of the nineteenth century and the belief
in the Latin motto. The model has rarely been confirmed by analysis. Goodfriend (1992) found that even in colonial New York City
there was not a melting-pot but a variety of ethnic institutions. Forms
of ethnic pluralism have persisted in the Republic. One of the most
important studies of the melting-pot model was undertaken by
Glazer and Moynihan in 1963 (1970). They studied Negroes, Puerto
Ricans, Jews, Italians, and Irish in New York City and found that
these principal ethnic groups maintained a distinct, if somewhat
changing, identity. In effect, the melting-pot did not occur. The
hypothesis was also called into question by the ethnic revival of recent
decades (Alba, 1990; Novak, 1972). This so-called revival, while
including a range of very diverse phenomena, suggested that ethnic
pluralism was not a temporary condition on the road to a unitary society but part of the fabric of US society (Fuchs, 1990; Lieberson and
Waters, 1988). A number of writers pointed to the persistence of ethnic identity, even in the third and later generations (Bouvier, 1992);
this identity has been given a variety of names, including voluntary
ethnicity (Farley, 1991), symbolic ethnicity (Gans, 1979), and imagined ethnicity (Yinger, 1994). Zelinsky (1992) asks us to imagine a
lumpy-stew metaphor for US society rather than a melting-pot.
Indeed the failure of the many to come together into the one, at least
in terms of a basic civil society, has led many commentators to decry
the centrifugal elements in contemporary US society (Schlesinger,
1992).

In this chapter the discussion of ethnicity will focus on the social
construction of ethnicity in urban United States. Three avenues will
be explored:

- the social construction of ethnicity by the US census;
- the representation of ethnicities in mass media;
- the self-construction of ethnic identity.

The census, race, and ethnicity

Despite the various definitions that make reference to physical and
cultural characteristics, race and ethnicity are not firm categories.
They are constantly changing, imposed, arbitrary definitions of identity. The arbitrary nature of these definitions is revealed whenever
they are measured, calibrated, or codified; as in censuses. The census
is the government's attempt to count and classify the country's

residents. The notion of racial and ethnic characterization is deeply embedded in the US census. Race and ethnicity are distinct from one another in that race refers to physical criteria while ethnicity refers to cultural criteria (Lee, 1993). The census acknowledges this distinction by including separate questions for measuring race and ethnicity. Ethnicity has been measured implicitly since 1850 and explicitly since 1980.

The chameleon-like character of racial and ethnic definitions is revealed in table 15.1, which shows how racial and ethnic identity have been categorized in the US census since 1810. Prior to 1970, the census enumerator assigned race identities to members of households on the basis of an interview and visual perception. These changing census category definitions mirror the country's changing obsession with racial identity and ethnic origin: the earliest census made a distinction between whites, Indians, and slaves; the census of 1820 added free colored people as a category; the census of 1830 introduced the notion of aliens by adding a question on place of birth; and in 1870 the birthplace of parents was also included, a question which remained in the census until 1980.

Table 15.1 reveals an abiding concern with race, ethnicity, and national origin of the population. What has changed, sometimes dramatically, over time has been the types of classification used. The censuses of both 1810 and 1990 had a simple structure of black and white, but from 1850 to 1920 the term "mulatto" was used. The census of 1890 made a finer distinction between mulatto, quadroon, and octoroon, and reflected the contemporary concern with the "scientific" basis of racial distinction. In 1930 these distinctions were dropped in favor of the "one drop of blood" idea that placed anyone with a trace of Negro blood as Negro (Wright, 1994). The categories used reflected the racial questions dominating the US: Chinese becomes a category in 1870, a time of rising anti-Chinese feeling in the country; in 1970 Koreans appear as an individual group.

Even a cursory examination of table 15.1 reveals the chaotic nature of changing categories. The categories often confused national origins with supposed racial identities. Mexicans, for example, were considered a separate race in 1930, counted as white in 1940, and in 1970 could be considered either whites or black depending on skin color. The past five censuses have all whites grouped together regardless of country of origin. The same is true for blacks. Yet Asians and Pacific Islanders are broken down by country of origin. Lee (1993: 91) attributes the mixing of ethnic and racial categories to "the political and ideological negotiations that underlie the decision-making process by which groups come to be defined as races or ethnic groups, and which groups get listed on census schedules."

TABLE 15.1 RACE AND ETHNICITY QUESTION IN THE US CENSUS, 1810–1990

1810
Free White males
Free White females
All other free persons except Indians not taxed
Slaves

1820
Free White males
Free White females
Free Colored persons
All other persons except Indians not taxed

1830
Free White persons
Slaves
Free Colored persons
Aliens – foreigners not naturalized

1840
Free White persons
Free Colored persons
Slaves

1850 and 1860
Schedule 1 – Free inhabitants
Color[1]
   White
   Black
   Mulatto
Place of birth, naming the state, territory, or country
Schedule 2 – Slave inhabitants
Color[2]

1870
Color[3]
   White(W)
   Black(B)
   Mulatto(M)
   Chinese(C)
   Indian(I)[4]

*Race, ethnicity,
and the city:
case study V*

Place of Birth, naming state or territory of US; or the Country, if of foreign birth[5]

Parentage[6]
    Father of foreign birth
    Mother of foreign birth

1880
Color[7]
    White(W)
    Black(B)
    Mulatto(M)
    Chinese(C)
    Indian(I)[8]
Nativity[9]
    Place of birth of this person, naming state or territory of United States, or the country, if of foreign birth
    Place of birth of the father of this person, naming the state or territory of United States, or the country, if of foreign birth
    Place of birth of the mother of this person, naming the state or territory of United States, or the country, if of foreign birth
Indian Division . . . Schedule 1 – Population
[This was an attempt at full enumeration of all Native Americans on tribal lands]
From "Personal Description":
    If this person is of full-blood of this tribe, enter "/." For mixture with another tribe, enter name of latter. For mixture with white, enter "W.;" with black, "B.;" with mulatto, "Mu."
    If this is a white person adopted into the tribe, enter "W.A.;" if a negro or mulatto, enter "B.A."

1890
Whether white, black, mulatto, quadroon, octoroon, Chinese, Japanese, or Indian[10,11]
Place of birth
Place of birth of father[12]
Place of birth of mother

1900
Color or race[13]
Place of birth of this person[14]

Place of birth of father of this person
Place of birth of mother of this person
Schedule No. 1 – Population: Indian population
Has this Indian any white blood; if so, how much? (0,½,¼,⅛)

1910 and 1920
Color or race[15]
Place of birth of this person[16]
Place of birth of father of this person
Place of birth of mother of this person
Schedule 1 – Population: Indian population
[Modified version of the 1900 Indian Population schedule. However, the proportion of Indian blood (as a fraction) was measured against three separate categories: Indian, White, and Black.]

1930[17] and 1940[18]

1950
Race
   White, Negro, American Indian, Japanese, Chinese, Filipino, Other

1960
Is this person:
   White, Negro, American Indian, Japanese, Chinese, Filipino, Hawaiian, Part Hawaiian, Aleut, Eskimo, (etc.)?[19]

1970
Color or race[20]
   White, Japanese, Hawaiian, Negro or Black, Chinese, Filipino, Korean, Other, American Indian[21]
Where was this person born?
Is this person's origin or descent:
   Mexican, Puerto Rican, Cuban, Central or South American, Other Spanish, None of the Above
What country was his [the respondent] father born in?

*Race, ethnicity,
and the city:
case study V*

What country was his [the respondent] mother born in?[22]

1980[23]

Is this person

White, Black or Negro, Japanese, Chinese, Filipino, Korean, Vietnamese, Asian Indian, Hawaiian, Guamanian, Samoan, Eskimo, Aleut, American Indian, and Other[24]

Is this person of Spanish/Hispanic origin or descent?

No, Mexican-American or Chicano, Puerto Rican, Cuban, other Spanish/Hispanic

What is this person's ancestry?[25]

1990

Race[26]

White, Black or Negro, American Indian, Eskimo, Aleut, Chinese, Japanese, Filipino, Asian Indian, Hawaiian, Samoan, Korean, Guamanian, Vietnamese, Other API

Is — of Spanish/Hispanic origin?[27]

What is this person's ancestry or ethnic origin?

Notes

1   From "Instructions to Marshals and Assistant Marshals – Census of 1850": "Under heading 6, entitled 'Color,' in all cases where the person is white, leave the space blank; in all cases where the person is black, insert the letter B; if mulatto, insert M. It is very desirable that these particulars be carefully regarded."

2   From "Explanation of Schedule 2 – Slave Inhabitants": "Under heading 5, entitled, 'Color,' insert, in all cases, whether the slave is black, the letter B; when he or she is a mulatto, insert M. The color of all slaves should be noted."

3   From "Instructions to Assistant Marshals": "It must not be assumed that, where nothing is written in this column, 'White' is to be understood. The column is always to be filled. Be particularly careful in reporting the class *Mulatto* [orig. emphasis]. The word is here generic, and includes quadroons, octoroons, and all persons having any perceptible trace of African blood. Important scientific results depend upon the correct determination of this class in schedules 1 and 2."

4   Native American Indians.

5   From "Instructions to Assistant Marshals": "Column 10 will contain the 'Place of birth' of every person named upon the schedule . . . If of foreign birth, the country will be named as specifically as possible. Instead of writing 'Great Britain' as the place of birth, give the particular country, as England, Scotland, Wales. Instead of 'Germany,' specify the State, as Prussia, Baden, Bavaria, Wurttemburg, Hesse Darmstadt, etc."

6   Questions to be answered simply "yes" or "no."

7   From "Duties of Enumerators": "It must not be assumed that, where nothing is written in this column, 'White' is to be understood. The column is always to be filled. Be particularly careful in reporting the class *Mulatto* [orig. emphasis]. The word is here generic, and includes quadroons, octoroons, and all persons having any perceptible trace of African blood. Important scientific results depend upon the correct determination of this class in schedules 1 and 5."

8   From "Duties of Enumerators": "Indians not in tribal relations, whether full-bloods or half-breeds, who are found mingled with the white population, residing in white families, engaged as servants or laborers, or living in huts or wigwams on the outskirts of towns or settlements are to be regarded as a part of the ordinary population of the country for the constitutional purpose of the apportionment of Representatives among the States, and are to be embraced in the enumeration."

9   Same as 1870.

10 From "Instructions to Enumerators – Census of 1890": "Write *white, black, mulatto, quadroon, octoroon, Chinese, Japanese,* or *Indian* [orig. emphasis], according to the color or race of the person enumerated. Be particularly careful to distinguish between blacks, mulattoes, quadroons and octoroons. The word 'black' should be used to describe those persons who have three-fourths or more black blood; 'mulatto,' those persons who have from three-eighths to five-eighths black blood; 'quadroon,' those persons who have one-fourth black blood; and 'octoroon,' those persons who have one-eighth or any trace of black blood."

[11] See note 8.

[12] From "Instructions to Enumerators – Census of 1890": "The names of *countries*, and not of cities, are wanted. In naming the country of foreign birth, however, do not write, for instance, 'Great Britain,' but give the particular country, as *England, Scotland* or *Wales* . . . If born in Canada or Newfoundland, write the word 'English' or 'French' after the particular place of birth, so as to distinguish between persons born in any part of British America of French and English extraction respectively. *This is a most important requirement and must be closely observed in each case and the distinction carefully made* [orig. emphasis]."

[13] From "Instructions to Enumerators": "Write 'W' for white; 'B' for black (negro or negro descent); 'Ch' for Chinese; 'Jp' for Japanese, and 'In' for Indian, as the case may be."

[14] From "Instructions to Enumerators": "If the person was born outside the United States, enter in column 13 the country (not city or district) in which he was born. By country is meant usually a region whose people have direct relation with other countries. Thus, do not write Prussia or Saxony, but Germany. To this rule, however, note the following exceptions . . . Write Ireland, England, Scotland, or Wales rather than Great Britain. Write Hungary or Bohemia rather than Austria for persons born in Hungary or Bohemia, respectively. *Write Finland rather than Russia for persons born in Finland* [orig. emphasis]."

[15] From "Instructions to Enumerators": "Write 'W' for white; 'B' for black; 'Mu' for mulatto; 'Ch' for Chinese; 'Jp' for Japanese, and 'In' for Indian, as the case may be. For all persons not falling within one of these classes, write 'Ot' (for other), and write on the left-hand margin of the schedule the race of the person indicated."

[16] See note 14. "*Do not rely upon the language spoken to determine birthplace* – This is especially true of German, for over one-third of the Austrians and nearly three-fourths of the Swiss speak German. In the case of persons speaking German, therefore, inquire carefully whether the birthplace was *Germany, Switzerland, Austria* or elsewhere."

[17] The 1930 Census was essentially the same but contained specific instructions for reporting race. "A person of mixed

White and Negro blood was to be returned as Negro, no matter how small the percentage of Negro blood; someone part Indian and part Negro also was to be listed as Negro unless the Indian blood predominated and the person was generally accepted as an Indian in the community. A person of mixed White and Indian blood was to be returned as an Indian, except where the percentage of Indian blood was very small or where he or she was regarded as White in the community . . . In order to obtain separate figures for Mexicans, it was decided that all persons born in Mexico, or having parents born in Mexico, who were not definitely White, Negro, Indian, Chinese, or Japanese, would be returned as Mexicans (Mex) . . . Any mixture of White and some other race was to be reported according to the race of the parent who was not White: mixtures of colored races were to be listed according to the father's race, except Negro-Indian (discussed above)."

[18] The 1940 census contained essentially the same questions as the previous three censuses. However, Mexicans were now to be reported as White unless they definitely had blood from Indian, Black, or a race other than White.

[19] "The instructions for completing P5 (race or color) by observation directed that Puerto Ricans, Mexicans, or other persons of Latin descent would be classified as 'White' unless they were definitely Negro, Indian, or some other race. Southern European and Near Eastern nationalities also were to be considered White. Asian Indians were to be classified as 'Other,' and 'Hindu' written in."

[20] A long "conversion" list was given to the enumerators as to how to score written-in entries. Examples include "Chicano," "LaRaza," "Mexican-American," "Moslem," and "Brown" which would be changed to "White" for census purposes and "Brown (Negro)" would be considered "Negro or Black" for census purposes.

[21] If the "American Indian" bubble was filled in, the respondent was asked to print the tribe name also.

[22] Under the blanks given for both of these questions is written "Name of foreign country; or Puerto Rico, Guam, etc."

[23] Enumerators were no longer allowed to mark a schedule by observation. The instructions were to mark the race according to the one the respondent most identified. If this was

*Race, ethnicity,
and the city:
case study V*

not possible, the race of the respondent's mother was to be identified. If this was unsatisfactory, the first racial group identified was to be reported. Unlike 1970, answers such as "Brown" and "Mexicano" could be entered as "Other" unless one of the listed categories was chosen.

24 A response of "American Indian" or "Other" required a write-in response of tribe or nationality.

25 Extensive directions were given as to how to report one's ancestry. Examples given underneath the space provided for the answer are: Afro-American, English, French, German, Honduran, Hungarian, Irish, Italian, Jamaican, Korean, Lebanese, Mexican, Nigerian, Polish, Ukrainian, Venezuelan, etc.

26 The full text of the question is as follows: "What is ——'s race? For example, White, Black, American Indian, Eskimo, Aleut or an Asian or Pacific Islander group such as Chinese, Filipino, Hawaiian, Korean, Vietnamese, Japanese, Asian Indian, Samoan, Guamanian, and so on. Fill ONE circle for the race that the person considers himself/herself to be. If response is "American Indian," ask – What is the name of ——'s enrolled or principal tribe? If response is an "Other API" group such as Cambodian, Tongan, Laotian, Hmong, Thai, Pakistani, and so on, fill the "Other API" circle and print the name of the group. If response is "Other race," ask – Which group does —— consider (himself/herself) to be?"

27 The same question as asked in the 1980 census, except a blank was provided for those marking "other Spanish/Hispanic."

Source: Bureau of the Census (1989)

Illustration 15.2
People of different shades of black, USA. In the US Census the young men could be classified as black, white or Hispanic (© Richard Levine)

Aside from the definitional problem, post-1920 censuses allow only one answer regarding an individual's race, which ignores the fact that there are many people of "mixed" racial backgrounds. The census makes the underlying assumption that people are of single, pure racial backgrounds, an assumption that, given the mixing in the United States, is at best optimistic and at worst simply incorrect (Wright, 1994). The census has not so much measured race and ethnicity as helped create categories of race and ethnicity.

The increasing reliance on racial and ethnic data for the allocation of government resources makes census questions on race and ethnicity of special importance. After a great deal of lobbying, primarily by Mexican-American leaders, a question on Spanish/Hispanic origin was added to the 1970 census although the question was present only on the long-form of the census, which was distributed to just 5 percent of the country's population. By 1980 the Hispanic origin question was on the short-form distributed to the entire population. Until the introduction of this question, the US Hispanic population was severely undercounted. Because Hispanic origin is not stipulated on birth and death certificates it had been impossible to estimate the

Hispanic undercount, as had been done for the black population since 1950 (Choldin, 1986).

The censuses of 1980 and 1990

The 1980 and 1990 censuses broke new ground in the way they approached the question of ethnicity. In 1980, in an attempt to gather more detailed ethnic information, the question "What is this person's ancestry?" replaced the parents' birthplace question. This open-ended question was included in the 1990 census in a slightly different form: "What is this person's ancestry or ethnicity?" Respondents could insert any term in the blank and were instructed to write the ancestry group with which they most closely identified and, because the US census is forbidden by law to gather information on religion, that the answer was not to be a religion. These questions were asked in addition to the separate questions of Spanish origin or Hispanic ethnicity.

The open-ended ancestry question permitted multiple listings of ancestry and allowed the respondents to fill in an ethnic categorization rather than choose from a set of groups predetermined by the Bureau of the Census (and Congress). However, a number of problems have arisen.

First, a significant problem with measuring ethnicity in the census is that no religious data can be collected. The Bureau of the Census is barred by law from asking questions regarding religion in any situation in which an answer is obligatory. Any entry of a religion as the first ethnicity in the open-ended question is therefore ignored. This presents an inherent flaw in the ethnicity data presented by the census because, for many, religion is an integral part of their ethnic identity. This is a particular problem for the Jewish population in the United States, many of whom count their religion as their most important ethnic identity. As evidence, Hout and Goldstein (1994) found religion to be the most influential factor in the intermarriage of ethnic groups.

Second, although the question permitted an unlimited number of entries, subsequent coding filtered this information. Only the first two were coded and, as shown in table 15.2, many answers were reassigned during the coding. For example, those who entered "Jewish" were designated as "other" while those who entered "British" were included in the count of "English," in effect ignoring the fact that Scotland, Northern Ireland, and Wales are also part of Britain.

Third, problems also arise because, as James Allen and Eugene Turner (1988, 3) point out, "there could be significant differences

**TABLE 15.2   US CODING PROCEDURES FOR THE 1990 OPEN-
ENDED ANCESTRY QUESTION NO. 13: 'WHAT IS THIS
PERSON'S ANCESTRY OR ETHNIC ORIGIN?'**

Respondent's Answer			*Coding by Census*	
German	Bavarian		Bavarian	
Polish	American		Polish	
British	English			
Scotch	Irish	English	Scotch-Irish	English
English	Irish	French	English	Irish
American[1]			American	
Jewish[2]			Other	
"Multi-national"			"Ancestry not reported"	
"Adopted"			"Ancestry not reported"	
"No idea"			"Ancestry not reported"	

Notes

[1] In 1980, an entry of "American" was coded as "Ancestry
not specified"

[2] An entry of any religion was designated as "Other"

Source: 1990 Census of Population and Housing, Guide Part
B: Glossary

between a person's actual predominant ancestral background and
what the person thinks is his or her predominant ancestry." The
ancestry question permits respondents to label themselves by country of origin (nationality) or by ethnic group. There is no measure to
identify the extent to which answers represent "real" ancestry as
opposed to symbolic or imagined membership. Lieberson (1985)
offers a four-tier classification system which is helpful when used in
conjunction with the concept of ethnic self-creation: true ancestral
origins, believed ancestral origins, self-identification, and imposed

Figure 15.1
*Lieberson's
typology of
ancestry reportage
as applied to the
US Censuses*
Source: Adapted
from Lieberson
(1985)

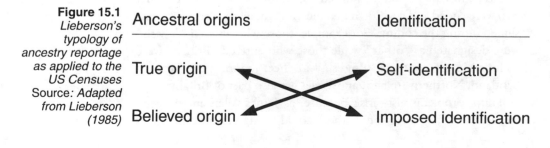

Ancestral origins — Identification

True origin — Self-identification

Believed origin — Imposed identification

identification (see figure 15.1). The first two refer to the actual bloodlines of one's family. The latter two refer to one's ethnic identification. The censuses before 1980 targeted the first and last conditions: ancestral origins and imposed identification. The 1980 and 1990 censuses targeted the second and third conditions: believed ancestral origins and self-identification.

The effect of these changes to the census can be seen in figure 15.2, which illustrates the percentage of Irish, Blacks, and Hispanics in the United States from 1900 to 1990 as measured by the census. Notice how the black population remains relatively constant between 10 and 12 percent. The stability is due in part to the stability of the population but also to the consistency of the category "black" in successive censuses. The Hispanic population increases dramatically, due partly

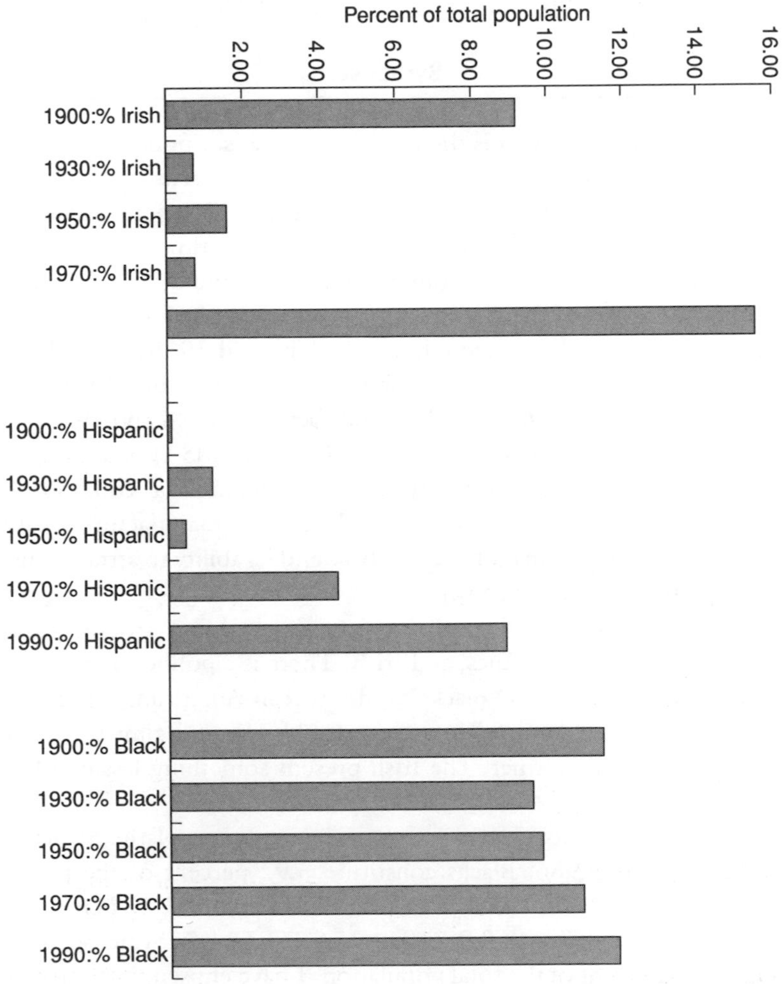

Percent of total population

	1900:% Irish
	1930:% Irish
	1950:% Irish
	1970:% Irish
	1900:% Hispanic
	1930:% Hispanic
	1950:% Hispanic
	1970:% Hispanic
	1990:% Hispanic
	1900:% Black
	1930:% Black
	1950:% Black
	1970:% Black
	1990:% Black

Figure 15.2
Selected ethnic groups in the US, 1900–90

to increased in-migration but also partly to the widening net of the census questions. The large increase between 1970 and 1990 is a result partly of the more open-ended ethnicity questions which appear in the 1990 census as well as of the Hispanic origin question added in 1970 and extended to the 100 percent short-form since 1980. The most dramatic result of the ancestry question is in the changing percentage of Irish, which increased enormously from 1970 to 1990, a time when in-migration of Irish was minimal. In effect, the census questions "created" an increased Irish population.

The census is a social construct subject to political pressure and reflects social concerns. The census does not so much measure racial and ethnic reality as much as it creates this reality. The census constructs race and ethnicity through the questions asked, the groups listed as choices, the answers permitted, and the way in which answers are coded and recorded.

Syracuse

The focus of this chapter is the city of Syracuse (see figure 15.3). For almost a hundred years, up until the 1970s, Syracuse grew as an industrial city with an economy initially based on chemicals and more recently on diversified manufacturing. During this time the city experienced successive waves of immigration from around the world and from other parts of the country. It was a typical north-eastern manufacturing city with a varied ethnic mix. The mid-1970s marked the beginning of a slump. Manufacturing employment fell by some 6,000 jobs from 1964 to 1984, and by 9,000 between 1984 and 1989. In 1990 the Syracuse metropolitan statistical area (MSA) had a population of 659,986 and the city had a population of 163,860. A thumbnail portrait of the city would reveal a manufacturing city losing its traditional manufacturing base and its ability to attract a significant number of newcomers.

In this chapter I will focus on three specific "ethnic" groups within Syracuse: Blacks, Hispanics, and Irish. There is a politics of naming, and I will use the terms "Blacks" and "African-Americans" as well as "Hispanics" and "Latinos" interchangeably. Through time the latter have replaced the former. The Irish present something less of a linguistic problem.

The 1990 census identifies the total population of the Syracuse MSA to be 659,986. Blacks constitute 5.92 percent of the population, with a total of 39,035 residents. Hispanics are 1.35 percent of Syracuse's population at 8,926. The 154,251 Irish in Syracuse make up 23.38 percent of the total population. I have chosen these groups

Figure 15.3
Location of Syracuse

for case study comparison because of the important differences between them. The Irish and Black populations represent old, established ethnic groups in Syracuse but with very different experiences, while the Hispanics are a much more recent immigrant group.

The data on the distribution of these three groups (figure 15.4) reflect the composition of many industrial north-east cities: the large population of Irish and those of Irish descent; from 1930, the steady increase in population of the other ethnic groups; and the huge jump in the Irish population since 1970, which, because there was no great increase in Irish immigration, is a result of the responses to the ancestry question in the census, a point I have noted with regard to the national data.

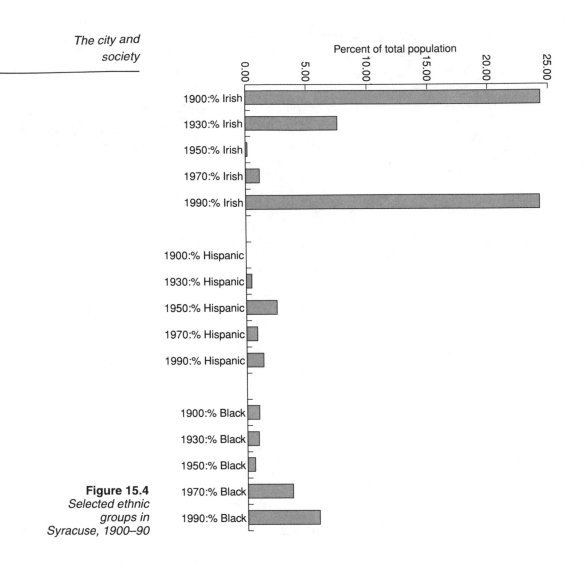

Percent of total population

Figure 15.4
Selected ethnic
groups in
Syracuse, 1900–90

THE REPRESENTATION OF ETHNICITY

Race and ethnicity are socially constructed in many ways. In this section I will explore the construction of ethnic characteristics through their representation in the print media. I will consider how the three different groups have been represented in the local press, restricting my analysis to Irish, African-Americans, and Latinos.

The news we receive is partial, filtered, and selective, and yet it is one of the most important ways that we garner information and opinion about "others" (Abron, 1990). The sources for this study were the newspaper clippings in the Onondaga Historical Association Research Center and the Onondaga County Public Library Local

History Collection. More than 1,500 articles on the African-American population, some 215 articles on the Irish population and approximately 150 stories on the local Latino population were examined.

As an example of the "loose" nature of this data source we can look at the files which portray the African-American population of Syracuse dating back to the mid-nineteenth century. The articles in the late nineteenth-century files contained only stories that involved Black individuals. By the mid- to late twentieth century, however, the files were filled with articles dealing with black issues and no longer contained pieces about daily occurrences involving Blacks in

---

TABLE 15.3   A SAMPLE OF HEADLINES IN THE SYRACUSE NEWSPAPERS

Irish
1 "Channel 9's Nancy Duffy brings the luck of the Irish to Syracuse" (1991)
2 "St James has the best float" (1992)
3 "Snow Rains on Parade: Syracusans bundle up" (1992)
4 "It's time for the wearing o' the layers of green" (1992)
5 "Gumby floats into Syracuse for parade" (1992)
6 "Parade veteran: former Syracusan returns as grand marshall of St Patrick's Day Parade" (1994)

African-American:
1 "Exclusive set bends its knee to dusky bride" (1908)
2 "No, it's not Harlem, it's a Syracuse block party" (1938)
3 "Increase in Negro youth population noted in Syracuse" (1953)
4 "Economic chains the barrier for blacks now" (1983)
5 "Black families: 'hidden strengths' " (1984)
6 "Chasing the American Dream: for an increasing number of blacks, happiness is living in the suburbs" (1991)

Cuban
1 "Tired Cuban refugees find friendship here" (1961)
2 "Win freedom from Castro" (1966)
3 "New career opens for Cuban refugee" (1966)
4 "For Cuban refugee, washing dishes is the American Dream" (1980)
5 "Cuban refugee accused in stabbing at Y" (1980)
6 "Transition for Cubans isn't easy" (1981)

Syracuse. Thus, examining the portrayal of African-Americans in the press over a large period of time becomes problematic. Librarians and archivists in charge of selecting the content of the files have changed over the years, and as trends in popular issues change, so do the kinds of articles they choose to preserve in the historical files. The sources were thus limited to those articles deemed important enough to clip by the individuals compiling the files. The clippings were examined with a wary eye, knowing that they were, both in terms of article and file content, partial. None the less, the images garnered from the *Syracuse Post Standard* and the *Syracuse Herald Journal* and their predecessors offer an array of interesting images and information on the city's many ethnic groups. Just by examining a series of headlines, we can see how different ethnic groups are portrayed in different lights (table 15.3). The strong positive and negative impressions are boldly displayed for the reader to take notice. From these headlines we can see that the Irish population is presented in a much more light-hearted, pleasant manner. On the other hand, the imagery evoked from such words as "chains," "dusky," and "Harlem" is not so favorable. Additionally, the constant reference to Cubans as "refugees," not simply as Cubans (or people, or men and women) imposes a somewhat lower status on the individual characters. But we must look more closely at the newspapers' contents to collect a more complete picture of their representation of different ethnic groups.

The Irish

Irish settlers first came to Syracuse in the early 1800s to work in the city's salt industry. More working-class Irish immigrants came to Syracuse in the 1820s to work on the Erie Canal, and many settled in Syracuse's West Side. So many settled in one West Side suburb that it become known as "Little Ireland." Another wave of Irish immigration to Syracuse occurred in 1848, after the Great Potato Famine. There were 2,000 Irish people living in Syracuse in 1855 and 3,000 in Onondaga County (McGuire, 1983). The population grew to 13,000 by 1930, and the main area of settlement in the city was around St Patrick's Church in a neighborhood called Tipperary Hill. In 1970 there were 7,000 first- and second-generation Irish in Syracuse. The 1990 census recorded approximately 150,000 Irish, a number more a function of the ancestry question than an actual increase in the number of Irish.

The Irish have been depicted in a generally favorable light by local newspapers during the past two centuries. They shared a similar skin color with the dominant groups in society. Their distinctiveness, which was commented upon in the press, related to the St Patrick's Day parade. The obvious focal point for public display of Irish ethnicity was and still is St Patrick's Day. The March 17 holiday has a long tradition of recognition in the United States. Celebrations date back as far as 1690 in Massachusetts, and at the time of the Revolution the day was universally observed. The first St Patrick's Day parade in Syracuse was around 1840, some 25 years after the initial arrival of Irish immigrants to the city. In 1843 feelings of hostility toward the Irish population in Syracuse erupted on St Patrick's Day, when a large dried codfish was placed atop the 150-foot liberty pole in downtown Syracuse. This was accompanied by a threatening crowd of "Yankees and Germans" shouting insults at the Irish who had come for the parade, prompting several leaders of the Irish community to chop down the pole with axes ("Tempestuous Path . . .," 1936). In 1861 St Patrick was hung in effigy in Clinton Square, and it was common in those days for Irish Americans to find an effigy of St Patrick with potatoes hung around his neck in the front yards of their houses. For many years, reports circulated about the presence of "awkward looking effigies" about town. These stories, however, ran concurrently with newspaper editorials which condemned the acts as being "indecent" and "outrageous," as "enemies to the peace and welfare of the community" (anonymous letter to the editor, *Syracuse Post Standard*, March 23, 1842).

Most reports of Irish community events portrayed positive images. The *Syracuse Post Standard* reported on March 18, 1854 that the participants of the St Patrick's Day parade "made a fine appearance and attracted much admiration." For the parade of 1867, the *Syracuse Journal* reported March 20) that "the crowd was immensely good natured, as American-Irish crowds always are." A St Patrick's Day banquet was also praised by the *Syracuse Journal* (March 18, 1862): "The entire proceedings were marked by the strictest propriety and the highest good feeling."

The *Syracuse Journal* reported on March 20, 1867, about the St Patrick's Day parade in New York City:

> *The well-to-do appearance of the people in the procession would surprise a stranger coming here with his head full of stories about suffering amongst the working classes of New York. Here were eight or ten thousand people, all dressed in nice broadcloth, and wearing silk hats and fine boots, most of whom, only a short time ago, had hardly a shirt to their backs, and most of them mechanics or day-laborers, yet they were dressed as expensively as many a gentleman, though not as well. I noticed on their banners the time-honored motto,*

*"Erin go bragh," and thought, as I looked at the comfortably-clad
and well-fed men who were carrying them, how obsolete, in this country, was Sydney Smith's famous sarcasm about "Erin go
bread-and-butter, Erin go cabins that keep out the rain, Erin go
clothes without holes in them!" Here our Irish brethren have all these
blessings, and are fast adding to them, and can join in the old cry
with a clear conscience.*

As Irish Americans moved up the class hierarchy and lost their association with the working class, they gained an image of respect and
admiration.

The earliest parades were always accompanied by religious services.
The significance of St Patrick's Day as a religious celebration, however, waned as it became increasingly a civic event. This was noted
early on in the Syracuse press, which in one article condemned this
changing significance for its nationalistic function. The *Syracuse
Journal* printed an editorial in 1869 which called the parade "an
annual nuisance," noting the disruptions the parade caused in the
city. On March 18, 1878, it printed:

*But the truth seems to be that, as a religious festival, St Patrick's day
has in these later days largely lost its power . . . The result has been the
gradual relegation of the occasion to a national celebration, and its
final degeneration into a factious political demonstration as widely
opposed in character and purpose to the holy spirit of St Patrick and
his beneficent work, as darkness is from the sun-light, as anarchy is
from peace. Irish patriotism is now, on this day, stirred to the very
depths of its impulsiveness. Instead of the gospel of peace, the gospel of
hatred is preached, not by bishop or priest indeed, but by arrant dem-
agogues, who under the guise of "liberty" appeal to the basest of
passions and religious hatred.*

The celebration of Irish *national* identity was deemed inappropriate,
although the day as a religious Irish celebration was acceptable.
Today, St Patrick's Day has taken its place as a civic tradition in which
all Americans can partake. In 1970, Syracuse's Mayor Lee Alexander,
who is not of Irish but of Greek descent, said, "This is a happy day
for all the Irish and for those who wish they were Irish on this day,"
as he hung the Irish flag from City Hall on St Patrick's Day ("The
green flies . . . ," 1970). County Legislator Gordan Ireland, also not
of Irish descent, said, "I suppose on St Patrick's Day we're all a little
bit Irish" (Rycraft, 1981).

In the media today, images of the Irish community involve the portraits of prominent individuals: "Channel 9's Nancy Duffy Brings the Luck of the Irish to Syracuse" and "Parade Veteran: Former Syracusan Returns as Grand Marshal of St Patrick's Day Parade" (*Tully Villager*, March 11, 1991; *Syracuse Post Standard*, March 14, 1994). Images of St Patrick's Day involve stories of the weather and the parade route and contentment: "Snow Rains on Parade: Syracusans Bundle Up," "It's Time for the Wearing o' the Layers of Green," "Gumby Floats into Syracuse for Parade" and "St James Has the Best Float" (*Syracuse Post Standard*, March 15, 1992; *Syracuse Herald Journal*, March 14, 1994; *Syracuse Herald Journal*, March 12, 1992; *Onondaga Valley News*, March 23, 1992). In these cases, being Irish seems to matter only with regard to St Patrick's Day, and it is never portrayed in a negative light.

The Irish community, once looked down upon for its working-class and Catholic characteristics, now enjoys an accepted status. This shift in image accompanied the gradual placement of many Irish Americans in jobs of civic service. Indeed, more people claimed Irish ancestry in the last census than would have been expected from an analysis of the projected natural growth rate of the Irish population, suggesting that there is an increase in the subjective identification with Irish ancestry (Hout and Goldstein, 1994, 64–5).

African-Americans

While reading approximately 1,500 articles from the clippings files of the Onondaga Historical Association's and Onondaga County Library's local history archives it is certainly possible to find an assortment of articles portraying Syracuse Blacks in a less-than-favorable light. Late nineteenth-century newspapers contained a great deal of negative publicity about the minority group. One article answers the question in its title "Will the Slaves Come North?" with "the colored man is a creature of the tropics, and all his aptitudes fit him for a warm climate . . . His skin is thirsty for sun . . . and is as much out of place in our cold temperate zones, as are oranges, plantains and palm trees" (*Syracuse Journal*, 1862). Similarly negative reports on local Blacks include stories on "Niggers in a Mess" and "A Colored Incident." In each of the stories on altercations involving Blacks, the newspapers ensure that the color of the man or woman's skin is prominently reported. The only time a white person's skin color is mentioned is to distinguish the different characters.

Subsequent archival clippings files contain precious little on the Syracuse Black community, though there are some examples of press coverage. One article comments on the group's social events. "No,

It's Not Harlem – It's a Syracuse Block Party" exhibits four large photographs of energetic, smiling Black couples dancing to the latest tunes in the 1930s (*Syracuse Herald Journal*, August 21, 1938). Although the photographs depict a happy and lively scene, the head-line posted on the top of the page sounds rather condemnatory of the gala affair.

Black issues once again take center stage in the press during the Civil Rights Movement of the 1960s. In the beginning of the decade, the Syracuse newspapers echoed a national call for action to create a more equal society for Blacks. Local headlines cited news that "Hughes Demands Action to Solve Negro Problems," "Apartment Owner Told to Let Negroes Rent," and "Negroes Urged to Employ Discrimination Remedies" (*Syracuse Post Standard*, July 3, 1962; *Syracuse Herald Journal*, July 11, 1963; *Syracuse Post Standard*, August 6, 1963).

During this time, "Black leaders and the news media were de facto allies" (Drummond, 1990). This changed, however, with advent of the urban uprisings later in the decade. The scene in Syracuse matched the national mood: Syracuse newspaper headlines that once promoted such items as "Stores Approve Negro Mannikins," "Employers Recognize Need for Negro Skills," and "Board Votes 34–0 to Aid Negro Aims" suddenly changed their tune: " 'Black Power' Demands May Slow Integration," "Mayor on Blacks: Double Standard," and "Youths Stone Windows in Scattered Incidents" (*Syracuse Post Standard*, May 8, 1964; *Syracuse Post Standard*, October 4, 1964; *Syracuse Herald Journal*, November 5, 1963; *Syracuse Post Standard*, October 4, 1967; *Syracuse Herald Journal*, September 15, 1970; *Syracuse Post Standard*, August 17, 1967). After the violence let up, the newspapers returned to the coverage of social issues, detailing every move made in the city's plan for integrating the school system in the seventies (*Syracuse Post Standard*, April 5, 1972).

Although the files from the past few decades fail to include the commonplace stories on daily problems in the inner city that had been in the files of the late nineteenth and early twentieth centuries, they do contain more than 200 positive pieces, especially portraying the Black population in a positive light. There are files devoted to articles on Black History Month and the city's most successful African-Americans. The Syracuse newspapers are now making a good-faith multicultural effort in their portrayal of the news. In a 1992 editorial essay, executive editor Timothy D. Bunn outlined the company's recent hiring and internship practices and programs, and expounded on the virtues of several minority staff members. He offered the details of a story that involved Professor Leonard Jeffries, the controversial chairman of the African Studies Department of City College of New York, and the Jewish Defense League and received criticism for portraying the Jewish Defense League in a "militant" light. The story, he said, had been written by a Latino, edited by a Jew, and reviewed by an African-American:

> *Throughout the day, an elaborate dance took place between these three wonderfully competent and thoroughly dedicated journalists from widely differing backgrounds. Through it, they fine-tuned the story so that each could agree it was sensitive and responsible. Meanwhile they had to accomplish this without trampling on one another's ethnic or professional sensibilities.* (Bunn, 1992)

While Bunn admits that not all stories get "treatment quite so thorough," he does say that daily "it does go on in more abbreviated fashion."

Leon Modeste, executive director of the Urban League of Onondaga County, echoes the remarks of Drummond and Abron. Modeste praises the Syracuse newspapers for their coverage of Black History Month and the contributions of the many local Black achievers and entrepreneurs. He complains, however, that the "local media coverage has either blatantly or tacitly portrayed teen pregnancy as a 'black problem.' . . . Such articles only serve to feed the myopic views of the prejudiced and uninformed reader." He also expresses dismay at the representation offered by the newspapers in their reporting of the relocation of tenants from a local housing development. One major cause of this "insensitive coverage is the small number of Black reporters and virtual lack of Black decision-makers on [the] news staffs" (Modeste, 1992).

Latinos

The terms "Latino" and "Hispanic' are broad and encompass several so-called ethnic groups. There are (at least) five distinct "Latino" groups in the United States: Mexican Americans, Puerto Ricans, Cubans, Central Americans, and other Caribbean Latinos, most of whom come from the Dominican Republic (Augenbraum and Stavans, 1993).

By lumping "Latinos" together as a single entity, it appears that the media have ultimately created one definition of these people, people who come from different backgrounds, cultures, and countries. Though no unanimous consensus has been reached, Latino is the current preferred term for the overall population (Shorris, 1992).

While Latinos have not immigrated to Syracuse at a rate comparable to cities such as New York, Miami, and Los Angeles, their numbers in this upstate New York city have increased in recent years, adding to its ethnic mix. In 1990, the Latino population in the greater Syracuse area reached 8,926, marking a 52 percent increase since 1980 (*Syracuse Herald American*, August 7, 1994). One of the first waves of Latino immigrants to Syracuse took place in the early 1960s, when about a dozen families arrived after fleeing Fidel Castro's communist Cuba. In 1961 and 1962, the local newspapers featured 12 articles on the city's newest immigrants. The photographs and texts of these pieces painted a happy picture: well-to-do Cubans who fled their Caribbean island state to escape the evils of communism were welcomed with open arms by the Syracuse community. Photographs of doctors, engineers, and their upper-middle-class families sitting smiling in their new homes illustrated articles that featured headlines such as "Tired Cuban Refugees Find Friendship Here," "Diocese to Welcome 11 Cuban families," and "Cuban Families Build New Life in Syracuse" (*Syracuse Post Standard*, March 2, 1961; *Syracuse Catholic Sun*, February 23, 1961; *Syracuse Herald American*, January 30, 1966). These newcomers had proven themselves worthy citizens and professionals in their homeland, and it was naturally assumed that they would assimilate nicely. Five years after their arrival the *Syracuse Herald American* followed up on the progress of the local Cubans only to report that, yes, they were doing quite well.

There was then a hiatus on local Cubans in the Syracuse newspapers until 1980, at which time the Mariela boatlift brought in a new group of Cubans to town. This group, however, embodied a different set of characteristics than their predecessors. "The Marielitos are often denigrated in this country because the boatlift included convicted criminals released from Cuban jails, but it also included blue-collar workers seeking a better life in the United States and people whose families were separated by the revolution" (Augenbraum and Stavans, 1993, xviii).

No longer were the immigrants well-educated professionals, but unskilled workers who had a more difficult time adjusting to life in the United States. This was made quite clear to local residents via the media's coverage of their arrival and settlement. 'For Cuban Refugee, Washing Dishes is the American Dream" claimed one article, automatically lowering the standard for assimilation and community contribution of the Cubans (*Syracuse Herald American*, November

9, 1980). Many of the initial articles failed to capture the same welcoming tone as the articles 20 years earlier.

"Refugees Working Out Well" claimed one headline, suggesting a touch of surprise that they would in fact work out well. This question simply was not raised when the well-educated Cubans arrived in the 1960s. Continued uneasiness about their settlement in Syracuse can be taken from articles titled "Transition for Cuban Refugees Isn't Easy" and "A Better Life for Some but not All" (*Syracuse Herald American*, November 9, 1980; *Syracuse Post Standard*, April 7, 1981; *Syracuse Herald American*, July 19, 1981). Though "YMCA's Helping Hand Reached Cuban Refugees" denotes assistance for the down and out, it is not much of a positive image for the local population to digest, especially when just 13 days later, the headlines shouted "Cuban Refugee Accused of Stabbing at Y" (*Syracuse Herald American*, November 2, 1980; *Syracuse Herald Journal*, November 15, 1980). It is interesting to note that the editors chose to single out the accused as a Cuban refugee and not simply as a Cuban or, even more simply, as a man.

In 1991, 30 years after their arrival in Syracuse, Tina and Carlos Saladrigas announced they were leaving, retiring to Little Cuba in Miami. Featured in the 1961 article "Tired Cuban Refugees Find Friendship Here," this family certainly lived up to the expectations the local media established for their new neighbors from the south. He became a teacher, she an associate buyer for a local department store, and they eventually moved to the upper-middle-class suburb of Fayetteville. Tina Saladrigas is proud of her Cuban heritage and actively seeks to dispel negative stereotypes of her people. Her friends are often stunned to hear her description of the Cuba in which she grew up. 'People think we were jumping from one tree to another, eating bananas." Her husband, on the other hand, is not always quite so bold. 'When Carlos recently told someone at a party he was moving to Miami, the person responded, 'You want to live there with all those Hispanics?' Carlos didn't say a word. He's tired of dealing with xenophobes – people fearful of anyone unlike themselves" (Rodriguez, 1991).

For many Cubans like Carlos Saladrigas, the portrayal of their people has long been associated with negative images – most of which are reported through the media. As we have seen in the analysis of newspaper coverage, there was positive media coverage of the Cubans who came to Syracuse in the wake of Castro's rise to power. But the refugees who followed them some 20 years later brought with them a less-affluent social status, one which the media prominently displayed in their coverage. The ensuing result was that, via the press, all Cubans seemingly took on the characteristics of the ex-convict Marielitos.

Ethnicities are neither fixed inheritances nor solely the result of external attribution; they are internally constructed. People can take an active role in constructing their own group identity. In this section of the chapter I will examine some examples of this construction, paying particular attention to the three groups already discussed.

The ethnic "revival" discussed by a number of writers (for example Alba, 1990; Novak, 1972) has its manifestation in Syracuse, where we can see the formation of many ethnic organizations and groups. The 1991–2 *Cultural and Ethnic Directory of Organizations and Groups in Central New York* (International Center of Syracuse, 1992) lists 101 entries. Of those, 60 are organizations with a general focus and are directed toward entire national groups, with names like the Polish Heritage Club of Syracuse, Inc., the Italian Cultural Association, the North American Indian Club, or the Kurdistan Cultural Center. Seventeen ethnic organizations in the Syracuse area are church-based, such as St Sophia's Greek Orthodox Church and the Sacred Heart Polish Church. And a dozen organizations are specifically directed at various types of performances or hobbies: Irish Cultural Dance Society of CNY and the Scandia Folkdancers. Other organizations have different foci: some political, like the Spanish Action League; some for business, such as the Syracuse Minority Business Development Center; or others, such as the Italian American Athletic Club.

The Festival of Nations

While ethnic and regional festivals are not new in this country (Mardi Gras in New Orleans and the St Patrick's Day parade in major cities have been around for a long time, for instance), "we are now experiencing a whole new breed of festival, one with many subcategories, but all involving the hawking of merchandise amidst a wide range of other activities" (Zelinsky, 1992, 176). Ethnic festivals today involve the staging of traditional songs and dances, and the selling of crafts and spectacle.

Every year, Syracuse hosts a Festival of Nations. The 1993 promotional brochure for the event states that its purpose is "to demonstrate that the folk traditions of the national heritage groups in the greater Syracuse area are an enduring source of community character, vitality and pride . . . The Festival reminds us of the distinctive human differences that enrich and unite our community." The festival consists of 35 groups (2,500 individuals) which participate in various exhibits and performances.

The festival was founded in 1969, when Syracuse's Cultural Resources Council was conducting a feasibility study for the new Civic Center and was struck by the numerous pockets of talent it found in the local ethnic communities. Long-time organizer of the festival Gloria Romeo (1994) says the council discovered that many Americans "were living two lives: American by day, when they go to work, and traditionally at home." The council wanted to bring these various groups together with the intention that a "better understanding of different ethnic communities will promote peace." When the festival first began 16 groups participated. Now there are 35. Asian groups equal the number of groups of European origin. Romeo suggests that the Festival of Nations is an attempt to "bring young people back" to the ways of their ancestors, noting that, despite the former trend toward Americanization, "we're not a 'melting pot' at all."

Ethnic festivals are important tools for understanding ethnicity in the city. They reflect the multicultural character of a place and reveal the changing cultural composition of cities. They also exist as performances and as consumer products to be purchased and consumed by the public.

Building an international image of the city which will attract international business is important for postindustrial cities such as Syracuse (see Short et al., 1993). Ethnicity and ethnic organizations become part of the new image of the city and assume a civic role in their interaction with capital:

> *Cities and places now, it seems, take much more care to create a positive and high quality image of place, and have sought an architecture and forms of urban design that respond to such need. That they should be so pressed, and that the result should be a serial repetition of successful models, . . . is understandable, given the grim history of deindustrialization and restructuring that left most major cities in with each other, mainly as financial, consumption, and entertainment centres. Imaging a city through the organization of spectacular urban spaces became a means to attract capital and people (of the right sort) in a period (since 1973) of intensified interurban competition and urban entrepreneurialism.*
>
> (Harvey, 1989, 91–2)

Such imaging of Syracuse is done in part by creating an atmosphere of internationalism and cultural diversity.

Guy Debord (1983, 1) notes that "in societies where modern conditions of production prevail, all of life presents itself as an immense accumulation of *spectacles*. Everything that was directly lived has moved away into a representation." He argues that in the period of industrialization and corporate capitalism since the Second World War, mass consumption has given culture and social organization a consumerist bend. Instead of being "lived," culture is now based on images and representation. In the same way, ethnic festivals take traditions that were once lived and transform them into consumer-based spectacles. In turn, these images or spectacles produce and reproduce social relations.

Irish

For the Irish-American community in Syracuse, the most well-known "ethnic" event is the annual St Patrick's Day parade. Parades have been a part of Syracuse's history since the mid-eighteen hundreds, with a 43–year respite between 1940 and 1983. As noted in the previous section of this chapter, although the parades were a common practice for the Irish community and were originally an extension of the religious holiday in Ireland, they were sometimes accompanied by attacks and mocking insults. In 1850 the Irish had to organize a chapter of the National Guard to protect themselves from violence during the parade. Since that time, however, the parades no longer incite mockery.

The parade has changed over the years, from a specific ethnic and religious event to a general, civic event, one whose crowds have occupied an increasing larger portion of public space and numbered upward of 100,000, depending on the weather (1987: 125,000; 1990: 130,000; 1992: 125,000). In fact, the Syracuse parade has been called "the largest St Patrick's parade per capita in the world" (Zych, 1993).

As a construction of ethnicity, the parade is a good example of a created ritual, taken out of the context of its origin in Ireland, where it is more important as a day to remember the saint credited with bringing Christianity to Ireland. The parade has become more an American institution than a traditional Irish one, created by Irish immigrants in America. Nancy Duffy, journalist and president of the Syracuse parade, said St Patrick's Day parades are a purely American tradition. 'When the Irish were the underdogs in this country, the parade was a way for the Irish to come together and say 'We're important.' It's more than an Irish thing, it's an all-community thing" (Knauss, 1986). Here, again, we can see that the parades are important as a civic institution.

There is also a degree of commercialization which goes with

St Patrick's Day. "Hallmark (Cards) has made St Patrick's Day as much as the Irish," said Irish native Carmel McColgan, a founder and member of the local Irish American Cultural Institute (Knauss, 1986). Today, ethnicity is more than just a chosen identity, it is also something which can turn a profit.

St Patrick's Day is not the only way Irish-Americans find to express their ethnicity. A television program called *The Irish Connection* has been aired on three local cable channels since 1991 with support from the Irish American Cultural Institute. The Institute also sponsors Project Children, a program in which children from Northern Ireland come to stay with a family in Central New York for a summer. There is a newsletter called *Everything Irish* (formerly *Irish Activities & News*) which is distributed to businesses located on Tipperary Hill and which promotes dance and language classes as well as information about meetings, advertisements from Irish-owned businesses, and pieces of Irish history.

A large concentration of Irish-Americans is located in the west side, on Tipperary Hill, and they frequently gather in a local restaurant called Coleman's Authentic Irish Pub. Decorated with shamrocks and photographs of Ireland and complete with its own gift shop, the pub promotes an image of Ireland. It is a well-known and central part of the Irish community in Syracuse. This 140–seat pub attracts some 3,000 people on St Patrick's Day. Most of the "regulars" at Coleman's are third-generation Tipperary Hill residents. Although they no longer have direct ties to Ireland, the symbols and the atmosphere help construct a sense of connection to Ireland, which is imagined in a particular way by those who claim Irish ancestry but who have never actually been to Ireland. The construction of an Irish identity, then, is facilitated by such places as Coleman's pub through symbols and a community whose members adhere to the same "traditions."

The significance of this bar lies in its place in the center of the Irish neighborhood called Tipperary Hill. Coleman's is often directly involved in civic events and hosts fund-raisers for building parks and for other activities in the neighborhood. In the autumn of 1994, there was fear that an old dilapidated house would contribute to the downgrading of the area, so the Irish-American community got together to raise the money to tear it down and change the lot into a park. Bricks for the park were sold at Coleman's, drawing local television media coverage and many local civic leaders, such as the mayor of Syracuse. This type of community, closely tied to City Hall, centers around an idea about shared heritage, around a particular idea about what it means to be Irish.

The history of self-constructed ethnicity and the establishment of self-serving organizations for the African-American community is different from that of the Irish. Due to the institutionalization of racism through slavery and the disadvantages this caused for Americans of African descent, self-sponsored organizations were important as tools for survival. The earliest support groups within the African-American community were churches. In 1841 the first Black church in Syracuse was founded by a runaway slave, the Reverend Thomas James, who had a congregation of 25 people. This church was a stopping point along the Underground Railroad, and its second pastor persuaded officials to make Syracuse an "open city," that is, a city where runaway slaves could settle without fear of reprisal (Cleaveland, 1982).

Throughout the rest of the 1800s, there was a wide variety of self-directed support organizations. Freedman's Relief Association sent money, clothes, and other aid for distribution in the south. Fraternal organizations, such as the Lodge of Colored Free Masons, the Colored Odd Fellows, and the Colored Knights of Pythias, and other social organizations like the Colored Young Men's Social Club hosted social activities, including balls, receptions, picnics, and socials. There were three Black political organizations in Syracuse: the Colored Republicans, the Colored Democrats, and the Colored Citizens League. Three Black churches existed: the AME Zion Church, Bethany Baptist, and St Philip's Episcopal Church (Davis, 1980, 12–17).

At the beginning of the twentieth century, political and social activities for the Black community declined. However, there were still churches which sponsored activities and the Dunbar Center, a Black community center which sponsored dances, lectures, teas, sports, and so on, from its establishment in the mid-1920s. Around the Second World War, life in the community "revolved primarily around church, home and neighborhood" as new churches were established (Davis, 1980, 20).

And so it remained until the 1960s, when a more explicitly cultural ethnic politics began to emerge. One example is the Black Youth United of Syracuse (BYUS), formed in 1968, which leased the premises of the former Danforth United Church and founded the Afro-American Youth Cultural Center in 1969. A newspaper article in the *Post Standard* from March 26, 1969 said of this organization:

In establishing its center, BYUS becomes the most recent of a number of local groups whose focus of interest has developed out of its

*Race, ethnicity,
and the city:
case study V*

*distinctive background . . . Earlier groups formed the Liederkranz
and established the Jewish Community Center, the Italian
Community Home Federation and the Polish Community Home.
"Black people are trying to find their lost identity," Fred Johnson, a
senior at Nottingham High School and a member of the BYUS
Planning Committee said in an interview. "Black people in Syracuse,
and especially black youth, need a place where they can identify themselves with their own culture. The center will offer this," he said.*

(Roseburgh, 1969)

As well as support organizations, African-Americans have established
newspapers for their own communities. In Syracuse, the history of
these newspapers dates back to the middle of the nineteenth century,
when the *Impartial Citizen*, then a leading voice for the abolitionist
cause, was published from February 1849 to June 1850. Another,
Chatscrip, appeared for six months in 1929 and 1930. The *Progressive
Herald* was founded in 1933 and ran for almost 30 years. More grew
out of the Civil Rights Movement, including the tabloid *Home Town
News*, which was published in the mid- to late 1960s (Davis, 1980).
"With increasing unemployment, discrimination and high illiteracy
among youths, Black-owned and -oriented newspapers are vital
because they are vigorous in their approach to those problems, publishers and editors of Black newspapers say," reported the *Syracuse
Post Standard* July 7, 1982). By choosing to represent themselves,
the Black community could address problems in its own neighborhoods instead of relying on the mainstream, white-dominated press
to do so for them. Today, there are few Black newspapers. Instead of
using their own newspapers to write for their own communities,
Blacks are left to express themselves through the mainstream media,
thereby letting the white-dominated press help decide how their
image will be constructed and portrayed to the entire population.

For African-Americans, one way of promoting a positive self-image
is through the active creation, pursuit and celebration of African-
American history and culture. Black History Month, now called
African-American History Month, was established in 1969 by the
Pan-American/Pan-African Association as an extension of its prede-
cessor, Negro History Week. Negro History Week was founded in
1926 by Dr Carter G. Woodson, a Black scholar and founder of the
Association for the Study of Afro-American Life and History. This
week-long event was adapted from the earlier Negro History Day,
which began in 1893 and was set up by Dr Dolores Harris, the president of the National Association of Colored Women's Clubs. The
growing emphasis on the event highlights its increasing significance

as a vehicle for self-expression and its increasing acceptance within society.

During African-American History Month there are many activities, including special programs in schools, lectures, films, conferences and colloquia, church services, theater plays, singing performances, dancing, poetry readings, and art exhibitions. Many articles appear in the local newspapers highlighting Blacks who either are prominent in the community at present or were leading figures in Black history. Some specific examples of events that have occurred in Syracuse during Black History Month include a 1980 photo exhibition entitled "A History of the Black Community of Syracuse," a large exhibition "Afro-American Abstraction" at the Everson Museum 1981, and a 1986 public ceremony to honor various Blacks who were or are pioneers in their fields (Chayat, 1980; Muck, 1981; Anderson, 1986). By promoting positive images and by looking at the cultural history of African-Americans in both the United States and Africa, the African-American community is constructing its own ethnic heritage and creating a basis for a collective identity and solidarity among a group that has traditionally been marginalized.

There are also ways within the African-American community for celebrating ethnicity through ritual. An example of such a celebration is Kwanzaa, the only nonheroic Black holiday created, observed, and celebrated by and for African-Americans. The holiday was created in 1966 by Maulana Ron Karenga, now chair of Black Studies at California State University in Long Beach. "He wanted to create something that would honor the cultural heritage of people of African descent while offering African-Americans a holiday that stresses family unity. Karenga based Kwanzaa on several different cultural traditions from all over Africa" (Burns, 1991). The word Kwanzaa means "first fruits" in Swahili, and the holiday is based on the African tradition of celebrating the harvest of the first fruits. It was created as a way of reminding African-Americans of their African heritage, reaffirming their roots and reinforcing bonds within that community. The holiday is celebrated for seven days, from December 26 to January 1. On each of the days participants are to reflect on important principles by which to guide their lives. In addition, one candle is lit each day to reinforce the principle of that day (day one is for unity, day two for self-determination, three for collective work and responsibility, four for cooperative economics, five for purpose, six for creativity, and seven for faith) (Kgama, 1993). Different sources estimate that anywhere from 5 to 13 million people in the United States celebrate Kwanzaa each year (Burns, 1991; "Kwanzaa celebrates . . . ," 1992). In Syracuse in 1993 the Southwest

Community Center sponsored a celebration of dance, poetry, and food which drew about 200 local residents. The holiday is an example of an explicitly created ritual recently brought into being which has developed an important meaning for those who participate.

As with the Irish, there is also a commercial side to the holiday. In 1993 "Hallmark released 12 Kwanzaa cards" (Kgama, 1993). The recent appearance of several African import and clothing stores in Syracuse also highlights the commercial value of ethnicity.

Latinos

While many US cities have long seen the influence of "Latino" culture, its emergence in Syracuse is relatively recent. In 1969 the Spanish Action League, more commonly known as La Liga, was founded to help immigrants with few English language skills to adjust to life amidst foreign sounds. Today the organization "provides advocacy, counseling and education for more than 4,000 local Latino families. League programs focus on housing, domestic violence, developmental disabilities, juvenile justice and education" (Carr, 1994, A1).

In August 1994 La Liga celebrated its twenty-fifth anniversary with a whole host of performances as part of the weekend festival called Las Fiestas de Santiago Apostal de Loiza Aldea. The program, among many events, included folk dancing demonstrations and Latin jazz concerts. The Syracuse Latino community further promoted their traditions during the annual September 15 to October 15 Latino Heritage Month. Panel discussions on Latino issues, Latino youth conferences, and several shows featuring Latin art and music were offered at various times and locales across the city. To top off the month-long celebration, a gala dinner dance, Una Noche Latina, was held at the Hotel Syracuse.

The Latino festival on Syracuse's near West Side in August 1994 was promoted to the general population and featured ethnic food, music, and dance. The Syracuse community was invited to come and share in this cultural celebration. Advertised as an ethnic festival, it took on the flavor of yet another holiday that all members of the community could enjoy. This event was small compared to such citywide events such as the St Patrick's Day parade and it has not yet attained the popularity of the city's annual Greek festival; it was, none the less, successful in attracting the attention of the general community. It is then curious to wonder whether, as the festival grows in years to come, local residents may call themselves Latin for a day.

The 1994 celebration also included the kickoff of a new Latino radio program titled *Radio Tropical.* As the Latino population in Syracuse has grown, so has their involvement in the popular media. Currently, there are two television talk shows specifically targeted to the local Latino population. Taking its name from a Puerto Rican legend involving a frog, *El Coqui Canta* is a Spanish-language program which focuses on Latino issues for local Latino residents. *Entre Vecinos*, on the other hand, is in Spanish and English and is designed to help promote education about and awareness of the Latino community in the wider population.

As part of a movement to continually maintain contact with nearby Latino communities, *Panorama Hispano Magazine* was created in 1992. The bilingual monthly periodical is published for the Latino communities of Buffalo, Dunkirk, Rochester, and Syracuse. In addition to advice on housing, medical and other social services available in each metropolitan area, it prints information about recently held and upcoming social events in the four cities and fosters the sense of a larger Latino community.

It is difficult to compare the Latino construction of ethnicity with those of the African-American and Irish populations, because their influx into this city has been so recent. For many of the local Latinos, participating in and promoting Latino food, song, and dance is perhaps a conscious maintenance of their ethnicity rather than a fabricated construction of it. Latinos have effectively developed ways and means to ensure that their adjustment to life in the United States does not mean a farewell to their cultural foundations. We might question, however, whether or not their ethnic culture was an important issue prior to their arrival in the United States. Perhaps it is simply a way of holding onto the past.

Who is the we?

In the internal construction of ethnicity there are ethnic entrepreneurs who mobilize ethnic identity. While ethnic leadership is certainly necessary to gather, motivate, and organize social movements, these leaders can paradoxically reinforce the minority group's "underclass" status. In her book *Out of the Barrio* (1991) Linda Chavez looks at the increasing establishment of Latino organizations and how Hispanic leaders have convinced politicians and policymakers that Hispanics want and deserve special treatment. She writes, "In doing so, these leaders have enhanced their own power, but their methods jeopardize the future integration of Hispanics into this society"(Chavez, 1991, 61).

Cornel West also calls to task the black leadership in the United

States in his book *Race Matters* (1993). He makes clear the point that black political and intellectual leaders are not by any means *the* voice of black America. Henry Louis Gates, Jr makes a similar point in a *New Yorker* article when he writes,

> *A theoretical politics of solidarity – of unity, of sacred covenants – must inevitably run up against the hard facts of political economy . . . black America isn't as fissured as white America; it is more so . . . the black middle class has never been larger. And never before have so many blacks done so poorly . . . We need something we do not yet have: a way of speaking about black poverty that does not falsify the reality of black advancement; a way of speaking about black advancement that does not distort the enduring realities of black poverty.*
>
> (1994, 80)

There are also leaders who more or less cash in on their people's ethnicity. Peter Coleman, for example, has promoted everything Irish in Syracuse for several decades. His Tipperary Hill pub has garnered significant local fame and is said to be *the* place to be on St Patrick's Day. His gift shop markets everything from mugs and postcards to boxer shorts and tee-shirts displaying the Coleman's logo. Indeed, one could call Coleman a professional Irishman.

Sam Velasquez has also done a good job of promoting the relatively small Syracuse Latino population to the public. As executive director of La Liga, Velasquez is responsible for helping the local Latino population improve their quality of life in the city. However, he has done much more than that, personally promoting things Latino all over Syracuse. Hosting such events as the annual La Liga gala dinner dance, Velasquez is certainly the most visible Latino in Syracuse. He has furthered this position by going on the air with his own television program, *Entre Vecinos*, which we mentioned earlier.

The point of making these comments is not to decry leadership of ethnic communities but to note that the agenda of the leaders may differ from that of the rest the population. Ethnic leaders help in the creation of ethnic identities.

Race and ethnicity are socially constructed. In this chapter I have noted this construction in three ways:

- how the US census helps create ethnic groups as much as it counts them;
- how different ethnic groups have been identified and recorded in the print media;

■ how ethnic communities created themselves through spectacle, ritual, and the activities of ethnic organizations and their leaders.

GUIDE TO FURTHER READING

This chapter is based on a joint paper:

Short, J.R., Hoyte, T., Marsh, A., Matthew, C. and Vogt, E. (1994) Race, ethnicity and the city. Department of Geography, Syracuse University, mimeo.

Works cited:

Abron, J. (1990) The image of the African American in the U.S. press, *Black Scholar* 21, 49–52.

Alba, R. (1990) *Ethnic Identity: The Transformation of White America*, New Haven, Con.: Yale University Press.

Allen, J.P. and Turner, E.J. (1988) *We the People: An Atlas of America's Ethnic Diversity*, New York: Macmillan.

Anderson, T. (1986) Community groups honor Black Pioneers for historic achievements, *Syracuse Post Standard*, February 27.

Augenbraum, H. and Stavans, I. (eds) (1993) *Growing Up Latino: Memoirs and Stories*, Boston, Mass.: Houghton Mifflin.

Bouvier, L. (1992) *Peaceful Invasions: Immigration and Changing America* Lanham, Md.: University Press of America.

Bunn, T. (1992) It's a multicultural effort: working hard to give all views fair airing, *Syracuse Herald American* March 1.

Burns, M.C. (1991) Let the festival begin, *Syracuse Herald Journal* December 26.

Carr, B. (1994) Spanish Action League marks 25 years of advocacy, *Syracuse Herald Journal* August 6.

Channel 9's Nancy Duffy brings the luck of the Irish to Syracuse (1991), *Tully Villager* March 11.

Chavez, L. (1991) *Out of the Barrio: Toward a New Politics of Hispanic Assimilation*, New York: Basic Books.

Chayat, S. (1980) Photos depict past of Syracuse's blacks, *Syracuse Post Standard* October 17.

Choldin, H.M. (1986) Statistics and politics: the "Hispanic issue" in the 1980 Census, *Demography* 23, 403–18.

Cleaveland, C.L. (1982) Church boasts of history of activism, *Syracuse Post Standard* February 15.

Clifford, J. and Marcus, G.E. (eds) (1986) *Writing Culture*, Berkeley, Cal.: University of California Press.

Davis, B. (1980) A history of the black community of Syracuse. Exhibit and symposium at Onondaga Community College, Syracuse, New York, October.

Debord, G. (1983) *Society of the Spectacle*, Detroit, Mich.: Black & Red.

Drummond, W. (1990) About face: from alliance to alienation: Blacks and the news media, *American Enterprise* 1, 22–9.

Farley, R. (1991) The new census question about ancestry: what did it tell us? *Demography* 28, 411–49.

Fuchs, L.H. (1990) *The American Kaleidoscope: Race, Ethnicity and Civic Culture*, Hanover, N.H.: Wesleyan University Press.

Gans, H.J. (1979) Symbolic ethnicity: the future of ethnic groups and cultures in America, *Ethnic and Racial Studies* 2(1), 1–19.

Gates, H.L. Jr (1994) The black leadership myth, *New Yorker*, October 24, 7–8.

Glazer, N. and Moynihan, D. (1970) *Beyond the Melting Pot*, 2nd edn Cambridge, Mass.: MIT Press (1st edn, 1963).

Goodfriend, J.D. (1992) *Beyond the Melting Pot*, Princeton, N.J.: Princeton University Press.

The green flies over City Hall (1970) *Syracuse Herald Journal* March 17.

Gumby floats into Syracuse for parade (1992) *Syracuse Herald Journal* March 12.

Harvey, D. (1989) *The Condition of Postmodernity*, Oxford: Blackwell.

Hirschman, C. (1983) America's melting pot reconsidered, *Annual Review of Sociology* 9, 397–423.

Hout, M. and Goldstein, J. (1994) How 4.5 million Irish immigrants became 40 million Irish Americans: demographic and subjective aspects of the ethnic composition of white Americans, *American Sociological Review* 59, 64–82.

International Center of Syracuse (1992) *A Cultural and Ethnic Directory of Organizations and Groups in Central New York, 1991–1992*, Syracuse, N.Y.: ICS.

It's time for the wearing o' the layers of green (1992), *Syracuse Herald Journal* March 14.

Katznelson, I. (1979) *City Trenches: Urban Politics and the Patterning of Class in the United States*, New York: Pantheon.

Keith, M. and Cross, M. (1993) Racism and the postmodern city. In M. Keith and M. Cross (eds), *Racism, the City and the State*, London and New York: Routledge 1–30.

Kgama, M. (1993) Kwanzaa celebrates spirit, unity, *Syracuse Herald Journal* December 22.

Knauss, T. (1986) Gaelic rites and green beer, *Syracuse Post Standard* March 14.

Kwanzaa celebrates African heritage (1992), *Syracuse Herald Journal* December 28.

Lee, S.M. (1993) Racial classifications in the U.S. Census: 1890–1990, *Ethnic and Racial Studies* 16, 75–94.

Lieberson, S. (1985) Unhyphenated whites in the United States, *Ethnic and Racial Studies* 8(1), 159–80.

Lieberson, S. and Waters, M.C. (1988) *From Many Strands: Ethnic and Racial Groups in Contemporary America*, New York: Russell Sage Foundation.

McGuire, D. (1983) American traditions enliven St Pat's Day, *Syracuse Herald Journal* March 17.

Modeste, L. (1992) African American coverage: papers score some hits, several misses, *Syracuse Herald American* March 1.

Muck, G.F. (1981) Afro-American exhibit depicts black heritage, *Syracuse Post Standard*, March 9.

Novak, M. (1972) *The Rise of the Unmeltable Ethnics*, New York: Macmillan.

Parade veteran: former Syracusan returns as grand marshal of St Patrick's Day parade (1994), *Syracuse Post Standard*, March 14.

Petersen, W. (1987) Politics and the measurement of ethnicity. In W. Alonso and P. Starr (eds), *The Politics of Numbers*, New York: Russel Sage Foundation, 187–233.

Rodriguez, C. (1991) Thirty years later, first Cubans head south, *Syracuse Herald Journal*, January 7.

Romeo, G. (1994) Personal interview, November 7.

Roseburgh, E. (1969) Afro-American Youth Cultural Center opens, *Syracuse Post Standard*, March 26.

369

Rycraft, P. (1981) Even Ireland is Irish today, *Syracuse Herald Journal* March 17.

St James has the best float (1992), *Onondaga Valley News* March 23.

Schlesinger, A.M. (1992) *The Disuniting of America*, New York: W.W. Norton.

Shorris, E. (1992) *Latinos: A Biography of the People*, New York and London: W.W. Norton.

Short, J.R., Benton, L.M., Luce, W.B. and Walton, J. (1993) Reconstructing the image of an industrial city, *Annals of the Association of American Geographers* 83(2), 207–24.

Smith, M.P. and Tarallo, B. (1993) The postmodern city and the social construction of ethnicity in California. In M. Cross and M. Keith (eds), *Racism, the City and the State*, London: Routledge, 61–76.

Snow rains on parade: Syracusans bundle up (1992), *Syracuse Post Standard* March 15.

Sollors, W. (1986) *Beyond Ethnicity: Consent and Descent in American Culture*, New York: Oxford University Press.

Tempestuous path carved by St Patrick in conquest of hearts of Syracusans (1936) (name of newspaper unknown), March 17.

US Bureau of the Census (1989) *200 Years of U.S. Census Taking: Population and Housing Questions, 1790–1990*, Washington, D.C.: US Government Printing Office.

West, C. (1993) *Race Matters*, New York: Vintage Books-Random House.

Wright, L. (1994) One drop of blood, *New Yorker* July 25, 46–55.

Yinger, J.M. (1994) *Ethnicity*, Albany, N.Y.: State University of New York Press.

Zelinsky, W. (1992) *The Cultural Geography of the United States*, Englewood Cliffs, N.J.: Prentice-Hall.

Zych, J. (1993) St Pat's parade grows, *Fayetteville Eagle Bulletin* March 17.

PART III
THE PRODUCTION OF THE CITY

CITIES ARE PRODUCED AND REPRODUCED. WE CAN EXAMINE THIS PRODUCTION IN A NUMBER OF DIFFERENT WAYS. WE CAN RESTRICT OUR ANALYSIS TO THE FINISHED PRODUCT. MANY STUDIES OF URBAN MORPHOLOGY, FOR EXAMPLE, ADOPT THIS NARROW APPROACH. WE CAN ALSO WIDEN OUR VIEW TO EXAMINE THE LINKS BETWEEN THE CREATION OF THE BUILT FORM AND WIDER SOCIAL PROCESSES. IN *THE PRODUCTION OF SPACE*, HENRI LEFEBVRE (1991) MADE A DISTINCTION BETWEEN THE PERCEIVED, THE CONCEIVED AND THE LIVED. THE PERCEIVED ARE THE SPATIAL PRACTICES INVOLVED IN PRODUCTION AND REPRODUCTION; THE CONCEIVED IS THE REPRESENTATION OF THE CITY TIED TO RELATIONS OF PRODUCTION; WHILE THE LIVED EMBRACES IMAGINATIVE REPRESENTATIONS OF THE CITY. LEFEBVRE'S TRIAD FORMS THE BASIS FOR THE NEXT THREE CHAPTERS. IN PARTICULAR I WILL EXAMINE:

- THE PRODUCTION OF THE CITY THROUGH CAPITAL FLOWS AND CONSEQUENT RESISTANCES (CHAPTER 16);

- THE PRODUCTION AND REPRODUCTION OF SOCIAL AND POLITICAL POWER AS EMBODIED IN THE FORM OF THE CITY (CHAPTER 17);

- THE PRODUCTION AND CONSUMPTION OF THE SYMBOLIC REPRESENTATION OF THE CITY IN MYTH, IDEOLOGIES, AND IMAGES (CHAPTER 18).

THE THREE CASE STUDY CHAPTERS DRAW ON RESEARCH PROJECTS IN SYRACUSE, USA (CHAPTER 19), THE SOUTH-EAST METROPOLITAN REGION OF ENGLAND (CHAPTER 20), AND BARCELONA, SPAIN (CHAPTER 21). THIS FINAL CHAPTER IS LESS FORMAL AND MORE SUGGESTIVE OF THE CONNECTIONS BETWEEN THE VIEWER AND THE VIEWED, THE SUBJECT AND THE OBJECT, THE CITY AS BOTH CONTEXT AND RECORDER OF PERSONAL EXPERIENCE. IN ITS EMBRYONIC FORM THE CHAPTER IS LESS A SUMMATION AND MORE AN INDICATION OF THE WORK THAT LIES AHEAD.

Chapter 16

CITY AS INVESTMENT

T HERE IS NOTHING SO HABIT-FORMING AS MONEY.
   DON MARQUIS, *THE MERRY FLEA* (1927)

The city is produced in many ways. One of the most important factors affecting contemporary cities is the pulse of investment flows. In
capitalist societies things become commodities, to be bought and
sold, traded and bargained. The land and buildings that constitute
the physical environment of the city are important commodities. As
a site of investment and disinvestment the city is affected by the flows
of capital investment and disinvestment. In this chapter I will examine some of the factors and consequences of these flows.

THE PULSE OF CAPITAL

Public investment

We can make a distinction between private and public investments.
Private investments tend to take a short- to medium-term horizon
and are primarily guided by profitability. Public investments, though
perhaps guided by short-term profit figures, also have the opportunity to take a much longer perspective. Public investments are
necessary when vital needs are not served by the private market. Many
of the big investments in the city are public investments, such as
roads, bridges, sewerage systems, housing, and telecommunication
networks. The capitalist city has a great deal of public investment.
And public investment can influence private growth. The case study
material in chapter 20, for example, highlights the connection
between public investment and private growth and in particular
shows how the growth and buoyancy of such areas as the south-east
of England, were and are partly a function of the huge amounts of
public investment which underwrites the growth of private investment. In an interesting edited book, Andrew Kirby (1992) shows
how the pattern of defense spending in the United States altered
regional economies and the economic fate of numerous metropolitan
areas.

Public investment in the city is never constant. When areas formerly seen as unprofitable become profitable then private investors seek privatization measures that open the way for profitable private investment. The argument used is that public investment is "crowding out" private investment. And when formerly private investments become unprofitable then the demand changes for public takeover: investors want investment winners to be privatized and losers to be nationalized.

Public investment in the built environment ranges in size from small increments to the urban fabric to large "lumpy" investments such as airports, new highways, and so on. These are huge investment projects fraught with potential conflict and risk. Conflict arises because they tend to be once-and-for-all decisions, not easily repeated or changed. Conflict over the why, where, and when of investment leads to the politicization of the issue. In his book *Great Planning Disasters* (1980) Peter Hall looks at a variety of such conflicts including the BART scheme in San Francisco and the debate over London's third airport.

The distinction between private and public is useful as a broad-scale analytical device but in reality the two go hand in hand. Speculative office development at the intersection of two interstate highways is a conjunction of both public and private: the private is not possible without the public. Investment patterns of both a public and a private type merge and intersect in the urban arena; the private often dependent on the public while public investment is influenced by private investment decisions.

Private investment

We can think of private investment as a series of decisions. The first decision is whether to invest in property or in something else. Property investment has to compete with other investment opportunities, including stocks and bonds, bank deposits, and government securities. Investment in the land and buildings of a city are dependent on a variety of factors. The most important is the relative rate of return. When investment in land and buildings yields a higher rate of return than alternative investments then capital will be invested. The surge of capital into and out of the built environment is a function of the relative rate of return. There are some provisos. Crude rates of return have to be assessed against risk. High rates of return with a substantial risk may be less attractive to some investors than lower rates with lower risks. For some, medium rates of return will be preferred to higher rates which have more risk. Many of the large financial institutions making investment decisions have security as much as return as their most important investment criterion. Property provides returns in the medium to long term that are attractive to institutions seeking a balanced portfolio.

The second decision is what type of property to invest in. We can picture different types of built-form investment: houses, hotels, offices, convention centers, and so on. The changing pattern of demand will influence this decision. If there is a growing demand for hotels, then capital will tend to flow into hotel construction.

The third decision is where to invest. In a global economy and with an international banking system, savings generated in Chicago, London, or Brussels can be invested in hotel construction in Miami, office development in Paris, or housing development in Arizona. Investment in property is volatile, and investors disinvest in a declining sector and reinvest elsewhere.

Speculative investment

Much of the larger-scale private investment in the city is of a speculative nature. When someone builds an office block or constructs new houses on the edge of the city for a general perceived demand rather than for a specific client they are making a speculative investment. They are betting on their ability to read the market. Much of the look, structure, and orientation of the city reflects patterns of speculative activity. Central London, for example, contains many remnants of speculative measures, from the neoclassical elegance of Bedford Square (construction started in 1775) to the town planning experiment of Hampstead Garden Suburb where building first started in 1907. David Cannadine (1980) shows the social as well as the economic importance of urban development by examining the connection between the British aristocracy and speculative developments in British cities.

The more successful speculators both read and control the market. In many cities of the United States, the classic form of urban land speculation was by wealthy speculators who assembled rural land cheaply and then constructed streetcars and other forms of urban transit. They brought the demand to the supply and in the process created fortunes for themselves as well as structuring the orientation of the city. The ideas of the economist Henry George (1839–97) were shaped by such processes. His experience as a newspaper man in San Francisco alerted him to the avarice of land speculation. In his most famous book, *Progress and Poverty*, first published in 1879, he argued that land-value increases in cities should not be privately appropriated. They were a result of collective forces and thus should belong to the community. He argued for a single tax on land to meet the costs of government. His ideas were very influential at the time and have percolated through the years to become part of such specific programs as the British New Town Movement and more general programs of government taxation of land and of land-value increases.

Land speculation is fueled by the big profits to be made from getting a change of use in the land. Buying land at rural prices then selling the same land for residential development is a source of great profit. To purchase residential land and then be able to turn the land into office development is another source of profit. In capitalist cities getting a change of use has been a powerful dynamic: legally and illegally, above-board or riven with corruption, the possibility of reaping the rewards has fueled and continues to fuel many of the major land-use changes in the city.

Consider the case of office development in London. Since 1945 there have been three major office booms. The first occurred after the buildup of demand and the restrictions on office supply in the 1950s. The result was a boom described by Oliver Marriott in his book *The Property Boom* (1967). The second occurred in the early 1970s and was fueled by easy credit. It forms the backdrop to the classic study by Peter Ambrose and Bob Colenutt entitled *The Property Machine* (1975). The third boom occurred in the mid- to late 1980s and was caused by increasing demand for financial services and the ability of developers to obtain planning permission in areas beyond the traditional office sector. This building boom extended into Docklands (see pp. 159–65) and north of the City. In each of the three periods the boom was fueled by increased demand, easy or cheap lines of credit, and a responsive planning system that allowed change of use. The booms were halted by a downturn in demand, increasing interest rates, or a combination of the two. While the exact nature of the office boom has varied over the years the underlying dynamic has remained the same: the enormous profits to be made from turning residential or industrial land use into much more profitable office development.

The psychology of investment

To understand banking, noted Kenneth Boulding, you have to be more of an anthropologist than an economist. Investment patterns are guided by economic considerations but take place in a social context. Investment is a social activity as affected by the herd mentality as all other collective practices. There are only a few market leaders, and the majority of investors are crowd followers. In his study of office construction in Houston Joe Feagin (1987, 183) makes a similar point:

> *A former Citibank executive pointed out that Houston's overbuilt environment shows that finance capital has a "herd mentality": lenders move to "hot" money cities. . . . In the boom period outside investors said to their banks and other brokers, according to one local expert, "if it's in Houston, I want it."*

What is rational for individual investors may become irrational for the collective. Let me explain. If there is a demand for office construction, then individual investors will put up money for office developments. Each of them is acting rationally. However, by their individual actions they may create an oversupply of offices, which leads to vacancies, a fall in rental income, and a decline in property values. Feagin's study of Houston and other studies point to this pattern of perceived demand, then investment flowing in to meet this demand, then the creation of an oversupply. Office development, in particular, follows this boom-and-bust pattern. As the title of one book has it, *Sydney Boom, Sydney Bust* (Daly, 1982).

Theories of investment

Patterns of investment have also been tied to broader theories of society. Let us consider three. First, David Harvey has extended the work of Henri Lefebvre (1970) to suggest that a secondary circuit of capital can be identified which is used to soak up surplus funds (see pp. 106–7). This theory is very dependent on an underconsumptionist model of the economy which presumes "excess" funds. Rather than assuming two distinct circuits, it is more useful to see property investment as one more investment opportunity.

Second, the English property analyst David Cadman has identified something he refers to as the mode of investment (Cadman and Payne, 1989). Cadman points to the growing importance of investing institutions. Either voluntarily or as part of their contracts, many people in Britain and North America have passed their savings to financial institutions, which use professional fund managers. These managers control huge sums of money. They are constantly seeking investment opportunities. Urban property is particularly attractive to these fund managers because large projects take up big chunks of money in relatively safe and secure investment. Cadman suggests that we now have a mode of investment which stresses size of project and

Illustration 16.1   *Office development in the 1970s: Commercial Union Building, London (© British Architectural Library, RIBA, London; photograph: A.C. Cooper Ltd)*

security of return. With only a small number of very large institutions the group mentality operates to define very narrow limits of what are acceptable investments. In effect, Cadman is pointing to the power of finance capital over and above its role in financing production and consumption.

Third, although perhaps not a theory in the strict definition of the term, the work of Sharon Zukin (1982, 1991, 1995) points to some of the wider connections of property investment. She identifies what she terms the interacting circuits of economic and cultural capital. Figure 16.1, for example, looks at the circuits of cultural capital involved in the process of gentrification. Zukin's work is suggestive rather than definitive, and the terms are more indicative than enlightening. However, she points to the cultural connections of capital

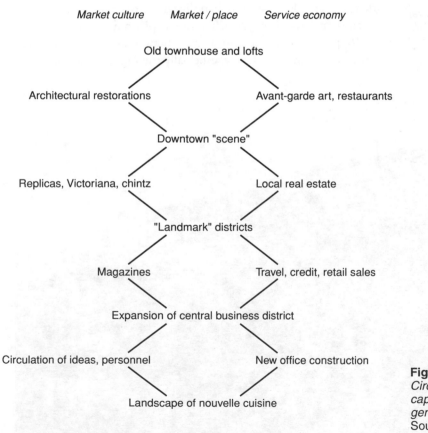

Market culture   *Market / place*   *Service economy*

Old townhouse and lofts

Architectural restorations   Avant-garde art, restaurants

Downtown "scene"

Replicas, Victoriana, chintz   Local real estate

"Landmark" districts

Magazines   Travel, credit, retail sales

Expansion of central business district

Circulation of ideas, personnel   New office construction

Landscape of nouvelle cuisine

Figure 16.1
Circuits of cultural capital involved in gentrification
Source: *Zukin (1991)*

investment and the myriad processes involved in the construction and reconstruction of particular places.

Whatever theoretical stance is adopted, an important starting point for any theorizing is the fact that urban property is now one of the favored investment sites of finance capital. The structure of cities is intimately bound up with the flows of capital while the health of capitalism is connected to the buoyancy of urban land markets.

The role of planning

The pulse of capital into and out of the built environment is affected by the planning system. We can identify two ends of a continuum. At one end are the more *laissez-faire* systems which allow development pressures to dominate; at the other are the more interventionist systems. The United States and the United Kingdom provide respective examples. We should be wary, however, of seeing one as pro-development and the other as antidevelopment. Aggressive capitalist markets can and do exist quite happily with strong planning systems. A detailed analysis of the British land-use planning system (Short et al, 1986) points to the accommodation between the planning system and the development industry, especially the big developers.

Illustration 16.2
Office development in the 1980s: Gateway 2 (© British Architectural Library, RIBA, London; photograph: A. C. Cooper Ltd)

By designating only certain parcels of land for specific purposes the planning system creates and maintains scarcity. The returns on capital invested in prime sites are thus secured by the planning system, which restricts the supply of building land and the size and number of development sites.

Planning has unintended as well as intended consequences. In their wide survey of the British planning system Hall et al. (1973) point out that although agricultural land had been protected, the result was increased separation between home and workplace and increased land and property prices. The distributional effects of British land-use planning were regressive: owners of land who were granted planning permission saw a dramatic rise in the market price of their land, while low- to middle-income homeowners had long journeys to work and expensive housing.

BUILDING CYCLES

Investment in the built environment occurs in distinct waves. One of the most palpable effects of such cyclical investment are building cycles. They have a distinct periodicity; they occur, on average, about every 20 years. We can identify four elements. In the *trough* of the cycle there is very little building. Supply of most building types exceeds demand. Higher returns are available in alternative investment opportunities. Following the trough comes the *upswing*. If the city is growing, even modestly, then demand for building and land for expansion will increase. Investment is attracted back and building increases. At the *peak* there is a building boom. Demand is so heavy that high returns can be obtained. There is a lot of speculative activity and much building. Eventually, the feverish activity creates an oversupply, and we slide into the *downswing* of reduced building and disinvestment, which leads us back to the trough, and another cycle is both completed and begun.

Transport and building cycles

Building cycles are associated with specific transport eras which gave shape, location, and size of the building cycle. John Adams (1970), for example, has developed a model of the building cycles and transport eras in a typical Midwest US city. Figure 16.2 shows six building booms from the 1890s to the 1960s. Different transport eras are also identified, from the walking city, to the electric streetcar, to the automobile. The predominant mode of transport in each era influences

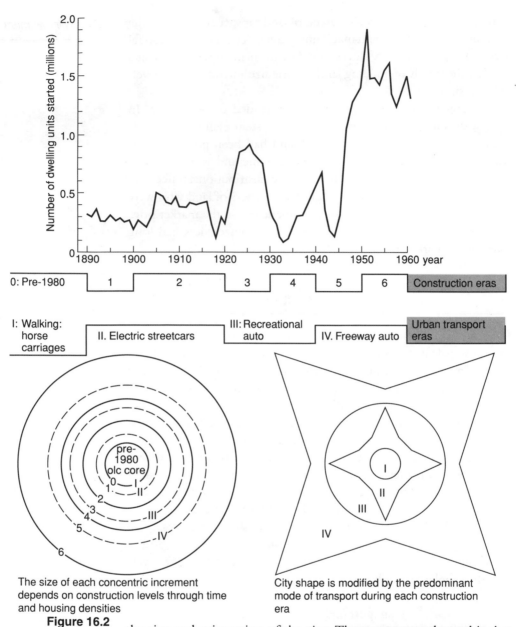

The size of each concentric increment depends on construction levels through time and housing densities

City shape is modified by the predominant mode of transport during each construction era

Figure 16.2
Building cycles, transport, and urban shape, pre-1800–1960
Source: *Adams (1970)*

the size and orientation of the city. The most general trend is that the evolving transportation systems allow successive building cycles to be at increasing distances from the city centre. The net effect is of a stretching out of the city along the predominant transport corridors.

The Adams model takes us to the 1960s. Since then another build-ing cycle has taken place in many US cities. In the 1960s and 1970s there was the malling of America as large retail clusters relocated from the downtown toward the suburbs. Giant indoor shopping centres were established on the accessible periphery of many cities. In the 1980s there was also the construction of what the journalist Joel Garreau (1991) refers to as *edge cities*. He defined these as centers with over 5 million square feet of feasible office space, 600,000 square feet of leasable retail space, more jobs than bedrooms, and situated where there was nothing like a city less than 30 years earlier. As you

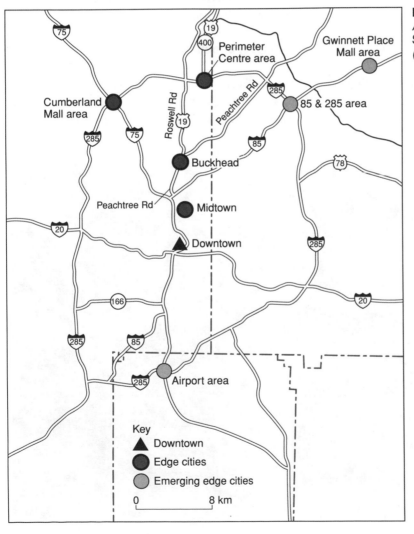

Figure 16.3
Atlanta
Source*: Garreau*
(1991)

can see, his definitions range from the precise to the vague. Garreau claims to have identified 120 edge cities. Figure 16.3, for example, indicates the edge cities in Atlanta. Notice how they cluster beside interstate highway connections. Although we may quibble with Garreau's assertions and his jarring nationalistic prose, his book does outline the nature of the most recent building cycle, a construction of built form at accessible points well away from the old city centers. These new centers include the construction of large prestige office complexes and up-market shopping centers that provide the focal point of new rounds of investment and building. Edge cities are not unique to the United States. Similar trends have been noted in Sydney, London, and other cities, but the decline of the downtown is more pronounced in the United States, as is the amount of investment going into the new edge complexes.

Impact of building cycles

Building cycles create the fabric of the city. The very largest cities will have examples of most building cycles. New York and London, for instance, have expressions of all the different building styles of the last

Illustration 16.3
*Investment in the
built environment
fluctuates over
time and space: an
unattractive
investment in
Syracuse, N.Y.
during a slump
(photograph:
author)*

hundred years; the time frame of London's building cycles stretches back over a thousand years.

Building cycles are the physical embodiment of the dominant architecture, location, and mode of transportation. Each building cycle thus has a specific character, an individual "feel" and "look" which marks it out from all the others, whether it be the straight lines of modernism, the whimsy of postmodernism, or the elegance of the neoclassical. In many cities dominant growth occurred at particular times, their character linked to particular styles: the Georgian splendor of Edinburgh's New Town, the contemporary look of much of Los Angeles, or the industrial/postindustrial feel of Pittsburgh. There are also silences. Seoul in South Korea is one of the most modern cities with only a few remnants of building before 1960. More poignantly, Hiroshima and Nagasaki in Japan have a very modern feel. Most of the pre-1945 urban fabric was destroyed by atomic bombs.

For a city to be associated with old building cycles is a sign of historical connection and, for some, intellectual depth. To be associated with the most recent is a sign of being on the edge, to use Garreau's phrase in a double sense. To be associated with neither the most recent nor the older vintages is to be caught in that most unfashionable lacuna between the contemporary and the old.

ACTS OF RESISTANCE

Capital investment and disinvestment is a social process as much as an economic transaction. The movement in and out of the built environment, the waxing and waning of building cycles have social implications as well as architectural consequences. In a previous section I described a series of office booms in London, England. The property boom meant the possible destruction of old buildings and the construction of new buildings; in effect, the destruction of certain communities and the construction of new communities. In some places this process was resisted. Take the case of Covent Garden. The site of this former fruit, flower and vegetable market was scheduled for redevelopment after the market's relocation to a less-congested area south of the river Thames. In 1968 the Greater London Council (GLC) announced plans to demolish a majority of the buildings in the area and build new roadways, offices, and hotels. The Covent Garden Community Association (CGCA) was formed by residents, planning students, and radical architects to fight these plans. At a public inquiry held in 1971 the CGCA proposed alternative plans which emphasized conservation and housing rather than demolition and commercial buildings. The CGCA also opened a social center in the area, published a newsletter and established a community theater. The GLC presented a revised plan in June 1976, but this was also deemed unacceptable by CGCA. Eventually the GLC bowed to community pressure and a new plan was announced in June 1977. The new agreed plan stressed rehabilitation of existing buildings, mixed uses, and maximization of housing. As one commentator noted:

> *The plan was the diametric opposite of the 1968–1971 plan and a substantial scaling down of the June 1976 proposals. It can only be viewed as a triumph for the defenders of the community, a major reversal for property speculators and a major concession by the planners and the GLC.* (Christensen, 1981, 121)

Illustration 16.4
Covent Garden, London, in the 1990s, now a setting for popular street performances. The church also appears in Illustration 2.4 (© Barry Lewis/ Network)

Today Covent Garden is one of the more humane places in central London, where visitors and locals wend their way past low-rise buildings, pubs and small shops, and the old market is used as a craft fair. Covent Garden was the success story for community resistance. There have also been failures. Ambrose and Colenutt (1975) paint a gloomy

picture of the property machine running over poorly organized communities in south London.

Fast forward a decade, and move a couple of miles east from Covent Garden and a similar story unfolds: Spitalfields, in the east end of London. The old wholesale fruit and vegetable market was also scheduled for relocation and this was an opportunity for the redevelopment of the fourteen-acre site. Rachel Woodward (1993) tells the story. To be more accurate two stories. The story told by the development company, Spitalfields Development Group (SDG), which in 1987 was granted planning permission to redevelop the site, was one of a much-needed cash and job transfusion into a decaying inner-city area. The Campaign to Save Spitalfields from the

Illustration 16.5
Office building in one of Atlanta's edge cities. This high-rise building sits in a greenfield site miles from the downtown (photograph: author)

Developers (CSSD) told another story. This was a group composed of activists in the local Labour Party and voluntary sector who sought to fight the redevelopment. Their story was of the destruction of a vibrant community. In this case one story "won" and another lost; SDG won its fight for redevelopment while CSSD was unsuccessful in preventing the relocation of the market and did not get the re-development plans halted.

Different places, different results. The examples represent either end of the continuum of community resistance to capital flows. Similar stories can be told for other cities. We could draw up a check-list of why some groups are successful, why some resistances are successful, and others not. These are matters already discussed in chapter 12. Here, the important point to note is that the form, location, size, and orientation of the built environment is not simply the result of economic forces; it represents and embodies individual and collective displays of power, contestation, and resistance.

GUIDE TO FURTHER READING

On investment in the built environment, see:

Ambrose, P. (1994) *Urban Process and Power*, London: Routledge.

Ambrose, P. and Colenutt, B. (1975) *The Property Machine*, Harmonds-worth, Middx: Penguin.

Cadman, D. and Payne, G. (1989) *Future Cities*, London: Routledge.

Cannadine, D. (1980) *Lords and Landlords: The Aristocracy and the Towns, 1774–1967*, Leicester: Leicester University Press.

Daly, M.T. (1982) *Sydney Boom, Sydney Bust*, Sydney: Allen & Unwin.

Fainstein, S. (1993) *The City Builders: Property, Politics and Planning in London and New York*, Oxford: Blackwell.

Feagin, J. (1987) The secondary circuit of capital: office construction in Houston, Texas, *International Journal of Urban and Regional Research* 11, 172–92.

Hall, P. (1980) *Great Planning Disasters*, London: Weidenfeld & Nicolson.

Kirby, A. (ed.) (1992) *The Pentagon and the Cities*, Newbury Park, Cal.: Sage.

Lefebvre, H. (1970) *La Révolution urbaine*, Paris: Gallimard.

Marriott, O. (1967) *The Property Boom*, London: Hamish Hamilton.

Willis, C. (1995) *Form Follows Finance: Skyscrapers and Skylines in New York and Chicago*, New York: Princeton Architectural Press.

Zukin, S. (1982) *Loft Living: Culture and Capital in Urban Change*, Baltimore, Md: Johns Hopkins University Press.

Zukin, S. (1991) *Landscapes of Power: From Detroit to Disneyworld*, Berkeley and Los Angeles, Cal.: University of California Press.

Zukin, S. (1995) *The Culture of Cities*, Oxford: Blackwell.

Ways in which the planning system affects and is influenced by investment in the British context are analyzed by:

Hall, P., Thomas, R., Gracey, H. and Drewett, R. (1973) *The Containment of Urban England*, 2 vols, London: Allen & Unwin.

Short, J.R., Witt, S. and Fleming, S. (1986) *Housebuilding, Planning and Community Action*, London: Routledge.

On building cycles, historical and contemporary:
Adams, J.S. (1970) Residential structure of mid-western cities, *Annals of the Association of American Geographers* 60, 36–62.
Garreau, J. (1991) *Edge Cities*, New York: Doubleday.

On acts of resistance:
Christensen, T. (1981) The politics of redevelopment: Covent Garden. In D.T. Herbert and R.J. Johnston, (eds), *Geography and the Urban Environment*, Vol. 4, London: John Wiley.
Woodward, R. (1993) One place, two stories: two interpretations of Spitalfields in the debate over its redevelopment. In G. Kearns, and C. Philo, (eds), *Selling Places: The City as Cultural Capital, Past and Present*, Oxford: Pergamon Press.

Chapter 17

CITY AS TEXT

[THE CITY] IS A POEM WHICH UNFOLDS THE SIGNIFIER AND IT IS THIS UNFOLD-
ING THAT ULTIMATELY THE SEMIOLOGY OF THE CITY SHOULD TRY TO GRASP
AND MAKE SING.

ROLAND BARTHES, *SEMIOLOGY AND THE URBAN* (1971)

THE CITY . . . DOES NOT TELL ITS PAST, BUT CONTAINS IT LIKE THE LINES OF
A HAND, WRITTEN IN THE CORNERS OF THE STREETS, THE GRATINGS OF
THE WINDOWS, THE BANISTERS OF THE STEPS, THE ANTENNAE OF THE LIGHT-
NING RODS, THE POLES OF THE FLAGS, EVERY SEGMENT MARKED IN TURN WITH
SCRATCHES, INDENTATIONS, SCROLLS.

ITALO CALVINA, *INVISIBLE CITIES* (1974)

The city is produced in many ways. In the last chapter, we looked at the influence of capital flows and acts of resistance in shaping the form of the city. This form, as the quotes by Barthes and Calvino suggest, tells us much about the wider society. Cities are systems of communications telling us who has power and how it is wielded. The configuration, use, size, internal layout, and external design of the city embodies the nature, distribution, and contestation of power in society. The power struggle fundamentally revolves around the meaning of the city, what it represents, what it could represent, and what it should represent. In a very real sense the city is a system of communication, a set of signs indicating power and prestige, status and influence, victory and defeat.

URBAN FORMS

Recurring elements

In a wide-ranging survey of urban patterns the architectural historian Spiro Kostoff (1991) identified five recurring elements. The first was the city organized on organic lines: the tight cluster of the medieval city, the picturesque of garden suburbs, or the new exurbia in the depopulating countryside are all examples of cities organized around organic shapes and functions.

The second element is the grid; it is found throughout the world and is particularly common in the New World. The grid has been used for a variety of purposes: as the guiding element in communitarian experiments to the easiest form for land speculators and builders. While some see the grid as an example of authoritarian control and lack of imagination, Kostoff takes a more neutral view, seeing it as a geometric form capable of multiple meanings.

The third element is what Kostoff terms the city as diagram. This is the city as military geometry, cosmic symbolism, utopian experiment. The city as diagram is a top-down imposition, and in the end, argues Kostoff, all these ideal city forms are dehumanizing because they are a cerebral concern with order and discipline.

Kostoff's fourth category is the grand manner composed of "heroic scale, visual fluency and the luxury of building materials. It speaks of ceremony, processional intentions, a regimented public life." Behind the grand manner is a strong state. From Babylon to Nazi Germany and from state capitals to national capitals, cities express the pretensions of political power. We can tell much about a political regime by the buildings it constructs.

Kostoff's final element is the skyline, what he terms "the shorthand of urban identity." From the spires of Gothic cathedrals to the flat

Illustration 17.1
The city as a text: a building in Seoul, South Korea (photograph: author)

tops of modernist blocks the vertical form of the city tells us as much about human aspirations as about building technologies. From cathedrals of God to cathedrals of commerce, the urban skyline in its individual buildings, as in its ensemble of buildings, indicates the recurring concerns of a society. The small urban setting with its dramatic Gothic spire tells us about the power of the Church, while the tall towers of a business district reveal the power of capital and business. Even the term *central* business district speaks of the centrality of commerce in contemporary life as in contemporary architecture.

The city and the body

Perhaps one of the most famous books on architecture is the ten-volume work by the Roman military engineer Vitruvius. Written some time between 31 BC and AD 14, *On Architecture* deals with a variety of topics including city planning, building materials, temple construction, public buildings, and private buildings. In the third volume, focusing on sacred buildings, Vitruvius suggests that buildings should have the proportion of a man. The size and geometry of the temple should reflect the human form. The ideas of Vitruvius were the chief classical authority relied upon in the Italian Renaissance. Architects such as Bramante, Michelangelo, and Palladio endorsed Vitruvius' demand that buildings be materially sound, functionally practical, and formally beautiful. The human body was important as a measure of both beauty and practicality. The famous drawings by Leonardo da Vinci indicate the formal proportions between body, square, and circle. Much of the continuing appeal of classical and Renaissance architecture is that the buildings are built to a human scale. Not simply are they smaller and more intimate than other building types but the human form was one of the basic measuring devices. We lose something when the individual human form no longer is one of the basic units of architectural measurement and organization.

The body was and continues to be reflected in the city. There is, for example, the phallic symbolism of high-rise tower blocks. The modern skyline of many big cities is often a solid metaphor for male virility and masculine strength. Sometimes the relationship is even more obvious. The design for a national monument by the English architect Sir John Soane in 1779 makes some of the connections between nation and the (gendered) body politic all the more explicit. There are feminine parallels. The beautiful soft roundness of Michelangelo's dome of St Peter's in Rome has the look and contours of the female breast. The parallel is even more clear in Michelangelo's drawing than in the final product erected in 1590.

The form is repeated in the baroque dome of St Paul's cathedral in London, designed by Sir Christopher Wren and completed in 1711. As one of the most basic forms, the human body has acted as a powerful template for imagining the city. Even some of the terms we use are indicative: for example the heart of the city, transport arteries and traffic circulation, healthy urban economies, sick buildings.

The relationship between city and body extends beyond the isomorphic mapping of the body onto urban structure and the metonymic use in architecture and urban planning to represent the human body. Elizabeth Grosz (1992) reminds us that the city has a vital part to play in the social production of gendered and racialized corporeality. And in a fascinating book Diane Ackerman (1990) summarizes a mass of material on the way our body's senses of smell, touch, taste, hearing, and vision interpret the external world. In a similar vein, Paul Rodaway (1994) develops the concept of sensuous geographies in which touch, smell, hearing, and sight structure the geographical experience.

One of the great silences of urban geography, indeed of much of the social sciences, is an explicit consideration of the body. The concentration with the mind, best expressed in Descartes' maxim "I think therefore I am," has meant that much social commentary ignores the body. But yet it is through the corporeal that we both perceive the world and move through the world. The sociologist Bryan Turner (1984) has summarized a lot of interesting general material. The work of David Seamon (1979), for example, elaborates on what he refers to as the geography of the lifeworld. This is a geography sensitive to the human body with notions of body ballets and the ways bodies have a sense of place. The connections between body and place are at last beginning to be recognized as important elements in our understanding of the urban experience (see Sennett, 1994).

The meaning of the built environment

The built environment embodies meaning. Rapoport (1990) identifies three levels of meaning: the high-level meaning relating cosmologies and worldviews; the middle-level meaning giving intimations of status and wealth; and the low-level meaning relating to the everyday use of space. Any building or group of buildings will condense the different levels of meaning. The United Nations buildings in New York signifies world cooperation and modernist architecture and is a significant element in the built environment of upper east side Manhattan. But meanings change. The Empire State Building in New York, for example, was built as a speculative venture during the depression; it was a symbol of business confidence at a time of economic gloom. It has since become an icon of New York, a much-loved place, a recognizable element in the skyline, and a symbol of skyscraper New York which as time passes has taken on an historical, nostalgic tinge. Meanings vary by status. For most people the Empire State Building is only something to look at, maybe even to visit. It is different for a real-estate mogul. Harry Helmsley once said of the Empire State Building, "There it stands, and every morning you would look out the window and the building is staring you in the face. So you'd say, well I gotta buy it" (quoted in Shachtman, 1991).

The built environment has meaning. But it is never fixed or constant. Any building, group of buildings, or urban ensemble has a variety of possible meanings which are not anchored permanently but float in a sea of competing ideas, differing values, and antagonistic political and economic forces.

Legibility

For meaning to be produced cities must be legible. Legibility depends on many things: a shared set of values and beliefs, a common "language," an easily understood architectural syntax. One of the most persistent themes of contemporary debates on urban form is the idea that the city is becoming less legible. Richard Sennett (1990, xi) compares the ancient and present urban world:

> *The ancient Greek could use his or her eyes to see the complexity of life. The temples, markets, playing fields, meeting places, walls, public statuary, and paintings of the ancient city represented the culture's values in religion, politics, and family life. It would be difficult to know where in particular to go in modern London or New York to experience, say, remorse. Or were modern architects asked to design spaces that better promote democracy, they would lay down their pens; there is no modern design equivalent to the ancient assembly. Nor is it easy to conceive of places that teach the moral dimensions of sexual desire that the Greeks learned in their gymnasiums. . . . The shopping mall, the parking lot, the apartment house elevator do not suggest in their form the complexities of how people might live.*

Sennett's thesis is that our cities have become more private, we have become obsessed with refuge, the inside, private spaces. We have become more and more frightened of other people, and this is reflected in the barriers of the city to intimacy between strangers, and the construction of neutral zones of public indifference. Anthony

Giddens (1992) makes a similar claim when he writes about the sequestration of experience brought about by the privatization of passion, the marginalization of difference, and the narrative of enjoyment in malls and theme parks. In multicultural, pluralistic societies there is no longer any common set of beliefs and values; in the postmodern world there are many languages and there is no longer a correspondence between architectural forms and social and political messages.

The illegibility is reinforced by our lack of connection with the built environment. Most of us live in other people's creations, in environments designed for us rather than by us. Contemporary cities are legible but the inscription is of signature architects: Michael Graves, Arata Isozaki, James Stirling, and Robert Venturi. Architects like John Portman in his exploded space of inner public spaces, such as hotel lobbies as found in the Hyatt Regency in Atlanta, Georgia, give us a spectacle of space that comes from the work of an individual architect rather than a shared language of architectural form and meaning. In that regard our cities are illegible, and that is what makes them so disorienting, so overwhelming; they are like reading a book in a foreign language – we can identify the letters but it does not add up to a sustained narrative. We have safe refuges but no public city.

WRITING THE CITY

In one sense the city can be seen as a set of signs, a nonverbal system of communication. The city is a container of messages, as well as the messages themselves, passed through society. The writing of the city also involves the reading of the city. There is no one-to-one correspondence between the production of the message and its consumption. There are alternative, different, and contestatory readings of the city. We can illuminate these points more clearly with reference to specific examples which provide a kaleidoscope of urban restructuring in the past 200 years in varied cities of the world.

Kandy

Kandy is the capital of Sri Lanka, formerly Ceylon. The last king of Kandy was Sri Vikrana Raja Sinha, who ruled from 1798 to 1815. Although he defeated the invading British army in 1803 his power was challenged by the nobles and the British. In the final years of his kingship he undertook a massive building program (see figures 17.1 and 17.2). Between 1809 and 1812 there was continuous rebuilding

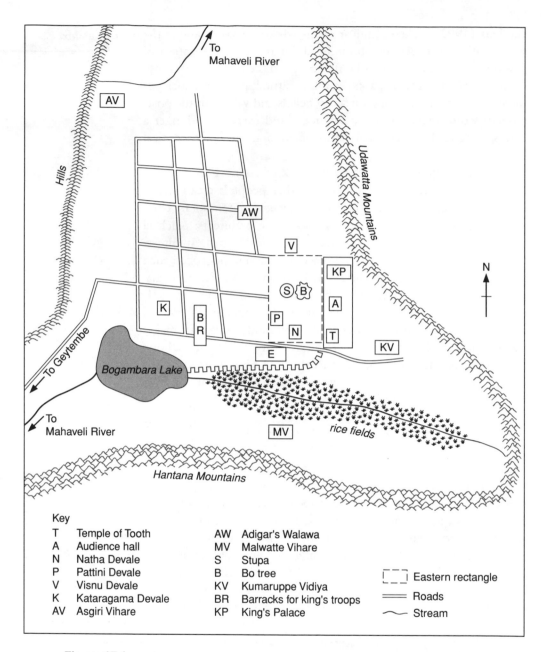

Figure 17.1
Kandy in 1765
Source: *Duncan (1990)*

Key

T	Temple of Tooth	AW	Adigar's Walawa
A	Audience hall	MV	Malwatte Vihare
N	Natha Devale	S	Stupa
P	Pattini Devale	B	Bo tree
V	Visnu Devale	KV	Kumaruppe Vidiya
K	Kataragama Devale	BR	Barracks for king's troops
AV	Asgiri Vihare	KP	King's Palace

[--] Eastern rectangle
══ Roads
〰 Stream

of city, palace, and royal gardens, including the construction of five new blocks of shops and residences, the construction of a stone rampart, and the creation of an artificial lake. Between 1810 and 1812 almost 3,000 men were forced to labor on this project. In the middle of the lake an island was built on which stood a rectangular pleasure house.

Jim Duncan (1990), in his detailed and careful deconstruction of

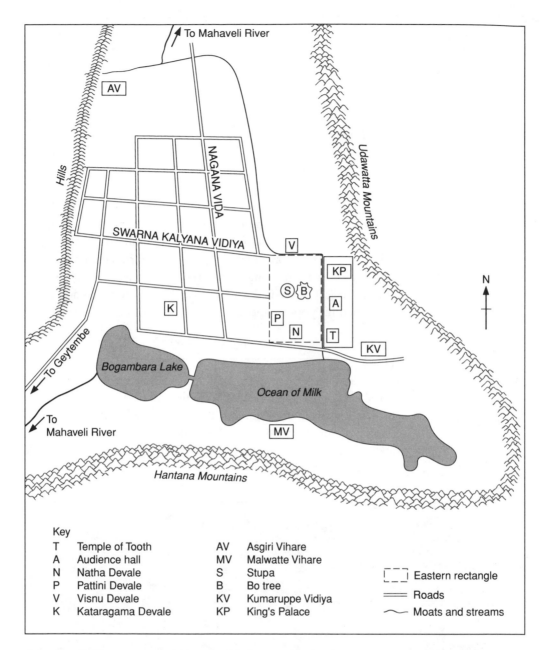

Key

T	Temple of Tooth	AV	Asgiri Vihare
A	Audience hall	MV	Malwatte Vihare
N	Natha Devale	S	Stupa
P	Pattini Devale	B	Bo tree
V	Visnu Devale	KV	Kumaruppe Vidiya
K	Kataragama Devale	KP	King's Palace

⌐¬¬ Eastern rectangle
═══ Roads
〜 Moats and streams

the urban landscape, argues that the king attempted to impress upon his subjects his power and prestige by the sheer magnitude of the building. The rebuilt city was a solid metaphor for the vigorous power of the king. But the buildings took a particular form. Duncan argues that there was a homology between the landscape of Kandy and the mythical city form of the gods. In the western rectangle of the city the king added two streets and extended three others, thereby

Figure 17.2
Kandy in 1815
Source: *Duncan
(1990)*

increasing the number of squares in the city to 21: the same number of administrative units in his kingdom. The additions and extensions also created a more rectangular form, a reference to the heavenly city of the gods. The urban form thus reflected the kingdom on earth and the kingdom in the heavens. Even the names used were important. The artificial lake was called the Ocean of Milk, the name used in the sacred texts to refer to the ocean at the center of the universe. The lake referenced the beginning of time. The city was an allegorical landscape. The parallels were used by the king to legitimate his reign with reference to divine comparisons.

There were different readings of the new city form. Many of the nobles saw the acts of an irrational tyrant; the peasants of the Western province also saw the building program as unjust and repressive, much of it based on forced labor, but also they ridiculed the whole pretension of an earthly king trying to emulate the divine gods. The building project, designed to increase his support, paradoxically undermined his popular appeal.

Edinburgh

For over 500 years this city was the capital of Scotland. It was the site of royal coronations, the seat of government, and the center of the Scottish Presbyterian Church. The old city clustered around the spine of land that led up to the castle, and names like Cowgate, Market Street, Lawnmarket, Grassmarket were indicative of trade and commerce, while Candlemaker's Row and Surgeon's Hall

Figure 17.3
Edinburgh's New
Town

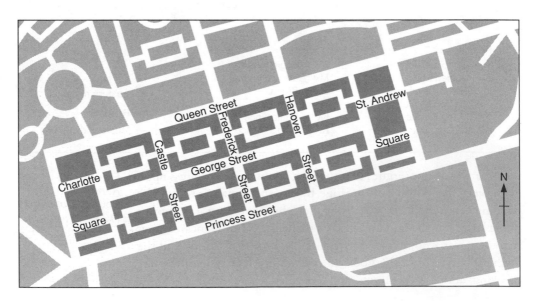

reflected the guilds and crafts of the city. The Old Town, as it was subsequently called, was a jumble of high-rise tenements, mixed land-uses with the smell of the markets and the trade of the countryside never far away.

In 1707 the Act of Union joined England and Scotland in an alliance that has persisted to the present day. Edinburgh was no longer the capital city of an independent country but the control center of a state centered much further south in London. In 1767 some land to the north of the Old Town came under the control of the city council and for the next 30 years an impressive building program created three parallel streets ending in elegant squares (figure 17.3). The building of the New Town contained many messages. The urban form of straight lines and rectangular squares, a counterpoint to the organic density of the Old Town, was a solid metaphor for an enlightened society. The geometric structuring of space paralleled the belief in a rational, ordered universe susceptible to human understanding and control (Reed, 1982). The New Town distanced the rich and powerful from the rest of society. In the Old Town social classes were mixed, often with horizontal differentiation in the same

Illustration 17.2
Part of Edinburgh's New Town (© British Architectural Library, RIBA, London; photograph: A. C. Cooper Ltd)

tenements, but the New Town separated out the powerful from the weak and the rich from the poor. It was the embodiment of an emerging social class making itself in and through urban reorganization. And then there were the names: Frederick Street, Hanover Street, Queen Street, George Street, Princess Street and Charlotte Square all spoke of a social class eager to align themselves with the English royalty and tie their fortunes to the English state. This was an important point, given the Jacobite Rebellion of 1745 and continued English fears that Scotland was a source of disloyalty to the House of Hanover. The prosaic names of the Old Town which spoke of trade and commerce and rude function were replaced in the New Town by names of the English royal family.

Today few people are aware of the specific messages of the New Town. The streets and squares indicate Georgian elegance while the names have long passed into such common usage that most people forget the allusions. The New Town is a symbol of the elegant past, a distinctive feature of the Edinburgh landscape and an integral part of the notion of the city as the "Athens of the North."

Vienna

In his meticulous study of Vienna at the turn of the nineteenth into the twentieth century the historian Carl Schorske (1980) draws attention to the importance of the Ringstrasse. This was an area of land encircling the old inner city, originally the site of fortifications. Inside the old inner city were the buildings of the old order: the residence of the emperor, the urban palais of the aristocracy, the Gothic cathedral and numerous churches. By the middle of the nineteenth century there was less need for fortifications, and by 1860 a political change saw the liberals in power. The emperor's decree in 1857 to open up the Ringstrasse for new urban building gave the new class a great opportunity. For the liberal intellectuals,

> *Vienna became their political bastion, their economic capital, and the radiating center of their intellectual life. From the moment of the accession to power, the liberals began to shape the city in their own image, and by the time they were extruded from power at the century's close, they had largely succeeded: the face of Vienna was transformed. The center of this urban reconstruction was the Ringstrasse.* (Schorske, 1980, 24)

The Ringstrasse became the visual expression of an ascendant social class, full of symbolic representation. It was not a total, uncontested victory. In the early years and particularly between 1857 and 1860 the forces of reaction had leverage. The military, for example, resisted the destruction of the old fortifications and argued the need for a continued military presence. In the first plans the military were given a new arsenal and two barracks close to the railway station. It argued successfully for a wide thoroughfare to enable easy troop movement and to make the construction of barricades much more difficult. As with the Haussmann plans for Paris the resulting wide thoroughfare was more a response to the fear of civil insurgency than a concern for architectural aesthetics. Thereafter, the building plans reflected the achievements and hopes of the urban bourgeoisie. Public buildings were constructed in representative styles: the university was constructed in Renaissance style to reference modern, rational culture arising from medieval darkness as the new liberal era emerged from absolutism; the Parliament had the look of a Greek classical temple, to remind people of the democratic nature of ancient Greece and, by extension, the contemporary society; the home of city government, the Rathaus, was built in massive Gothic "to evoke its origins as a free medieval commune, now reborn after a long night of absolutist rule." The size, style, and location of the buildings were a message proclaiming a new social order and the virtues and values of an ascendant social class. The Ringstrasse was the blank page onto which the liberal bourgeoisie wrote its hopes and its dreams.

Similar social changes were happening throughout Europe. The rise of the middle class was a more general phenomenon. But while the social changes were similar, the spatial reconstructions varied. Donald Olsen (1986) has looked at the experience of Vienna, Paris, and London over the period from 1814 to 1914. The Ringstrasse was a blank page, in Paris there was the radical surgery of Baron Haussmann, while in London changes were more gradual and limited, such as the construction of Regent Street. And while flats were constructed in Paris and Vienna for the rising middle class, in London the dominant form was single-family dwellings. In chapters variously entitled "The City as Monument," "The City as Home" and "The City as Pleasure," Olsen identifies the differences. London was a place of hidden pleasures and interiors, Paris boasted the garden and the street while Vienna gave a stage for display and self-representation:

> *Each responded to the aspirations of its dominant classes with institutions and built environments intended to serve their interests and reinforce their values: in London the gentlemen's club and villa suburbias; in Paris the boulevard with all its attendant pleasures; in*

*Vienna, the creation of a vast stage set on which its more fortunate
citizens could pursue their daily lives in a manner that partook of the
quality of grand opera.* (Olsen, 1986, ix)

Beijing

The impact of changing social forces on the built environment, as
well as the power of enduring forms and designs, can be illustrated
with reference to Beijing (Samuels and Samuels, 1989). Formerly
called Peking, since 1271 this city has been the capital of a united
China. Under the Ming rulers (1368–1644) it became the seat of
imperial authority. To represent universal Confucian order as well as
imperial power, the city was based on the geomantic square with
inner and outer rectilinear walls oriented along a north–south axis.
At the center was the walled rectangle of the imperial palace, known
as the Forbidden City. Although symbolism was sometimes sacrificed
to practicality, as when the perfect rectilinearity was disturbed in the
north-west corner of the outer wall to accommodate essential water

Illustration 17.3
*Tiananmen
Square, Beijing:
Museum of the
Chinese
Revolution and
Chinese History*

supplies, the shape, orientation, and structure of the city was built to
symbolize order, hierarchy, and the universal system of governance
defined by the Confucian order.

By 1644 there were four separate walled cities: Outer, Inner,
Imperial, and Forbidden. The year 1860 marks a major change

because in that year British and French forces invaded the city. The "foreigners" established a legation quarter just south of the Imperial City. The imposition of a foreign presence signified and embodied the Western influence in China and Beijing. Confucian order was now affected by the presence of the West. However, Western influence was much greater in the coastal cities, such as Shanghai, and the solid reminder of a confident, united China was perhaps one reason why the city was selected as the national capital when the People's Republic of China was established on October 1, 1949.

As a center of the new socialist society, Beijing was transformed. Manufacturing industries were introduced into the city, and the urban form was reshaped most noticeably in the construction of Tiananmen Square, completed in 1959. The square was built south of the Forbidden City; it covers 50 hectares and is able to accommodate almost a million people. On the west of the square was built the 172,000 m² Great Hall of the People; on the east the Museum of the Chinese Revolution was constructed; and in the middle of the square was erected a granite obelisk 37 m high, designed as a Monument to the People's Heroes (Figure 17.4). The square symbolized the power, authority and legitimacy of the Chinese Communist Party. This socialist transformation used a similar geometry to the old city, reinforcing the link with the past, but

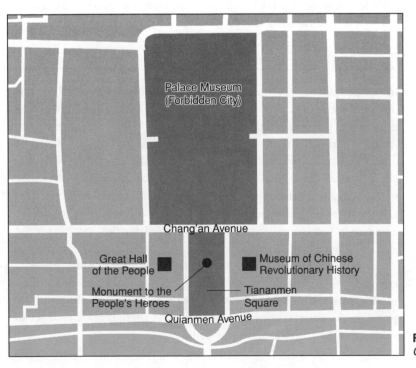

Figure 17.4
Central Beijing

by demolishing some old buildings and breaking through the north–south axis the new rulers symbolized their break with the feudal past. The result was the capital of Chinese socialism, combining elements of the modern socialist present with the "Chinese" past.

Urban form provides the setting for human behaviour and social interaction. In Beijing, Tiananmen Square was constructed as a symbol for a socialist China. In the West, however, the name is synonymous with resistance to this system. In spring of 1989 university students staged a sit-in in Tiananmen Square. They were protesting for many reasons: falling standards of living, corrupt party officials, and the lack of political freedoms. Throughout May and June a festival-like atmosphere prevailed in the giant square. At times there were almost 150,000 people there, their protest seen around the world courtesy of television coverage. On the night of Saturday, June 3, the army moved along the Avenue of Eternal Peace into the square to disperse the crowds. The army fired into the crowd. Almost 300 people were killed and over 3,000 were wounded (Fathers and Higgins, 1989). While communist power fell in Eastern Europe and the Soviet Union, in Tiananmen Square communist rule was re-affirmed. The name of Tiananmen became associated with brutal repression and out-of-touch, aging, political leadership. The square built to commemorate Chinese communism had become a symbol of its tarnished reputation.

Los Angeles

In his analysis of contemporary Los Angeles Mike Davis (1990) has one chapter entitled "Fortress LA." In it he notes that "this obsession with physical security systems, and collaterally, with the architectural policing of social boundaries, has become a zeitgeist of urban restructuring, a master narrative in the emerging built environment of the 1990s" (1990, 223). The background to this new narrative is the creation of a dual city of very different life experiences and the increasing marginalization of an increasing number of people. The city in the United States now has more homeless people on the streets. The urban other has become a more ubiquitous presence. There is also a loss of community in the sense that within the same city widely diverging life paths are being created, and this is nowhere more evident than in LA, where the wealthy are superwealthy and the poor are thus all the poorer. In this context there is no shared set of values and, by extension, no safe public space.

This "master narrative" has many different forms. There is the destruction of public space as traditionally conceived. In its place comes public space that is controlled, with accessibility restricted to the respectable. Public parks are closed to all but the locals, and urban redevelopment schemes reduce contact with the street people. Sadistic street environments are created, such as benches where fully stretched sleep is impossible, there are signs that tell people to stop loitering, and inner-city malls that are constantly policed. The concern with security has led to the creation and reinforcement of gated communities, fortress cities where the outsider is kept at bay by armed guards, fences, walls, and security stations. In LA the system is policed by a force which is technologically sophisticated but has little connection with the streets. In a prescient analysis Davis described LA as a riot about to happen. He summarizes the process:

> *The carefully manicured lawns of Los Angeles's Westside sprout forests of ominous little signs warning: "Armed Response!" Even richer neighborhoods in the canyons and hillsides isolate themselves behind walls guarded by gun-toting private police and state-of-the-art electronic surveillance. Downtown, a publicly-subsidized "urban renaissance" has raised the nation's largest corporate citadel, segregated from the poor neighborhoods around it by a monumental architectural glacis. In Hollywood, celebrity architect Frank Gehry, renowned for his "humanism," apotheosizes the siege look in a library designed to resemble a foreign-legion fort. In the Westlake district and the San Fernando Valley the Los Angeles Police barricade streets and seal off poor neighborhoods as part of the "war on drugs." In Watts, developer Alexander Haagen demonstrates his strategy for recolonizing inner-city retail markets: a panoptican shopping mall surrounded by staked metal fences and a substation of the LAPD in a central surveillance tower. Finally, on the horizon of the next millennium, an ex-chief of police crusades for an anti-crime "giant eye" – a geo-synchronous law enforcement satellite. . . . Welcome to post-liberal Los Angeles where the defense of luxury lifestyles is translated into a proliferation of new repressions in space.*
>
> (Davis, 1990, 223)

The book was published two years before the riots/uprising of 1992. Without the benefit of hindsight Davis predicted those riots. (For his analysis in hindsight, see Frommer, 1993).

Los Angeles may be extreme. To look at Los Angeles is not always to look at the future, for urban America, much less for the rest of the world. But the trend identified by Davis has parallels around the world. The partial eclipse of the liberal-democratic consensus, heightened by global recession, can make big cities more fractured. The loss of shared public space is both cause and effect of the general loss of community. While the extremes of LA may not be replicated elsewhere, this city does indicate one possible, if frightening, possibility for a new master narrative of urban restructuring.

READING THE CITY

If the city is written, it is also read; it is consumed as well as produced. Literary theory in the last 20 years has been concerned with the consumption of texts as well as with their production. Creativity is not restricted to the authors of texts; reading is also a creative act. If reading is creative there will probably be multiple readings. The readings will vary across the society. The city is not a shared text with equality in writing and reading. The examples quoted in the previous section provided different readings. In the case of Kandy, the king's readings of his works was very different from those of the peasantry or the nobles. Vienna's Ringstrasse was seen as a positive endorsement of liberal attitudes, but for the emperor and the military it was a mark of defeat, a collapse of the old order, a sign of social disintegration. And readings will change over time. Edinburgh's New Town was produced as a symbol and embodiment of the Scottish Enlightenment, with names explicitly used to reference the English royal family. Although the elegant order remains, the loyal allusions to the House of Hanover are now long forgotten by most people, and the names of the streets have lost their original function and their historical specificity. Between the production of urban form and its consumption falls the intervention of multiple, contested, changing readings.

Urban structure and social process

The city is used by people: daily routines, civic rituals, sociospatial movements, and the ebb and flow of social usage all give meaning to the city and its constituent elements. There is an ongoing relationship between, on the one hand, urban and structure and, on the other, individual and collective social behavior. We make the city as much as we live in the city. Indeed we make the city by living in the city. The British sociologist Anthony Giddens (1981) has drawn attention to the connection between agency and structure. He seeks to avoid the pitfalls of functionalism and the dangers of voluntarism. The functionalist fallacy reads off actions and events from a preconceived structure while voluntarism sees society as simply the products of human intentions. To focus on the agency–structure nexus is to generate social theories between structural determinism and idealism and to highlight the evolving recursive relationships between action and context. In one sense it is the modern version of Marx's phrase that people make their own history but not in circumstances of their own making; not only history but also geography.

The agency–structure nexus is often discussed in the abstract, but we can ground it in very concrete, physical things. Space and particularly urban space and places are a point of contact between human agency and social structure. This opens up new avenues of research as well as resuscitating traditional lines of inquiry. When the elements of the built environment, such as the shop, the home, the workplace, are no longer seen simply as building forms but as sites of connection between social structure, political power, and human agency then important lines of inquiry are opened up. An important stimulus to this kind of analysis of the built environment has been the work of Michel Foucault (1972, 1976, 1977). One of Foucault's many enterprises was to avoid total histories; he eschewed the use of metanarratives and concentrated on the local, the particular, and the specific. Space was central to his concern and was seen as a major aspect of (and in) the exercise of power. Much of his work involved identifying the social practices and discourses related to particular sites: his work on madness and illness, for example, was concerned not only with the ideas of mental and physical health but also with the sociospatial practices involved in the development, change, and variation within these discourses.

Foucault has informed as well as stimulated a whole variety of work. Chris Philo (1989) and Thomas Markus (1982), for instance, take Foucault as a primary source and point of reference, respectively, in their discussions of the evolution of the asylum. The enormous prestige of Foucault reinforced the importance of specific histories and particular geographies.

Discourses are anchored in sites, and places embody and reflect wider social discourses. Some of the more interesting work in urban geography is taking up these themes. Jon Goss (1993) examines the US mall in terms of retail strategy, liminal space, transaction space, as well as meaning and signification. Work of this kind theorizes the built environment while grounding social theory. Social change is a recorder in the changing form, function, and meaning of particular sites. Table 17.1 identifies some of the possible links between social processes and institutions, sites, and places. This is a rudimentary grid, but it is indicative of important connections. An examination of these connections is one of the most important agendas for urban geography.

TABLE 17.1 SOCIETY, SPACE AND PLACE		
Society	*Space*	*Places*
Family and kinship	The dwelling	3 Audubon Drive, Cazenovia, NY
Economy	Factory, office, warehouse, farm	AT&T corporate headquarters
Religion	Temple, church	Amritsar Temple, Vatican
Death	Cemetery	Arlington National Cemetery
Social control	Prison, school	Syracuse University

Source: After King (1980)

Space and power

Power is a relationship between people. Power does not have to be visibly exercised to be influential. Power relationships can be built into the context of human interaction. Let's look at this with respect to work places, residences, and general urban structure.

In the typical corporation, position in the hierarchy is registered by the size, location, and function of people's workplaces. Routine office workers share large rooms with little privacy. People seek to personalize their little spaces – soft toys and photographs on desks are just some of the ways in which people make their mark on their surroundings. Chief executives and managing directors get the biggest offices at the top of the building. Entry into this room is through an office guarded by a secretary. You can't just walk in. You have to make an appointment and wait outside until they can see you. Your time has to match their convenience. Zones of space are traversed, from the corridor through the outer and inner offices, until the sanctum is reached. Here, far from the ground and close to the sky, noise is kept to a minimum by the dampening effect of thick carpets and walls shrouded with pictures and expensive wallpaper. People move slowly, they talk in hushed tones. This is a "top-executive space." Down below the densities increase, the noise level is higher, and the furnishings are more utilitarian.

Power relationships within organizations are given an explicit spatial manifestation. In firms dealing with the public, say a shop selling clothes, the lower-status salespeople are out front, more accessible to the public, on the edge of the public–private space. The higher up the hierarchy people are, the further from the public, and the more protected in private offices they become. To ask to see the manager, to bring someone out from this private back space to the public front space, is a sure sign that something is seriously wrong.

Space and time are important coordinates of power. In most university departments, for example, academics have greater spatial freedom than secretaries do. Typists have to work specified hours and usually have to be there five days a week, including the summer holidays, even when the undergraduates are gone. Academics, in contrast, have less-rigid time constraints and greater freedom. The distinction reflects and maintains the status difference.

Given the technology now available it is possible, in theory, for people to work together from different places. People in one office could all specify a time for working but stay at home and communicate by telephone, fax, and computer networks. One powerful reason for inhibiting this development is the need for status differences. If communication is only by electronic mail the spatial character of power relationships would not be visible.

In chapter 9 I discussed the concept of a housing life-cycle whereby people move from apartment to house then to bigger house as space requirements and income increase. Houses give off messages about the status of the occupants. They register change. When council houses are sold to tenants, the tenants are eager to reflect their new status. Bottle-glass windows, new hardwood doors, different color paint and pebbledash finish are all used to show that this house is now "owned." The changes show it is no longer rented.

Groups of similar types of houses form neighborhoods. All cities have their ethnic areas, their poor areas, the area for slumming students, the area for people on the way up, and the way down. The residential mosaic of the city is a subtle indication of where people are in the socioeconomic hierarchy. Sometimes changes occur. The process of gentrification has involved certain middle-income groups buying up the older property in selected inner-city areas. The change is signified by the skip in the street, the exposed brickwork, the antique pine furniture, and eventually the opening of a local health-food shop. The new middle class is keen to reflect its occupancy and mark out its territory.

Even the basic structure of a city reveals the distributions of power. In capitalist societies it is the *business district* that is central. Commerce and money-making are the hub of the city, the focal point of social endeavors, the defining center of the city. In other societies the church, mosque or temple was and is the biggest building in the most central location. In Western Europe and North America the commercial office block has become the temple of capitalism, the cathedral of commerce, and like the giant cathedrals of the more religious Gothic period, it stands tall and proud above the rest.

Cities reflect the distribution of power in more specific ways. For example, cities are now dominated by the needs of the car user rather than the pedestrian. The more affluent car owners have their needs inscribed into the smooth functioning of the city – most transport plans are concerned with removing traffic jams, in other words, allowing traffic to move freely. The free flow of vehicular traffic is the ultimate goal. Can you imagine urban transport plans where issues of health, safety, and conservation were top of the agenda?

Power is built into the way we organize space. And spatial organization reflects and embodies the operation of power, its distribution, and its presence.

The urban landscape

The urban landscape contains a variety of clues and messages about social order, social control, political power, and cultural dominance. We can learn much about these things from reading the urban landscape. Let me end this chapter with two case studies which justify this claim.

The urban landscape is often inscribed with the power of the elites. In the residential development of London, for example, the power of the big landowners was written into the nature of developments. To maintain the status of Bloomsbury the landowner, the Duke of Bedford, vetted all goods sold in shops in the area and built gates at the entrance to the estate to keep out the lower classes travelling to and from the newly built railway stations of King's Cross and St Pancras. Elsewhere and at different times the power of the elites is somewhat modified. In an interesting study Peter Hugill (1995) looked at the urban landscape of a small town in upstate New York and its development from the late 1790s. Elite power was evident in the early years, reinforced by landholdings and economic power and reflected in controlled land sales, the layout of the settlement, and the construction of appropriate public buildings. The home of the elite family (Lorenzo) was constructed on an imposing site with an uninterrupted view of the local lake. However, the elite power could never be as strong as London's landowners. Land was sold, not leased, and there was the powerful rhetoric of democracy. Hugill suggests that the success of the elite in Cazenovia lay in the more subtle way in which consensus was arrived at. The town in its layout and look was a landscape of restricted authorship. Hugill uses the term gesture rather than text, and sees the landscape as a set of gestures to communicate the presence of an old elite to successive generations of newcomers. Even in the contemporary period when the old elite had lost much of its economic power it re-established control over the village through the construction and adoption of strict zoning laws, the sale of Lorenzo to the state and its use as a state historic site, and informal controls over alterations to existing houses through peer pressure and community standards. The look, feel and atmosphere of the town.

> *reflects an unbroken elite concern with landscape aesthetics that can be documented over two hundred years, and which reflects strongly English and aristocratic roots going back well before that. The elite have never deviated from their purpose of constructing an elite landscape, and even when they lost ground, as during the Depression, they made it up later. Only the elite have had the sense of history, the sense of purpose, the continuity and the economic base to construct an entire landscape in this.* (Hugill, 1995, 231)

In a wider-ranging study James Howard Kunstler (1993) uses the contemporary urban landscape in the United States as a peg on which to hang a broad social critique of US society. There is a long tradition of social commentary through meditations on the built form. And vice versa. Edward Relph's (1987) detailed commentary on the modern urban landscape tells us as much about contemporary society as about the contemporary city. For Kunstler, the landscape of strip developments, shopping malls, dead city centers, and congested suburbs all reveal the problems of a society dominated by quick profits, a love affair with the automobile, and a lack of aesthetic sensitivity. Through detailed case studies he tells the story of environmental degradation, social fracturing, loss of place, and decline of community. He writes:

Born in 1948, I have lived my entire life in America's high imperial moment. During this epoch of stupendous wealth and power, we have managed to ruin our greatest cities, throw away our small towns, and impose over the countryside a joyless junk habitat which we can no longer afford to support. Indulging in a fetish of commercialized individualism, we did away with the public realm, and with nothing left but private life in our private homes and private cars, we wonder what happened to the spirit of community. We created a landscape of scary places and became a nation of scary people.

(Kunstler, 1993, 273)

These two examples, one a detailed analysis, the other a well-written polemic, reveal the extent to which the urban landscape can be used to read specific messages and grand narratives. The city, its particular buildings as well as general form and layout, is a vast library, or ensemble of gestures to use another metaphor, to be read and studied for its own sake and for the insights it gives to the operation and reproduction of society.

GUIDE TO FURTHER READING

On urban form:
Ford, L. (1994) *Cities and Buildings: Skyscrapers, Skid Rows and Suburbs*, Baltimore, Md: Johns Hopkins University Press.
Giddens, A. (1992) *The Transformation of Intimacy: Sexuality, Love and Eroticism in Modern Societies*, Stanford, Cal.: Stanford University Press.
Jackson, J.B. (1984) *Discovering the Vernacular Landscape*, New Haven, Conn.: Yale University Press.
Kostoff, S. (1991) *The City Shaped: Urban Patterns and Meanings through History*, Boston, Mass.: Little, Brown.
Markus, T. (1993) *Buildings and Control: Freedom and Control in the Origin of Modern Building Types*, London: Routledge.
Rapoport, A. (1990) *The Meaning of the Built Environment*, 2nd edn, Tucson, Ariz.: University of Arizona Press.
Sennett, R. (1990) *The Conscience of the Eye*, New York: Alfred A. Knopf.
Shachtman, T. (1991) *Skyscraper Dreams: The Great Real Estate Dynasties of New York*, Boston, Mass.: Little, Brown.
Vale, L.J. (1992) *Architecture, Power and National Identity*, New Haven, Conn.: Yale University Press.

On the connection between the city and the body:
Ackerman, D. (1990) *A Natural History of the Senses*, New York: Random.
Grosz, E. (1992) Bodies–cities. In Colomina (ed.), *Sexuality and Space*, New York: Princeton Architectural Press.
Rodaway, P. (1994) *Sensuous Geographies: Body, Sense and Place*, London: Routledge.
Seamon, D. (1979) *A Geography of the Lifeworld: Movement, Rest and Encounter*, London: Croom Helm.
Sennett, R. (1994) *The Body and the City in Western Civilization*, New York: W.W. Norton.

Turner, B.S. (1984) *The Body and Society*, Oxford: Blackwell.

On examples of writing the city I have drawn extensively on the following case studies:

Davis, M. (1990) *City of Quartz: Excavating the Future in Los Angeles*, London: Verso.

Duncan, J.S. (1990) *The City as Text: The Politics of Landscape Interpretation in the Kandyan Kingdom*, Cambridge: Cambridge University Press.

Fathers, M. and Higgins, M. (1989) *Tiananmen*, London: Independent.

Frommer, M. (1993) An interview with Mike Davis, *Chicago Review* 38, 212–43.

Olsen, D.J. (1986) *The City as a Work of Art*, New Haven, Conn., and London: Yale University Press.

Reed, P. (1982) Form and context: a study of Georgian Edinburgh. In T.A. Markus (ed.), *Order in Space and Society: Architectural Form and its Context in the Scottish Enlightenment*, Edinburgh: Mainstream.

Samuels, M.S. and Samuels, C.M. (1989) Beijing and the power of place in modern China. In J. Agnew and J. Duncan (eds), *The Power of Place*, London: Unwin Hyman.

Schorske, C.E. (1980) *Fin-de-siècle Vienna*, New York: Alfred A. Knopf.

On reading the city, see:

Foucault, M. (1972) *The Archaeology of Knowledge*, London: Tavistock Publications.

Foucault, M. (1976) *The Birth of the Clinic: An Archaeology of Medical Perception*, London: Tavistock Publications.

Foucault, M. (1977) *Discipline and Punish: The Birth of the Prison*, London: Allen Lane.

Giddens, A. (1981) *A Contemporary Critique of Historical Materialism*, London: Macmillan.

Goss, J. (1993) The "magic of the mall": an analysis of form, function and meaning in the contemporary retail economy, *Annals of the Association of American Geographers* 83, 18–47.

King, A.D. (1980) Introduction. In A.D. King (ed.), *Buildings and Society: Essays on the Social Development of the Built Environment*, London: Routledge & Kegan Paul.

Markus, T.A. (1982) Buildings for the sad, the bad and the mad in urban Scotland, 1780–1830. In T.A. Markus (ed.), *Order in Space and Society: Architectural form and its Context in the Scottish Enlightenment*, Edinburgh: Mainstream.

Philo, C. (1989) "Enough to drive one mad": the organization of space in 19th-century lunatic asylums. In J. Wolch and M. Dear (eds), *The Power of Geography*, Boston, Mass.: Unwin Hyman.

On the urban landscape, see:

Hugill, P.J. (1995) *Upstate Arcadia*, Lanham, Md: Rowman & Littlefield.

Kunstler, J.H. (1993) *The Geography of Nowhere*, New York: Touchstone.

Relph, E. (1987) *The Modern Urban Landscape*, Beckenham, Kent: Croom Helm.

Chapter 18

CITY IMAGES

Clearly ideas of the country and the city have specific contents and histories, but just as clearly, at times, they are forms of isolation and identification of more general processes. People have often said "the city" when they meant capitalism or bureaucracy or centralized power. . . . We need to put these ideas to the historical realities: at times to be confirmed, at times denied.

Raymond Williams, *The Country and the City* (1973, 350)

Cities are produced; in a variety of ways. In the previous chapters of this section I have looked at the production of the built form of the city. In this chapter I want to look at the production of city images. The city is more than just a physical entity, more than a place where people live and work. The city is a place symbolic of many things, representative of many things. The city is a work of imagination, a metaphor, a symbol. The production of these imaginings, metaphors, and symbols is the topic of this chapter.

URBAN MYTHS

I use the term "myth" to refer to ideas which are part fact, part fancy, and totally a product of social construction. Myths resonate through time, and can be heard over space and through time.

Let us begin with a crude, though still effective, distinction between pro- and anti-urban myths. The anti-urban myth has a number of elements:

- the unnatural city is compared unfavorably with the countryside and the wilderness;
- the anonymity of the city is contrasted with the warm community found in villages and small towns;
- the city is a place of sin, disease, and moral corruption;
- the city is a threat to social order.

414

In the last 200 years the level and pace of urbanization has increased. Around the world more people now live in cities than ever before. Contemporary society is an urban society. Despite, or perhaps because of, this trend the dominant social thought has portrayed urban living as an unnatural act. This is a comparatively new orientation. In the classical world urban society was the pinnacle of human civilization. The term "civilization" shares the same Latin root as "city". However, the rise of Romanticism displaced urban living from its prime position. The benefits of living close to nature were supposed to include a more authentic, more spiritual, better life. From this perspective, living in the city was an unnatural act, only suitable for those who had no other choice. This negative view of the city has been a consistent theme in social thought for many centuries; however, it has been strengthened during the last century. A lack of belief in social progress, a cynicism about social institutions, the failure of utopian schemes, and the trenchant criticism of the modernist enterprise have all led to a loss of belief in collective progress and a consequent disquiet over the city. When you lose confidence in society you tend to lose faith in the city. When attention turns to the lauding of the natural world and when social evolution is portrayed as a regress from a more Edenic state, then the most human of constructions, the city, loses its appeal and becomes the repository of social criticism.

The anonymous city

The sociologist Geoffrey Pearson (1975) refers to the line of social thought that berates the city as a place of shallow, ephemeral, and functional relationships as the "sociological pastoral." This body of thought contrasts the city with the supposedly deep, long-lasting, and varied relationships found in the countryside, village, and small towns. The pastoral has a long history in Western social thought, but the sociological pastoral has emerged most strongly in the last 150 years. Pearson (1975, 178) notes:

> *pastoral contrasts the corruption of manners in the sovereign's court with innocence of shepherds. . . . However, in the transforming of the Industrial Revolution pastoral adopts new forms which provide a creative comment on the modern city, the factory system and a money economy.*

The criticism of the city as a site of anonymous interactions, a place of no community, is in many ways a broader attack on the emergence of an industrial capitalist system. The city is a convenient peg on which to hang these assertions.

Sin city

In 1880 the English artist and critic John Ruskin wrote, in a letter, that cities were "loathsome centres of fornication and covetousness – the smoke of sin going up into the face of heaven like the furnace of Sodom." Ruskin's phrase echoes down through the years. The notion of the city as Sodom has been a consistent theme of Western social criticism. The tradition of the ascetic priest, to use Nietzsche's phrase, has long looked askance at the city as a place of loose morals, sin, and debauchery. The city as a place of bodily contact, human pleasures, and the pursuit and display of desire and enjoyment has made it a vehicle for the advancement of moral judgements and social criticisms.

The city as threat

Cities are places where people congregate and come together. The fear of the city is very often the fear of the crowd. The city provides a setting and often an opportunity for marginalized groups to take an active role; even the term "taking to the streets" is indicative of the urban bias of popular unrest. The historian E.P. Thompson (1971), in a famous essay that looked at eighteenth-century England, identified something he called the moral economy. This was traditional rights of custom, the values of the broader community. He showed that food riots in the towns and cities of England were not spasms of anger based on hunger but well-organized forms of popular action. They were concerned with the workings of the moral economy rather than of the money economy. Urban crowds throughout history have been concerned with the moral economy as much as the market economy.

For the rich and powerful the urban crowd was a danger, a threat to the existing order. In 1835 the most astute observer of the United States, Alexis de Tocqueville, noted:

> *in cities men cannot be prevented from concerting together and awakening a mutual excitement that prompts sudden and passion-ate revolution. Cities may be looked upon as large assemblies of which all the inhabitants are members; their populace exercise prodigious*

influence upon the magistrates and frequently execute their own wishes without the intervention of public officers.

When he visited New York and Philadelphia he observed:

> *The lower ranks which inhabit these cities constitute a rabble. They consist of freed blacks and a multitude of Europeans [who] are ready to turn all the passions which agitate the community to their own advantage.*

Cities constitute a stage, a setting, and an opportunity for the dispossessed, the poor. and the marginalized to exercise street power, collective action, and disruptive behavior. Revolutions, uprisings, and just plain riots have an urban bias. The city is a potential threat to the existing order. From the revolutions in Russia and France to the more recent uprisings in Los Angeles, the city has been the storm center of social tension and social discontent.

There are also pro-urban views. We can identify the following:

- the civilized city;
- the soft city;
- the free city;
- the radical city.

The civilized city

For the ancient Greeks, city living was synonymous with a civilized life. In Greek art, politics, and social commentary it was taken as axiomatic that social life rather than the natural world was to be preferred. It is the human form that adorns Greek vases; and when Aristotle said that people are essentially political animals he was reinforcing the importance of social contact and collective debate to Greek views of the good life.

Bit cities, especially in the rich countries, do contain a range of goods and services not available in smaller towns and rural areas. The big art galleries, the opera house, the fancy shops, the extensive libraries all have an urban bias. Culture and civilization may not be a product of big cities, but it is associated with them. And when these cities become linked with the residences of the local and international elites, the city as civilization becomes part of the image of the place.

The city as a civilized place is often contrasted with the backwardness of the small town and countryside. Many of the inhabitants of

New York City think civilization ends at the boundaries of the city. The term "upstate", when used by New Yorkers, conjures up images of the wild, a place where electricity is intermittent and good bagels are hard to find. Most big cities have those creative cartographic depictions of their view of the world where city neighborhoods take up most of the map and other parts of the country consist of small cliché-ridden parts in the far distance. These maps give graphic illustration of the selective worldview of the citizens of many big cities, a view which contrasts the culture of their city with the backwardness of the rest of the country. When France is described as *Paris et la déserte française* we know it comes from an urban commentator.

The soft city

Whereas the anti-urbanists see the anonymity of the city as a cause for concern, the pro-urbanists see it as something to celebrate. The writer Jonathan Raban (1974) has written of the soft city, the city in which people have the ability to choose their identity, express their individuality, and seek their own personal, as opposed to social, definition of happiness. The anonymous city is a city free from social constraint and community sanction.

Neither the anonymous city of the anti-urbanists nor the soft city

Illustration 18.1
*Alternative visions
of the good city:
country and town
combined;
Letchworth Garden
City, UK
(© Letchworth
Garden City
Corporation)*

of the pre-urbanists describes the whole city. Both are depictions of city living that concentrate on the inner-city, transient neighborhoods. In the urban villages of the poor, the rich, and the ethnics, and in the more settled neighborhoods of the city, social life has neither the anonymity nor the freedom that most commentators espouse.

The free city

In the feudal period there was a German saying that, roughly translated, means "city air makes men free." At that time many cities were free from the political and social power of the local aristocracy. Although not functioning democracies, the people of the city were freer than the inhabitants of the surrounding countryside, tied by force and custom as they were to the feudal hierarchy.

Cities, and especially the very biggest cities, have a freedom from local and national conventions because of their wider connections and intercourse of trade, people, and ideas from around the world. They are less tied to the restrictions of the country than are small towns and villages. While only some parts of the city have this cosmopolitan feel, the whole city is touched by these wider connections. Over 2,000 years ago Cicero described the coastal cities of imperial Rome thus:

> *These towns become adulterated with strange languages and habits, and import not only foreign cargoes but foreign morals which inevitably prevent their national tradition.*

This prevention of a "national tradition" liberates the big cities from the conventions of the surrounding countryside.

The radical city

Whereas the anti-urbanists bemoan the city as a threat to the existing social order, the pro-urbanists take this same characteristic as something to celebrate. In *Manifesto of the Communist Party*, first written in 1848, Marx and Engels wrote:

> *The bourgeoisie has subjected the country to the rule of the towns. It has created enormous cities, has greatly increased the urban population as compared with the rural, and has thus rescued a considerable part of the population from the idiocy of rural life.*

For many radicals, both before and since Marx and Engels, the city has been a place that has coalesced individual experiences of exploitation into the perception and mobilization of collective strength. In this perspective, the city is a source of radical impulses which have the ability to shake the existing power structure. While anti-urbanists bemoan the subversive potential of the city, the radicals encourage its radical energy.

There are two dominant myths of the city which embody elements of these city types: Babylon and Jerusalem. Babylon is the city as place of sin and debauchery, a cesspool of iniquity, a place of social disorder. The designation of Babylon is more than a description of cities, it is moral condemnation of what the city represents, and this may include a whole variety of things: modernity, capitalism, the contemporary,

Illustration 18.2
Alternative visions of the good city: the modernist version; Le Corbusier's Unité d'Habitation, *Marseilles (© Roger-Viollet, Paris)*

the importance of money, the decline of social values. The city has been used as a vehicle to carry a load of social ills and cultural failings. The city as Jerusalem, in contrast, holds forth the possibility that it can be the vehicle for social emancipation, the framework and embodiment of a better world. History is full of attempts to build better cities by constructing new cities. In the last hundred years, from the communitarian experiments of the nineteenth century to the modernist enterprises of the twentieth, there have been many attempts to construct a new order. In my book *The Humane City* (1989) I looked at ways in which we could conceive of cities in which ordinary people could lead dignified and creative lives. This was less an attempt at building new cities than of imagining better cities. After looking at the forces which make this goal difficult – cities as if only capital matters, cities as if only professionals matter, and cities as if only some people matter – I discuss ideas and themes which could lead to a liberation of our thoughts on how to think about cities. This book is just one example of a rich tradition of utopian thinking which is fueled by the eternal belief in our ability to create better cities and better societies. This tradition has been responsible for some of the best urban schemes and many of the worst.

URBAN IDEOLOGIES

The different strands of pro- and anti-urban sentiment discussed in the previous section rarely present themselves in such simple, stark terms. More often they are found wrapped together in a denser, more complex response to the city and the whole process of urbanization.

Myths of the city are often part of what I have termed national environmental ideologies. These are myths mobilized in the course of state formation and nation-building; they are myths which reference particular territories and specific societies. As an example: in the 1920s the German Nazi Party was promoting a Nordic image of a predominantly rural Germany. The party newspaper described the big cities as

> *the melting pot of all evil . . . of prostitution, bars, illness, movies, Marxism, Jews, strippers, Negro dancers, and all the disgusting offspring of so-called "modern art".* (Quoted in Lane, 1968, 155)

In this example, general anti-urban myths are used against specific targets. Ideologies give myths a time and a place by recruiting general arguments to particular purposes.

Urban ideologies are part of broader national environmental ideologies. Attitudes to cities are bound up with attitudes to the wilderness and the countryside. Consider the United States. In the early years of the Republic the dominant notion was one of creating and maintaining an agrarian democracy. Many of the founding fathers, such as Thomas Jefferson, were very concerned at the rise of cities. The family farm was an early icon of quintessential America; cities were considered dangerous to the stability of the Republic. Anti-urban feeling increased because subsequently the cities, and especially the big cities, became the destination point for waves of migrants from Europe and more recently from Mexico, South America, and Asia. The cities were the locale of the foreign-born, the American other, not yet rendered safe by US citizenship; the place of foreign languages, different religions, alternative beliefs. The cities, in some quarters, were a threat to the traditional picture of the United States. There was an alternative depiction: the cities as the starting point of the American dream, the place where people arrived to begin their scramble up the ladder of success. And all the time attitudes to the cities were counterpoised to the wilderness, the open spaces of the West, and the social conformity and tight community of small towns. Urban ideologies are tied to broader social considerations; they are embedded in particular histories and specific geographies.

Urban ideologies are not monolithic attitudes toward all cities. In many countries different cities evoke very different attitudes. In Britain, for example, one of the biggest contrasts is the distinction between London and all other cities. Britain has an urban hierarchy that is best described as one of urban primacy. London dominates in terms of numbers, cultural weight, political power, and elite residences. I have discussed much of this in chapter 3. Here I can note that this bias is reflected in a celebration of London by the metropolitan intellectuals, many of whom assume that civilization does not extend beyond the M25 motorway, which encircles the capital. London is a world city while the other cities in Britain are often associated with industrialization and deindustrialization, for example, Newcastle, Birmingham, Glasgow, and thus become symbolic of a different discourse. In other countries different cities come to represent different sets of values. In Israel, for example, the big contrast is between Tel Aviv, which has a reputation as a cosmopolitan, secular, partying kind of town, and Jerusalem, with its religious significance, its theocratic feel and setting for religious expression of three major religions. Babylon and Jerusalem. In Australia the big contrast, as well

as the axis of urban rivalry, is between Melbourne and Sydney.
Melbourne prides itself on its culture, its sophistication, its arts and restaurants. Sydney is often represented in a more hedonistic light, the place of warmer weather, better beaches, and racier night life. All of these ideas are part fact, part fancy. The cities come to represent broader notions and become the vehicles for wider social debates, the container of deeper meanings than the empirical character of the individual city.

Meanings and values are apportioned to cities. And also to particular parts of cities. The term "city" is too broad to capture the different types of cities. Thus the term "inner city" is often used to cover a variety of issues from race and conflict, poverty and wealth, social disintegration and the urban underclass. The suburbs, in contrast, are more associated with discourses of the family, community, middle class, stability, and social order. These are less factual reports than broader, deeper, hazier representations. Spatial adjectives and nouns such as suburb, inner city, and city refer as much to the social world as to the spatial world.

Representing the city

One of the most important topics of recent scholarship has been the issue of representation. A number of geographers have begun to explore the relationships involved in the representations of places, spaces, and landscapes (Aitken and Zonn, 1994; Barnes and Duncan, 1992). Urban myths and ideologies are represented in particular forms. They are not free-floating; rather, they are expressed in specific texts. Texts include books, films, jokes, adverts, products and, as discussed in the previous chapter, built form. Cities are re-presented in a variety of ways. An important area of contemporary urban scholarship is now looking at urban representation. In my book *Imagined Country* (1991), for example, I examined the way urban myths are represented in films, paintings, and novels. Also, Simpson-Housley and Preston (1994) look at writings of the city in terms of innocence, of an Eden now lost, a threat of sinful Babylon, and the promise of a new Jerusalem. Let us consider specific examples of different forms of representation.

Naming the city

On April 24, 1990 the residents of a city in what was formerly East Germany voted on the name of that city. By a three to one majority they decided to change its name from Karl-Marx-Stadt to Chemnitz.

After 37 years the old name of the city was restored, the change in name just one more act in the dismantling of the communist system.

Place names are important. There are, of course, the simple descriptive names. Many of the towns in Britain, for example, are geographic descriptions. Penarth in Wales means "headland on the hill," the name of the coastal town of Oban in Scotland means "little bay," while Henley is Old English for "high clearing." Church Lane and Railway Street give us a good idea of what to expect. But many place names are more, much more, than simple identifiers of place – they resonate with feelings and emotions, hopes and desires, they conjure up the past and intimate the future. Names are not just neutral handles we stick on to places to differentiate them from one another, the naming of places is a social act reflecting and condensing the struggle for power, status, and influence.

Place names reflect power. In the United States and Australia, for example, place names reflect the power of the colonists to impose their linguistic impression on the landscape. In 1781 a group of Spanish missionaries in southern California settled in a place they called *El Pueblo de Nuestra Senora la Reinade los Angeles de la Porciuncula* (The City of Our Lady of the Angels of the Little Portion). It was shortened, thankfully, to Los Angeles and is now often known simply as LA. On the east coast the English victory over the Dutch was reflected in 1664 when New Amsterdam was changed to New York. In Australia the English named many places after rich and powerful people. Sydney was named in 1788 after the English Secretary of State, Lord Sydney, while Adelaide was named in 1836 in honour of Queen Adelaide, wife of William IV.

Names of places often reflect a struggle for power. In 1914 St Petersburg was renamed Petrograd; ten years later, after the Bolsheviks had gained control, the name was changed to Leningrad to commemorate their leader. When Ayer's Rock (named after a premier of South Australia) was handed back to the aboriginal owners in 1985 in was given its old aboriginal name of Uluru ("great pebble"). In 1990 a street in the city of Harare (Salisbury) in Zimbabwe (formerly Southern Rhodesia) called National Avenue was renamed Josiah Tongogare Avenue after the former head of the Zanu armed forces that had fought for independence. The rise and fall of power is reflected in names. Whatever happened to Stalingrad?

Places names are evocative. They are used to commemorate events (Waterloo Station), to recall the past (all those classical names in the United States from Troy and Syracuse to Memphis and Athens), to remember the old country (Nova Scotia in Canada and Perth in

Australia), to condense hopes for the future (New Harmony in the United States and Peacehaven in England). Names conjure up specific images. Every builder of new suburban housing seems to feel it necessary to market the product by referencing the rural. Table 18.1 lists the names of areas in Lower Earley, a big new housing development just south of Reading in Berkshire. To sell the contemporary urban it seems you need to reference the nostalgic rural.

TABLE 18.1 NAMES OF AREAS IN LOWER EARLEY, BERKSHIRE		
Hunters Walk	Ryhill Copse	Upper Paddock
Badgers Walk	Abbey Lea	Pipers Dell
Greenbanks	Mead Ridge	Swallows Meadow
Millers Green	Meadow Vale	Hedgefield
Upper Wood	Meadowbank	Spring Field

Names communicate more than just the location of places. Washington is more than just a city in the United States, and to say Paris is to generate a whole set of expectations. Names are powerful. They tell us things about a society. Some names enter into the language, as in "to be sent to Coventry." The ultimate accolade is for a place to become an adjective, "very Hollywood," "East Coast intellectual," "West Coast sound," "Mersey beat," "Paris style," "New York look." Some are so powerful they become words in their own right, for example, "Armageddon."

Names turn spaces into places. They are one of the ways we humanize the world around us. Names of places reflect the operation of power, the need for connections with the past, hopes for the future. Place names give color, meaning, symbolism to the world around us. We make the world by giving it a name.

And in the beginning was the word.

Cities and the mass media

Cities are represented in the mass media. In the case of news reporting, individual cities are the site and context of news. The portrayal of cities is not a neutral, innocent process. In a fascinating study Thomas Klak (1994) compared the news coverage in major US newspapers of two cities in the Caribbean: Havana (Cuba) and Kingston (Jamaica). Both cities face problems: Havana has severe shortages of basic goods and services such as food and fuel, while Kingston has extensive poverty, high crime, and shares with Havana a deteriorating infrastructure and housing stock. These conditions are contextualized very differently in US newspapers. There is heavier coverage of the crisis in Havana, and reports describe the problems arising from the failures of Castro in particular and communism in general. Kingston receives less coverage, and when it is reported the city's problems are not connected to either the political-economic system or the political leadership. The differential coverage has an obvious ideological context. Two cities with similar problems are represented and "explained" very differently because they occupy different ideological sites in US geopolitics.

Reel cities

Film is one of the most popular forms of representation. The connection with cities and urban imagery has been considered in a number of studies, as in Larry Ford's (1994) analysis of the depiction of cities in US cinema. In the very early silent movies cities were unidentified stages for action because the emphasis was on actors. Subsequently, urban representation in the US cinema was influenced by the genre known as *film noir*. In Fritz Lang's very influential film, *Metropolis* (1926), the city is a threatening presence. Like a German expressionist painting, the movie paints a dark scene of the urban future. It depicts a modernist disutopia, a machine-controlled totalitarian future. In the classic *film noir* of the late 1940s and 1950s the city is tense, brooding, ill-lit, a place of personal isolation and collective anomie. More contemporary movies which have elements of *film noir* include *Blade Runner* (1982), *Blue Velvet* (1986), *Batman* (1989), and *Shadows and Fog* (1991). This last movie is interesting because the director, Woody Allen, is much better known for his concentration on middle-class Manhattanites and his celebration of New York life in such movies as *Annie Hall* (1977), *Manhattan* (1977) and *Hannah and Her Sisters* (1986).

In her concentration of filmic descriptions of Los Angeles, Lisa Benton (1995) examines three movies all released in the same year, 1991: *Grand Canyon, LA Story*, and *Boyz 'n the Hood*. She shows that, while there are differences in each of the films (table 18.2), they share a similar concern with LA as a place of simulations, a place obsessed with crime, surveillance, and security.

Geographers have come relatively late to questions of cultural representation. It is only in the last decade that urban geographers have been looking at the way cities are represented and the problems involved in dissecting texts. There are many difficulties, including issues of divergence between the production and consumption of messages,

TABLE 18.2 CHARACTERISTICS OF THE VARIOUS GEOGRAPHIES OF LOS ANGELES	
Film	*Visual images and experience of place*
La Story (1990)	LA as Utopia or Autopia Exaggerated, satirized Yuppie LA A Disneyfield landscape Land of eternal sunshine and prosperity Creative mobility Romance is ever-present
Boyz 'n the Hood (1991)	LA as city under siege LA as bitter realism "Hood" as place of epidemic violence, fear, the eclipse of hope, death and grief Landscape of black lower-middle class Collapse of meaning Random, chaotic violence Blacks killing blacks Economic decline imposed by powers outside the "hood" Disregard for human life and property Women depicted as weak and inconsequential
Grand Canyon (1991)	LA city of impending conflict and increased contact Overlapping space Apprehensive space Ambiguity and contradictions: affluence/ poverty, violence/safety, white/black Reaching across the chasm of race and class to form new relationships

Source: Benton (1995)

the role of collectively authored texts such as films, and the whole issue of intertextual relations. These are thorny issues, but they are not insurmountable and they should not prevent a more careful analysis of the cultural production and social consumption of urban images.

Illustration 18.3
*Still from Fritz
Lang's* Metropolis
*(© The Kobal
Collection, London)*

URBAN IMAGES

A recent advert for a Canon camera had the slogan, "Image Is Everything." Whether true or not, the phrase captures an important element in the cultural production of cities: the creation of urban imagery. The construction of favorable urban images to encourage civic boosterism, tourism, inward investment, and in-migration has a long history. More recently, however, because of interurban competition and increasingly footloose industry and capital investment, cities have to compete with each other in selling themselves. Urban image is of particular importance in an era of intense competition between cities for business, investment, tourists, conventions, and industry. The analysis of city promotion is now an important area. Significant topics include the analysis of the city promotion industry, the strategies used, the decoding of the messages, and an assessment of the campaigns' successes and failures. The papers in Gold and Ward (1994) and Kearns and Philo (1993) cover some of these topics and suggest that describing, understanding, and explaining the selling of cities is a rich vein of contemporary urban scholarship.

In this section I want to look at the range of urban images for different types of cities. Let us begin at the very top of the hierarchy.

World cities

At the level of the global hierarchy we can identify three world cities: London, New York, and Tokyo. They constitute a cross-section of the three most recent economic powers: Britain of the nineteenth-century Empire, the United States of the American Century, and the emerging Japanese superpower.

There is both competition and collusion between these three. They both compete for business and do business together. They provide a temporal coverage of incessant business. They need each other to provide a wide time coverage for international dealing in stocks, shares, bonds, futures, currencies, and commodities.

The stability and relative security of their position allows them the luxury of a *metropolitan provincialism* – a belief that the world is their city and a comforting sense that if you stand in Covent Garden, Fifth Avenue or the Maranouchi district, the world's most important business deals, cultural commentators, and social movements will pass through.

Illustration 18.4
Still from Woody Allen's Manhattan *(© The Kobal Collection, London)*

429

It is below this level that the greatest competition takes place. We can identify three groups. I will call them:

- ■ wannabee world cities;
- ■ clean and green;
- ■ look! no more factories.

Wannabee world cities

Wannabee world cities include Paris, Los Angeles, Chicago, Milan, Frankfurt, Melbourne, and Toronto. A good, though not infallible, guide is to look at the cities who have applied to host the Olympic Games or who have hosted the games in recent years. These include Seoul, Los Angeles, Atlanta, Barcelona, and Birmingham in the United Kingdom. To host the games is to achieve media coverage of a global spectacle; it implies that you need and want media coverage. It means you have world city pretensions, even if you're not quite there. The desire is prompted by the growth machine in individual cities – politicians, business leaders, developers, local elites often in association with organized labor. The lure is status, income, development, wealth, and power. The drive for world city status is prompted by the feeling that there are footloose business opportunities, from conventions to corporate relocations, which can be attracted to successful cities. Get the right world city image and the business will come.

Wannabee world cities are marked by a kind of edgy insecurity combined with a rather brittle cultural boosterism. They have an acute concern with their role and position in the global network of global cultural capital. Hence the importance given to art galleries, big-name architects, academic schools, art traditions. An edgy sense of not being at the center permeates these cities.

Clean and green

In the advanced capitalist countries the annihilation of space and time allows a more serious consideration of smaller towns and cities as places to do world and national business. One important selling point for places with good accessibility is that they are not big cities like London or Paris or Atlanta. They are clean and green. Unpolluted, closer to nature. The "old" image of such cities as Seattle and Portland or the emergence of the technology-based areas in Provence is of non-cities. They have the advantages of cities without the disadvantages. The "purity" of these cities is not only their relationship with nature; it implies pre-urban, pre-industrial. In the United States in particular this implies places where there is no organized working class, no strong regulatory bodies or redistributional interventionist states. New definitions of purity are constantly introduced as clean and green cities become "developed."

Look! no more factories

There is now a large, and increasing, number of cities in the advanced capitalist world whose economic growth and prosperity was based on manufacturing employment. Examples range from Pittsburgh to Glasgow, Syracuse to Scranton. The global shift of manufacturing has left these cities in need of a new economic base, a whole new image. They are associated with the old as opposed to the new, the polluted in contrast with the clean, work in comparison with leisure. The phrase "look! no more factories" encapsulates their attempt to create a postindustrial image. This image involves a distancing from the industrial legacy, sometimes even a conscious distancing through the historicizing of industrial districts, the creation of factory museums and industrial heritage sites.

The physical reconstruction of parts of the city become crucial metaphors for the phoenix-like rise from the ashes of industrialism. Old harbor fronts turned into leisure districts, old industrial districts transformed into postmodern business parks. There is a powerful financial incentive to these land-use changes. But there is also an important symbolism – saddled with a negative industrial legacy these cities seek to restructure their image. Even the terms "renewal," "revitalization," "renaissance" all bespeak redemption through change.

Another important element in this transformation is the renegotiation of the contract with the physical environment. One of the most important legacies of their industrial past was a polluted and disfigured environment. Lakes and rivers which previously were considered dumping grounds now become central to a new discourse. Cleaning up pollution is not only a mandated responsibility, it becomes an act of redemption, the forging of a new contract, the reconstruction of a new place. The clean air of Pittsburgh becomes a peg on which to hang a whole range of transformative discourses. When a *National Geographic* reporter wrote about the city, "Pittsburgh's air is cleaner than ever, and its waters run clear" (Miller, 1991, 133) he was telling a tale of a born-again city.

Cities compete for business, trade and investment. They struggle for corporate attention. What sells the city is the image of the city. In a very real sense the city becomes the image. Business journals are full of urban images. The images can be realistic, imitative, mocking or stereotypical (and counter-stereotypical). There are several different devices and marketing strategies. Here I am concerned with the super images that can be identified. These are the dominant images which are often superimposed one on another and cut across the different categories of cities. Four main images can be identified:

- fun city;
- green city;
- culture city;
- pluralist city.

Fun City

Fun city is the conspicuous consumption of leisure, it is the beach, where only the beautiful can be seen. The city, like the predominance of body shots of attractive young women used in much of the advertising, is laid before the consumer, eager to meet their needs, willing to satisfy their fantasies. It is a place where the sky is blue, people smile and laugh. There are no problems to wrinkle the landscape or the lifestyle of the hyperfun city. This is an image used not only by tourist places but also by cities eager to attract business. Come to work in fun city and it won't seem like work.

Green city

Then there are the green cities where a nature safely controlled and manicured provides a close though comforting experience with the semi-wild, while also providing room service and fax. As in the fun city, water is an important icon, along with fresh air, mountain vistas, and lack of traffic.

Culture city

Here the emphasis is on a manicured and sanitized cultural experience, from high-class shopping malls, and symphony orchestras to art galleries. It involves the representation of the city as a cultural festival. Music festivals for the small cities, resident world-famous conductors for the bigger cities. The underlying message is to assure the discriminating that this is no hick town; this is a place of a sophistication, well wired to the flow of global culture.

The pluralist image is associated with the culture theme. Now the message is: Come and experience the rich mix of different life-styles. It also links in with the pleasure theme; the urban experience is just one round of different ethnic holidays; constant fun-filled days with a never-ending cycle of festivities and celebrations.

This is the upside of multiculturalism: the pluralist dream of different ethnic groups adding to each other's experience but with no struggle over scarce resources or battles over cultural identity; mixed but nice, varied but safe. It is the definition of multiculturalism as the blending of sushi bars with rap music and Armenian holidays. It is the reduction of cultural identity to modes of consumption.

The example of Glasgow

Let us consider some of the themes outlined above with reference to a specific example: the city of Glasgow in Scotland (Boyle and Hughes, 1991; Damer, 1990).

The name of the city derives from the Celtic *Glasghu*, which can be translated as "beloved green spot". Its first surge of growth came after the Treaty of Union between England and Scotland in 1707. The treaty allowed Glasgow to trade with the colonies of the West Indies and North America. Like the other British west coast ports of Liverpool and Bristol, Glasgow did well from this trade, particularly with the import of tobacco. In 1768 the Clyde was deepened, allowing ships to come further up the estuary and dock in the center of the city. Glasgow became a rich mercantile city where wealthy merchants displayed their affluence. Visitors to Glasgow in the eighteenth and very early nineteenth centuries all commented on the beauty of the city. In 1730 Edward Burt described it as "the prettiest and most uniform Town that I ever saw," and even as late as 1771 the novelist Tobias Smollett could see it as "one of the prettiest towns in Europe."

From the late eighteenth century Glasgow became one of the epicenters of the industrial revolution. In 1799 bleaching powder was patented in the city, and in 1822 the first blast furnace was put into operation. The city was transformed by the new economic order. Ship-building, iron and steel production, the manufacture of locomotives, chemical works, printing and dyeing, whisky blending and bottling, flour milling, and engineering. The city developed an international market for its products. Its growth was dramatic. Between 1780 and 1830 the population of the city increased fivefold. Yet the urban fabric remained the same. The effects were huge population densities and the overwhelming of such public services as roads, sewerage, and sanitation. The "beloved green spot" was transformed. In 1820 the diarist Benjamin Haydon noted that the city had "the look of manufacture and abomination."

Throughout the nineteenth and early twentieth centuries Glasgow grew. It became one of the leading heavy engineering centers of the British Empire. Locomotives built in the city were driven in Canada, Australia, and India. Ships built on the Clyde sailed the seven seas. In 1801 the population of the city was 77,385; by 1901 this had risen to 761,709, a tenfold increase over the century. By 1931 the figure was 1,088,417. Glasgow was the second biggest city in the country and one of the most important industrial cities of the British Empire.

The postwar era saw a downturn in the city's economic fortunes. The whole manufacturing and ship-building basis of the city was undercut by shrinking markets and sharper foreign competition. Just as Glasgow had been one of the leading centers of industrialization so it became one of the more dramatic sites of deindustrialization. The city was also losing some of its vitality in the massive housing program that gave people better housing but on the giant public housing estates on the periphery or in new towns such as Cumbernauld and East Kilbride. The population of the city had fallen to 774,008 by 1989.

Things looked bleak. The city found it difficult to attract employment or capital investment. It had a reputation for hard drinking, violence, and poor housing. Throughout the 1960s and 1970s Glasgow was regularly portrayed as a city of declining industry and rising violence; an economic and social basket case. Film crews would come up from London to point the camera at some remaining slums and get some young thugs to speak into a microphone about their violent acts. Exit film crew with the old Glasgow image unexamined and reinforced. There were even people in Glasgow who subscribed to this image. Local writers and filmmakers also helped to reproduce these images; it was their local creative seam to be mined and refined.

The dominant images began to change in the 1980s. In 1983 the city was bombarded with the elided message "Glasgow's Miles Better" (say it quickly to get the double message). This message was for internal consumption, to get the citizens to believe in the city. Later a wider marketing campaign was launched to change the external perception of the city. Then in 1987 the city was designated the European City of Culture for 1990. This announcement did more than anything to shift public opinion. Glasgow was now sharing the same stage as Athens, Amsterdam, Florence, and Paris. During 1990 there were 13,000 cultural events attended by 9 million people. People began to talk about opera almost as much as soccer, and more people attended Pavarotti concerts than the Glasgow Rangers football matches.

The total effect was staggering in the swing of perception. Gone was the old image of Glasgow with the gangs, the violence, the hard men, and the heavy drinking. Glasgow was now seen as a pleasant, cultured city. The new man displaced the hard man.

The message of Glasgow is that images are important. In the early nineteenth century cities needed cheap fuel and labor, easy access to raw materials, and good transport links to achieve economic growth. In the late twentieth century they need a successful advertising campaign.

The advertising campaign was an exercise in rhetoric, a successful attempt to shift the meaning, perception, and symbolism of the city from a drab, industrial image to the sexier, culture-rich image of a postindustrial city. It was more than just rhetoric. Buildings were cleaned up, tourism was boosted, there was a renewed confidence in the city. However – and there is always a however – a cultural campaign does not fill in all the gaps left by economic disinvestment. The economic base of Glasgow is still shaky, unemployment is high, and life chances for many inhabitants are limited and constricting. The image campaign often brought these limitations into sharper relief as the people in the peripheral public housing schemes saw money spent by and for the cultural intelligentsia.

There are two responses. The first is to see the recent Glasgow experience as a successful campaign, an advertising rhetoric that worked, a turnaround in image. The second is to see it all as a cynical, superficial exercise that did not shift the economic realities or the political facts of life for a city that, despite the cleaned-up buildings, is still a black hole of contemporary capitalism. Even if successful, the selling of places is not the same as living in places. There is a dichotomy between the rhetoric of the advertising campaign and the texture of everyday life.

Comparing Cities

An important goal of urban promotion campaigns is to improve the relative standing of a city in comparison with others. In consequence, there have been various attempts to represent cities in terms of their comparative ranking (for example Scott, 1990). Of the numerous examples let me consider just one.

One of the most comprehensive studies, the *Places Rated Almanac* by Boyer and Savageau (1989), looks at 333 metropolitan areas in the United States and rates and ranks these areas on nine factors. I will consider only five.

Cost of living

Indicators include cost of housing, food, transportation, and health care. The range is enormous; if we take the US standard housing cost as 100 then Stamford, Connecticut, comes out as 407, while Brownsville in Texas costs only 53. One is a rich enclave, the other a dirt-poor town in the middle of nowhere.

Employment

This dimension includes quality of jobs, rates of pay, and rates of employment growth. Anaheim-Santa Ana in California is the biggest job-creating area, while poor old Casper in Wyoming may have its good points but it is not the place to go if you are looking for a job.

Crime

The violent-crime rate and property-crime rate are combined to give a measure of the overall safety of the 333 areas. Top of the list, the most crime-ridden place, is Miami, Florida. In a typical year over 200,000 violent and property crimes are reported to the police. *Miami Vice*, it seems, is not a complete work of fiction.

Other dimensions include *health care and environment, transportation, education, recreation, the arts*, and *climate*. Let us end by looking at the last two.

The arts

People don't live by bread alone. Variables used to measure the quality of artistic life include the hours of fine arts broadcasting and the number and size of public libraries, art museums and galleries. Jackson, Tennessee, comes out worst, perhaps giving substance to the notion of "rural hick town," while top of the list is New York. However, New York's artistic excellence has to be offset against its high crime statistics, which rank it second behind Miami. You may not be able to see the ballet, symphony orchestra or the latest European movies in Jackson, but you have much less chance of being mugged.

In small countries like Britain quality-of-life studies rarely take climatic differences into account. They should. Oxford has fine buildings, but its wet, humid climate makes it one of the unhealthiest places in Britain to live compared to, say, the bracing windiness of Norwich or Aberdeen. The sheer size of the United States makes climatic differences significant. The study has a complicated set of measures including number of hot and cold months, number of freezing days, seasonal temperature variation, number of days over 90°F. The "best" place is Oakland, California. In contrast, with four months of below-freezing average temperature and very hot summers, Grand Forks in North Dakota comes out as the worst place, climatically speaking, in the United States.

A composite index of all the dimensions shows that the three best places in the United States to live are Seattle, San Francisco and Pittsburgh. Bottom of the list is Pine Bluff, Arkansas.

These studies are interesting in different ways. First, the attributes used reveal much about the value systems employed. No measure of community or social justice is employed; rather, the emphasis is on the performance of private households; for example, the cost of living is an important variable. Second, the study has an inflated notion of value-free, objective measurements whereas the process is very subjective, the seemingly solid data confirming presupposed ideas rather than examining them. Third, despite all the criticism and qualifications (see Cutter, 1985), many people use it to find out where their own place figures. Syracuse comes twenty-first out of 333. Not bad. It would be even higher were it not for the cold winters. But I like them. The snow allows you to go skiing. But I suppose everyone has a rider to add about their own place. There must be people in Pine Bluff who actually like living in the place. There must be . . . surely . . .

These are difficult times for cities. The competition is now global, not just national or regional. In recession and downturns the competition becomes even more severe. What becomes of crucial importance is for the city to identify its market niches and construct the appropriate images. The right combination of powerful images will not solve all the problems, but it sure does help. Maybe the Canon advert got it right.

GUIDE TO FURTHER READING

This chapter draws heavily upon one of my previous books:

Short, J.R. (1991) *Imagined Country: Environment, Culture and Society*, London: Routledge.

On different aspects of urban myths and ideologies, see:

Lane, B.M. (1968) *Architecture and Politics in Germany, 1918–1946*, Cambridge, Mass.: Harvard University Press.

Lees, A. (1985) *Cities Perceived: Urban Society in European and American Thought*, New York: Columbia University Press.

Pearson, G. (1975) *The Deviant Imagination*, London: Macmillan.

Raban, J. (1974) *Soft City*, London: Hamish Hamilton.

Short, J.R. (1989) *The Humane City*, Oxford: Blackwell.

Thompson, E.P. (1971) The moral economy of the crowd in the eighteenth century, *Past and Present* 50, 76–136.

On general issues of representation and places, see:

Aitken, S.C. and Zonn, L.E. (1994) *Re*-presenting the place pastiche. In S.C. Aitken and L.E. Zonn (eds), *Place, Power, Situation and Spectacle*, Lanham, Md: Rowman & Littlefield.

Barnes, T.J. and Duncan J.S. (eds) (1992) *Writing Worlds: Discourse, Text and Metaphor in the Representation of Landscape*, London: Routledge.

Duncan, J.S. and Ley, D. (eds) (1993) *Place/Culture/Representation*, London: Routledge.

On specific examples or urban representation:

Benton, L. (1995) Will the real/reel Los Angeles please stand up, *Urban Geography* 16(2), 144–64.

Ford, L. (1994) Sunshine and shadow: lighting and color in the depiction of cities on film. In S.C. Aitken and L.E. Zonn (eds), *Place, Power, Situation and Spectacle*, Lanham, Md: Rowman & Littlefield.

Klak, T. (1994) Havana and Kingston: mass media images and empirical observations of two Caribbean cities in crisis, *Urban Geography* 15, 318–44.

Simpson-Housley, P.A. and Preston, P. (eds) (1994) *Writing the City: Eden, Babylon and the New Jerusalem*, London: Routledge.

On urban images and place promotion, see:

Boyer, R. and Savageau, D. (1989) *Places Rated Almanac*, New York: Simon & Schuster.

Boyle, M. and Hughes, G. (1991) The politics of the representation of the "real": discourses from the left on Glasgow's role as European City of Culture, *Area* 23, 217–28.

Cutter, S. (1985) *Rating Places: A Geographer's View of Quality of Life*, Resource Publication in Geography, Washington, D.C.: Association of American Geographers.

Damer, S. (1990) *Glasgow: Going for a Song*, London: Lawrence & Wishart.

Gold, J.R. and Ward, S.V. (eds) (1994) *Place Promotion: The Use of Publicity and Marketing to Sell Towns and Regions*, Chichester, Sussex: John Wiley.

Kearns, G. and Philo, C. (eds) (1993) *Selling Places: The City as Cultural Capital, Past and Present*, Oxford: Pergamon Press.

Miller, P. (1991) Pittsburg – stronger than steel, *National Geographic* December, 125–45.

Scott, T.G. (1990) *The Rating Guide to Life in America's Small Cities*, Buffalo, N.Y.: Prometheus.

Chapter 19

RECONSTRUCTING THE IMAGE OF A CITY: CASE STUDY VI

At five o'clock we arrived at Syracuse. I do detest these old names vamped up. Why do not the Americans take the Indian names. They need not be so very scrupulous about it; they have robbed the Indians of everything else.

Captain Frederick Marryat, *A Diary of America* (1839)

In chapters 16, 17 and 18 I considered different ways in which the city is produced. In this chapter some of the different ways are brought together by examining the reconstruction of the image of an industrial city. The pattern of deindustrialization and economic decline sets the context for a range of processes involving the built form and the urban imagery of the city.

Because of the globalization of production and new systems of flexible production, there is intense competition between cities for investment, both public and private. Competition is particularly severe for the traditional industrial cities; they are subject to competition from newly industrializing countries, regions, and cities which have lower labor costs, lower taxes, and are considered to have a more "business-friendly" environment. In this chapter I will examine one of the consequences of this competition; namely, the attempt to "reconstruct" the image of an industrial city.

CITY AS TEXT

To call a city "industrial" in the present period in the United States is to associate it with a set of negative images: declining economic base, pollution, a city on the downward slide. Cities with more positive imagery are associated with the postindustrial era, the future, the new, the clean, the high-tech, the economically upbeat, and the socially progressive. We can identify a number of polarities in the division between industrial and postindustrial. Industrial cities are associated with the past and the old, work, pollution, and production. The postindustrial city, in contrast, is associated with the new, the future, the unpolluted, consumption and exchange, the world of leisure as opposed to work.

The terms are loose and vague. They are meant to be. We are discussing the hazy world of images and rough mental maps, not the hard solid outlines of empirical reality. Neither are we testing, for the moment at least, these images against existential experience; we are limiting our observations to the restricted and partial world of vague ideas and loose connotations. The most important point to note is that business elites and civic leaders in industrial cities, because of the intense competition, are considering ways to change their image, to move away from the negative connotations of "industrial" and to tap the positive imagery of "postindustrial." Cities, like all environments, are texts in which are inscribed values, beliefs, the exercise of and struggle for power. But if the city is a text it is also written as well as read, (re)constructed as well as (re)interpreted and (re)produced as well as consumed. I will use the term "reconstruction" to refer to changes both in image and the physical environment.

The reconstruction of a city occurs for many different reasons and can take many forms. We can identify at least three reasons and associated forms. First, there is the attempt to change the image of the city for external consumption (Ashworth and Voogd, 1990; Bailey, 1991; Philo and Kearns, 1993). This is the realm of traditional civic boosterism, the aim being to promote the name and the positive image of the city. Civic boosterism has an important role to play in the urban development of the United States but is not restricted to the United States. One of the most successful campaigns of recent years has been the selling of Glasgow, Scotland (see chapter 18, and also Boyle and Hughes, 1991; Damer 1990). This city, whose economic base was founded on ship-building, heavy engineering, textiles and chemicals, was ravaged by the deindustrialization of the British economy. In Britain it was widely perceived as an economic disaster area, a place of hard drinking, slums, and violence. In the 1980s a very successful advertising campaign turned around the image of the city. When Glasgow became the 1990 European City of Culture the transformation was complete, from industrial wastelend to postindustrial cultural center in less than a decade. Around the world competition between cities is leading civic leaders to develop city image campaigns.

Second, the promotion of new city images for external consumption is also a cause and a function of a changing internal debate between different groups within the city. The reconstruction of a new image for a city means a realignment of the internal debate between those groups. To promote a postindustrial image involves, for example, a devaluation of the industrial base and a possible reduction of the power of local industry.

Third, there is the construction of a new urban imagery through the production of new urban spaces either through the recycling of old buildings and districts or through the construction of new buildings and physical layouts. Large schemes such as Baron Haussmann's Paris or US postwar urban renewal schemes are more than just rearrangements of physical space; they are a new way of visualizing the city, new distributions of power. The conscious physical transformation of a city is both a demonstration and a consequence of economic and political power; it is an attempt to reinforce, change or contest the social and political meaning of the city.

The focus of this chapter is Syracuse, New York. Syracuse was selected because it is a classic example of a north-east US industrial city experiencing deindustrialization; it is a good example of a Rustbelt town, a city whose economic fortunes were tied to industry. In particular, I will focus on three elements of reconstruction:

- the changing message of civic boosterism;
- the internal debate over pollution and the city's relationship with the physical environment; and
- the changing iconography of the downtown.

These elements are found in most cities seeking to transform their image from industrial to postindustrial. Thus, while the material is specific to Syracuse, it has wider significance.

SYRACUSE

For almost a hundred years up until the 1970s Syracuse grew as an industrial city with an economy initially based on chemicals and more recently on diversified manufacturing. In the early twentieth century Syracuse led the world in the manufacturing of bicycles and produced more typewriters than any other city in the world. Syracuse was well-positioned as a medium-sized industrial city in the heartland of an expanding industrial America (figure 15.3). The mid-1970s marked the beginning of a slump and a changed position for the United States in the world economy. The change impacted on the Syracuse economy. Manufacturing employment fell by some 6,000 jobs from 1964 to 1984 and by 9,000 between 1984 and 1989. In 1990 the Syracuse metropolitan statistical area (MSA) had a population of 659,986 and

Illustration 19.1
Abandoned factory in Syracuse, N.Y.: a symbol of deindustrialization as a former typewriter factory grows weeds (photograph: author)

the city had a population of 163,860. While the MSA had experienced a modest growth of 3.5 percent from 1970 the city's population fell by almost 17 percent over the same period.

A thumbnail portrait of the city would reveal a formerly dynamic, diverse manufacturing city losing its traditional manufacturing base and losing out in the competition for new jobs and investment. In the world of hypermobile capital Syracuse needed to refashion its image. While this reconstruction took many forms, I will examine three important and interrelated elements:

- selling the city;
- coping with the industrial legacy;
- changing the downtown iconography.

I will focus on selected items within these three broad headings and taken an historical approach to show the more important changes.

An important agent in civic boosterism is the chamber of commerce, the main institutional representation of local business interests. The US Chamber of Commerce was established in 1912, at the prompting of President Taft, to better coordinate the lobbying efforts of business. By 1991 the national chamber had 400 full-time employees and 50 full-time lobbyists who seek to influence federal policy. They work with local chambers to foster "business interests." The local chambers are independent bodies with a longer history. They are a vital element in what Logan and Molotch (1987) refer to as the "urban growth machine" which dominates public debates and defines civic issues.

Syracuse Chamber of Commerce: 1879–1960

The Syracuse Chamber of Commerce (COC) was first established in 1889, much earlier than the national chamber. Speaking of Syracuse in 1898 the COC president John Marsellus said:

> *For fifty years those tributary conditions of splendid location, natural resources, enterprising pioneers and business elements, which have laid so well the foundations of our present and which guarantee so clearly the future of this fair city, have been gradually attracted and conserved. Here are busy lines of transportation, up-to-date newspapers, solid banking institutions, handsome business emporiums, attractive public buildings and hives of industrial activity.*
>
> (*Syracuse Standard*, 1898)

The words sound like typical booster rhetoric, but they also suggest an elite certain of the prosperity of its home city. A careful analysis of the COC prior to the 1960s points to business leaders who were quite content with the position Syracuse had attained within their region and the nation. They saw their role as civic boosters maintaining the positive images that were being associated with Syracuse. Unlike their counterparts today, whose work is more heavily oriented toward attracting new business investment or staving off the departure of businesses currently in Syracuse and contemplating moving elsewhere, the COC during the late nineteenth and first half of the twentieth centuries had a broader civic mission. Indeed, many of the activities of the COC in the early part of this century had little direct connection with business activity. Throughout the 1910s and 1920s the COC regularly helped organize fire prevention and safety classes, and summer swimming classes that taught as many as 1,000 children. They established relief funds for dependents who were left without wage-earners owing to the war effort. They had yearly lawn contests, awarding cash prizes to the best-cared-for lawns. They encouraged homeownership and even dabbled in state politics. In 1917, when Buffalo interests were protesting Syracuse's drawing of drinking water from nearby Skaneateles Lake on the grounds that it was destabilizing the Erie Canal, COC members went to the state capital in Albany to argue their case.

Syracuse, under the guidance of the COC, also developed a model program to hasten the process of assimilation of foreign immigrants newly arrived in the United States. Fears that many Europeans, particularly Germans, would be sympathetic to the efforts of their homelands during the war fueled strong nativist sentiments throughout the United States during this period. The COC-sponsored assimilation program was so successful that representatives from the Department of Naturalization and the Bureau of Commerce and from many of the nation's cities visited Syracuse to see its "Americanization" program in action. The chamber also worked closely with the War Industries Board to ensure that wartime production schedules were met. The COC coordinated this effort and assumed a major role in discouraging any industrial dissension that might have occurred during the war production years. During the 1920s the chamber organized the Community Chest, an annual campaign for charitable purposes, which fueled efforts to have Syracuse adopt more stringent health regulations.

In summary, the COC's agenda during this first period was made possible by the growth of the national and regional economies. The COC could take growth as a given and concentrate on reproducing the social order necessary to ensure the continued buoyancy of the Syracuse economy.

Greater Syracuse Chamber of Commerce: 1960–1982

In 1960, the COC approved the formation of the Business and Industrial Development (BID) committee. BID was given the task of trying to persuade Syracuse businesses not to leave the area. To achieve this goal, BID committee members personally met with the executives of 237 area manufacturers to determine what they perceived to be the most serious problems they were facing. They persuaded city politicians to create a central clearinghouse of information on local industrial programs in the hope that area manufacturers would use local subcontractors rather than the services

of firms from distant locations; in effect, a "Buy Syracuse" plea. They
launched a national advertising campaign extolling Syracuse's favorable transportation setting in *Plant Location Magazine*.

*Reconstructing a
city's image:
case study VI*

The emergence of BID signaled the beginning of a new period of
civic boosterism in Syracuse. Previously, attention had been focused
inward, on maintaining the social order of a successful urban economy. But by 1960 boosterism was becoming far more critical for
survival. The COC had to sell the virtues of the city; they were no
longer so obvious to potential investors, especially in the harsh glare
of fierce competition. With this competition in mind, the COC began
a new period of assertive marketing in order to persuade outsiders to
invest in Syracuse or to buy Syracuse-made products.

In 1964, recognizing that people and investment dollars were leaving the city and heading for the suburbs, the COC renamed itself the
Greater Syracuse Chamber of Commerce. In 1965, 20 Syracuse businessmen spent three weeks in Europe, armed with color brochures
and persuasive facts and figures. The COC had entered the international arena. Later that years, 23 local businessmen went to
Montreal on a similar mission. "The entire endeavor was a striking
example of the new spirit of salesmanship," wrote a local reporter
(Sparrow, 1965). Other "prospecting" groups went to Chicago,
Atlanta, Toronto, and frequently to California. Selling the virtues of
Syracuse was now a necessity. It seemed that every other city had
aggressive marketing efforts underway and Syracuse would have little hope of attracting any growth if it didn't join in. When asked
which other states had tried to entice away a planned $14-million lab
expansion, the chairman of Carrier Corporation, one of Syracuse's
largest and best-known companies, responded simply, "The other
forty-nine."

"We're Growing Greater": image building since the 1980s

In the early 1980s, as in other cities such as Baltimore, Cleveland,
Pittsburg, Houston, Denver, and Atlanta, Syracuse embraced the
marketing of a new image. In June 1982 the COC undertook its most
ambitious endeavor to date. The Greater Syracuse Program was a
$3.2 million marketing campaign aimed at bringing 20,000 jobs and
$500 million of capital investment to Syracuse by the end of 1985.
The plan for the program was first developed in 1979 by Melvin
Eggers, the chancellor of Syracuse University and the then-president
of the COC. The program was funded by a coalition of local business
interests, including Agway, Carrier Corporation, General Electric,
Syracuse China, Allied Chemical Company, and Canadian Pacific

Enterprises. Financing the Greater Syracuse Program was accomplished entirely through pledges from local businesses. Carrier Corporation pledged $400,000 and was one of the top aid-givers. Other executives willingly offered enough to reach the $3.2 million goal, no small accomplishment for a city the size of Syracuse. Maria Russell, one of the directors of the newly formed COC Communications Department, said there really was no choice in the matter. "If you're not going to do that for your city, you're going to sit on the shelf like a product that isn't promoted" (Gallagher, 1983). Over 50 local businesses were urged to "invest in the future of the community."

The program drew inspiration from similar schemes elsewhere. The company that developed the Forward Atlanta campaign, National Community Development Services, was hired to identify industries which could be expanded, improved, or brought to Syracuse. The program also carefully examined the very successful campaigns of civic promotion used by Dallas and the 1965 marketing plan for Denver. A New York public relations firm, Development Counsellors International, was chosen to coordinate public relations for the Greater Syracuse Program. This company was handling similar accounts for other cities. Place imagery was being marketed according to a set formula, urban imagery was an advertising construction to be bought and sold; in effect, the commodification of the image.

The project leaders hoped to "alter dramatically the image of Syracuse in the minds of 'decision makers' in growth industries, particularly in the high technology field" (Porcello, 1981, B1). Noting that Sunbelt locations were losing their appeal for many industries due to rising costs, local leaders (public and private) felt that the north-east stood to profit and that Syracuse could take the lead with an aggressive marketing plan. Borrowing heavily from earlier successful image promotion campaigns in Atlanta and Denver, national and local advertisements, including full-page spots in *Business Week* and *Fortune,* urged new and existing firms to "Take Stock in Syracuse" and "Profit from our Assets." To encourage local pride and enthusiasm, buttons were distributed declaring "I've Got a Share in Syracuse" and "We're Growing Greater." It was, however, essentially a top-down promotion concerned with changing the external image of the city to potential investors outside the city.

The years of aggressive promotion resulted in several relocations, new jobs, and a new industrial park downtown. Employment did rise by almost 20,000 between 1982 and 1985. How much of this would have occurred without the marketing is very difficult to assess. What is more certain, however, is that Syracuse entered an era of unprecedented competition for investment dollars in the 1980s. The image campaign was a sign of the problem facing the business community as much as its attempted solution.

DEALING WITH THE INDUSTRIAL PAST

The successful transformation of a city's image from industrial to postindustrial involves effectively dealing with one of the worst legacies of the industrial era – pollution. In Syracuse the issue of pollution was concentrated around Onondaga Lake, four and a half miles long and one mile wide and bordering on urbanized Syracuse (see figure 19.1). The lake is important in the reconstruction of the city on two counts. First, it highlights some of the pressure from the nonbusiness community. So far I have concentrated by analysis on the business leaders and civic elite, their perceptions and their influences. A study of Onondaga Lake shows how grass-roots pressure has also had a role in the new discourse. Second, the lake has been central to the image of the city, not only as a body of water whose transformation into usable space is vital to a number of development schemes but also as a symbol of and for the whole city. Though the physical

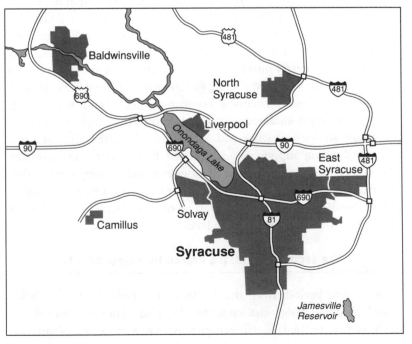

Figure 19.1
Onondaga Lake

configuration of the lake has remained constant, its symbolic importance has changed dramatically, and in this regard the history of Onondaga Lake can be characterized in three periods:

- the lake as an economic reservoir bereft of social significance;
- a juncture of ambiguity, in which only a few people in the community contested the predominant image of the lake as an economic commodity and called for a rethinking of its symbolic and cultural value;
- a time of reassessment as a postindustrial city; Syracuse redefines its identity, deals with the polluting effects of its industrial past, and gives new meaning to its landscape.

The first period: a lake lost

In 1881 Solvay Process Company began soda ash production; this requires cool water during manufacture and a location for dumping by-products. The byproducts of this process, calcium and chloride, were dumped into the tributaries that led into Onondaga Lake. Before the decade was over, other major industries such as steel, machinery and pottery manufacturing set up business on the lake or its tributaries. By 1901 pollution of the waters was so bad that New York State prohibited the cutting of ice for consumption.

Until 1940, both industry and the community shared in the use of Onondaga Lake. In the 1920s, lakeshore development boasted a popular summer resort where tourists and locals could fish, swim, and boat; on the other side sat the smoking stacks of industry. Industrial waste flowed directly into the lake, and as the city grew the lake also served as an inexpensive dumping ground for municipal sewerage and refuse. The biggest chemical company, Allied, and the city of Syracuse reached an agreement which allowed the city to pump its sewerage sludge onto the beds of industrial wastes; the resulting chemical action supposedly neutralized both wastes. Despite this "solution," the twin problems of industrial and municipal waste further degraded the lake, and eventually it was closed to swimming in 1940. By 1950 the pollution levels were such that is was no longer safe to eat the fish caught in the lake.

The second period: the search for responsibility

The second period, from the 1940s to the early 1980s, is distinguished by a rising challenge to the unquestioned commercial exploitation of the lake. Citizen groups were formed to pressure for environmental cleanup, but they struggled to be heard over the cacophony of industrial and civic leaders.

A grass-roots group organized after 1943 when the dike holding back Allied Chemical Company waste broke on Thanksgiving Day, inundating homes and burying the State Fairgrounds. The victims filed lawsuits, and the community held an open forum. Prompted by this disaster, a trio of environmental activists rallied to the lake's defense. Walter Welch, Crandall Melvin, and William Maloney, founders of the Onondaga Lake Reclamation Association, ushered in the second period of discourse in the community. They wrote letters, called community meetings, organized press releases, initiated their own surveys of the lake, and pressed for state action against the industrial polluters. Contesting the privileges of capital, Welch remarked, "The important thing is that Syracuse, Solvay [Process], and the environs on Onondaga Lake belong to all the people; not just to stockholders of Allied Chemical and Dye Corp." (*Syracuse Post Standard*, 1946).

An important distinction to note, however, is that the association did not call for industry to cease operations. Rather, they hoped that cleaning up the lake waters would rekindle business interests and investment. Their concern not only with the aesthetic aspects of the lake but with the restoration of its "usefulness" to the community is significant. It reveals how strongly intertwined economic needs are with the cultural values of an industrial community.

The crusaders continued their fight to reclaim Onondaga Lake, and although not successful they remained a countercurrent to the predominant view throughout the 1940s, 1950s and 1960s. By 1970 the chartering of the Environmental Protection Agency brought renewed energy to the environmentalists in the community. John Hennigan Jr, deputy commissioner of the Onondaga County Department of Public Works, feared "the new legislation is going to provide such strict requirements for effluent discharge that it will adversely affect the 140 or so 'wet industries' which discharge into Onondaga Lake." He echoed the sentiments of many who feared "the new law will make it so tough to do business that many industries will have to build their own treatment facilities or move out of the country" (Ganley, 1972). Local politicians and industry claimed more studies were needed, and state and local government responded by appropriating funds for continued surveys. By 1979 over 245 studies, dissertations, and articles on water quality in Onondaga Lake had been written. Over three-quarters of these studies had been done either by the Army Corps of Engineers or by faculty at Syracuse University and at the College of Environmental Science and Forestry, part of the State University of New York, located in Syracuse. The rest were done by consultants. To date, despite the enormous body of data, there has not been any positive action.

The second period is characterized by ambivalence. The need to begin cleanup efforts surfaced, yet the desire for continued economic well-being was at odds with the necessary steps. It is only in the third period that we find the community reorienting itself toward and rethinking its attitudes about the lake.

The third period: Onondaga Lake reclaimed

Dreams of reviving the lakefront area surfaced in the mid-1970s and again in the mid-1980s in an attempt to lure new businesses to the lake and to restore the public domain. During this time, the lake assumed its new position as both public and private space. This is exemplified in the new logo adopted by City Hall in 1986 (Figure 19.2). The Old logo portrayed salt fields and belching smokestacks. It represented the old industrial image. In 1972 Mayor Lee Alexander organized a design contest to replace the 100-year-old image. There was a lot of community resistance. Typical was the president of the Onondaga Historical Association, who in a letter to the mayor wrote: "We do not throw out the portraits of our ancestors because their clothes are out of style." The scheme floundered. Perhaps Syracusans were not yet ready to jettison their history, and while the economy seemed relatively secure there was little apparent popular desire to dissociate community identity from the depiction of an industrial landscape. In 1986 a new mayor, Tom Young, succeeded in introducing a design contest for a new city logo. With the decline of the local economy and a pressing need to attract as well as to retain

Figure 19.2
*Changing images:
(a) Syracuse's
logo, c.1848;
(b) the new logo for
Syracuse sets the
lake as "front yard"*

(a) (b)

investment, city leaders were in the market for a new image. An advisory council of advertising executives from central New York chose three finalists from 50 submitted designs. With the co-operation of local newspapers, the three designs were published and the community voted. The winning logo (figure 19.2) was designed by Bob Ripley, art director of a local design firm Paul, John & Lee. The designer has acknowledged that discussions of lakeside development influenced his decision to include the lake as part of the design. In a recent telephone interview he commented that by silhouetting the lake in the graphic design he consciously portrayed it as clean. In comparing the two logos, notice how the image of an industrial city has been transformed. Factory chimneys are replaced with a modern skyline reflected in the lake. Onondaga Lake is "reclaimed," now central to a new image of the city, it is no longer the dumping ground for industry. The positive images of water as a visual and recreational amenity are harnessed to promote a new postindustrial image of the lake and the city. The message to the community: picture Onondaga Lake as the heart of the city. The message to outsiders: Syracuse has a dramatic skyline, a festive waterfront, a sleek look. The deletion of factories in favour of high-rise office buildings silhouetted in the background suggests the transition from industrial to postindustrial, polluted to pristine, and Fordist to post-Fordist.

Discussions in this period focus on the lake as a unifying element for the city. As Emanual Carter, principal planner for the city's Department of Community Development, remarked:

> With regard to attitude, I think that one of the first things the city has to do is to acknowledge the lake is there, and that although the lake is in its current state not a good condition – it is not a lost cause. It has to acknowledge that lake improvement is something that is desirable and worthy of local government resources. . . . I think we're going to have to begin to see ourselves as somehow physically, visually, and image-wise associated with Onondaga Lake.
>
> (Carter, 1984, 64)

In 1983 Samuel Sage created the not-for-profit Syracuse-based Atlantic States Legal Foundation for the purpose of suing industrial and municipal polluters under the federal 1972 Clean Water Act. Since its founding, affiliated environmental activists have filed more than 200 suits across the United States, forcing polluters to fund cleanup projects. In January 1988, Atlantic States brought a $50 million lawsuit against Onondaga County over sewer pollution of

Onondaga Lake. Sage's goal was to force the county to spend the millions that would be necessary to free Onondaga Lake of pollution. The attorney general and commissioner of the New York State Department of Environmental Conservation joined in this suit. In 1989 US Senator Daniel Patrick Moynihan demanded that state officials take some action against Allied: "Allied dumped a quarter of a million pounds of mercury in the bottom of that lake. . . . They poisoned our lake for a century. When are we going to bring Allied into court or before our committee. . . . We never should have let them get out of town. We should have locked them up" (Sanders, 1989).

As Bluestone and Harrison (1982) noted, a community in the midst of deindustrialization confronts a deep sense of insecurity which grows out of the collapse all around them of the traditional economic base of their community. Attempts to reclaim the lake as "social space" can be viewed as one attempt to redefine the community in the wake of deindustrialization.

There was very little conflict within the various communities of Syracuse over the redefinition of the lake. A long-term hegemonic image of the lake as an adjunct to industry has been replaced by an equally hegemonic vision of the lake as a shared space whose visual and recreational appeal is vital for the reconstruction of the city's image. In the first and third period there was a consensus between capital, labor, and local government. In the interregnum of the second period, community groups protested against polluting industries. This was relatively short-lived because of the departure of these industries from the scene; they no longer provided employment, a tax base, or a local political force. The industry that remained shared the belief of community groups and civic leaders that a cleaned-up lake was essential for the city. Today there is a consensus between business and political leaders and the various concerned community groups that a cleaned-up, nonpolluted lake is a shared community objective. While there may be disagreements over the specific timing and particular methods of assigning costs, there is a large measure of community agreement over the symbolic position and cultural importance of the lake to the city.

DONNING THE CARNIVAL MASK

The deindustrialization of many cities is also a time of opportunity for developers. The exodus of industry, plant closures, the discontinued use of big railway yards and harbor facilities all create development potential close to the central-city areas of industrial cities. In the 1980s a new phase of investment in the built environment was inaugurated by investment-hungry capital, increased demand, and the myriad development opportunities afforded by deindustrialization. It is against this broader background that parts of downtown Syracuse were reconstructed in an attempt to write a new text for the city with postindustrial syntax.

To overcome the city's limiting industrial image Syracuse civic leaders also focused on a revitalized downtown. In their desire to outcompete other cities, these leaders initiated or proposed a series of public–private partnerships designed to create an "amenity infrastructure" and a "new city" look. This was part of a more general landscape transformation in contemporary cities: the creation of *festival settings* in downtown districts. Tacit agreement seemed to have been reached among civic leaders, investors, and developers that the future should be fun, frivolous, and festive, and that if you build it, people will come (or rather, if you promote it people will participate). Cities across the nation acquired the new iconography of convention centers, cultural centers, stadiums, festive malls, and "theme" retail districts. Terms such as "renaissance" and "rebirth" often appeared in project names as well as "frontier" and "pioneer," and water, as an amenity rather than as an industrial commodity, was a common and powerful motif.

In Syracuse the plans to "revitalize" the CBD include a new convention center (Onondaga County Convention Center), a refurbished indoor arena (War Memorial), a renovated ballpark (MacArthur Stadium), a regional mall (Carousel Center), two "historic" residential and retail districts (Armory and Franklin Squares), urban cultural parks, a science and technology museum, a light rail system to connect the diverse elements of the new downtown, a new downtown mall (The Galleries), and a rehabilitated farmers' market (see figure 19.3).

The following discussion examines the dynamics behind some of the more significant projects. It seeks to tell the "story" behind three out of the many proposed or completed projects, which together will impose a lasting postmodern architectural imprint on the visual landscape and reorient the function and structure of the traditional CBD. To examine this issue, I will look closely at the "context of generation" of each of these developments and interpret their underlying strategies and target beneficiaries.

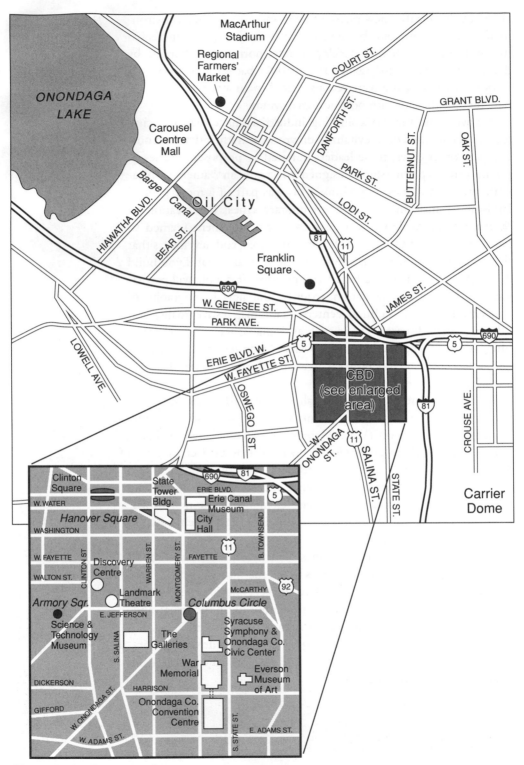

Figure 19.3 *Downtown Syracuse*

Reconstructing a
city's image:
case study VI

The Carousel Center: round and round the money goes

Carousel Center, built on a toxic-waste site on the southern shore of
Onondaga Lake, opened in October 1990. It was a joint venture
between the city and a local developer, Robert Congel (through his
Pyramid Companies), the largest mall developer in the north-east.
Carousel is the lakefront anchor of Congel's "Oil City" project (see
figure 19.3). This is an ambitious project involving the $1 billion
development of a 700–acre site from the northern edge of the downtown to Onondaga Lake. Plans include the construction of at least
2,000 residential units, a light industry park, a hotel, restaurants, and
small shopping centers. A marina is planned to extend into Onondaga
Lake, and the city would create parks and bike paths along the lake

Illustration 19.2
*Carousel Mall,
Syracuse, N.Y.
(photograph:
author)*

and the Barge Canal, which runs through the center of Oil City. The mall, a massive quarter-billion-dollar, glass and marble shopping center, includes cinemas, stores and restaurants, banquet and convention facilities, a "skydeck," and a restored 1909 carousel. Three Syracuse malls now have carousels – supporting the "carnival mask" hypothesis about contemporary urbanization (Knox, 1991, 202). The mall's postmodern architecture and festive interior epitomize the 1990s' monument to retail. Free concerts and entertainment are used to publicize the mall and create a fun-filled ambience.

Carousel is a superregional mall, and its economic feasibility is predicated on its ability to draw 1 million people, each spending $104 per year. Significant revenue is expected from people living beyond this area. Advertisements in the Syracuse newspapers enjoining retailers to "Open your doors to Canadian shoppers!" and a "Shop Syracuse" tabloid section distributed in Canada reveals that target customers are not only local residents, who have access to over six other large malls in the same vicinity, but "tourist" shoppers from as far away as Canada.

Creative financing by the city was implemented in a system of "payment in lieu of taxes" (PILOTs). Instead of property taxes for the next 25 years, Pyramid will pay the city a certain amount directly. Using this as collateral, the city plans to borrow other money in bonds to develop the lakefront. (Although it originally planned to clean up the toxic waste on which the mall was built, the city recently decided to let the toxins lie in perpetuity in clay containers under the mall parking lot). The city will also pay Pyramid for any "public improvements" it undertakes in the Oil City corridor in furthering its private development plan. Under the agreement, any extra money will go back into the lakefront development project, which in turn will help bolster Pyramid's investment. It is an especially attractive deal for Pyramid, which managed to build its mall on a toxic-waste scrapyard without having to clean up the site or pay taxes for 25 years.

Onondaga County Convention Center

The downtown convention center proposal originated in 1984 with a fanfare greeting. It was a joint venture between City Hall ($12 million), county government ($30 million), and the New York State Urban Development Corporation ($40 million). In addition to the 180,000-square-foot center, the largest exhibition space ever built in the county, plans included a parking garage, a hotel renovation or new construction, and renovation of the adjacent War Memorial building (which would have been torn down had not several local cit-

Illustration 19.3
Carousel Mall, Syracuse, N.Y.: interior (photograph: author)

izens succeeded in getting it placed on the National Register of
Historic Places). After dropping the original state-required hotel element, resolving partisan conflicts in the county, and getting past the
War Memorial hurdles, the project was finally approved and ground-
breaking began in November 1990. Before work had even begun on
the new structure, at least $2.7 million had been paid to consultants,
including an accounting firm, an environmental firm, a design con-
sultant, three architectural companies, and a project construction
manager. In addition, a senior vice-president of Syracuse University,
Harvey H. Kaiser, took partial leave of absence during 1989 to direct
the project and cut through "mountains" of bureaucratic red tape.
Kaiser, an architect, hailed the facility as a "classic piece of civic architecture" which promised new economic opportunities for Syracuse
and Onondaga County. Kaiser suggested that Syracuse University
and its Carrier Dome represented the "institutional vision" of the
community, that Carousel Center represented the "private vision" of
the community, and that the Convention Center would represent the
"civic aspiration" of the community.

The Galleries

When The Galleries opened in 1987, it was heralded as the "Saviour
of downtown retailing." The seven-story, glass and masonry postmodern building situated in the heart of the downtown was expected
to house offices, movie theaters, and up to 75 stores. Also, under a
"unique partnership between private industry, the City of Syracuse,
and Onondaga County," the county central library became a major
anchor of the mall, occupying five major office spaces. The Galleries
became one of the first victims of the Carousel Center. After Carousel
opened in 1990, it seemed a hopeless case to lure retailers and shoppers into this brand new wasteland. New suburban malls and factory
outlets also worked against the mall; it was an idea whose time had
come and gone. In 1991 the faltering $50 million downtown mall
was put up for sale, at a significantly discounted price.

The three stories echo a common theme. Local and county governments are becoming involved in the city's economy on an
unprecedented level. The reconstruction of the postindustrial city
involves a high level of public–private cooperation. Today's "private
vision" is rarely private. Moreover, rapid and drastic changes in the
iconography and the spatial configuration of the city creates a very
unstable climate. Specific sites and particular buildings may find
themselves suddenly bereft of economic *raison d'être* as the new city

is created and re-created at bewildering speed. When private visions, civic aspirations, and profit motives coincide there will be winners and losers as the development machine transforms the profit surface of the city.

The "entrepreneurial city," together with private capital, is creating a postindustrial downtown. This new architecture, despite the claims of postmodernist architecture to reclaim the vernacular past, references the successful present rather than the industrial past. The architecture of the reconstructed downtown has that "postmodern anywhere" feel that can be found in many cities in the United States and around the world. This can result from the use of "signature" architects whose look is immediately apparent. What you buy is the look, the style for which the architect has become well known. In the case of Syracuse, for example, the Convention Center was designed by the highly successful New York firm of Mitchell-Giurgola. Big-name architects leave their signature on the landscape. "Postmodern Bland' also results from the conscious attempt to mirror and copy successful schemes elsewhere. Syracuse's Inner Harbor is modeled specifically after Baltimore's Harbor Place. The end result is, as Harvey (1989, 92) notes, "a serial repetition of successful models . . . understandable, given the grim history of deindustrialization and restructuring that left most major cities in the advanced capitalist world with few options except to compete with each other."

CONCLUSIONS

Economic restructuring sets the context for the attempt of civic leaders to change a city's image. The increasing mobility of capital and the growing competition between cities to attract capital is the economic backdrop to the new rounds of civic boosterism, public relations campaigns, and the "renaissance' of the downtown that now figure so largely in contemporary America. Industrial cities are refashioning their image against a wave of deindustrialization and disinvestment. This involves rewriting the very meaning of the city, replacing the discourse of modernity and industry with the postmodern and the postindustrial.

In this chapter I examined the attempted reconstruction of an industrial city through the new images promoted by the civic boosterism of the Chamber of Commerce. the renegotiation of the social contract between the city and the lake and the physical reconstruction of parts of the downtown. In effect, they are all attempts to "rewrite" the meaning of the city and replace a negative industrial image of the city with a more positive postindustrial image.

I have shown that the boosterism of the Chamber of Commerce has been transformed from an initial concern with the local social order, because growth was taken for granted, toward a more aggressive promotion of the city's positive image to attract investment. In the first half of the twentieth century Syracuse was not competing so much with other cities. Civic boosters considered their job well done if they accomplished a reproduction of the social order so as to keep an expanding economy moving forward at the highest possible rate. External promotion was not necessary. By the 1960s things had changed. The work of BID and the Greater Syracuse Program were all attempts to re-create the image of the city, to position the city in the mental map of investors as a place where money could be made and business could be done.

I also examined the changing use and symbolic significance of Onondaga Lake. Initially seen as a dumping ground for industrial effluent, it became the subject of community attempts to reclaim its broader social role, and finally there was broad agreement that the reclamation and purification of the lake was essential to the city's new image. The story of the lake is capable of broader interpretation as other industrial cities renegotiate their relationship with their physical environment. Purifying polluted land and water becomes a symbol for the new, postindustrial city. The rewriting of the city took on a more literal form in the case of the change in the city's logo. An image of factories, of thriving industry was replaced by a crisp, clean image layered with meaning: the importance of an unpolluted, recreational lake for the city, the downtown as a thriving, modern place, and a freeway junction indicating a fine location.

Finally, I discussed the conscious attempt by business and civic leaders to reconstruct the iconography of the downtown from a work-oriented atmosphere to one of display, consumption, and fun through new construction and an intensified promotion with special social and cultural events. A new text for an older city cannot be created on a blank page. In Syracuse the industrial era left behind the poisoned chalice of Onondaga Lake and the relict industrial landscape of Oil City. The reclamation of the lake, in both environment and symbolic terms, and the proposed redevelopment of Oil City have been central to the elite's new image of the city.

As shown in the discussion of three developments, there is a symbiotic relationship between the public and private sectors with often heavy public subsidies to corporate interests. The new entrepreneurial city consists of, on the one hand, aggressive, market-oriented city governments and, on the other, corporations eager to have their costs underwritten by the public sector. In Syracuse, as in other cities undergoing deindustrialization and disinvestment, the fiscal emphasis on attracting investment means civic authorities have to provide attractive packages to potential investors. As other industrial cities compete to offer the most attractive packages, the net effect is to maximize the advantages to capital and, given the fiscal constraints, to reduce socially redistributional spending and to make for a more regressive form of municipal spending and investment.

The discourse of transforming the image of an industrial city to a postindustrial one has its utterances. It also has its silences. The dominant images being constructed for the cities of America show places ripe for investment, places of profit, sources of benefit to capital. Alternative images of the city – notions of cities as places where all people can lead dignified and creative lives – are squeezed out, marginalized to the periphery of the debate. The new image of Syracuse, as of other industrial cities, is partial, selective and, despite the claims to speak for the whole community, contains implications which have markedly different redistributional consequences for different sectors of the population. For example, there is little discussion of housing for low-income groups or of the declining employment opportunities for the unskilled or those skilled in redundant industrial techniques, and there is little said about cutting transfer payments to the poor while increasing subsidies to corporate interests.

GUIDE TO FURTHER READING

This chapter was based on:
Short, J.R., Benton, L.M., Luce, W.B. and Walton, J. (1993) Reconstructing the image of an industrial city, *Annals of the Association of American Geographers* 83, 207–24.

On selling the city:
Ashworth, G. and Voogd, H. (1990) *Selling the City*, London: Belhaven.
Bailey, J. (1991) *Marketing Cities in the 1980s and Beyond*, American Economic Development Council.
Boyle, M. and Hughes, G. (1991) The politics of the representation of the "real": discourses from the left on Glasgow's role as European City of Culture, *Area* 23, 217–28.
Damer, S. (1990) *Glasgow: Going for a Song*, London: Lawrence & Wishart.
Logan, J. and Molotch, H. (1987) *Urban Fortunes: The Political Economy of Place*, Berkeley, Cal.: University of California Press.
Philo, C. and Kearns, K. (eds) (1993) *Selling Places: The City as Cultural Capital* London: Pergamon.
Watson, S. (1991) Gilding the smokestacks: the new symbolic representations of deindustrialized regions, *Society and Space* 9, 59–70.

Other works cited include:
Bluestone, B. and Harrison, B. (1982) *The Deindustrialization of America*, New York: Basic Books.
Carter, E. (1984) *Proceedings of a Community Symposium on Onondaga Lake: The Inside Story*, Syracuse, September 15.
Gallagher, J. (1983) Will Syracuse get its share?, *Syracuse Post Standard* September 19, D9.
Ganley, J. (1972) Hennigan pessimistic over pollution control, *Syracuse Herald Journal*, March 17, 15.
Harvey, D. (1989) *The Condition of Postmodernity*, Oxford and Cambridge, Mass.: Blackwell.
Knox, P. (1991) The restless urban landscape: economic and sociocultural change and the transformation of metropolitan Washington, DC, *Annals of the Association of American Geographers* 81, 181–205.
Porcello, J.A. (1981) New look urged to sell area, *Syracuse Herald Journal*, January 25, B1.
Sanders, B. (1989) Senator Moynihan says Allied should atone for "rape of the lake", *Syracuse Post Standard*, April 28.
Sparrow, K. (1965) Syracusans woo industry in Canada, *Syracuse Herald Journal* December 5.
Syracuse Post Standard (1946) Expansion of present site for Fair advocated: Welch suggests Solvay pay for waste reclamation, September 8.
Syracuse Standard (1898) Commerce Chamber's ninth banquet February 11, 10.

Chapter 20

CONFLICT AND COMPROMISE IN THE BUILT ENVIRONMENT: CASE STUDY VII

Houses live and die: there is a time for building.
T.S. Eliot, 'East Coker' (*Four Quartets*, 1940)

In this case study I want to explore some of the themes touched upon in previous chapters. In particular, I want to explore how the built environment is produced. In this case study the focus is on housing production in an area of growth in Britain.

In mixed economies the production of the built environment is rarely either the simple unfolding of market forces or the pure outcome of state actions. Rather, there is conflict, negotiation, and tension between sets of agents working with different principles, goals, and strategies. In this chapter, I will examine the interaction between the main agents involved in the production and management of one element of the built environment: privately owned housing. The work is drawn from a much larger case study (Short et al., 1986).

A great deal has been written about the two functions of the state in capitalist society: maintaining capital accumulation and ensuring social legitimacy (see O'Connor, 1973). There have been far fewer studies of how these two pressures are articulated and resolved, if at all, through state action. My approach here focuses upon some of the key agents involved with the residential built environment – house builders, local resident groups, and local planning authorities – and their interactions at a specific place and time: central Berkshire, United Kingdom, in the early to mid-1980s.

House builders aim to derive profit from the construction and sale of new houses. Existing residents frequently campaign to protect or improve the quality of services and the environment in their localities. The state represents the arena for the competition between these sets of agents and between the accumulation and consumption demands that they represent. The state itself, however, is neither neutral nor a single body, and the conflict between house builders and community groups through the planning system produces conflict between central and local government.

THE CONTEXT

Growth in central Berkshire

Central Berkshire forms one of three "structure plan" areas within Berkshire, comprising the district councils of Bracknell, Wokingham, Reading, and the eastern part of Newbury. It is an area that has been designated for substantial growth since the early 1970s, in sharp contrast to most of the adjoining structure plan areas. Its location (figure 20.1) and transport links with London and Heathrow airport have been important factors underlying the growth and prosperity of the area. Unemployment rates are only half the national average, and the population grew from 251,000 in 1961 to 373,000 in 1980. Half of this increase resulted from in-migration from other areas.

Figure 20.1
Central Berkshire
in its regional
context

Growth and development pressure has taken three main forms: industrial, commercial, and residential. Central Berkshire lies within the M4 Corridor, which has received much media and political

Illustration 20.1
Aerial view of M4 and rail link in Reading, UK (© Aerofilms)

attention for its high-tech development. Berkshire had the highest rate of high-tech employment growth in the country between 1975 and 1981, especially in the computer electronics sector. A survey by Berkshire County Council indicated that high-tech companies provided 14 percent of the county's private-sector employment, with 31 percent for Bracknell district (Berkshire County Council, 1984).

The focus upon high-tech has partially obscured the importance of commercial development, especially in Reading and Bracknell. The service sectors of insurance and producer services grew by 77 percent and 82 percent respectively between 1971 and 1981, and Reading is now the third largest insurance center after the City of London and Croydon. Although office rents in Reading are similar to those in London (outside the City), rates (local property taxes) were generally less than half the level in the capital. Property developers thus received similar returns on their investment, while users obtained cheaper premises.

Finally, there has been a high rate of housing construction, particularly on large greenfield sites. Effective demand has been high because of the general affluence of the area, declining household size and the inflow of population from other parts of the United Kingdom. Local employment opportunities have been plentiful in the healthy sectors, and good transport links facilitate commuting into London.

In summary, this is an area of absolute growth in some sectors and of relative growth within the national economy. Central Berkshire forms a prosperous suburban district of the metropolitan system. Jobs in traditional manufacturing industries have been lost, as elsewhere, but the growth in a number of service sectors and in high-tech manufacturing has largely compensated, at least in aggregate terms.

The main agents

The main agents involved with the residential built environment and some of their linkages are shown in figure 20.2. There are the *house builders*, who are concerned with building and selling dwellings, and existing *local residents*, who in central Berkshire are largely opposed to high levels of residential growth and its environmental and social consequences. Then there are the different levels of the *state*. The production and control of the built environment involves negotiation through the land-use planning process. The planning system

Figure 20.2
Agent interactions

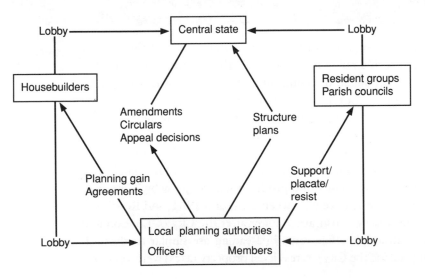

introduced in Britain in 1947 was primarily intended to regulate and direct development. It has since been transformed into a system of negotiation. Three elements are important. First, there has been increasing use of *planning gain,* by which local planning authorities secure some public advantage from the granting of planning permission. Second, more room has been afforded to the public. The 1968 Town and Country Planning Act introduced *public participation* into structure planning, and greater public involvement in development control was made possible in 1972. Finally, there has been growing *developer participation.* Since the late 1970s government circulars have given developers the right to be involved in the identification of developable housing land and have altered the provisions of the planning system to reflect more closely the demands of house builders.

In figure 20.2 only one planning authority is depicted, but in practice, prior to the reorganization of local government in 1996, county councils were responsible for structure plan preparation, while the district councils had responsibility for most local plans and development control decisions. Two major agents constitute local planning authorities: planning officers, whose position is based on a claim to professional experience, and elected representatives, whose power lies with their mandate from the local electorate. Competing pressures and demands upon the planning authorities are frequently transformed into conflict between these two groups. These main agents will be examined in turn, with emphasis placed upon their interactions.

The structure plan

The planning context for the conflict within the area has been the Central Berkshire Structure Plan. Preparation began in 1974, and the plan was submitted in 1978. The key factor in its preparation, modification, operation and review was the attitude of central government toward growth levels in the subregion. In accordance with legislation there was a public participation exercise, in so far as the county council's alternative strategies were advertised, exhibited, and debated. The three options were for restricted, limited or high levels of growth, with midrange population forecasts for the mid-1980s of 408,000, 428,000 and 461,000 respectively.

The consultation document outlining the alternatives concluded that only the limited-growth strategy provided a realistic solution to the dual and conflicting demands of growth and containment. The restricted-growth option was considered to be untenable, despite the recognition that this would reflect dominant local opinion. Central government, having designated central Berkshire as part of Growth

Area 8 in the South-East Regional Strategy (1970), would not coun-tenance a restrictive strategy. Despite this conclusion, 13 percent of the 1,242 individuals and 19 percent of the local organizations that submitted views opted for restricted growth (Berkshire County Council, 1978). Only the Housebuilders' Federation and a local estate agent articulated support for the high-growth option.

The structure plan was submitted to the Department of the Environment (hereafter DOE) in June 1978 and a public inquiry held in 1979. Approval was granted on April 14, 1980, but important modifications were made. An extension of the Metropolitan Green Belt westward to the edge of Reading was rejected, and the DOE required the county council to identify land for an extra 8,000 houses on major sites for release after 1982. The submitted plan had envis-aged that the stock of land with permission outstanding (for 31,600 dwellings in 1976) would suffice until 1986. The amendment, stem-ming from the objections and demands of the Housebuilders' Federation at the public inquiry, was intended to allow for higher building rates than the submitted plan had assumed. There was to be no risk of the local planning authorities dampening central Berkshire's growth by limiting land release for the necessary housing.

Illustration 20.2
*Commercial
development
around the M4 in
Reading, UK:
Arlington Business
Park, Theale, at
Junction 12
(© Sir Robert
McAlpine)*

The additional 8,000 houses represented an extra population of at least 20,000, the equivalent of a small town. It was soon dubbed "Heseltown" by the local press, after the then-Secretary of State, Michael Heseltine. The modification followed similar actions in respect to other areas in the south-east. Land for an extra 7,500 people had been required in south Buckinghamshire, and for a further 12,000 to 13,000 dwellings in the Surrey Structure Plan. Given the power of the DOE to enforce structure plan amendments by overturning refusals of planning permission, the central Berkshire authorities had little option but to accept the 8,000 houses. In 1983, the county council formally challenged the amendment (seeking a reduction from 8,000 to 4,000 dwellings), but this was, not surprisingly, rejected by the DOE. Faced with the prospect of development proceeding on the basis of appeal decisions, the local authorities argued that their most responsible course of action was to plan for the extra housing and ensure orderly and planned development.

In effect the structure plan modification demonstrates the imposition of central control upon local representation. The public participation exercise had proved to be a sham, and extra evidence was given to the Saunders (1980, 551) hypothesis that

> *the tensions between economic and social priorities, between rational planning and democratic accountability and between centralized direction and local responsiveness, tend to underlie one another.*

HOUSE BUILDERS

The pressure for residential development from speculative house builders is most directly expressed by the submission of planning applications. A computer printout of residential applications submitted between 1974 and 1981 produced by Berkshire County Council provided a sampling frame of 175 firms. Only multisite applicants were chosen, thus excluding the many individuals who sought new dwelling planning permission for a single site, and 40 applicants were randomly selected for interviewing. Comprising local, regional and national companies, the sample included individual operators, family and corporate firms, and both specialist and nonspecialist builders. The size classification, although seemingly arbitrary, represents quite distinct modes of operation between firms of different sizes (table 20.1). It is a composite criterion, making wider reference to firm structure, levels of capital provision, and policies of land search and acquisition (Fleming, 1984).

TABLE 20.1 THE HOUSE-BUILDER SAMPLE			
Number in sample	*Classification*	*Annual dwelling completions*	*1981 turnover limits (£)*
10	Very small or occasional	0–4	0–290,000
9	Small	5–20	290,000–700,000
7	Medium	21–100	1,400,000–3,500,000
14	Large	100+	12,000,000+

The nature of the development process in Britain, with its need for planning permission, ensures that developers must interact with the planning system. The form and extent of such contact is highly variable, however. Some house builders deliberately keep interaction to a minimum, often little more than the submission of an application and essential correspondence with planning and highways officers. Others invest considerable resources in attempting to obtain favorable outcomes. This may involve detailed negotiation with officers, the lobbying of planning committee members, and the use of the appeal mechanism. A few of the large house builders may also interact with the policy process, attempting to influence the level and location of future land releases.

One crude but readily available measure of the outcome of house-builder–planning-authority interaction is the success rate of planning applications. It is evident from figure 20.3 that most of the 40 interviewed house builders achieved a success rate of more than 70 percent. Surprisingly, a high proportion (principally the very small and large developers) enjoyed complete success.

A critical factor is the extent to which a developer probes and explores the limits of planning. It is relatively easy for a company to achieve very high success rates if all its applications are for safe sites or merely for the details of a development that has already received outline permission. It is much more difficult if attempts are made to challenge planning policies or to obtain permission for difficult or controversial sites. This latter factor is closely related to a house builder's mode of profit-making. There is an important distinction

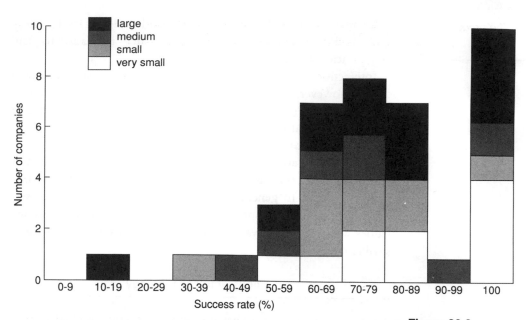

Figure 20.3
Planning application success rate of surveyed house builders in central Berkshire, 1974–81
Source: *Berkshire County Council*

between those who concentrate upon production to obtain favorable returns upon capital and those who stress the importance of bringing forward land for development.

The land element in the house-building process can produce profit in a number of ways: rises in land value between land purchase and house sales; higher sales income from a site than that estimated at the time of land purchase or betterment. Land acquired at or near agricultural use value that subsequently receives planning permission for housing produces a substantial profit. Some developers therefore acquire sites that have not been allocated or perhaps even considered by a planning authority and attempt to obtain planning permission. Periodic applications may be submitted to test the strength of a local authority's (and also the DOE's) commitment to refusal. A "landfinder" strategy, however, is both long term and risky. Land purchased years ahead of likely development may involve loans and long-term interest charges. Option agreements, postponing purchase until outline permission is received, are widely used to reduce the risk of misjudged purchase and the costs of holding land for many years. In these situations the bargaining between developer and landowner over the value of the land is crucial.

The majority of companies rely largely or entirely upon profits from output (the constructors). Long-term planning delays and uncertainty are incompatible with their mode of operation, although many construction companies may have some speculative sites in the land bank. For them "cheap land is dear land, and dear land is cheap land," and their applications are generally "safer" in relation to planning policies and criteria.

Interaction with the planning system and application success rates cannot, however, be simply read off from these structural differences. A house builder's mode of operation is also influenced by attitudes to consumers and the planning system, and knowledge of the planning process. Some developers perceive planning as a system of negotiation and are prepared to test the positions of local planning authorities. Others regard planning in terms of certainty and as a regulatory process. In general it is the larger firms that, of necessity, adopt the negotiation approach. However, there are some large companies with very conservative attitudes and also some sophisticated smaller operators.

A house-builder typology

A matrix can be envisaged that attempts to integrate residential application success rates and the extent to which house builders probe the limits of planning. A fourfold typology may be conceived (figure 20.4).

The *Cautious* house builder has a high application success rate, but involvement with the planning process is low. The conservative style of these firms restricts them to safe sites: they often limit their land purchase to sites with existing outline permission. Contentious applications are seldom submitted because the house builder usually wants quick approval with a minimum of planning interaction. Few surprising decisions are therefore encountered.

To some extent smaller firms are more likely to be classified as Cautious simply because their fewer developments require less contact with the planning system. However, a lack of resources and sophistication are undoubtedly the main factors. Very few large firms appeared within this category; their access to greater resources eventually prompts a probing of the system and thus a degree of negotiation. The one large Cautious company in our sample was in fact a finance house that had been drawn into housing production through land inherited from collapsed creditors. It would not be surprising if this company eventually concentrates more upon the planning aspects of house building.

The *Naïve* house builder is rare and, almost by definition, is restricted to the very small operators. They have little interaction with the planning system beyond the required minimum, often unaware of planning procedures and the scope that exists for discussion and

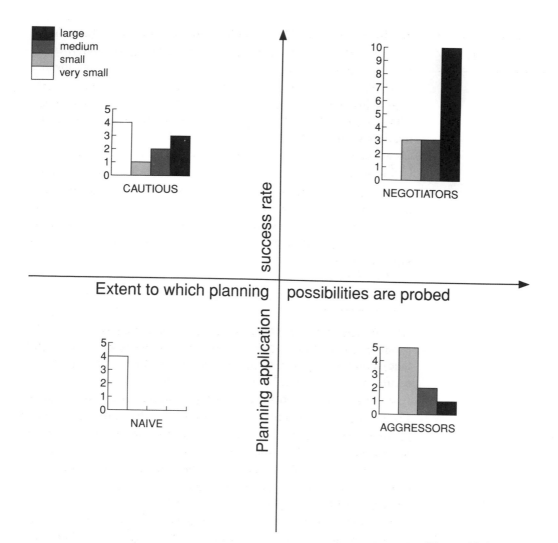

negotiation. Through naivety they may submit hopeful and careless proposals without sounding out the planning authorities in advance, and therefore suffer a relatively high level of refusal. Even when faced with refusal, their lack of familiarity with the system precludes a negotiated compromise, unless initiated by the planning authority. A lack of confidence and resources discourages the use of the appeal mechanism; less than half of the very small firms had lodged an appeal, in contrast to all but two of the twenty large and medium developers.

Both the Naive and the Cautious developers have minimal contacts with district planning officers and probably none with the perceived periphery of the planning system: county council officials and the DOE. Some use may be made of the elected representatives, but lobbying tends to be either in desperation or undertaken in an

Figure 20.4
A typology of housebuilder approaches to the development control system

aggressive, and therefore counterproductive, manner. Only rarely will the Cautious developers employ planning agencies, and even then the agencies either are of a Cautious type themselves or are given a restricted brief.

The *Negotiators* stand in stark contrast to the previous two groups. They have relatively high success rates and a close involvement with the development control process. The planning system is regarded as an arena for negotiations that extends to all aspects of house-builder–planning-authority interaction. Preapplication discussion is a standard procedure, and in some cases quite detailed proposals may be presented before a house builder has purchased a site. Negotiation will often continue after a refusal, either to seek a compromise before an appeal is heard or to attempt to undermine the authority's case by satisfying its strongest grounds for refusal.

Negotiators encompass the full range of house-builder size and are concerned with a wide range of sites, not merely those that are deemed safe. On certain sites the interaction with the planning system may span many years, with regular applications to test the position of the council or DOE in the light of changing planning and land-supply situations. At the detailed stage, firms will attempt to secure more profitable densities or mixtures of house types. The trade-offs with the planning authorities are many and varied. Planning gain agreements are very much the symbol of this group.

The final group are the *Aggressors*: those with the high degree of knowledge (and interaction) but non the less relatively low success rates. They are not necessarily unsuccessful negotiators but may be impatient or overambitious, or they concentrate their resources upon the appeal rather than on the local authority decision. Their interest in negotiation is therefore rather variable. The line between the Aggressors and the Naive developer may be a fine one, but the Aggressors usually have the ability and the resources to take applications to appeal. In this way the perceived arbitrariness of the appeal system is being exploited. Aggressors usually concentrate upon outline applications, often relying to some extent upon profit from the land element rather than solely from turnover. They are most evident in the small-size category, although some of these border upon the Naive. This may indicate the pressures being exerted by the large companies in central Berkshire and the trend since the 1970s toward larger sites. Their stance may be something of a desperation measure in an attempt to obtain suitable small, but not single-plot, sites.

It is the Negotiators and the Aggressors who invest most resources in tackling the planning system. It is they who have actively changed the nature of the system at the local level and who have given greatest impetus to the assault upon the system undertaken at the top through individuals and house-builder organizations.

RESIDENT GROUPS

Residents are affected by additions and changes to the built environment. The construction of a road or a new housing estate has both a direct impact upon the local environment and various externality effects, such as reducing local property values. To influence events, usually with the aim of maximizing positive externalities and minimizing negative ones, residents band together in resident groups.

From a range of information sources, a total of 149 resident groups in central Berkshire were identified and contacted; 92 of these were interviewed successfully and provide our sample. All these groups were established after 1960, the frequency of formation increasing during the 1960s and peaking in the mid-1970s, and with fewer additions in the period to the early 1980s. This picture is consistent with increasing owner-occupation, the encouragement of public participation in planning issues, and the rise of articulate middle-income groups that are related to resident-group formation and action. The cumulative effect was to generate a large number of groups seeking to influence planning outcomes.

A resident-group typology

All resident groups are concerned with their local environment. The term "environment," however, needs careful inspection. Robson (1982) identifies three types of environment. The physical environment is, as the name implies, the form and distribution of buildings, roads, open space, and other features that constitute the natural and built environment. The social environment relates to the social and demographic characteristics of the local population, whereas the resource environment refers to the location, distribution, and accessibility of public and private goods, such as shops, schools, and recreational facilities. Resident groups are concerned in varying ways with different environments. From the responses to questions probing the "why" of group formation, it became clear that groups desired both to prevent developments in the physical and social environments and to obtain facilities or services in the resource environment. These two characteristics can be crudely summarized as stopping (or protecting) and getting (or enhancing). The balance between them varied, and three broad categories were identified.

Forming 43 percent of the sample, *stopper* groups were primarily concerned with protecting local areas from further development. Just over half of these groups described their aims as stopping or modifying unwanted development, while the remainder saw their chief goal as protecting the quality of the existing environment. Two-thirds of Stoppers were located in rural central Berkshire, with the others in middle- and upper-income parts of the major towns. In 83 percent of cases, group formation was initiated by a specific threat to the locality.

The concerns of Stoppers reflected both environmental and economic calculations, and also specific social valuations. Residential growth is perceived to impose negative externalities in the form of increased noise, traffic congestion, and construction activity, and to lead to loss of local open land and landscape quality. But there is a hard core of material interest underneath the environmental concern which relates to the impact of new development upon house prices. This calculation also involves the social composition of an existing neighborhood and any new development. Many households were attracted to certain villages or the more salubrious urban neighborhoods because of their exclusivity. Particularly in the rural areas there is a powerful ideology that sees in a village location the hope of restoring a moral Arcadia away from the anonymity of mass urban society. The concern with community here is an attempt to face up to modernity by asserting definable positions within a small, local, social hierarchy.

The defense of villages from development came mainly from residents of less than 20 years' standing who wished to maintain the physical village on the ground as much as the village in the mind. Defense is greatest when developments are proposed that lead to either the coalescence of villages or the submersion of a village by a large town. Such changes strike not only at the material base but also at the emotional heart of the Stoppers.

Getters, forming 37 percent of the sample, were mainly concerned with the enhancement of the local area in terms of both the social and the resource environments. This involved pressing for improvements in the quality of local services, opportunities, and facilities, and might also take the form of self-help. Community participation, often allied to demands for community centers, was seen as an essential part of community provision. The great majority (88 percent) were found in recently constructed private-sector estates, with only three (9 percent) in areas of public housing.

It was the middle-income groups in "average" areas who were the most vociferous in their pursuit of improved services and facilities. A few may have had close links with local political organizations and overlapping core membership; most, however, stressed the nonpartisan nature of their activities and campaigns. Self-help represents a step outside the formal political system when the state cannot or will not meet the demands of a locality.

There were some groups, 20 percent of the sample, that were concerned in equal measure with both the protection and enhancement of their locality. These *Stopper-Getters* were grounded in both old, established urban neighborhoods and new estates. In only one case did a group's area constitute a predominantly local authority housing area, and in only three cases did it include both public and private housing. Owner-occupation dominated the other 14 Stopper-Getter groups.

The questionnaire survey provides only a snapshot of resident groups in central Berkshire and their roles. Group aims may alter over time, and thus a particular group will move between categories. For older neighborhoods a typical progression is from Stopper to Stopper-Getter, whereas for new estates the sequence may be from Getter to Stopper-Getter to Stopper, as more recent in-migrants seek to restrict further development. Groups representing highly valued urban or rural areas are more likely to retain a basically antigrowth role.

TABLE 20.2 DOMINANT TENURE TYPE OF MEMBERSHIP					
		Resident association			
	Central			*Stoppers/*	
Tenure	*Berkshire (%)*[a]	*All*	*Stoppers*	*Getters*	*Getters*
Owner-occupation	65	68.4	88	67	47
Council housing	22	5.4	6	12	—
Private renting	8	—	—	—	—
Mixed	—	26.2	12	27	41
Other[b]	5				
	100.0	100.0	100.0	100.0	100.0
Absolute numbers		92	40	18	34

Notes:

[a]Figure refers to households in permanent buildings (*Source:* 1981 census)

[b]Includes housing associations and housing linked to employment

In summary, the voice of the Stoppers is the voice of middle-class, middle-aged owner-occupiers seeking to protect their physical and social environments. This voice is also strong in the other two types of resident groups, but it is not the only one (table 20.2). If you listen, you can hear the sound of younger owner-occupiers in new estates and inner-city areas, and the demands of tenants' associations on council estates. Here the concerns are not only with protecting but also with enhancing the local physical and social environments.

Contact with the planning system

The resident groups of central Berkshire interacted with the planning system in a number of ways. The most common form was the monitoring of and reaction to planning applications (table 20.3). Such monitoring is vital for any group wishing to restrict or modify developments in their area. It was hardly surprising to find that this was undertaken by over four-fifths of Stopper groups, but it was also carried out by over one-half of the Getters. When a group was opposed to a development, it would submit a formal objection to the local planning authority and might also contact planning officers by telephone to obtain more details and to reinforce their opposition. Pressure was often applied on councilors, particularly those on the planning committee, both directly and through the local press.

TABLE 20.3   RESIDENT GROUPS AND THE PLANNING SYSTEM

Type of involvement	Percentage of groups involved
Planning application	72
Local plans	50
Development briefs	46
Public inquiries	42
Structure plans	41
"Heseltown"	33

The impact of resident-group opposition is very difficult to evaluate. In only 14 percent of cases were applications refused in line with group objections, and a causal relationship cannot be attributed to even this correspondence. Planning officers in general have low opinions of community organizations, and it was claimed that officials of the Reading Borough Council referred to resident and amenity associations as "Mickey Mouse" groups. The relationship between

TABLE 20.4 LOCAL GROUPS' RESPONSE TO INITIAL STRUCTURE PLAN PROPOSALS	
Organization	*General comments*
Meadow Residents Association (Wokingham)	Supports a national policy of conserving energy and the principle that growing communities should be socially and economically self-supporting. Ideally, therefore, there should be no growth in central Berkshire, but limited growth is supported based only on unavoidable commitments.
Hurst Village Society	Supports limited growth but is concerned about the tendency for growth to lead to the coalescence of adjacent settlements. Committed to preservation and enhancement of separate communities.
Cavesham Parish Council	Prefers restricted growth but accepts that limited growth may have to be adopted.
Binfield Parish Council	Accepts limited growth but feels that restricted growth should be adopted in rural areas and villages.
Twyford Parish Council	Supports limited growth because of the need to catch up on the provision of amenities due to the recent rapid growth.

Source: After Berkshire County Council (1978)

groups and their ward councillors was highly variable, although community groups were ranked second (behind the planning officers) by planning councillors in terms of their influence over development control decisions (Witt and Fleming, 1984). Opposition to development often continued to the planning appeal stage, with 42 percent of the sampled groups having participated in at least one local inquiry.

Many resident groups also interacted with the local planning system in the policy arena. This contrasts with the low level of house-builder participation, which was limited to the large firms and the Housebuilders' Federation. Groups made known their views through formal public participation procedures, in plan preparation (table 20.4), at examinations in public, and also through the local media. The majority (76 percent) used the media, chiefly the local newspapers. The importance of publicity was widely recognized and exerted extra pressure upon the other actors in any issue. The most successful group in this respect were the Stoppers, who managed to link their own local aims with the wider public interest through the medium of general environmental concern.

Resident-group impact in central Berkshire

While it is relatively easy to note the aims, structure, and external contacts of resident groups, it is very difficult to ascertain their impact. Between the goals of a group and final outcomes lie a myriad of conflicts and other interests. A precise balance sheet cannot be drawn up, but three general points can be made.

First, the Stoppers were influential in creating an articulated and powerful no-growth lobby in central Berkshire, which sensitized many local politicians to the issues of resisting and deflecting growth. The actions of the Stoppers placed growth minimization higher than growth generation on the planning agenda of central Berkshire.

Second, the importance of the Getters was increasing. On the one hand, they might well have become the Stoppers of tomorrow. On the other, considering their capacity for community self-help, they might be least affected by a reduction in certain public services. Given the emphasis of recent public policy on control of expenditure and public service provision, the ability of communities to generate self-help will create further patterns of inequality. This distinction will be based not simply on income and status but also on length of residence, gender, stage in the life-cycle, and other factors that create a strong sense of community within an area. With their success in mobilizing internal resources and experience of campaigning for additional public provision, the Getters may be best placed to counter some of the effects of public service decline.

Third, we can note that resident groups represented specific interests. Their concerns were those of many owner-occupiers and some public-sector tenants: restriction of further growth or the generation of community facilities. They did not fully articulate the interests of the homeless or the unemployed, and the voice of private-sector tenants was scarcely heard. Not all issues that affect local communities are thus placed on the agenda for public discussion and political decision-making by resident groups.

THE STATE

The central Berkshire situation has been one of high development pressure, strong resident opposition to further growth, and a land-use planning system differentially accessible to public and builder participation. The state, or more precisely the planning system, is the arena where the conflict over residential growth is expressed. Many theorists have identified two principal functions of the state: maintaining the economic conditions necessary for the profitability of capital, and maintaining social order and cohesion through policies of coercion and/or legitimation. The former function comprises policies and expenditure in both production and consumption spheres; social investment and social consumption, to use the terminology of O'Connor (1973).

The state itself, however, is not a single entity but comprises local and national elements. In parallel with the increase in the strength and scope of state intervention since the nineteenth century, there has been a trend toward centralization of state power. There are tensions between different levels of the state, which Saunders (1979) suggests overlie the competing claims of accumulation and legitimation. Local government has lost responsibility for social investment, with the transfer of major infrastructural functions (gas, electricity, water supply and sewerage) to private companies. In the field of social consumption, however, local government has retained control of a number of services that have increased in scope and importance (education, housing, social services), although ultimate control remains with central government. The contradictory functions of social investment and consumption have progressively come to be located at different levels of the state. In addition, the mode of policy development and implementation is markedly different. In many cases social investment is determined within a corporate sphere of interest mediation (Saunders, 1985), whereas consumption issues lie more within the open sphere of local politics.

Land-use planning involves, directly at least, relatively little public expenditure. The division of state action and expenditure into investment and consumption is useful, however, in our examination of conflict in central Berkshire. First, there is the context of central–local government conflict over public expenditure and the rate support grant. Since the mid-1970s, central government fiscal policy has been dominated by the control of public and particularly local authority spending. Berkshire's block grant, for example, was reduced from £66.6 million in 1981–82 to only £45.7 million the following year. This cutback has to be related to burdens imposed by additional development. The costs of growth are high. In the long term the new developments produce extra taxes and hence revenue. But in the short or medium term there is a disparity between costs and income, because some infrastructure and service provision is required before and during construction. The gap between costs and revenue has not been bridged by the central state and, if anything, will widen. Part of the shortfall can be met by extra local taxes, and the county precept for 1982–3 was increased by 27.5 percent, but there are political limits to such a response. Local electors are particularly sensitive to such increases and vote accordingly. Thus, while some of the developers' costs are socialized through public provision of roads, drainage, schools and other forms of infrastructure, local residents face both higher taxes and poorer levels of service provision.

Second, the demands of house builders, local community groups and the different levels of the state can be expressed in terms of accumulation and consumption. The granting of planning permission to a house builder is an essential part of a process of obtaining profit. The enjoyment (and retention) of open areas, woods, views, tranquility, particular local social structures and the like are part of the consumption of the physical and social environment by residents of an area. Central government places greater emphasis upon accumulation and the provision of sufficient housing to meet the needs of those taking new jobs in the buoyant subregional economy. The local state is primarily involved with consumption issues and is much more open to pressure from voters and local groups. This is particularly the case with planning conflicts, which can arouse strong locality-based feeling and community action.

The role of local planning authorities

Local planning authorities consist of two sets of agents: elected councillors and salaried officials. These two groups work together but have different organizational structures, perspectives, priorities, and roles. While the salaried officials have to serve the elected representatives, they also have reference to an ideology of professional planning practice. Decision-making ultimately lies with the planning councillors, who directly face the whole range of conflicting demands. The competing pressures of accumulation and legitimation noted earlier are crystallized in and through the actions and roles of planning councillors. Our concern with central Berkshire planning authorities will therefore be concentrated upon planning committee members.

Planning authorities respond to the conflicting pressures in central Berkshire in a number of ways. Five approaches can be identified, usually occurring in combination rather than in isolation:

- resistance to growth;
- deflection of development;
- deflection of blame;
- control over development;
- planning gain.

Absolute resistance by planning authorities has been severely limited by the power of the DOE to overturn refusal decisions. The Berkshire authorities, however, were not stampeded into immediate compliance with the structure plan amendment. Widespread public consultation was undertaken by the county council, against DOE advice, regarding the location of the extra 8,000 houses, and Wokingham District Council carried out local studies and consultation for the chosen areas within its boundary. The county's consultation exercise was resented by house builders, who viewed it as purely a delaying tactic. Their challenges against the delay, however, were not supported by the DOE, and major residential appeals determined during this period were dismissed on the grounds of prematurity. Local opposition to growth continued despite the Heseltown defeat, and the cumulative effect of such pressure upon local politicians was evident in the 1985 decisions of both Bracknell District and Berkshire County Councils to formally oppose the 4,000-dwelling Heseltown allocation for north-east Bracknell.

Outright rejection of growth pressures has proved to be at most a delaying tactic. Within the area, however, the *deflection of residential growth* has been much more apparent. Development often takes the line of least resistance, and intensity of local opposition can influence the location of new housing. There was considerable competition between Bracknell and Wokingham District Councils, the two major recipients of housing growth. Wokingham consistently and vehemently opposed the principle of the additional 8,000 houses and at one stage formally resolved to refuse any of the dwellings before 1986. Bracknell DC by contrast took a more reasoned approach, proposing that the allocation be shared evenly. This approach and the implicit view of many councillors from more rural areas that Bracknell was always intended for expansion and could hardly be spoiled were factors in the allocation of 6,150 of the 8,000 houses to the district. Local opposition to the north-east Bracknell decision (4,000 houses) continued, however, led by the Binfield and Warfield parish councils and resident groups. With strong support from a newly elected Bracknell Member of Parliament, the cumulative effect of the pressure was a Bracknell DC decision in 1985 to formally oppose the allocation, even though a local plan for the area was in preparation. Pressure upon the county council led to a proposed reduction in the north-east Bracknell figure (to 2,650) in the review of the structure plan. Concern grew in Wokingham at the prospect of development being redirected from Bracknell, and a senior Wokingham planning councillor publicly referred to the Bracknell decision as a "dereliction of duty." Worried parish councils and local groups in Wokingham formed an action group to give greater backing to their district's fight against development, especially against any redirected from Bracknell.

The third response was *deflection of blame*. Where applications are approved despite local opposition, and often the personal conviction of councillors, a planning committee must make clear its dilemma. Speeches are required condemning the impact of the application, stressing the reluctance of councillors to grant permission, and pointing to the threat of an appeal. The choice between principle and the realities of central government power must be explained via speeches, reported by the local press, to affected residents and the local electorates alike. Blame is transferred totally to Whitehall. This is merely a public relations exercise to disguise district impotence but is usually linked with one or both of the remaining approaches.

The emphasis upon local authority *control* over the details of development can be expressed in the phrase "if it cannot be refused it must be planned." Negotiation with applicants over details is a standard feature of the modern planning system; the key factor is the extent of committee involvement and the accompanying publicity. Where councillors have accepted the principle of development, albeit reluctantly, they may become closely involved with the density, layout, design and, in the case of any of the 8,000-house allocations, the precise location of a development. The greater the influence of the planning authority, but particularly of councillors, upon a scheme the greater the justification for permitting it despite the local opposition.

This approach is easily extended into the sphere of *planning gain*, which involves a legal agreement between an applicant and the local authority to provide certain benefits or financial contributions as part of the planning consent. All but one of the planning councillors interviewed supported the principle of extracting some form of gain or recompense from a developer in view of the costs or dis-benefits imposed on a local community by a new development. The extent of planning gain varied widely. Offsite drainage and highway improvements are often required for large sites; additional public open space, new footpath links, accommodation for elderly people, "village greens," and the free provision of sites for schools are common community gains from residential developments. On some sites a community hall or leisure facilities have been obtained.

The offering of benefits to the local authority, the cost of which can invariably be passed on to the landowner, is a common feature of the development process within central Berkshire. Planning gain is often a key means of facilitating development for the house builder, whether to encourage the granting of planning permission or to enable development to proceed. The demand to build in central Berkshire gives planning authorities a strong position from which to bargain with developers even if they do not possess the authority to prevent growth. Given that development through the appeal mech-

Illustration 20.3
New housing construction in Lower Earley, Reading, UK (© Woking District Council)

anism merely demonstrates the impotence of planning authorities in the face of central government and the house builders, planning gain gives local politicians tangible achievements with which to confront the locally powerful antigrowth lobby.

The pursuit of planning gain has a number of consequences. In seeking to maximize it, the local authorities have tended to look favorably upon large sites involving a few major developers, where planning gain can be more easily achieved and implemented. The decision to locate 4,000 houses in north-east Bracknell, for example, was at least partly influenced by the planning gains, particularly over road and sewerage networks, which could effectively be reached on such a large development. The extent of planning gain and the conviction with which it is pursued by a planning authority often depends upon the influence of the local lobby by elected representatives, community groups and parish councils.

Earlier I posed the question of how the state resolves the dual pressures of maintaining capital accumulation and ensuring social legitimation. In this particular case the central state's concern with accumulation was twofold. On the one hand, the demands of developers were met in central Berkshire in the early 1980s mostly by the imposition of central government control over local planning outcomes. On the other hand, the concern with reducing public expenditure, was translated into allowing local planning authorities to pass some infrastructural costs on to private developers and frequently, in turn, on to landowners.

The local state was responsive to the demands of the no-growth lobby but, given the structure of the land-use planning system, had to accept central directives, albeit under protest. The successful pursuit of planning gain to some extent legitimizes the position of the local authorities, especially the councillors. Such gains neatly mesh local political interests with central government macroeconomic policies. This is not, however, to present a neat functional solution to the tensions confronting the state. The convergence of planning gain and negative externalities was not uniform: areas with planning protection or influential local lobbies were more successful in limiting or channeling residential growth.

The central state is concerned with the macroscale issues of national economic growth. Local authorities are much more responsive to local opinion. The resulting tension reflects the competing functions of the state, while the results indicate the distribution of power.

GUIDE TO FURTHER READING

The material presented here is drawn from previous work:

Fleming, S.C. (1984) *Housebuilders in an area of Growth: Negotiating the Built Environment of Central Berkshire*, Reading University Geography Paper no. 84, Department of Geography, University of Reading.

Short, J.R., Fleming, S.C. and Witt, S.J.G. (1986) *Housebuilding, Planning and Community Action*, London: Routledge & Kegan Paul.

Witt, S.J.G. and Fleming S.C. (1984) *Planning Councillors in an Area of Growth: Little Power but All the Blame?*, Reading University Geography Paper no. 85, Department of Geography, University of Reading.

Other works cited include:

Berkshire County Council (1978) *Central Berkshire Structure Plan: Report of Public Participation*, Shinfield, Berks.: County Planning Office.

Berkshire County Council (1984) *Survey of Employers*, Shinfield, Berks: County Planning Office.

O'Connor, J. (1973) *The Fiscal Crisis of the State*, New York: St Martin's Press.

Robson, B.T. (1982) The Bodley barricade: social space and social conflict. In K.R. Cox and R.J. Johnston, (eds), *Conflict Politics and the Urban Scene*, Harlow, Essex: Longman, 45–61.

Saunders, P. (1979) *Urban Politics: A Sociological Interpretation*, London: Hutchinson.

Saunders, P. (1980) Local government and the state, *New Society* 50 (March), 550–1.

Saunders, P. (1985) The forgotten dimension of central–local relations: theorizing the regional state, *Environment and Planning C: Government and Policy*, 3 149–62.

Chapter 21

POSTSCRIPT: BARCELONA

IT TAKES ALL KINDS OF CITIES TO MAKE BARCELONA. IT TAKES AMONG OTHERS A ROMAN CITY, A GOTHIC CITY, A MARITIME CITY, AND A CITY OF COSMOPOLITAN PLEASURE.

KENNETH TYNAN, *TYNAN RIGHT AND LEFT* (1969)

Places are important to us. As individuals we attach meaning and symbolism to particular places. Our childhood, for example, is not only a time but also a place, a place constantly revisited as we recall our past, conjure up our earliest memories, and relive our first experiences.

Our life is a journey through different sets of places – home, school, perhaps college and various workplaces. Our different dwellings from a small room to a larger house mark our housing career while the size of our office registers our rise or fall in the firm hierarchy. Our life-cycle is recorded in important places. The first house, apartment or room we have outside of our parent' place marks the beginning of our adult life. Specific places related to important events come to highlight certain times in our lives.

Our attitude to places also changes. What was once our dream house becomes good but not great, then adequate, and finally it is seen as constraining. What was once a perfectly adequate house, if we get richer or more ambitious, becomes cramped, a place to leave rather than stay in. We can identify a model of the housing life-cycle from first apartment to small house to bigger and bigger houses. The demand is driven by changing space requirements as the family gets bigger. But it is also fueled by rising expectations of place.

Places that we live in take on the aura of normality. We become indifferent to our surroundings as we slide into the deep rut of habit. "Other" places become exotic, strange, a source of mystery. There are the "dark" exotic places. Previous generations projected demons onto the wilderness of forest, fen, and mountains. The Victorians could see savagery in "darkest" Africa. The native other was the uncivilized other. More recently, the perceived dark places are the inner areas of the big cities. In popular imagination they occupy the territory of fear, the landscape of neglect, the home of the other.

Illustration 21.1
Barcelona. In the middle distance Gaudí's Church of the Sagrada Familia stands erect (photograph: author)

There are also the "friendly" exotic places. I live in the United States, and people hearing my Scots accent are always keen to recall their holiday trips to Scotland. For most of them Scotland is remembered as romantic, less hurried and more sociable than their present place. Of course, it was they rather than Scotland who were romantic, less hurried and more sociable. They were on holiday, taking a break from their usual selves. Scotland was the setting for their other, different self. Places cast an influence but, in large measure, the creation of the meaning of places lies within rather than without. An exotic place for some is ordinary for another. Tahiti is exotic if you live in Neasden but southern England is exotic to most Tahitians.

Different places mean different things to different people. When both the place and the person change, complex relationships are created. Let me elaborate with reference to my own experience of Barcelona.

I first visited the city in 1974. I was a poor graduate student. With limited experience of foreign places Barcelona was at the same time strange, very foreign, very exciting, very threatening, and strangely welcoming.

I stayed in an incredibly cheap hotel in the medieval heart of the city just off the Ramblas. This was the Barcelona of the all-night cafés and cheap wine; it stayed on the margin of the city's everyday life. My

Illustration 21.2 *Barcelona: the Old Quarter (photograph: author)*

Illustration 21.3 *Gaudí's Barcelona. The city contains many examples of the work of the Catalan architect Antoni Gaudí (photograph: author)*

Barcelona friends were political dissidents struggling under the
shadow of the Franco dictatorship.

I visited the city a number of times, both Barcelona and I changing together, the visits a reminder of how we were developing. My
most recent visit was in 1990 when I went to give some lectures at
the Autonomous University. I could now afford to eat in fancy restaurants. My friends were now part of the established order with a nice
house in Bellaterra. I was more traveled, more experienced in visit-
ing foreign cities. And Barcelona was becoming less Catalan and more
international. It was a world city grown bigger and more cosmopolitan, more used to meeting people like me, and preparing for the 1992
Olympic Games. We had become more grown up. But like all maturing experiences something had been lost as well as gained, and I could
never recapture that wide-eyed, open-mouthed wonder at first arriving in the city.

Place captures space by registering our times, embodying our identities, and reflecting our lives.

My attitude, my experiences, my very sense of Barcelona changed.
It varied according to where I was, when I was, even who I was.

GUIDE TO FURTHER READING

This chapter is based on:
Short, J.R. (1991) So what is place?, *Geography Review* 5, 9.

There are many good books on Barcelona. A small selection of some
    of the most interesting include:
Hughes, R. (1992) *Barcelona*, New York: Alfred A. Knopf.
King, C. (1968) *Barcelona*, South Brunswick: Barmes.
Orwell, G. (1938) *Homage to Catalonia*, London: Gollancz.

CONCLUDING COMMENTS

Now that you have come to the end of this book, I hope you will want to explore further the urban condition. Let me make a number of suggestions.

Look Examine with your eyes the cities that you know. See the changes and the stabilities in the built form. Watch the television coverage in news reports and documentaries. Movies and television drama also give an artistic depiction of urban living that supplements the non-fiction narratives.

Listen In conversation and the media urban fears and dreams are discussed and analyzed. Be open to these conversations. Listen to what is being said. And by whom.

Read Much is written about the city. There are the formal books and journals. I have cited a number of books and articles in this text. To keep abreast of the latest research look at some of the following journals: *Environment and Planning* (A, B, C and D), *International Journal of Urban and Regional Research*, *Journal of Urban Affairs*, *Urban Affairs Quarterly*, *Urban Geography*, and *Urban Studies*. Also read the newspapers, and popular journals. The dynamics of urban living are often revealed by good journalists. The city itself is also a text, to be read and reread. Read your own city or the city nearest to you. How would you characterize it? What are the biggest changes you have noticed?

Write Keep a journal. Describe the city in your own words, especially when you visit a new city or town. By writing down your thoughts you give shape and structure to your ideas.

Participate We are all citizens. There is no surer way of understanding the city than by being an active participant; this could be by taking part in formal or informal politics, community organizations and neighborhood activities. Understand the city by changing it.

INDEX

Rutherford, Jonathan, 313
Rybynski, Witold, 259

Sage, Samuel, 451, 452
Sahlins, Marshall, 14
St Paul's Cathedral, 393
Sassen, Saskia, 70
Saunders, P., 469, 481
Schama, Simon, 21
Schorske, Carl, 400
Scotland, 489
    Edinburgh, 398–400, 406
    Glasgow, 5–6, 433–5
Seabrook, Jeremy, 243–4
Seamon, David, 393
Segal, Lynn, 313–14
Semiology and the Urban (Barthes), 390
Sennett, Richard, 394
service employment, rise in, 153, 154
service strategies, 269–70
sexual identity, 233–4, 235, 236
shantytowns, 114, 115
shopping
    patterns, 56
    see also retailing
sin city, 416
skylines, urban, 391–2
small towns, 52
Smith, Neil, 182–4
Smith, Susan, 253
Smollett, Tobias, 433
Soane, Sir John, 392
social arena, 207–38
social change, and masculinities, 313–14
Social Justice and the City (Harvey), 105
social process, and urban structure, 406–8
socialist cities, 109–11
socialization, and the home, 197–8
society and the city, 2–3
society/space relationship, 13
soft city, 418–19
Soft City (Raban), 239
Sommers, Christina Hoff, 310
South Africa, 196, 222–3
South America
    informal economy, 245–6

as primate urban hierarchy, 42–3
space
    and the city as stage, 252–3
    creating, and business lobbying, 278–9
    and gender, 231, 233, 307–29
    mode of regulation over, 116
    and power, 320–4, 407, 408–10
    privatization of, 394–5
    see also public space
space–time
    citizens as travelers in, 254–8
    and shrinkage of the urban network, 65
spaced times, 259–61
Spain, Daphne 324
spatial restructuring, world cities, 159–65
sports clubs, allegiance to, 56
Spurling, Andrea, 307, 324
Sri Lanka, Kandy, 395–8, 406
SSA (social structure of accumulation), 97
stage, city as, 251–3
state, the, 280–9
    and business, 277–80
    and land-use planning systems, 481–2
    and social reform, 280–1
    and urban governments, 281–9
States of Desire (White), 233
Steinem, G., 315
Stoker, G., 289
Stone Age Economics (Sahlins), 14
Stone, Clarence, 288
street people, 258
Streetwise (Anderson), 252–3
structure planning, in Central Berkshire, 467–9
Stuttgart, 54
suburbanization, 62, 98, 99, 114, 230
Sweezy, P., 98
Sydney, 48, 50, 51, 423, 424
    Green Bans, 122, 131–4, 135, 136, 137–8, 138–9, 142–51
    property cycle, (1968–74) 125–6
    and capital-labor relations, 128–39
symbolic regimes, 289
Syracuse
    ethnicity in, 346–67

EXCEPTIONALLY GIFTED CHILDREN

Exceptionally Gifted Children examines the origin, development and school histories of 15 Australian children who are among the most remarkably gifted young people ever to be identified and studied in any country. Covering the first ten years of a longitudinal research project which will trace the children through to adulthood, the book examines in detail the children's early lives and influences, their families and personal characteristics. More importantly, it explores the school experiences of these remarkable children, the opportunities offered, and more often denied, to them and the effects of their early school life on their educational and social development – how the normal school environment can affect exceptionally gifted children's self-esteem, self-concept, motivation, capacity to find and form friendships, and the children's own attitudes towards their unusual abilities and achievements.

Miraca U.M. Gross is Senior Lecturer in Gifted Education at the University of New South Wales, Australia.

EXCEPTIONALLY GIFTED CHILDREN

Miraca U.M. Gross

London and New York

To John

First published 1993
by Routledge
11 New Fetter Lane, London EC4P 4EE

Simultaneously published in the USA and Canada
by Routledge
29 West 35th Street, New York, NY 10001

Reprinted 1993

Typeset in Baskerville by Michael Mepham, Frome, Somerset
Printed and bound in Great Britain by
Mackays of Chatham PLC, Chatham, Kent

British Library Cataloguing in Publication Data
A catalogue record for this book is available
from the British Library.
Library of Congress Cataloging in Publication Data
Gross, Miraca U.M.   Exceptionally gifted children / by
Miraca U.M. Gross.
p.   cm.
Includes bibliographical references and index.
1. Gifted children—Education—Australia—Case studies.
I. Title
LC3999.4.G76 1993   92–23118
                                                  CIP

ISBN 0–415–06416–3 (Hbk)
ISBN 0–415–06417–1 (Pbk)